Anonymous

Indian Records

With a commercial View of the Relations between the British government and etc.

Anonymous

Indian Records
With a commercial View of the Relations between the British government and etc.

ISBN/EAN: 9783337062217

Printed in Europe, USA, Canada, Australia, Japan

Cover: Foto ©ninafisch / pixelio.de

More available books at **www.hansebooks.com**

HIS HIGHNESS THE
NAWAB NAZIM OF BENGAL
BEHAR AND ORISSA.

INDIAN RECORDS,

WITH

A COMMERCIAL VIEW

OF THE

RELATIONS

BETWEEN

THE BRITISH GOVERNMENT

AND THE

NAWABS NAZIM OF BENGAL, BEHAR AND ORISSA.

"Render unto Cæsar the things which are Cæsar's."

LONDON:
G. BUBB, 167, NEW BOND STREET.
1870.

TO

HIS HIGHNESS SYUD MUNSOOR ULLEE,

NAWAB NAZIM OF BENGAL, BEHAR AND ORISSA.

THIS WORK IS RESPECTFULLY DEDICATED

BY HIS OBEDIENT SERVANT,

THE AUTHOR.

CONTENTS.

	Page
Original Treaty of Alliance with Meer Jaffier, June 1757.	6
Second Treaty and Agreement between Nawab Meer Jaffier and the East India Company, 10th July, 1763.	9
Demands made by Nawab Meer Jaffier for the establishment of his rights in perpetuity, 10th July, 1763.	12
Nawab Meer Jaffier's note of hand for the expenses of the Army, 16th September, 1764.	13
Additional Treaty and Agreement with Nawab Nudjm-ul-dowlah, 25th February, 1765.	15
Firmauns of the Emperor of Delhi conferring the office of the Dewanny upon the East India Company, 12th August, 1765.	19
Supplementary Agreement with Nawab Nudjm-ul-dowlah accepting a fixed sum for "the expenses of the Nizamut," 30th September, 1765.	22
Additional Treaty and Agreement with Nawab Syef-uf-dowlah, 19th May, 1766.	23
Additional Treaty and Agreement with Nawab Mobaruk-ul-dowlah, 21st March, 1770.	25
Order from Court of Directors to reduce the stipend of Nawab Mobaruk-ul-dowlah during his minority to sixteen lakhs, 26th April, 1771.	31

CONTENTS.

	Page
Order from Court of Directors to provide for the support and dignity of Nawab Mobaruk-ul-dowlah by augmentation of his stipend, 21st July, 1786.	34
Letter from the Governor-General Lord Cornwallis to Nawab Mobaruk-ul-dowlah, making proposals for reduction of his liabilities and the support of his dignity, 22nd September, 1790.	34
Letter from the Governor-General Lord Cornwallis to the Paymaster of Nizamut stipends, conveying instructions relative to Nizamut Family Fund and future distribution of Nizamut stipends, 30th September, 1790.	38
Letter from Marquis Wellesley to Nawab Bubber Jung, "the Pillar of State and Defender of the Realm."	46
Proposals for absorbing Munnee Begum's stipend after her death for general purposes, 9th November, 1802.	48
Letter from Lord Minto to Nawab Zynudeen Ali Khan, on his accession to the throne, 26th May, 1810.	49
Proposals of Mr. Edmonstone for the establishment of an office of Agent to the Governor-General at the Court of the Nawab, 23rd July, 1816.	52
Deputation of Mr. Monckton to Moorshedabad.	55
Mr. Monckton's Report of his conference with the Nawab 19th October, 1816.	56
Instructions to Mr. Monckton on the subject of the Agency Fund.	60
Instructions to Accountant-General to invest the money for Agency Fund.	60
Letter from Mr. Monckton to Sub-Treasurer, Fort William, respecting transmission of money for Agency Fund, 19th December, 1816.	61
Letter from Mr. Monckton to Accountant-General, Fort William, regarding investment of money for the Agency Fund, 19th December, 1816.	61
Letter from Mr. Monckton to Acting Chief Secretary to the Government, Fort William, explaining matters connected with Agency Fund, 26th December, 1816.	63

CONTENTS.

	Page
Instructions from the Governor-General in Council to Mr. Monckton regarding reinvestment of money for Agency Fund	66
Instructions from Governor-General in Council to the Government Agent regarding reinvestment of Agency Fund in Government Securities	67
Letter to Mr. Monckton appointing him to the Office of Agent Governor-General, 22nd February, 1817	67
Instructions regarding the distribution of the interest of the Agency Fund for the office of the Agent Governor-General, 10th May, 1817	68
Instructions to Mr. Monckton regarding his office and establishment, 10th May, 1817	69
Details of Agency Fund from 1817 to 1860	70
Letters from Marquis Hastings to Nawab Ahmad Ali Wallah Jah, 10th August, 1821	75
Proposals of Mr. Monckton to appropiate accumulation from the Nizamut Fund, 31st December, 1822.	77
Letter from the Governor-General to the Nawab regarding the several appropriations from the Nizamut Stipend for different objects, such as Deposit Fund, &c.	79
Instructions from the Governor-General in Council to the Accountant-General and Government Agent respecting the investment of money forming Munnee Begum's Fund.	80
Letter from H. T. Prinsep, Esq., Persian Secretary to Government, to the Agent Governor-General, Moorshedabad, regarding the formation of the Munnee Begum's and the Nizamut Deposit Fund, 28th Jan., 1823.	81
Letter from the Governor-General, Lord Amherst, to Nawab Humayoon Jah after his succession to the throne, 14th January, 1825.	89
Letter from the Governor-General, Lord William Bentinck, to Nawab Humayoon Jah, 24th January, 1835.	90
Letters from the Governor-General, Lord Auckland, to	

viii   CONTENTS.

                                                                               Page

Nawab Humayoon Jah, dated 7th March, 1836, 11th September, 1837, and 20th October, 1837.   . . . 91

Letter from C. E. Trevelyan, Esq., Deputy Secretary to the Government, to H. Paulin, Esq., Attorney to the Honourable Company, regarding the Independence of the Nawabs of Bengal, and the inability of any Court of Justice to exercise jurisdiction over them.   . . 93

Letter from the Honourable C. T. Metcalfe, Acting Governor-General, to Nawab Humayoon Jah, respecting the Agreement of 1834.   95

Agreement entered into in 1834 for the future regulation of the Nizamut Affairs.   96

Correspondence which led to the execution of the Agreement of 1834.   97

Proposal of Sir Charles Trevelyan for absorbing all stipends that might lapse on the decease of the Nawab's relatives.   100

Instructions issued to the Agent Governor-General on the subject of Lapsed Stipends of the Nawab's relatives, 1st March, 1836.   101

Proposal of the Deputy-Governor of Bengal to absorb all the stipends of servants and dependents on the death of the holders, 18th July, 1838.   106

Order of Court of Directors on the subject of Lapsed Stipends, and their opinion that the Nizamut Deposit Fund is not public money, but a part of the "Assignment by Treaty of the Family."   107

Proclamation and General Order on the accession of the present Nawab Syud Munsoor Ullee.   109

Official Letter addressed to the present Nawab Syud Munsoor Ullee on his accession.   110

Statement of the extraordinary transactions of Mr. Torrens, Agent Governor-General, with Correspondence relating thereto.   112

Letter from Lord Dalhousie to the present Nawab Syud Munsoor Ullee, informing His Highness of his own

CONTENTS. ix

	Page
appointment to the office of Governor-General, 12th January, 1848.	125
Correspondence and Law Reports relating to the Murder Case, upon which Lord Dalhousie based an attack upon the rights and privileges of the present Nawab.	129
Letter from Lord Canning to the present Nawab, on his assuming the office of Governor-General, 11th March, 1856.	194
Proclamation of Her Majesty the Queen in 1858.	196
Correspondence setting forth the valuable services rendered by the Nawab to the Indian Government on the occasions of the Santhal Rebellion in 1854, and the great Indian Mutiny of 1857.	199
Narrative of Nizamut Affairs, compiled in 1858-9 by Colonel Colin Mackenzie, Agent Governor-General, setting forth in a most truthful manner the relations between the Nawabs of Bengal and the British Government.	211
Letter from Colonel Colin Mackenzie to the Secretary to the Government of Bengal regarding the claims of the present Nawab Syud Munsoor Ullee, 25th May, 1859.	231
Correspondence relating to an affront supposed to have been offered to the Agent Governor-General, which brought about an estrangement between the Nawab and that officer.	239
Correspondence relating to the dismissal of the Dewan by the Nawab, and the action taken in the matter by the Agent Governor-General and the Government of India.	241
Correspondence regarding the loss sustained by the Nawab through the unwarranted stoppage of his Stipend by the Agent Governor-General, and the singular procedure of the Government in the matter.	265
Extract from letter to the Secretary to the Government of Bengal, conveying the opinions of the Governor-General in Council regarding the claims of the Nawab	

	Page
as set forth in his Memorial of 1857 to Her Majesty's Secretary of State for India in Council, dated 14th January, 1862, forwarded to the Nawab for his information.	269
Extract from a Despatch, dated 17th June, 1864, from Her Majesty's Secretary of State for India in Council to His Excellency the Governor-General in Council, conveying the Sentiments of Her Majesty's Government on the claims of the Nawab of Bengal as advanced in his Memorial of 1857.	279
Memorial addressed by His Highness Syud Munsoor Ullee, the present Nawab of Bengal, Behar, and Orissa, to His Grace the Duke of Argyll, K.T., on the 28th July, 1869.	289

PREFACE.

On whomsoever may devolve the unthankful task of compiling records of any episode in the Government of India, or whatever may be the prejudice with which he commences by exhibiting the severe necessity for unrestricted rule over a people incapable of constitutional institutions, his narrative, whatever its historical pretensions may be, will invariably degenerate into a story beginning with intrigue, continuing in spoliation, and terminating in confiscation. Such, for the most part, is the history of all Indian Princes in connection with the British Government of India, nor is the present work an exception to a rule so general.

The first centenary of the last Treaty with the Nawab of Bengal was completed on the 21st March last. A hundred years in the history of Europe, where the progress is gradual, can hardly be realized; but a century in the history of British India unfolds a panorama commencing with the establishment of a few factories in comparatively insignificant parts of the coast, and terminating in the efforts to consolidate and improve one of the largest and most powerful empires in the world.

To Englishmen, the value of this vast Imperial possession is of paramount importance, for with this Dependency we have acquired a position amongst the Nations of the Universe, which, from our insular and isolated position, it would in vain have taxed Anglo-Saxon energies to have gained. India affords a ready market for our manufactures, an almost inexhaustible store-house for the supply of raw material wherewith is provided employment to British labour, supported and encouraged by British enterprise and British capital; it also furnishes an ample field for the development and profitable use of the talents and energies of our young men, which would otherwise only help to overstock our market of intellect at home. Yet with all these advantages, and despite this universally acknowledged importance, how small is the interest displayed by Englishmen in matters relating to the welfare and prosperity of this vast Dependency. A debate on Indian Affairs in the House of Commons is invariably marked with the characteristic feature of "empty benches," and not unfrequently with what is worse, a "Count Out."

To right-thinking men the injustice of this apathy has been not only bitterly felt, but has led to remonstrance, yet we doubt not from our daily growing closer connection by telegraphs and railways, India and Indian questions will not only form subjects of general notice but of absorbing interest. The apathy of which we have complained has doubtless led in many instances to the Government of India adopting a course of policy which, to Englishmen, lovers of Truth, Justice, and Freedom, is abhorrent, and would in our individual capacities be shunned equally with a deadly plague.

But that which Englishmen, as individuals, would blush to hear themselves charged with, much less be guilty of committing, they in their collective and corporate capacity, sometimes unhesitatingly accomplish; and English talent and genius are, we regret to say, too often prostituted in support of the cause of wrong and injustice.

It has been assumed by a few eminent statesmen and writers, that the secret of British success in India is entirely dependent upon the extinction of Sovereign rights and sway amongst the Native Princes of that land; that, in fact, for the English rule in India to be secured upon a firm and sound basis, the policy of the Indian Government must be "Annexation." Without discussing the soundness, or otherwise, of this doubtful policy, it has at no time been maintained that we should not only deprive the Princes of India of their possessions, but also rob them of their moveables and moneys; this doctrine we are happy to say, whatever may have been the private practice of our Indian Administrators, has never been expounded with authority.

The Great Mutiny of 1856—7 was an outbreak entirely due, not to a general discontent of the people at the disturbance of their landed tenures, or an insubordination of the military occasioned by interference with their religious prejudices, for these were but instruments, not causes of rebellion, but to the now well-known determination of certain powerful natives no longer to endure the insidious treachery of Indian Government policy, and their fixed resolution to put a stop to, and to revenge the continuous course of accumulated, although almost insensible, injuries and encroachments perseveringly carried on against them by the East India Company's officers. The severe lesson then administered by such a remonstrance in arms, would, doubtless, have induced the Company to conduct their Government of India upon more just principles, had not a knowledge of the cause and effects led to a wise resolution of Her Majesty to take from the corrupt hands of a Commercial Body the sceptre of empire over two hundred millions of human beings, and no longer to expose the British rule to the odium of a narrow-minded and mercenary policy. The hopes of India rose with the generous Proclamation of Her Majesty in 1858, and the native Princes of India were gladly folded under the wings of their encompassing Angel "British Empire."

Since that time, year after year has seen documents set forth on official authority, gratulatory of the material improvements effected in the managment of Indian affairs. But the moral policy of the Council in India has remained the same. There has been no cessation of the trenching towards confiscation as regards the Indian Native Princes that was left behind in the official desks of the Company—what was commenced in 1760, counselled in 1816, connived at in 1834, determined upon in 1854, and directed in 1862, was approved in 1864, and would have been effected in 1869 but for the bold determination of the intended victim, no less a personage than His Highness the Nawab of Bengal, Behar and Orissa—the oldest ally and greatest friend in India of the English power—to appear in person before Her Majesty, the Parliament, the People, and the Law of England, and to appeal for redress in the present for himself, and protection in the future for his family.

Thus the knowledge has been forced upon the English public—hitherto careless of Indian circumstances—that although the leading idea of the governing power in India was outwardly changed in person as in expression, the bureaucratic idea remained identical. So that it has happened that things have been done in the name of Her Majesty as Empress of India which are intolerable in any country subject to British laws, and governed according to British principles of justice.

That such things were possible under the sway of the East India Company there is no unwillingness to confess, but that it may be possible to suffer injustice from British Indian Imperial Government such as His Highness the Nawab of Bengal comes to complain of at the foot of the throne of England, some might feel inclined to doubt. To such, a painful spectacle must have been presented on the 1st March last in the Judicial Committee of the Privy Council, when their Lordships gave judgment on the Appeal "Her Majesty's Secretary of State for India *versus* Mussamat Khanzadee," a short quotation from which is annexed:

"The Government was much in the wrong in taking "possession as they did, and that this Appeal never "ought to have been brought. Their Lordships will "therefore humbly advise Her Majesty that it be dis-"missed. The dismissal should be with costs."

The Government alluded to is that of India as controlled by Her Majesty's Secretary of State and the Indian Council, which Council is thus described by Sir William Denison :—

Council of India:—" The gentlemen composing this
" Council can only give the Secretary of State the record
" of their past experience; they dream of the India of the
" present day as that of their youth; they can give no
" information which cannot be obtained in a much more
" perfect and correct form from the local authorities in
" India; their advice is disregarded by the Secretary of
" State when it does not harmonise with his own views,
" and is merely made use of by him to shelter himself
" from the responsibility which ought to devolve upon
" him of thinking out and deciding questions submitted
" to him from India; questions, I may say, which would
" be, in most instances, better dealt with by a fresh mind
" than by a body constituted like that of the Indian
" Council."

It is against the unjust and arbitrary decision of this tribunal in 1864 on the subject of his legitimate and hereditary rights that the Nawab Nazim of Bengal now appeals to the enlightened British Public.

"Can it be possible," an English gentleman would ask, "that on the termination of a contest for disputed sovereignty in which essential services had been rendered by those noblemen to the victor, after receiving from the head of a noble family, say the Dukes of D———e or A———ll, the management of his estates and the administration of his territories on condition of supplying a certain sum annually as revenue, the potentate, acting as steward—

after obtaining through such administration a complete command over the property—should turn round upon the family of his original employer and styling him—the Duke of D——e or A——ll—a 'titled stipendiary,' should declare the settlement (after a lapse of a hundred years) to have been only a personal agreement with his ancestor, and propose to cut away his rank, and lop off his revenue, leaving him only a bare annuity in the residue called a life-interest, but secured only on his (the payer's) caprice or convenience, with the addition of an insulting offer for the apprenticing of his sons to some trade?"

Such, nevertheless, is the object, intent, meaning and history of the following passage relating to the Nawab of Bengal, which occurs in a Despatch addressed by Sir C. Wood as Secretary of State for India to the Governor-General in Council in India—a passage no doubt purposely concealed and omitted in the copy supplied to the Nawab himself.

"I am of opinion that the future position of Nawab
" Nazim's sons should be fixed and defined with as little
" delay as possible. Her Majesty's Government desire to
" have the views of Your Excellency on this subject.
" Your Excellency *is aware that this Government are fully*
" *sensible of the* INCONVENIENCE OF PERPETUATING IN THIS
" OR ANY OTHER FAMILY A LINE OF TITLED STIPEN-
" DIARIES *without power and responsibility, and without*
" *salutary employment, &c., &c.,* it would seem to be the
" wish of the Nawab Nazim that his sons should be
" trained to some useful occupations. I should be glad
" if arrangements could be made for enabling them to
" become useful members of society. *The accumulation in*

"*the Nizamut Deposit Fund* MIGHT afford permanent endowment to a certain extent."

A similar proposal submitted to the House of Commons by the Chancellor of the Exchequer, as Dewan of the United Kingdom, in regard to Her Majesty's Civil List, would not be more absurdly illogical or flagrantly unjust.

To impose some check by public opinion on the continuous urging of such a policy is the main object of the present compilation of documents in regard to the Case of His Highness the Nawab of Bengal. In defence of his children's rights, he appears in this country as a Petitioner of Right. It was in his country and through his ancestor's services that the English secured a permanent footing in India in 1757; it was by his own loyalty that they were enabled to maintain it in 1857. That any such power will again fall to the hands of an Indian Native Prince is not probable. Her Majesty's rule as Empress has grounded a far different policy than what led up to the deplorable events of that sad period. But before the effects of such an improved policy can be realized to their full extent, it will be necessary that the old principles that have formed the ground-work of Indian official action should be entirely eradicated.

Surely, when all is said, " honesty is the best policy." What is called the English Government of Bengal was established upon commercial principles by commercial men. The East India Company never received any authority to *govern* the Provinces of Bengal, Behar, and Orissa; they were appointed first by the Nawab and afterwards by the Emperor of Delhi Chancellors of the Exchequer under the Nawabs' Government. Whatever authority the English Government of Bengal now possesses, has been *assumed*. In all their relations with the Nawabs of Bengal descended from Meer Jaffier the East India Company treated the Nawabs as Independent Princes, for it was a well known fact that they had purchased their independence by paying a fixed tribute of twenty-six lacs of rupees a year to the Emperor of Delhi, and were therefore *de facto* Independent Princes, and could only be treated as such. No revolution of the people has overthrown their power, nor have they committed any breach of Treaty with the English by which they could legally be said to have sacrificed their honour, or the protection to which they are entitled at the hands of the British Government. What was stipulated in the original Treaties and Agreements with the Nawabs is justly due to them, and should —speaking in a commercial sense alone—be paid over to them without further chaffering or unjust question.

Even in its best form, the present policy of the Government of India has attained no higher range than that of standing by injustice, and doing no more wrong. This idea was clearly set forth by Sir William Denison while acting temporarily as Governor-General in 1864, nor does he disguise the present condition of things, nor seek to conceal the wrong done.

" The more I see of the state of things in this country, " the more earnestly do I wish for alterations and reform ; " yet the growth of abuses has been so natural and so gra-

"dual, each step having been almost a necessary conse"quence of the preceding one, that it is difficult to know "where to begin, and having begun, equally difficult to "know where one is to stop. Many matters come before "me which involve a consideration of the treatment dealt "out by us to the great men of the land in former times, "and which impress me with the conviction that we acted "towards them most nefariously; but were I to attempt to "grant redress to the children of these, where could I stop? "I should have to give over a large slice of the Madras "Presidency to others who, ignorant and full of native "prejudices, would bring back a state of things, which, "if not past, is, at all events, passing away. I have made "up my mind, therefore, not to attempt to redress here"ditary injustice; but taking what happened before my "time as a *fait accompli*, to be careful that no complaint "is made against me."

However plausible and superficially politic such-like sentiments may be, they are neither commonly honest nor just. They resemble the simple idea of the "cateran" set in action on a large scale over an empire of two hundred millions of people,

"The robber's simple plan
That they should take who have the power,
And they should keep who can."

In the present instance of the claim now submitted to the patient investigation of the reader, the present Nawab Nazim has come to this country to seek at the hands of the British Government and Nation, that justice and redress which have been denied him in India. His claims are based entirely upon Treaties, public official Letters and Proclamations of the Government of India, and that also of Her Majesty. He seeks no favour, but simply desires a public and patient enquiry and investigation of his *just* claims, and he does this as a faithful servant and loyal adherent of Her Most Gracious Majesty. If those claims, on public and patient investigation, should prove just and legitimate, it is beyond the question to evade payment by pleading inexpediency. His Highness has at all times shown a desire to meet the Government in a friendly spirit, and to settle his claims amicably without embarrassing them. Had he been met in an equal spirit, there is no doubt that the vexed question of the " Claims of the Nawab of Bengal" would have been settled long ere this.

London, 2nd May, 1870.

GLOSSARY.

Aanut—Assistance.
Amils—Collectors.
Asamee—Defendants.
Ashur Khana—Department relating to the celebration of the Mohurran.
Baboo—A Hindoo gentleman.
Bahadoor—Brave or noble.
Bakshi—Controller of the Army.
Banchoot—A term of abuse.
Batta burdar—A man who attends an Indian Prince to supply him with spices, beetle leaf, &c.
Batta—Discount or difference in exchange.
Bazar—Market place.
Beea—Interested.
Bester—Bedding.
Begum—Princess; now used as a complimentary title only.
Behala—Treasury, or paymaster's department.
Beyt—Switch or cane.
Bhaebunds—Intimate acquaintances.
Bhatjee—A Hindoo physician holding a diploma.
Bheestee—Water carrier.
Burkundauzes—Military police; constabulary.
Chelah—Disciple or follower.
Chobdar—Mace bearer.

GLOSSARY.

Chokedar—Policeman.
Chuckla—A district or part of a province.
Chunam—Lime.
Circar—Government.
Coss—Two English miles.
Cutcha—Raw or green.
Darogah—Superintendent.
Dewan—Collector of Revenue and paymaster.
Dewanny—Office of Collector of revenues.
Dewanny Sherista—Dewan's office department.
Dohay—Help.
Domdeen—A humbug or deceiver.
Dustuck—Passport.
Emaruth—Building department.
Fakeer or *Faquir*—Mendicant.
Farashkhana—Tent department.
Firmaun—Letters patent or royal charter; edict.
Foujdar—A magistrate or collector.
Foujdarry—Magistrate's court or collectorate.
Futwa—Decision given by a Mahomedan law officer.
Garries—Carriages or carts.
Gareewan—Coachman or carter.
Gatch—Tree.
Gentoos—Hindoos.
Ghurries—Hours.
Golam—Slave.
Gomastah—Agent.
Hakeem—Mahomedan physician.
Hath—A measure of 18 inches.
Hookah—A native pipe.
Humlogko dhoopme doorawa—You have made us wander about under the hot sun.
Humko nahuk marta—He is beating me unjustly.
Hurkara—Commissioner or messenger.
Hurumzadur—A term of abuse.
Husbulhookum—A customs pass.
Huzoor—Your Honour: a term of respect applied by an inferior to a superior.

Imteazy—Superior.
Jaghire—A pension in land for services rendered; a fief or freehold.
Jaghirdar—Fiefholder or freeholder.
Jemadar—Head of a department of servants.
Jharoo—Birch or broom.
Jugy—Jugged.
Jungle—Wild place; forest.
Kanat—Side wall of a tent.
Karkhanah—Place where work is done; department.
Keories—Husbandmen.
Khalsa Shereefa—Freehold.
Khana—Department or room.
Khas Khawas—A chosen servant or personal attendant.
Khavas—Valet or footman.
Khazanchee—Treasurer.
Kheema—Tent.
Khoonrays—Executioners.
Kistbundy—Instalment.
Kooberaj—A Hindoo physician without a diploma.
Koob maro—Beat very much.
Korah—Whip.
Kullumdan Khana—Privy purse.
Lakh—One hundred thousand.
Latteals—Men who fight with sticks.
Licka ap—Did you write this.
Lushkar—Camp.
Mahout—Elephant driver.
Majholee—A kind of cart.
Mamoolat—A customary allowance.
Marhrohe or *Mohurrir*—A clerk or writer.
Maro—Beat.
Meah—Eunuch or chamberlain.
Meeanah—A conveyance, like a Sedan chair, for invalids and women.
Meer—The distinctive appellation of a descendant of Mahomed.
Meer Samana—Commissariat department.
Mehal Serai—Seraglio.
Mehter—Scavenger.
Mofussil—Country: opposed to town.

Mohafez khanah—Record room.
Mohurrum—Celebration of the Martyrdom of the grandsons of Mahomet.
Mohurrir—Scribe.
Molazum—Courtier.
Molazuman Imteazy—Officer of the Court of an Indian Prince.
Moojrayee—Crier of a Court.
Mookbarah—Tomb or Mausoleum.
Moonshieff—An Indian subordinate Judge.
Moors—Mahomedan.
Mosahib—Aide-de-Camp.
Muftee—Law officer.
Musnud—Throne.
Mutaynat—An appointed perquisite.
Muttasuddees—Accountants.
Naib, Naib Soubah—Deputy, Nawab's deputy.
Nawab or Nabob—Ruler of a Province of the Empire.
Nawab Nazim—Originally Deputy Ruler or Viceroy of the King of Delhi, but subsequently an Independent Tributary Prince.
Nawab Nazir—Chamberlain, an office usually held in the East by eunuchs.
Nautch girl—A dancing girl.
Nazirs—A title generally applied to eunuchs or other people holding responsible service appointments.
Nizamut—Nawab Nazim, his Court Family and Government.
Nizamut Adawlut—The highest Indian Appellate Court.
Nukeeb—A crier, herald.
Nutthee—A bundle of papers.
Nuzzer—A homage gift.
Omrahs—Noblemen.
Oomedwar—A hanger-on waiting for employment.
Pal—A gipsy tent made of matting.
Pandish bearer—A servant-in-waiting upon an Indian Prince with spices, perfume, &c.
Peadah—A foot soldier of the body-guard employed as a servant.
Peons—Commissionaire or messenger,
Peruneeah—One who writes down evidence in a Court.
Pergunnah—A parish or part of a district.

GLOSSARY.

Perwannah—An order or pass in writing.
Pheel Khana—Elephant department.
Rajah—A title of Hindoo nobility.
Razdarre—Councillor.
Reiat or *Ryot*—A tenant.
Robokarunavees—Writer of summary decisions.
Rowana—A customs pass.
Rupee—Two shillings; florin.
Russee—A rope used as a measure about 30 feet.
Ruth—A kind of covered bamboo carriage on four wheels.
Sahib—Gentleman.
Sepoys—Native soldiers.
Shagerd Pesha—Menial servants.
Shurrah—Tenets of Mahomedanism.
Siccas—The old Indian rupees of about one-sixteenth more value than the English rupees.
Sircar—A government or head of a department.
Sirdar—A governor or chieftain. Head man.
Soubah—Government; a division of the Empire.
Soubahdar—Head of the Government of a division of the Empire.
Soubahdarry—Kingdom, Division of the Empire.
Sooruthal—The first process of instruction in a Criminal Court.
Suddar Nizamut—The highest Indian Appellate Court.
Suggurgarree—A two-wheeled bullock-cart.
Sultanut—Empire.
Sunnud—Royal Warrant.
Suwarry—Retinue.
Syce—Groom.
Talka pal—Awning, generally made of mats.
Talookdars—A land holder.
Tamasha—An amusing entertainment.
Tazeer—Guilty.
Teen duffa ya haluth hooa—This occurred three times.
Thanna—Police station.
Ticca—Temporary employment.
Toshakhana—Robe department.
Ukroba or *Akrobah*—Relations.
Urzbeggy or *Aruzbegy*—Usher in waiting on an Indian Prince.

Vakeel—Agent.
Verandah—Portico.
Vizier—Prime Minister.
Wogherah—Et cetera.
Zemindar—Landholder.
Zemindary—Leasehold Estate subject to ground rent.
Zillah—County or shire.
Zimmum—Bond or surety.
Zulen—Oppression or tyranny.
Zumistanee—Seasonable gifts.

INTRODUCTION

The relations between the Nawab Nazim of Bengal and the British Government may be classified under three heads, viz.: Political, Commercial, and Social.

The Political relations are consequent on the Treaty of Alliance offensive and defensive entered into with Meer Jaffier by the Representatives of the British Government in 1757 (Page 6), confirmed by the Treaty of 1763 (Page 9) and ratified by the subsequent Treaty with Nudjm-ul-Dowlah in 1765 (Page 15). The true spirit, intent and meaning of those Treaties have been clearly evinced by the recognition of the descendants of Meer Jaffier as Soubahdars and Nawabs Nazim of Bengal, Behar and Orissa, up to the present day, and although they have since 1772 been *deprived* of the power vested in them, as also many of their rights and privileges, no legitimate reason can be adduced in support of such an arbitrary course of procedure.

The Commercial Relations are grounded upon the Firmaun of the Emperor of Delhi in 1765 (Page 19), and the Agreement (Page 22) with Nawab Nudjm-ul-Dowlah, who made over the Freehold of his own personal estates as well as that of the Imperial Lands to the Company as a Feud, and agreed to accept a round sum of about £570,000 per annum as the Nizamut share of the Revenues to be regularly paid as long as the East India Company's Factories continued in Bengal. This arrangement was subsequently modified by mutual consent, and by a Treaty and Agreement in 1766 (Page 23), and at last definitely fixed by the Treaty and Agreement of 1770 (Page 26), "for ever." Since that time no formal Treaties have been entered into to regulate this allowance, and it does not follow that because the Nawabs Nazim, as powerless Princes, were unable to exact the full amount then agreed upon, and were obliged perforce to accept whatever sum their powerful Allies chose to pay them, that they are in consequence not legitimately entitled to the sum fixed by mutual arrangement in 1770! Such a conclusion would be both unjust and, commercially speaking, untenable.

The Social relations are those by which society is regulated, whereby men of rank are entitled to a certain amount of respect as becomes their position. These relations have been sadly departed from by the officers of the British Government in their dealings with the present Nawab, and right-thinking men may satisfy themselves of the truth of this assertion by a perusal of the Correspondence from Page 238 to Page 268. Notwithstanding the repeated assurances of Governors-General to support the happiness, dignity and high station of the Nawab, even his private rights have been invaded, his income has been arbitrarily curtailed, and the management of his own family, the dismissal of his own servants, and even the religious services over his ancestors' tombs have been successively interfered with, each invasion being quoted as a precedent for another. His Highness has thus been subjected to indignities which no man, however humble his position, would brook without remonstrance! Is it, then, to be wondered at that the Nawab

Nazim is now appealing to the British Government for redress and protection?

With regard to the Nawab Nazim's political and commercial privileges it has been plausibly asserted that "under the Treaties (with his ancestors) the Nawab Nazim has no acquired rights," and "that the Family of the Nawab Nazim of Bengal have under the Firmaun of Shah Allum, no claim upon the British Government," but these assertions are unsupported by legal authority, or by the conditions under which the Company acquired the Fief of the Provinces of Bengal, Behar and Orissa; for when the office of the Dewanny was conferred upon the Company, they became Chancellors of the Exchequer only, and were not invested with any *governing* powers. All such powers were reserved for the Nawabs Nazim with a stipulation in the Firmaun that their expenses and those of their family and court should first be provided for out of the revenues of the provinces. The following extract of a letter from the Court of Directors themselves dated 17th May, 1766, clearly exhibits the relative duties of the Company and the Nawab: " We conceive the " office of Dewan should be exercised only in " *superintending* the collection and disposal of

"the Revenues, which office though vested
"in the Company should officially be executed
"by our Resident at the Durbar under the
"control of the Governor and Select Com-
"mittee, the ordinary bounds of which control
"should extend to nothing beyond the super-
"intending the collection of the Revenues,
"and receiving the money from the Nawab's
"Treasury to that of the Dewannah or Com-
"pany. . . . . . This we conceive to be the
"whole office of the Dewanny. The Admin-
"istration of Justice, the Appointment of
"Offices, Zemindarries, &c., in short what-
"ever comes under the denomination of Civil
"Administration we understand is to remain
"in the hands of the Nawab and his ministers."
(*vide* Page 469 of Long's "Selections of Unpublished Records of the Government of India.")

This letter explains the dualistic form of Government which united the interests of the East India Company and the Nawabs Nazim of Bengal, Behar and Orissa, and no legal authority was ever given to the East India Company which entitled them to control the whole Administration of the Provinces. This usurpation of power took place in 1772 during the minority of the young Nawab Mobaruck-ul-dowlah, while his affairs were conducted in Trust by the Prime Minister Mahomed Reza Khan who had been appointed to that office by a former Nawab, and even allowing that the Company were obliged to assume the temporary management of the Nawab's Government during his minority, as Regents they were morally bound to restore to him the management of his affairs when he was old enough to govern. The Judicial Branch of the Administration alone was restored and continued under the control of the Nawabs Nazim until 1838-40, when in consequence of the non-age of the present Nawab, that also was taken up by the Company for their own purposes, thus leaving the Nawab against his own will "*without power and responsibility, and without salutary employment.*" This fact was ungraciously taken up in 1864 by Her Majesty's Secretary of State for India, and dwelt upon as a reason for depriving the children of the present Nawab Nazim of those rights, dignities and privileges which have been guaranteed to the family by solemn Treaties, and these Princes have been ignominiously styled " Titled Stipendiaries," liable at any moment to have their means of subsistence taken from them, although their rights were secured "for ever" by the provisions of a mutual agreement based upon the stipulations of the Imperial Firmaun, which while it constituted the Company Fiefholders and Chancellors of the Exchequer, especially provided for the support of the Nizamut.

The Revenues of the Provinces of Bengal, Behar and Orissa were only made over to the East India Company in Trust on certain conditions, and it is the breach of those conditions which is clearly hinted at in the Despatch of 17th June, 1864 (Page 279). Such a narrow-minded Policy, however, is opposed to all the rules of morality, and to the magnanimous principles of the British Government, and if carried out would throw a slur on the good name of the British Nation, and expose our credit to justifiable attacks from foreigners, which it is the duty of every Englishman to carefully guard against.

Commercially speaking, such an act of confiscation would be analogous to that of a banker or agent, holding the control of certain moneys or lands placed in his custody under a proviso that a portion thereof should be paid for the support or benefit of a ward in Chancery, refusing to meet the claim on a plea of inexpediency or from self-interested motives.

The British Government would be as much justified in repudiating the claims of all those who now hold the bonds and securities of the East India Company in the form of Company's Papers, &c., as in cancelling the Treaties and engagements made with the Nawabs Nazim of Bengal, Behar and Orissa. Both were given for value received by the East India Company, and as the British Government bound itself by Royal Proclamation to abide by all such engagements and to maintain them scrupulously, surely no State Policy should dictate the abrogation of the one without the other, or in other words, make the *weak* suffer while supporting the *strong*.

The present Nawab Nazim, as a powerless Prince, relies entirely on the moral support and protection of the British Public against a premeditated act of injustice to himself and his family. He asks for no favour, and the fact of his seeking a public investigation and inquiry into his claims, which have not yet been controverted by the Government, will naturally lead thinking men to the conclusion that he has *justice* on his side, and that "his weakness is his strength."

A COMMERCIAL VIEW

OF THE

RELATIONS

BETWEEN THE

BRITISH GOVERNMENT

AND THE

NAWABS NAZIM OF BENGAL, BEHAR AND ORISSA.

That commerce is one great source from which national importance is derived, is unquestionable, for history points out that the energies of many great nations have been directed to the protection of it, and that with the decline of their commerce, such nations as the Dutch, Spanish, and Portuguese lost their influence, and sunk into obscurity, yielding the palm of greatness to other Powers, foremost among which now stands England. The British nation is essentially commercial, and to this fact may in some measure be attributed our position as the leading Power of the world, since our influence has been derived from the enormous resources of our country, accumulated to a great extent by the importation of the material wealth of other lands over which we hold sway. The greatest and wealthiest of our possessions is India (which has been very appropriately styled "the brightest jewel in our Regal Crown"), it is to a part of India, therefore, and an Indian question, founded upon our commercial relations with that country, that this paper is particularly dedicated.

The first Europeans we read of who obtained a settlement in India for the purposes of trade were the Portuguese, whose example was followed first by the Dutch, and afterwards by the French and English. Without entering into historical details, connected with the Charter granted by Queen Elizabeth to the English merchants trading to the East Indies, it will be sufficient for our purpose to give an outline of the Government of India, and more particularly of that portion of it to which we wish to draw public attention (the Provinces of Bengal, Behar, and Orissa) from the year 1636, when, through the influence of an English surgeon named Boughton, a few enterprising British merchants obtained a Firmaun (Patent) from the reigning sovereign, Shaw Allum, to trade free of customs throughout all his dominions. India had at that time, after many and great revolutions, become subject to the Emperor of Delhi, commonly known as the Great Mogul, and was divided into several provinces or kingdoms called soubahdarries, the government of which was entrusted by the Emperor either to his sons or to viceroys of Royal lineage, called Nawabs, who, as rulers of the Soubahdarries, were styled Soubahs or Soubahdars. These Soubahs paid tribute to the Royal

Court at Delhi, but exercised full power in their own Provinces as Independent Princes, so that it became incumbent on our traders to obtain their consent as well as that of the Emperor before they could carry on their commercial operations in the several provinces. Thus circumstanced, our merchants were occasionlly interfered with by some of the Nawabs, and having been at last expelled from the country, they appealed to King James the Second, who sent out some ships with troops to protect the rights and interests of his subjects, and secure the establishment of that commercial body known to us as the Old East India Company, who prosecuted their trade with varied success until the year 1698, when another Company of merchants was formed in England, under the auspices of King William III., for the purpose of trading with India. This new establishment excited the jealousy and indignation of the old traders, who exerted all their power to overthrow it, but without effect, till 1705, when, after much discussion, a union of the two interests was agreed upon, and a Royal Charter was obtained for the United Company of English Merchants trading to the East Indies. This union of the two Companies was the first step towards the establishment of British power in the East, for their combined efforts and joint capital enabled them to enlarge their operations by buying land, building factories and forts, hiring troops, and putting themselves in a position to defend themselves in cases of emergency. The commerce of Bengal—the richest Province in India, and which at that time, together with Behar and Orissa, was governed by Prince Azim-ul-Shan, grandson of the

Emperor Aurungzebe—became their chief study, and they accordingly obtained permission from the Nawab for carrying on their operations in that Province, even under heavy restrictions. The trade of the Company, however, increased but slowly until the time (1741-1756) of Nawab Aliverdy Khan (the fifth in succession after Prince Azim-ul-Shan), who, being well disposed towards the English, entered into a Treaty with them, and granted them many concessions which enabled them by right of purchase and other means to establish themselves permanently as traders in the country, in which capacity they might have existed up to the present day, had not circumstances occurred after the death of Nawab Aliverdy Khan, which roused the indignation of the British Government, and led to those events which opened out a new era in the history of Bengal, and gave birth to the policy by which, under cover of Solemn Treaties and Engagements, the Company eventually secured for themselves the Supreme Administration of the three Provinces of Bengal, Behar, and Orissa, and the way was thus opened for the introduction of the Wise Laws and Noble Institutions of our country into a land that for many ages had been the scene of political intrigue, massacre, and bloodshed. But while admiring the great results of that policy as exhibited in the improved condition of the country and also in the advantages gained by it for the British Nation, we should not lose sight of the faithful representatives of our oldest ally, Meer Jaffier to whose influence and co-operation alone can be attributed the success which has accompanied it. It is, therefore, to His Highness Syud Munsoor Ullee, the present Nawab of

Bengal, Behar, and Orissa, that we would now draw public attention, and, after giving a brief account of his ancestors their position and relations with the East India Company, their loyalty, and faithful attachment to the British Crown, notwithstanding the arbitrary measures of the Government of India which have resulted in their humiliation, and which will be fully set forth herein, we will introduce for public consideration His Highness' grievances as set forth in his Memorial to Her Majesty's Secretary of State for India in Council, wherein he describes the unjust treatment he received at the hands of the local Government of India—which led to his leaving his home and his family and visiting our country in the hope of obtaining from Her Most Gracious Majesty and Her wise and just Government and People that justice and redress for his wrongs for which he and his loyal Predecessors have vainly applied in India!

Nawab Aliverdy Khan (who left no male issue) had three years before his death nominated his grandson Mirza Mahomed (better known as Suraj-ul-dowlah) his successor. This Prince, being of a sullen, cruel, and tyrannical disposition, was quite unfit for the position he occupied, and he was in consequence disliked by his own people, and by everybody with whom he held intercourse; it may, therefore, be readily conceived that he soon made himself obnoxious to the English Company, whom he had determined to drive out of the country. His success against the English and his cruel acts which terminated in the dreadful tragedy of the Black Hole in Calcutta (too well known to need comment here) led the Company to enter into an intrigue with his relatives and their supporters for the purpose of dethroning the tyrant and placing another member of the Royal House on the musnud. Accordingly, negociations were commenced with Meer Jaffier Ali Khan, the son-in-law of Nawab Aliverdy Khan—a nobleman of Royal lineage, and great influence, and Commander-in-Chief of the Army, who had always shown himself a zealous friend and supporter of the English. He undertook to make good the losses the Company had sustained if they would lend him their assistance and co-operation as feudatories in obtaining possession of the throne; this the Company agreed to do, and drew up the famous red and white treaties under the direction of Colonel Clive, who afterwards, through the instrumentality of Meer Jaffier Ali Khan, succeeded in defeating Suraj-ul-dowlah at the memorable battle of Plassey, on the 15th June, 1757, and on the accession of Meer Jaffier Ali Khan, concluded the Treaty with the new Nawab, of which the following is a acknowledged to be a true copy. The original was supposed to have been subsequently destroyed by Colonel Clive for his own protection, when he was accused of having forged Admiral Watson's name on it.

Translation of the Public Treaty made with ADMIRAL WATSON, COLONEL CLIVE *and the other counsellors,* MR. DRAKE *and* MR. WATTS, *as written in Persic, &c., &c., and signed by* MEER JAFFIER ALI KHAN *with his own hand.* (*Vide Orme's* " *History of Indostan.*" *Vol. II., Page* 161.)

"I swear by God, and by the Prophet of God, to abide by the terms of this Treaty whilst I have life."

Article 1.

Whatever Articles were agreed to in the time of peace with the Nabob Surajah Dowlah, I agree to comply with.

Article 2.

The enemies of the English are my enemies, whether they be Indians or Europeans.

Article 3.

All the effects and factories belonging to the French in the province of Bengal, the paradise of nations, and **Behar, and Orixa, shall** remain in the possession of the English, nor will I ever allow them any more to settle in the three provinces.

Article 4.

In consideration of the losses which the English Company have **sustained by the** capture and plunder of Calcutta by the Nabob, and the charges occasioned by the maintenance of the forces, I will give them one crore of rupees.

Article 5.

For the effects plundered from the English inhabitants at Calcutta, I agree to give fifty lacs of rupees.

Article 6.

For the effects plundered from **the Gentoos, Moors, and other in**habitants of Calcutta, twenty lacs **of rupees shall be given.**

Article 7.

For the effects plundered from **the Armenian inhabitants of Cal**cutta, I will give the sum of seven lacs of rupees. **The distribution of** the sums allotted to the English, Gentoo, Moor, **and other inhabitant,** of Calcutta, **shall** be left to Admiral Watson, **Colonel Clive, Roger Drake,** William Watts, James Kilpatrick, and Richard Beechers Esquires, to be disposed of by them to whom they think proper.

Article 8.

Within **the ditch** which surrounds the borders of Calcutta, are tracts of land belonging to several Zemindars; besides these, **I will** grant to the English Company 600 yards without the ditch.

Article 9.

All the land lying south **of Calcutta,** as far as Culpee, shall be under the Zemindarry of the English Company : and all the officers of these parts shall be under their jurisdiction. The Revenues to be paid by the Company in the same manner as other Zemindars.

Article 10.

Whenever **I demand the** assistance of the English, **I will be at the** charge of **the maintenance** of their troops.

Article 11.

I will not erect any new fortifications near the River Ganges below Hughley.

Article 12.

As soon as I am established in the three provinces, the aforesaid sums shall be faithfully paid.

Dated the 15th of the month of Ramagan, in the fourth year of the present reign.

This Treaty as written by the English, contained the sense of the above Articles, though in different words, and concluded with an additional clause to the following effect :—

Article 13.

On condition, Meer Jaffier Cawn Bahadur solemnly ratifies and swears to fulfil the above Articles, we, the underwritten, do, for and in behalf of the Honourable East India Company, declare on the Holy Evangelists, and before God, that we will assist Meer Jaffier Cawn Bahadur with our whole utmost force to obtain the Subahships of the Provinces of Bengal, Behar, and Orixa, and further, that we will assist him to the utmost against all his enemies whatever, whensoever he calls upon us for that purpose, provided that when he becomes the Nabob, he fulfils the above Articles.

This Treaty was signed by

        ADMIRAL WATSON,
        COLONEL CLIVE,
        MR. DRAKE,
        MR. WATTS,
        MAJOR KILPATRICK,
        MR. BECHER.

The donations to the Army, Squadron, and Committee were written in another Treaty.

We need not dwell upon the flight and miserable death of Suraj-ul-dowlah, suffice it to say that Nawab Meer Jaffier Ali Khan was duly installed as his successor, and was confirmed in the office by a sunnud (patent or proclamation) from the Emperor of Delhi, without which he must have been looked upon as a usurper—for though long before this time the power of the Great Mogul had been on the decline, and most of the Nawabs had ceased to obey the Royal mandate, yet the form of applying to the Royal Court for sunnuds (patents) confirming any changes that might take place in the direct line of succession of the Nawabs had not been quite abolished. The right of succession, therefore, of the family of Nawab Meer Jaffier Ali Khan having been confirmed by the Emperor of Delhi, no grounds could thereafter be adduced for interfering with them without *cruel injustice;* yet, because the Nawab Meer Jaffier was unable to meet the exacting demands of the Company's servants, a conspiracy was formed against him while Clive was away, and he was induced to retire from public life, and make over the Government of the Provinces to his son-in-law, Meer Cossim Ali Khan, whom the servants of the Company used as an instrument for carrying out their ends. But Meer Cossim Ali Khan did not long enjoy his position, for the Directors in England ordered their servants to reinstate the legitimate Nawab, Meer Jaffier Ali Khan, which they accordingly did by an additional Treaty and Agreement, (which is still in the possession of the present Nawab) under which they secured for themselves and the Company many unlooked-for advantages—such as gifts of lands, &c.

Articles of a Treaty and Agreement between the Governor and Council of Fort William, on the part of the English East India Company and the NABOB SUJAH-UL MULCK, HOSSAIN-Ô-DOWLAH, MEER MAHOMED JAFFIER KAHN BAHADUR, MAHABUT JUNG, 1763.

| Company's large Seal. | The Seal of the Nabob Meer Mahomed Jaffier Khan, Bahadur, Mahabut Jung, &c. |

On the part of the Company.

We engage to reinstate the Nabob Meer Mahomed Jaffier Khan

Bahadur in the Soubahdarry of the Provinces of Bengal, Behar, and Orixa, by the deposal of Meer Mahomed Kossim Khan; and the effects, treasure, and jewels, &c., belonging to Meer Mahomed Kossim Khan, which shall fall into our hands, shall be delivered up to the Nabob aforenamed.

On the part of the Nabob.

Article 1.

The Treaty which I *formerly* concluded with the Company upon my accession to the Nizamnt, *engaging to regard the honour and reputation of the Company, their Governor and Council as my own*, granting perwannahs for the Currency of the Company's business, the same Treaty I now confirm and ratify.

Article 2.

I do grant and confirm to the Company, for defraying the expenses of Troops, the Chucklas of Burdwan, Midnapore and Chitagong, which were before ceded for the same purpose.

Article 3.

I do ratify and confirm to the English the privilege granted them by their Firmaun and several Husbulhookums, of carrying on their trade by means of their own dustuck, free from all duties, taxes, or impositions in all parts of the country, excepting the article of Salt, on which a duty of $2\frac{1}{2}$ per cent is to levied on the rowana, or Hooghly market price.

Article 4.

I give to the Company half the Saltpetre which is produced in the country of Purnea, which their Gomastahs shall send to Calcutta. The other half shall be collected by my Foujdar, for the use of my offices; and I will suffer no other person to make purchases of this article in that country.

Article 5.

In the Chuckla of Sylhet, for the space of five years, commencing with the Bengal year 1170, my Foujdar and the Company's Gomastah, shall jointly prepare chunam, of which each shall defray half the expense, and half the chunam so made shall be given to the Company, and the other half shall be for my use.

Article 6.

I will maintain twelve thousand horse and twelve thousand foot in the three Provinces. If there should be occasion for any more, the number shall be increased by consent of the Governor and Council proportionably to the emergency; besides these, the Force of the English Company shall always attend me when they are wanted.

Article 7.

Whenever I shall fix my Court, either at Moorshedabad or elsewhere, I will advise the Governor and Council; and what number of English Force I may have occasion for in the management of my affairs, I will demand them, and they shall be allowed me, and an English Gentleman shall reside with me to transact all affairs between me and the Company, and a person shall also reside on my part at Calcutta to negociate with the Governor and Council.

Article 8.

The late Perwannahs issued by Kossim Ally Khan, *granting to all merchants the exemption of all duties for the space of two years, shall be reversed and called in*, and the duties called in as before.

Article 9.

I will cause the Rupees coined in Calcutta to pass in every respect equal to the Siccas of Moorshedabad, without any deduction of batta, and whoever shall demand batta, shall be punished.

Article 10.

I will give thirty lakhs of Rupees to defray all the expenses and loss occurring to the Company from the war and stoppage of their investment; and I will reimburse to all private persons the amount of such losses, proved before the Governor and Council, as they may sustain in their trade in the country. If I should not be able to discharge this in ready money, I will give assignments of land for the amount.

Article 11·

I will confirm and renew the Treaty which I formerly made with the Dutch.

Article 12.

If the French come into the country, I will not allow them to erect any fortifications, maintain forces, hold lands, Zemindarees, &c., but they shall pay tribute, and carry on their trade as in former times.

Article 13.

Some regulations shall be hereafter settled between us for deciding all disputes which may arise between the English Agents and Gomastahs, in the different parts of the country, and my Officers.

In testimony whereof, we, the said Governor and Council, have set our hands and affixed the seal of the Company to one part hereof, and the Nawab aforesaid hath set his hand and seal to another part hereof, which were mutually done and interchanged at Fort William, the 10th of July, 1763.

(Signed)   HENRY VANSITTART,
      "   JOHN CARNAC.
      "   WILLIAM BILLERS,
      "   WARREN HASTINGS,
      "   RANDOLPH MARRIOTT,
      "   HUGH WATTS.

Before signing this Treaty, the Nawab Meer Jaffier Ali Khan, fearing the Company's servants might again disregard the solemn pledges they had given him to remain his firm Allies, made several demands upon them which were duly agreed to in the following terms :—

Demands made on the part of the Nabob Meer Mahomed Jaffier Cawn to the Governor and Council at the time of signing the Treaty.

1st. I formerly acquainted the Company with the particulars of my own affairs, and received from them repeated letters of encouragement and kindness, with presents. *I now make this request, that you will write in a proper manner to the Company and also to the King of England, the particulars of our Friendship and Union, and procure for me writings of encouragement, that my mind may be assured from that quarter, that no breach may ever happen between me and the English, and that every Governor, Counsellor, and Chiefs of the English that are here, or may hereafter come, may be well disposed and attached to me.*

2nd. Since all the English gentlemen assured of my friendly disposition confirm me in the Nizamut, I request that to whatever I may at any time write they will give their credit and assent; nor regard the stories of designing men to my prejudice, that all my affairs may go on with success, and no occasion may arise for jealousy or ill-will between us.

3rd. Let no protection be given by any of the English gentlemen to any who may fly for shelter to Calcutta or other of your districts, but let them be delivered up to me on demand. I shall strictly enjoin all my Foujdars and Amils, on all accounts to afford assistance and countenance to such of the Gomastahs of the Company, as attend to the lawful trade of the Factories. And if any of the said Gomastahs shall act otherwise, let them be checked in such a manner as may be an example to others.

4th. From the neighbourhood of Calcutta to Hooghly and many of the Pergunnahs bordering upon each other, it happens that on complaints being made people go against the Talookdars, *Reiats* and Tenants of my towns to the prejudice of the business of the Sircar. Wherefore let strict orders be given that no Peons be sent from Calcutta, on the complaint of any one upon my Talukdars or Tenants; but on such occasions let application be made to me, or to the Naib of the Foujdarry of Hooghly that the country may be subject to no loss or devastation. And if any of the *Merchants* Traders, which belonged to the Bucksbunder and Azimgunge, and have settled in Calcutta should be desirous of returning to Hooghly and carrying on their business there as formerly, let no one molest them. Chandernagore and the French factory were presented to me by Colonel Clive, and given by me in charge to Omer Beg Cawn. For this reason, let strict orders be given that no English gentleman exercise any authority therein, but that it remain as formerly under the jurisdiction of my people.

5th. *Whenever I may demand any forces from the Governor and Council for my assistance, let them be immediately sent to me and no demand made on me for their expenses.*

The demands of the Nabob Shujan-ool-Mulck Hissam o'Dowlah, Meer Mahomed Jaffier, Cawn Bahad'r Mohabut Jung, written in five articles. *We the President and Council of the English Company do agree and set our hands to—*

Fort William, 10th July, 1763.

	(Signed)	HENRY VANSITTART.
	,,	THOMAS ADAMS,
	,,	JOHN CARNAC,
	,,	S. BATSON,
	,,	WM. BILLERS.
	,,	JOHN CARTIER,
	,,	WARREN HASTINGS,
	,,	RANDH. MARRIOTT,
	,,	J. L. WATTS.

But in 1764 the Company's servants again infringed the Nawab's rights by demanding from him a note of hand for the expenses of their army, which, by the terms of the Treaty, they had no right to ask for.

NAWAB MEER JAFFIER ALLY KHAN's *Note for five Lakhs of Rupees per month for the expenses of the Army, 1764.*

Account of money settled for the expenses of the Europeans and Sepoys, the Artillery and raising of the Cavalry, which shall be paid a month sooner or later, according to the particulars undermentioned from the beginning of the month Sophar (31st July, 1764,) of the 5th year of the reign, till the removal of the troubles with the Vizier, viz.

In the Province of Bengal at Moorshedabad	.. 3,00,000
In the Province of Behar, at Patna	.. 2,00,000
Total Rupees	5,00,000

Written the 19th of Babbie-ul-Awul, the 5th year of Jaloos, 16th September, 1764.

N.B.—I will include in the aforesaid sum whatever balance may be due from me on account of my former agreement with the Company.

It is reasonable to suppose that the Company's servants, having by this time acquired everything that they could *reasonably* expect, by Treaty or otherwise, *in return for their services*, and also for the purpose of carrying on the legitimate trade of their employers, would have been satisfied in allowing the Nawab Meer Jaffier Ali Khan and his successors to retain possesion of the throne without further interference on their part, except in so far as they had bound themselves by Treaty to protect the rights and interests of the Nizamut; but (and we blush to say it) the foretaste of power and annexation led them to forget the principles of truth, honor, and justice (the characteristic virtues of Englishmen), and they sacrificed the credit of the British Nation by departing from their integrity, and breaking faith with their firm and confiding Allies for pecuniary considerations!

When Nawab Meer Jaffier Ali Khan died, his eldest surviving son, Nawab Nudjm-ul-dowlah, ascended the throne, and the Company's servants taking advantage of the confidence reposed in them by the Nawabs, embraced this occasion for obtaining from the new Soubahdar additional benefit for themselves and the Company, by drawing out another Treaty, in which the Nawab was induced, after ratifying and confirming those made with his father, to make further concessions in favour of the Company, and *to place part of the military administration of the country in their hands*, besides entertaining a creature of the Company, Mahomed Reza Khan, as his Vizier or Prime Minister.

Articles of a Treaty and Agreement concluded between the Governor and Council of Fort William, on the part of the ENGLISH EAST INDIA COMPANY, *and* NABOB NUDJUM-UL-DOWLA.

On the part of the Company.

We, the Governor and Council, do engage to secure to the Nabob Nudjum-ul-Dowla all the Soubahdarry of the Provinces of Bengal, Behar, and Orissa; and to support him therein with the Company's Forces against all his enemies. We will also, *at all times, keep up such force as may be necessary effectually to assist and support him in the defence of the Provinces; and as our troops will be more to be depended on than any the Nabob can have, and less expensive to him, he need, therefore, entertain none but such as are requisite for the support of the Civil Officers of his Government, and the business of his collections* through the different districts.

We do further promise, that in consideration the Nabob shall continue to assist in defraying the extraordinary expenses of the war, now carrying on against Shujah-ul-Dowla, with five lacs of Rupees per month, which was agreed to by his father, whatever sums may be hereafter received of the King, on account of our assistance afforded him in the war, *shall be repaid to the Nabob.*

On the part of the Nabob.

In consideration of the assistance the Governor and Council have agreed to afford in *securing* to me *the succession* in the Soubahdarry of Bengal, Behar and Orissa, heretofore held by my Father, the late Nabob Meer Jaffier Ally Khan, and supporting me in it against all my enemies, I do agree and bind myself to the faithful performance of the following Articles:—

Article 1.

The Treaty which my father *formerly* concluded with the Company upon his first accession to the Nizamut, *engaging to regard the honour and reputation of the Company and of their Governor and Council as his own*, and granting perwannahs for the currency of the Company's trade, *the same Treaty, as far as is consistent with the Articles hereafter agreed*, I do hereby ratify and confirm.

Article 2.

Considering the weighty charge of Government, and how essential it is for myself, for the welfare of the country, and *for the Company's business*, that I should have a person who has had experience therein to advise and assist me, I do agree to have one fixed with me, with the advice of the Governor and Council, in the station of Naib Soubah, who shall accordingly have immediately under me the chief management of all affairs. And as Mahomed Reza Khan, the Naib of Dacca has in every respect my approbation and that of the Governor and Council, I do further agree that this trust shall be conferred on him, and I will not displace him without the acquiescence of those gentlemen; and in case any alteration in this appointment should hereafter appear advisable, that Mahomed Reza Khan, provided he has acquitted himself with fidelity in his administration, shall in such case be reinstated in the Naibship of Dacca, with the same authority as heretofore.

Article 3.

The business of the collection of the revenues shall, under the Naib Soubah, be divided into two or more branches, as may appear proper; and *as I have the fullest dependence and confidence on the attachment of the English, and their regard to my interest and dignity, and am desirous of giving them every testimony thereof*, I do further consent, that the appointment and dismissal of the Muttaseddees of those branches, and the allotment of their several districts shall be *with the approbation of the Governor and Council;* and *considering how much men of my rank and station are obliged to trust* to the eyes and recommendations of the servants about them, and *how liable to be deceived*, it is my further will that the Governor and Council shall be at liberty to object and point out to me *when improper people are entrusted*, or where my officers and subjects are oppressed, and *I will pay a proper regard to such representations, that my affairs may be conducted with honour, my people everywhere be happy, and their grievances be redressed.*

Article 4.

I do confirm to the Company, as a fixed resource, for defraying the ordinary expenses of their troops, the Chuklas of Burdwan, Midnapore and Chittagong, in as full a manner as heretofore *ceded* by my father. The sum of five Lakhs of Sicca rupees per month for their maintenance was further agreed to be paid by my father; *I agree to pay the same out of my treasury, while the exigency for keeping up so large an Army continues. When the Company's occasions will admit of diminution* of the expenses they are put to on account of those troops, *the Governor and Council will then relieve me from such a proportion of this assignment*, as the increased expenses incurred by keeping up the whole Force necessary for the defence of the Provinces will admit of; and as I *esteem* the Company's troops entirely equal thereto and as my own, *I will only maintain such as are immediately necessary for the dignity of my person and Government, and the business of my collections* throughout the Provinces.

Article 5.

I do ratify and confirm to the English the privilege granted to them by their Firmaun and several Husbulhookums of carrying on their trade by means of their own dustuck, free from all duties, taxes, or impositions, in all parts of the country, excepting in the article of Salt, on which a duty of 2 per cent. is to be levied on the rowana or Hooghly market price.

Article 6.

I give the Company the liberty of purchasing half the Saltpetre produced in the country of Purnea, which their Gomastahs shall send to Calcutta; the other half shall be collected by my Foujdar for the use of my Offices; and I will suffer no other persons to make purchases of this article in that country.

Article 7.

In the Chuckla of Sylhet, for the space of five years, commencing with the Bengal year 1171, my Foujdar and a Gomastah, on the part of the Company, shall jointly provide Chunam, of which each shall defray half the expenses, and half the Chunam so made *shall be given* to the Company.

Article 8.

Although I should occasionally remove to other places in the Provinces, *I agree that the books of the Circar shall be always kept, and the business conducted at Moorshedabad, and that it shall, as heretofore, be the seat of my Government;* and wherever I am, I consent that an English gentleman shall reside with me to transact all affairs between me and the Company, and that a person of high rank shall also reside *on my part* at Calcutta *to negociate* with the Governor and Council.

Article 9.

I will *cause Rupees coined in Calcutta to pass in every respect equal to the siccas of Moorshedabad, without any deduction of batta;* and whosoever shall demand batta shall be punished; the *annual loss on coinage,* by the fall of batta on the issuing of the siccas, *is a very heavy grievance to the country;* and, after mature consideration, I will, in concert with the Governor and Council, pursue whatever may appear the best method for remedying it.

Article 10.

I will allow no Europeans whatever to be entertained in my service, and if there already be any, they shall be immediately dismissed.

Article 11.

The Kistbundee for payment of the restitution to the sufferers in the late troubles as executed by my Father, I will see faithfully paid. No delays shall be made in this business.

Article 12.

I confirm and will abide by the Treaty which my Father formerly made with the Dutch.

Article 13.

If the French come into the country I will not allow them to erect any fortifications, maintain forces, or hold lands, Zemindarees, &c., but they shall pay tribute, and carry on their trade as in former times.

Article 14.

Some regulations *shall be hereafter settled between us for deciding all disputes* which may arise between the English Gomastahs and my Officers, in the different parts of the country.

In testimony whereof we, the said Governor and Council, have set our hands, and affixed the seal of the Company to one part hereof, and the Nabob before named hath set his hand and seal to another part.

(A true copy.)
(Signed   W. MAJENDIE,
Secretary.

MEMO.—This Treaty was executed by the President and Council of Fort William, on the 20th February, 1765, and by the Nabob on the 25th of the same month.

The success which attended the above measure evidently led the servants of the Company to look forward to still further gain, for after they had acquired the influence consequent on their having been recognized by the *confiding* Nawab as the controllers of his Army, they determined to turn their power to a profitable account, and if possible to improve their financial position by obtaining the *administration* of his revenues also. Accordingly, acting upon the suggestion of Lord Clive, who in one of his despatches to the Home Board had expressed his opinion that "*All must belong either to the Company or to the Nawabs,*" they decided on using the power entrusted to them by the Nawab as the means for carrying out this object; and as the country was at the time the scene of a civil war, an opportunity was soon afforded them of using the Nawab's troops in conjunction with their own for rendering valuable assistance to the Emperor of Delhi, which Clive did not fail to take advantage of.

The Emperor felt very grateful to the Company for the services they had rendered him in his hour of need, and (at the instance of Colonel Clive, who was much esteemed for his bravery) was induced to confer upon the English Company by a Royal Firmaun (Edict) "*the gift of the Dewanny* (Office of the Collection of the Revenues) *of the three Provinces of Bengal, Behar, and Orissa, as a free gift and ultumgah for ever and ever*," granting them for their own use and profit as a *conditional* Jaghire "*Whatsoever may remain out of the Revenues of the said Provinces, after remitting the sum of twenty-six lacs of Rupees per month to the Royal Circar, and providing for the expenses of the Nizamut*," i.e., the Nawabs Nazim, their Court, and their families.

Firmaun from the **KING SHAH AALUM** *granting the Dewanny of the Khalsa Shereefa of Bengal, to the Company in 1765.*

At this happy time Our Royal Firmaun, indispensably requiring obedience, is issued, that and *in consideration of the Attachment Services* of the High and Mighty, the Noblest of Exalted Nobles, the Chief of Illustrious Warriors, Our Faithful Servants and Sincere Well-wishers, worthy of Our Royal favours, the English Company,— We have granted them as a free gift and ultumgah *agreeably to the Zimmum*, from the beginning of the Rubby Tuccacooy-ul of the Bengal year, 1172, *the office* of the Dewanny of the Khalsa Shereefa of the Province of Bengal (the Paradise of the Earth), *with the conditional Jaghire thereof*, without association of any other person. It is requisite that our Royal descendants, the Viziers, the Bestowers of dignity, the Omrahs high in rank, the great Officers, the Muttasuddees of the Dewanny, the Managers of the business of Sultanut, the Jaghirdars, and Khoonrays, as well the future as the present, using their constant endeavours for the establishment of this Our Royal command, leave *the said Office* in possession of the said Company from generation to generation, for ever and ever, looking upon them to be assured from dismissal or removal, they must on no account whatsoever give them any interruption, and they must regard them as excused and exempted from the payment of all the Customs of the Dewanny and demands of the Sultanut.

Knowing Our orders on this subject to be most strict and positive, let them not deviate therefrom.

Written the 24th of Suphar, of the 6th Year of the Jooloose, the the 12th of August, 1765.

Contents of the Zimmum.

Agreeably to the Paper which has received Our Sign Manual, we have granted the office of the Dewanny of the Khalsa Shereefa of the

Province of Bengal (the Paradise of the Earth), *with the conditional Jaghire thereof*, as a free gift and ultumgah to the High and Mighty, the Noblest of Exalted Nobles, the Chief of Illustrious Warriors, Our Faithful Servants and Sincere Well-wishers worthy of Our Royal Favours, the English Company, without the association of any other person from the beginning of the Rubby Tuccacooy-ul of the Bengal year 1172.

Fort William, 30th Sept., 1765.

Note.—Similar separate Firmauns were given for Behar and Orissa.

Firmaun from the KING SHAH AALUM *granting the Dewanny of Bengal, Behar and Orissa, to the Company in* 1765.

At this happy time Our Royal Firmaun indispensably requiring obedience, is issued, that whereas *in consideration of the Attachment and Services* of the High and Mighty, the Noblest of Exalted Nobles, the Chief of Illustrious Warriors, Our Faithful Servants and Sincere Well-wishers, worthy of Our Royal favours, the English Company,—We have granted them the Dewanny of the Provinces of Bengal, Behar, and Orissa, from the beginning of the Fussel Rubby of the Bengal year, 1172, as a free gift and ultumgah, without association of any other person, and with an exception from the payment of the customs of the Dewanny which used to be paid to the Court. *It is requisite that the said Company engage to be security for the* Sum of Twenty-Six Lakhs of Rupees a-year for our Royal Revenue, which sum has been appointed from the Nabob Nudjum-ul-Dowlah Behadoor and regularly paid by the same to the Royal Circar: and *in this case, as the said Company are obliged to keep up a large Army for the protection of the Provinces of Bengal, &c., we have granted to them whatsoever may remain out of the Revenues of the said Provinces, after remitting the sum of Twenty-Six Lakhs to the Royal Circar, and providing for the expenses of the Nizamut.* It is requisite that our Royal descendants, the Viziers, the Bestowers of dignity, the Omrahs high in rank, the great Officers, the Muttasuddees of the Dewanny, the Managers of the business of Sultanut, the Jaghirdars, and Khoonrays, as well the future as the present, using their constant endeavours for the establishment of this our Royal command, leave *the said Office* in possession of the said Company from generation to generation, for ever and ever, looking upon them to be assured from dismissal or removal, they must on no account whatsoever give them any interruption, and they must regard them as excused and exempted from the payment of all the Customs of the Dewanny and Royal demands.

Knowing Our Orders on this subject to be most strict and positive, let them not deviate therefrom.

Written the 24th of Suphar, of the 6th Year of the Jooloose, the 12th of August, 1765.

Contents of the Zimmum.

Agreeably to the Paper which has received Our Sign Manual, **Our** Royal Commands are issued, that *in consideration of the Attachment and Services* of the High and Mighty, the Noblest of Exalted Nobles the Chief of Illustrious Warriors, **our** Faithful **Servants** and Sincere

Well-wishers, worthy of Our Royal favours, the English Company,— We have granted them the Dewanny of the Provinces of Bengal. Behar, and Orissa, from the beginning of the Fussel Rubby of the Bengal Year 1172, as a free gift and ultumgah, without the association of any other person, and with an exemption from the customs of the Dewanny which used to be paid to the Court, *on condition of their being security for the sum of Twenty-six Lakhs of Rupees a-year from Our Royal Revenue, which sum has been appointed from the Nabob Nudjum-ul-Dowlah Bahadoor; and after remitting the Royal Revenue and providing for the expenses of the Nizamut, whatsoever may remain We have granted to the said Company,*

          The Dewanny of the Province of Bengal.
          The Dewanny of the Province of Behar.
          The Dewanny of the Province of Orissa.

The East India Company having thus obtained all they asked for, (to be made the stewards or collectors of the Nawab's revenues) and having engaged to fulfil the conditions expressed in the Royal Firmaun—by virtue of which alone they held *the office*— were in duty bound to supply the Nawabs with any monies they might require for themselves, their families, and the expenses of their Courts; but as they did not know whether the Revenues of the three Provinces of Bengal, Behar, and Orissa would furnish them with the means of carrying out their obligations, and also repay them for their trouble and expenditure in collecting them, *they as men of business and the responsible financiers of the State deemed it advisable instead of allowing the Nawab to draw whatever sums he wished from the exchequer, to offer him a fixed amount in full of all demands as the Nizamut share of the Revenues* of the Provinces. The following additional Agreement was therefore drawn up by which the Nawab consented " *to accept* Sicca Rupees 53,86,131-9 (£580,693) *as an adequate allowance for the expenses of the Nizamut, to be regularly paid* (under the blessing of God) *as long as the English Company's Factories continue in Bengal.*"

AGREEMENT *between* the NABOB NUDJUM-UL-DOWLAH *and the* COMPANY.

The King having been graciously pleased to grant to the English Company the Dewanny of Bengal, Behar, and Orissa, with the revenues thereof, as free gift for ever, *on certain conditions,* whereof one is that *there shall be a sufficient allowance made out of the said revenues for supporting the expenses of the Nizamut,* be it known to all it may concern, that I do agree to accept of the annual sum of Sicca Rupees 53,86,181-9, as *an adequate allowance* for the support of the Nizamut, which is *to be regularly paid,* as follows, *viz.,* the sum of Rupees 17,78,854-1 *for all my household expenses, servants,* &c., and the remaining sum of Rupees 36,07,277-8 *for the maintenance of such horses, sepoys, peons, burkundauzes,* &c., as may be thought necessary *for my suwarry and the support of my dignity only,* should such an expense hereafter be found necessary to be kept up, but on no account *ever* to exceed that amount, and having a perfect reliance on Maeen-ul-Dowla, I desire *he may have the disbursing of the above sum* of Rupees 36,07,277-8 *for the purposes above mentioned.* This agreement (by the blessing of God) I hope will be inviolably observed, as long as the English Company's factories continue in Bengal.

(A true Copy.)

(Signed) ALEX. CAMPBELL,
S. S. C.

30*th* September, 1765.

All the arrangements having thus been concluded by which the Company, under the Nawabs became the custodians and responsible managers of the Revenues of the three Provinces of Bengal, Behar, and Orissa,—having only to render an account of their issues and receipts to the Nawabs as the titled heads of the Government,—there was no just cause why the East India Company should thereafter have departed from the obligations imposed on them by the above **Solemn Agreement**, unless indeed **they had found, and** had convinced **the** Nawab, that the **Revenues of the Provinces were** entirely inadequate for **the fulfilment thereof, which they** were not; yet, on the **accession of Nawab** Syef-ul-dowlah, **they** again took **advantage** of their position of trust by putting a pressure **on the** Nawab and effecting a gain for themselves. The **Nawab, who** "*having an entire confidence in them and in* *their servants settled in the country, that nothing whatever would be proposed or carried into execution by them derogating from his honour, dignity, interests, and the good of his country,*" was induced, to agree "*that the protecting of the Provinces of Bengal, Behar, and Orissa, and the force sufficient for that purpose, should be left entirely to their discretion and good management,*" and also—as the Company would have to provide for the maintenance of *extra troops*—to accept the reduced annual allowance of Company's Rupees 41,86,131-9 (£418,613) for himself and his successors, evidently *in the hope* that by making these further concessions, and retiring altogether from the Executive Administration of the Provinces, "*this Agreement would be inviolably observed as long as the English Company's Factories continue in Bengal,*" for he no doubt thought that the Company, whom he believed to be upright and honest men, would have nothing further to gain from him or his successors, since, by this Agreement, they had *deprived the Nizamut of all real power.* The Nawabs thus, in a commercial point of view, gave up their authority in the Executive, and became annuitants in perpetuity.

Articles of a Treaty and Agreement concluded between the Governor and Council of Fort William, on the part of the ENGLISH EAST INDIA COMPANY *and the* NABOB SYEF-UL-DOWLAH.

On the part of the Company.

We the Governor and Council, do engage to secure to the Nabob Syef-ul-Dowlah, the Soubahdarry of the Provinces of Bengal, Behar, and **Orissa**, and to **support** him therein with **the** Company's Forces **against all his enemies.**

On the part of the Nabob.
Article 1.

The Treaty which my father *formerly* concluded with the Company upon his first accession to the Nizamut, *engaging to regard the honor and reputation of the Company, and of the Governor and Council as his own,* and that entered into with my brother, Nabob Nudjim-ul-Dowlah, *the same Treaties, as far as is consistent with the true spirit, intent, and meaning thereof,* I do hereby ratify and confirm.

Article 2.

The King has been graciously pleased to grant unto the English East India Company the Dewannyship of Bengal, Behar. and Orissa, as a free gift for ever; and *I, having an entire confidence in them and in their servants settled in this country that nothing whatever be proposed or carried into execution by them, derogating from my honour, dignity, interest and the good of my country, do therefore,* for the better conducting the affairs of the Soubahdarry, and promoting my honour and interest, and that of the Company, in the best manner, *agree that the protecting the Provinces of Bengal, Behar, and Orissa,* and the force sufficient for that purpose, *be entirely left to their discretion and good management, in consideration of their paying the King,* Shah Aalum, by monthly payments *as by Treaty agreed on, the sum of* Rupees 2,16,566-10-9, *and to me, Syef-ul-Dowlah, the annual stipend of* Rupees 41,86,131-9, *viz.,* the sum of Rupees 17,78,854-1 *for my house,* servants, *and other expenses indispensably necessary;* and the remaining sum of Rupees 24,07,277-8 for the support of such sepoys, peons, and burkundauzes as may be thought proper for my suwarry only; but on no account *ever* to exceed that amount.

Article 3.

The Nawab Minauh Dowla, who was, at the instance of the Governor and Gentlemen of the Council, appointed Naib of the provinces, and invested with the management of affairs, in conjunction with Maha Rajah Doolubram, and Juggat Seat, shall continue in the same post and with the same authority; and having a perfect confidence in him, I, moreover, *agree to let him have the disbursing of the above sum of* Rupees 24,07,277-8 *for the purposes above mentioned.*

This agreement (by the blessing of God) I hope will be inviolably observed as long as the English Company's factories continue in Bengal.

Dated this 19th day of May, in the year of our Lord, 1766.

(Signed)	W. B. Sumner.
,,	H. Verelst.
,,	Randolph Marriott.
,,	H. Watts.
,,	Claud Russell.
,,	W. Aldersey.
,,	Thomas Kelsall.
,,	Charles Floyer.

A pecuniary gain of £162,080 per annum having by this Agreement also been effected for the Company, and the *whole* of the Military Administration (as well as the Civil) having been made over to them by the Nawab, it might have been expected that with the resources in their hands, derived from *the rapidly increasing Revenues* of the Provinces, they would have been content in letting the Nawabs retain and enjoy for ever their rank, dignity, and privileges as then agreed upon, and which they had bound themselves to protect as long as they remained in Bengal; but though their ambition might have been satisfied, their cupidity was not, for on the accession of Nawab Mobaruck-ul-dowlah—a boy of tender age—the work of spoliation by the servants of the Company advanced apace—and in concert with the young Nawab's stepmother, Munnee Begum (who was familiarly styled " the Mother of the Company," in consideration of her attachment to their solid interests), and Nawab Minauh Dowlah (*alias* Mahomed Reza Khan), a creature of their own making—they drew up another Treaty and Agreement with the young Nawab by which they reduced the Annuity to Rupees 31,81,991-9 (£318,199), and thus deprived him and his successors of £100,414 per annum of their just due.

TREATY WITH MOBARUK-UL-DOWLAH.

The Company's Seal.

(Signed)   E. BARBER,
Secretary.

Articles of **Treaty and** *Agreement between the Governor and Council* **of Fort William** *on the part of the* EAST INDIA COMPANY *and* NAWAB MOBARUK-UL-DOWLAH, *dated 21st March,* 1770.

On the part of the Company.

We, the Governor and Council, do engage to secure to the Nawab Mobaruk-ul-Dowlah the Soubahdarry of the Provinces of Bengal, Behar, and Orissa, and to support him therein with the Company's Forces against all his enemies.

On the part of the Nawab.
Article 1.

The Treaty which my father *formerly* concluded with the Company upon his first accession to the Nizamut, *engaging to regard* **the** *honour and reputation of the Company, and of the Governor and Council as his own,* and that entered into with my brothers, the Nawabs Nudjun-ul-Dowlah, and Syef-ul-Dowlah, the same Treaties, *as far as is consistent with the true spirit, intent, and meaning thereof,* I do hereby ratify and confirm.

Article 2.

The King has been graciously pleased to grant unto the English East India Company, the Dewannyship of Bengal, Behar and Orissa as a free gift for ever; and *I, having an entire confidence in them and in their servants settled in this country, that nothing whatever be proposed or carried into execution by them derogating from my honour, interest, and the good of my country,* do therefore, for the better conducting the affairs of the Soubahdarry, and promoting my honour and interest and that of the Company, in the best manner, agree that the protecting the Provinces of Bengal, Behar, and Orissa, and the force sufficient for that purpose, be entirely left to their direction and good management, *in consideration of their paying the King* Shah Aalum, by monthly payments, *as by Treaty agreed on,* the sum of Rupees two lakhs, sixteen thousand, six hundred **and** sixty-six, ten annas, and nine pie, (Rupees 2,16,666-10-9): **and to me,** Mobaruk-ul-Dowlah, *the annual stipend* of Rupees thirty-one **lakhs,** eighty-one thousand, nine hundred **and** ninety-one, and **nine annas,** (Rupees 31,81,991-9,) *viz.,* the sum of Rupees fifteen lakhs, eighty-one thousand, nine hundred and ninety-one, and nine annas, (Rupees 15,81,991-9), *for my house, servants, and other expenses, indispensably necessary;* **and** *the remaining sum* of Rupees **sixteen** lakhs, (Rupees 16,00,000) *for the support of such sepoys, peons,* **and** *burkundauzes, as may be thought proper for my suwarry only;* but on no account ever to exceed that amount.

Article 3.

The Nawab Minauh Dowlah, who was at the instance of the Governor and Gentlemen of the Council, appointed Naib of the Provinces, and invested with the management of affairs, in conjunction with Maharajah Doolubram, and Juggat Seat, shall continue in the post and with the same authority; and having a perfect confidence in him, *I moreover agree to let him have the disbursing of the above sum of Rupees sixteen lakhs, for the purposes above mentioned.*

This Agreement (by the blessing of God) shall be *inviolably* observed *FOR EVER.*

Dated this 21st day of March, in the Year of Our Lord, 1770.

(Signed)   JOHN CARTIER,
,,   RICHARD BECHER,
,,   WILLIAM ALDERSEY,
,,   CLAUD RUSSELL,
,,   CHARLES FLOYER,
,,   JOHN REED,
,,   FRANCIS HARE,
,,   JOSEPH JEKYLL,
,,   THOMAS LANE,
,,   RICHARD BARWELL.

This last **Treaty**—which reduced the Annuity of the Nizamut to such a sum as could always be paid without encumbering the resources of the State, and also secured for the Company every advantage that they could hope to obtain from their Allies (or co-partners) the Nawabs—was concluded in the unmistakeable words : " This Agreement, by the blessing of God, *shall* be inviolably observed *" for ever ;"* it can, therefore, only be looked upon as a sacred and perpetual bond under which the **East** India Company engaged to pay the sum of Rupees 2,16,666-10-9 (£21,666) per month to the Court at Delhi, and Rupees 31,81,991-9 (£318,991) per annum to the Nawab or his heirs-at-law *" for ever,"* in return for the many and great concessions they had made to them.

It is worthy of notice that the several Engagements made by the **Honourable East India Company** with the **Nawabs** Nazim of Bengal, Behar, and Orissa have a twofold heading, viz., *Treaties* and *Agreements*. The word *Treaty* is evidently used to signify that certain *Political Relations* existed between the contracting parties, whereas the word *Agreement* must refer to the *Commercial Relations* set forth, whereby either the Nawabs or their successors agreed to give the Company certain lands, sums of money, &c., or, on the other hand, the Company guaranteed to pay the Nawabs or their heirs-at-law for certain periods stated in the body of the respective Agreements (the last of which was binding "*for ever*") annuities fixed by mutual arrangement.

Under such circumstances, although the East India Company might think themselves entitled, to exercise the *arbitrary power* they had *assumed*, and by infringing upon the Sacred Rights guaranteed by the *Treaties* find means to deprive the Nawabs Nazim of their *Political Status* and their rank and dignity, yet this done, they were legally liable for the due fulfilment of their pecuniary obligations under the respective *Agreements*, by virtue of which the *social status* of the Nawabs was fully secured under the provisions therein named; and the British Government having by Royal Proclamation in 1858 (Paras. 5, 6, and 7, Page 116) taken over all the obligations of the Honourable East India Company, is therefore now responsible not only for the Political Rights of the Nawabs guaranteed by that August Body, but also for all the debts contracted by the Company, and all the money due to the heir-at-law of Nawab Mobaruck-ul-Dowlah for arrears of the Nizamut Annuity, which were withheld by the Company, besides the payment "for ever" of such sums as are named in the ever-during Agreement of 1770, which was legally sealed, signed, and settled by the Representatives of the two Governments.

In a Political point of view the British Government would be just as much entitled to interfere with the rank and dignity of the Nobility of this country who derive their titles from their ancestors for services rendered to the Crown, as with the Political Rights of those Indian Princes from whom the Representatives of the Government obtained the authority to administer the affairs of that country, under cover of *Solemn Treaties;* and if a Political precedent is admitted in the latter case it will surely follow in the former; but in a *Commercial* point of view the Government cannot under any circumstances legally exercise its prerogative to infringe the terms of the *Agreements* entered into with the Nawabs by its Representatives, and by which it has guaranteed the payment of certain sums for certain advantages conferred and value received from those Princes in lands or otherwise. If such a commercial precedent as the violation by the Government of an ever-during Agreement could be entertained, there would be an end to all security, for private individuals holding contracts from Corporative Bodies for the supply of goods, lands, or other materials at prices agreed on—or for pensioners, annuitants, and others who forfeit certain advantages and rely entirely on the provisions made for them under arrangements with the Government, or other Corporative Bodies. Then again the control which has been arbitrarily exercised by the Government of India over the personal annuity of the Nawabs and their families since 1770, which it could not claim under the provisions of the Agreement, would not have been tolerated in this country by either the aristocracy or people who derive their support in a similar manner directly or indirectly from the Government; hence on this ground alone the Nawabs Nazim have had just cause of complaint against the Government of India, for as the Government only reserved the right of controlling that portion of the annuity assigned for *State purposes* (Pages 22, 24, 27), the Nawabs were legally entitled to redress for the wrongs inflicted on them by an undue interference in their personal affairs. With regard to the existence and validity of the Treaty of 1770, the Government of India has itself acknowledged both, as will be shown hereafter although its officers have up to the present time evaded the terms therein contained.

During the lifetime of Nawab Nudjm-ud-Dowlah, the tribute to the then reigning Emperor of Delhi was paid by the Company—and his successors claimed the same until the year 1857, when the Representative of the Great Mogul—by supporting the rebellion of the Native troops, broke faith with his Allies the East India Company, and thus forfeited all claim to further consideration at the hand of the British Government, which at that time interposed for the protection of its own subjects in India—and after overthrowing the dominion of the Emperor of Delhi, took upon itself the Supreme Administration of the country, cancelled the Charter of the Honorable East India Company, and bound itself to carry out all the obligations contracted by that August Body, while holding the Administration of the Affairs of Native Princes in the East.

But the Nawabs descended from Meer Jaffier Ali Khan never rebelled; how then did the East India Company fulfil their engagements to those Princes, through whose instrumentality and confidingness they had gained so much, and to whom alone can be traced the rapid development of British power in the East? How was Mobaruck-ul-dowlah dealt with? And how has the Government of India treated the present Nawab Nazim who rendered it such great assistance during the Indian Mutiny of 1857, and saved not only the country but the lives and property of so many of our countrymen by his influence and good example? The sequel will shew.

When the Treaty of 1770 was concluded, the sum agreed upon, £318,199 per annum, was paid to the new Soubahdar, and the servants of the Company, in their Despatch to the Court of Directors, took great credit to themselves for having secured a *permanent settlement* with the Nizamut on such advantageous terms to the Company, and expected to be complimented by their employers for their zeal and success; but praise was not in store for them, as the following extract of a Despatch dated 20th April, 1771, from the Court of Directors to their Governor-General, Mr. Cartier, will show:—

"In noticing the encomiums you pass upon your own "abilities, we cannot but observe with astonishment, "that an event of so much importance as the death of "Nawab Syef-ul-dowlah, and the establishment of a "successor in so great a degree of non-age, should not "have been attended *with those advantages to the Company* "which such a circumstance affords to your view. We "mean not to disapprove *the preserving the succession of* "*the family of Meer Jaffier;* on the contrary, *both justice and policy recommended the measure*, but when we consider the state of minority of the new Soubahdar, we know not on what ground it could have been thought necessary to continue to him the stipend allowed to his adult predecessor; convinced as we are, that an allowance of sixteen lacs per annum will be sufficient for the Nawab's state and rank, *while a minor*, we must consider every addition thereto as so much to be wasted. You are, therefore, *during the non-age of the Nawab*, to reduce his annual stipend to sixteen lacs of rupees."

The validity of the Agreement of 1770 is not questioned in the above Despatch, hence it is difficult to understand why the Court of Directors while agreeing in *the justice and policy of supporting the succession of the family of Meer Jaffier*, thought fit to order their servants to still further reduce the annuity of the new Soubahdar *during his non-age* to sixteen lacs, unless, as expressed in the Despatch, they *really* feared that the relatives and friends of the young Nawab would take advantage of his inexperience, and waste the money during his minority, and they (as his Trustees) might afterwards be held responsible for not having protected his interests. Accepting this view of their position, which is borne out by the instructions they gave to the Governor-General in 1786 (Page 34) we may naturally suppose that when the young Soubadhar attained his majority, all the accumulations during his minority would have been restored to him, and the full amount of the annuity, as by Treaty agreed on—and which he had enjoyed for more than a year—would then have been paid by the Company to him and his successors; but this was neither done during the lifetime of Nawab Mobaruck-ul-dowlah, nor have his successors and heirs-at-law since reaped the advantages secured to them by that Treaty and Agreement of 1770, which "by the blessing of God" was to be "inviolably observed *for ever*." The Nawab Mobaruck-ul-dowlah frequently applied to the Company's servants for the restoration of what he rightly considered was his just due; but they, having once been discountenanced by the Court of Directors for having made what they themselves considered *an excellent bargain*, were no doubt indisposed to again run the risk of being censured by their employers; and although the Governor-General, Mr. Warren Hastings, had, when on a visit to Moorshedabad, promised the Nawab and his stepmother, Munnee Begum, to restore the withheld rights, no further notice was taken of the matter by the Government in India. Meanwhile, the Nawab Mobaruck-ul-dowlah had to support a large and rapidly increasing family, and a numerous retinue which he was expected to maintain as became his rank and position; it is, therefore, not difficult to understand how, with the annuity reduced from £318,199 to £160,000 per annum, the Nizamut, which had to be supported on the same scale of magnificence, very soon became involved in debt, so much so, that in 1786 the Court of Directors, feeling it *incumbent* on them (under the conditions of the Royal Firmaun, by virtue of which they held office) "*to provide for the expenses of the Nizamut*," at once ordered their Governor-General to render the Nawab every assistance in extricating him from his pecuniary difficulties, and even authorized "*an immediate augmentation of his stipend*" (Civil List); which was certainly the most just and equitable measure that could have been adopted, notwithstanding the Company's affairs had through either misfortune or mismanagement become, for the time being, slightly embarrassed.

Extract of General Letter, dated 21st July, 1786, from THE HONOURABLE COURT OF DIRECTORS *to their Governor-General in India.*

> "To provide for the support and Dignity of the Nawab Mobaruck-ul-Dowlah *either by efficacious checks which may secure to His Highness the clear and undiminished receipt of the real stipend allotted to him*, or by an economical arrangement of his Household, Dependents, and other expenses, or *even by an immediate Augmentation of his stipend*, having a due consideration of his real necessities, and *at the same time an attention to the embarrassments of the affairs* of the Company."

But the Governor-General disregarded the suggestion to pay the real stipend or to augment it, which would have been a just and equitable measure, and in 1790, adopted the rather singular alternative for reducing the debts of the Nizamut by a further curtailment of the *moiety* of the "Allowance by Treaty of the Family," which had before been paid. The following proposals, which were forced upon the Nawab, will exhibit the one-sided manner in which the affairs of the Nizamut have been administered by the Governors-General in India, regardless of bonds and agreements by which they agreed *to support the rights, dignity, honor and interests* of the Nawabs as their first and chief care.

Extract of a letter from the Governor-General, LORD CORNWALLIS *to* NAWAB MOBARUCK-UL-DOWLAH, *dated* 22*nd September,* 1790.

> Your Highness will easily recollect the correspondence which passed between us, and the conversations that took place while Your Highness

was in Calcutta upon the subject of the arrangement of the affairs of Your Highness's household and the Nizamut, and no necessity now exists for a recapitulation of those particulars, but influenced by a strong desire to form such plans *as shall tend to your prosperity*, and to impress you with the *sincere intention* entertained by the Company in England and the Government here *to secure to you the undiminished receipt of your stipend*, and to recommend such a system for the better management of your household affairs, as shall not only add to your reputation and respect by the discharge of the heavy incumbrances on your Sirkar, but enable *you*, by an economical and judicious arrangement of the internal disposition of your household, so *to distribute the stipend paid by the Company as shall fully answer all the expenses of your Sirkar, provided Your Highness is equally well inclined with myself for a prudent and attentive superintendence over your own affairs.* I have taken into mature consideration the plan for these purposes submitted to Government by Mr. Ives, notwithstanding that gentleman's assiduity in the execution of the duty entrusted to him claims my approbation, yet as part only of what he suggested have my concurrence, I have the pleasure now to communicate to Your Highness such particulars as in *my judgment* will answer the ends so earnestly wished by the Company and myself.

It is my wish Your Highness should know me to be *your friend*, and that you should be convinced that *I have no object in view but your happiness and comfort*, and I trust that Your Highness will require no further assurance on this subject than the conduct I have pursued since my arrival. *It is the Company's orders and the intention of this Government that you should not only receive the stipend paid by the Company, but that the disposal of it should lodge in your own hands*, not doubting but your disposition will point out to you how much *your dignity and respect are concerned in the wise administration of your own affairs*, sensible that your judgment will lead you to put a confidence in my endeavours for your welfare, I cannot doubt *your ready acquiescence to my sentiments*, and that you will immediately put in execution the plan I have formed for the management of your affairs.

It is unnecessary to point out to you that in order *for your future comfort and respect*, the first measure is the discharge of those incumbrances which you at present labour under, and upon this subject *I feel a further inducement to urge the measure* to your notice, for I consider *the Company's credit* at stake even with your own, since by the regulations of the Company's Government in the administration of justice, *a due attention is paid to your dignity* by not admitting any claims upon Your Highness to be decided in the Court of Justice established to give every one their right. In this situation these claims rest upon Your Highness's justice, and as a friend, I conceive it a great reflection upon your credit that they have remained so long unpaid, confident of your wish that they should be discharged. I advise that a certain sum be stopped monthly from the sums paid on account of the stipend to be appropriated for the purpose of paying the just demands made against you. The amount of these demands on all accounts, I understand, is very heavy. *As it is my desire that you should in every respect be considered the master of your own affairs*, I therefore do not wish that any debts shall be considered just, but when decided as such with your acquiescence, I recommend that Your Highness issue a Proclamation in the form that Mr. Harrington will propose to you, accompanied by your support, of a regulation which he will also lay before you for the decision of disputed claims among the creditors. When the whole amount of these demands shall have been ascertained, a next remedy will be formed according to particular instructions which I have given to Mr. Harrington, which include proposals to be tendered to the creditors for a just compromise of their demands, and for the payment of the debt of Jugget Sett, the particulars of which Your Highness is already well acquainted with.

I have considered the situation of Your Highness's Family, and acccordingly *on the means for its support* as far as can be, *from the stipend allotted to the Nizamut*. These means, *though small*, with an economical management and a due consideration of the large sums allotted to other purposes, I cannot but consider as sufficient, especially as they will increase in proportion to the want of them. The sum to be *stopped* monthly as above described, for these two purposes, is *fixed* at 18,000 Rupees, and to be divided as more fully expressed in the accompanying account, part for the payment of the debts, and part for the expenses of Your Highness' Family.

While attentive to the discharge of the heavy incumbrances on your Sirkar, I have not overlooked other circumstances equally conducive to your honour and happiness, to the attainment of which I consider your own dignity in the eyes of the dependents on the Nizamut materially necessary. This cannot be secured but by a strict adherence to justice, and attention to the proper administration of your affairs. From a view of past years, *I am certain that the present encumbered situation of your affairs has arisen from the interference of interested and designing people*, and as Your Highness is arrived at that age when the knowledge of your own affairs can be easily obtained, I am first to advise that you exert yourself in searching into the various departments of your household and the Nizamut, and form such clear and true sentiments of each establishment as shall lead to a regular payment of them, and that *you do not admit the counsels and suggestions of self-interested people* to have any weight in your own determination. It is my wish that *you should be the uncontrolled manager* of such parts of your stipend as can with justice and due attention to the relative situations of others be left to you, and I therefore have directed that, of the sum of 16,000 Rupees, *the annual stipend*, the following sums be under your own management without any other interference in the disposal of them than such as, by any particular circumstances, should require the interference of Government, either by means of *applications from Your Highness for authority* over your own dependents, or by their representation of improper influence in your servants, which may tend to acts of injustice equally contrary to Your Highness's credit to admit, as to the Company's not to remedy.

These sums are as follows:—

Head officers or Mulazuman Imteazy	.	.	.	10,576 8 0
Menial servants or Shagerd Pesha, &c.	.	.	.	15,389 9 0
Marhrohe or Tosha Khana	.	.	.	19,452 4 5
Mier Samanee	.	.	.	7,893 8 12
Repairs or Emaruth	.	.	.	4,550 0 0

Moharrum Expenses or Ashur Khana	150	0 0
Privy purse or Kullumdan Khana	12,000	0 0
Women's apartments or Mehal Serai	7,707	0 0
Salary to Your Highness's son	2,000	0 0
Ukroba or variable Establishment	3,327	14 0
Imteazi or principal officer of Behala	948	0 0
Per Mensem	82,344	13 18
Per Annum	9,88,134	6 16

This sum being deducted from the stipend, will leave the sum of per mensem 50,988 7 8, two-thirds to be appropriated as follows:—

Pensions

Munnee Begum	12.000	0 0
Bubboo Begum	8,000	0 0
Mir Sidoo	4,000	0 0
Saleha Begum	1,000	0 0
Begums, &c., Pensioners on Behala	1,782	0 0
Ukroba Huzoor or your relations	5,917	0 0
The sums to be stopped as before mentioned for the payment of the Debt	18,000	0 0
Per Mensem	50,699	0 0

which sums are to be under the management and control of Mr. Harrington; of the stipend there still remains a small sum, which, as appertaining to no particular department, Your Highness will dispose of as you may think proper, being 289 7 8 ⅔ per mensem.

Your Highness will have observed that, of the 18,000 Rupees to be stopped from the monthly divisions of the stipend, part is to be applied to the Fund for the discharge of the debts, and part for the disbursements of Your Highness's Family, as more fully explained in the account accompanying. As there will be a necessity, during the period in which this sum is to accumulate, for sundry disbursements to be made for the exigencies for your Family, and which are of a nature that the internal disposal cannot be regulated but by yourself, *I have directed that the part of the stoppage, which is intended for this purpose, be also left to Your Highness's disposal,* which by the account you find to be 1,000 Rupees per mensem for the first year, 2,000 Rupees per mensem for the second year and so on, increasing 1.000 Rupees every year for the first nine years, and decreasing in that proportion from the Fund appropriated to the discharge of the debts. Upon this subject I have to observe to Your Highness that *as your annual stipend* and the amount of your debts *will not admit* of a large proportion for the purposes of your Family, the strictest economy will be necessary, and particularly as *the Company for various reasons will not have it in their power* to consider of any further provision for this object.

Wishing to relieve *Your Highness from the burthen upon your stipend of several pensions which have been added to the list from causes arising with the ancestors of those who at present enjoy them, I recommend that Your Highness shall continue them during the life of the present incumbents, and that at their death you will determine whether they shall be continued, as at present paid to the heirs of the deceased, or only in* part. In case of any death, I advise you to communicate such circumstance to the gentleman who may fill the office of Paymaster of the Nizamut stipends and inform him whether the pension paid to the deceased is to continue or not. *Should Your Highness be pleased to withdraw it altogether or in part, whatever is withdrawn I recommend you to add one-half thereof to the Tosha Khana Department, and the other half to the fund for the payment of your debts.*

The pensions here alluded to are as follows :—

Behala (variable establishment).......	3,327	14 0
Inteazi, or principal officers on the Behala ..	948	0 0
	4,275	14 0

Your Highness must be sensible that **by a saving** in this respect an increase may be added to the Fund for the payment of your debts, and even if the whole so withdrawn be applied to this purpose, the incumbrances will be sooner removed. and *I expect from Your Highness's confidence in my wish for your welfare* that you will be particularly careful in communicating any demise of the present pensioners as above requested.

For further particulars, I beg to refer Your Highness to Mr. Harrington, who is furnished with a copy of the plan as proposed by Mr. Ives, in order that he may converse with Your Highness more fully on the particulars of the several establishments which have come under my consideration, as presented by Mr. Ives. Mr. Harrington has my positive instructions to explain any particulars to Your Highness; to assist you in the adjustment of the plan for the discharge of the incumbrances *on your sircar*, and to arrange your household affairs according to the sentiments here laid down *on any intimation from Your Highness of a want of his assistance.*

I have *already experienced* **Your Highness's confidence** in my regard for you *by your ready compliance with such matters as I have had occasion to recommend to your notice*, and upon this ground I have no doubt but *what I have recommended will meet with an equally cheerful and ready acquiescence.* You must be sensible that by the mode *I have from pure motives of friendship urged to your notice*, when *superintended by yourself* with care and economy, and when rigidly adhered to, *your reputation and dignity will increase in the eyes of the world,* and yourself and dependants will live happily and with comfort. Relying, therefore, on your cheerfulness to accede to my advice, I shall conclude with wishing that your **own** discretion will add to the advice of your best friends, and that henceforward *the self-interested* **suggestions** of evil-minded men will have no weight in preventing you from rigidly adhering to *the only system by which you can ever secure the* **happiness and respect** *which the Company and myself sincerely* **wish you should enjoy.**

NIZAMUT FAMILY FUND.

To J. E. HARRINGTON, ESQ., *Paymaster of Nizamut Stipends, at Moorshedabad.*

Sir,

Having taken into consideration the plan proposed by Mr. Ives, in consequence of our instructions to him in June 1787, we have thought proper to adopt the following Resolutions concerning the Nizamut of Moorshedabad.

1st. To *provide a Fund* for the payment of the debts due by His Highness, the Nawab Mobaruck-ul-Dowlah, *out of the stipend allowed* to him by the Company.

2nd. To *provide a Fund* for the **maintenance of a future increasing** Family *out of the stipend allowed* to the Nawab by the Company.

3rd. *To leave the Nawab master over his affairs and his stipend,* as shall be hereafter more fully explained.

4th. To provide a maintenance for his eldest son.

5th. To regulate the several Departments of the Nizamut under separate heads, *according to which the stipend allowed* to His Highness by the Company *is to be hereafter* **appropriated***.

The following particulars are communicated to you for your guidance, and a copy of Mr. Ives's report and its Appendix is transmitted to you for your immediate information.

You **will** *endeavour to impress His Highness with the sincere desire of the Company* to extricate him from difficulties and incumbrances, which are a check upon His Highness and tend to diminish the respect of the Nizamut; and you will observe to him that in consequence of this wish, *they have come to a determination* to make themselves in some degree responsible for the discharge of his debts, deducting a certain monthly sum for that purpose.

The amount of these debts are computed by Mr. Ives at **Rupees 22,86,666-12-3**, as set forth in the Appendix to his report, (No. **15)**, and consist of arrears to his servants and other dependents on the Nizamut, as well as money borrowed at different times.

The **following** *measures are to be adopted* for the **discharge of this** sum. *You will set apart the sum of* 18,000 *Rupees per* **month from** *the stipend;* you will communicate to the Nawab that the Board, considering him **in all** matters concerning his own debts as the acting person, recommend to him to issue the Proclamation, a draft of which is herewith **sent** you in English and Persian, to call upon all his creditors of every description **to** deliver in their demands within the period limited in the Proclamation, **and at the expiration** of that period, you will, in conjunction with **the Nawab, or any** of his officers, form a kistbundy, or account **of instalments, having** first ascertained the amount of the debts, in **doing** which you **are** to attend to the instructions given to Mr. **Ives on the** subject; **and** having submitted to the notice of the creditors, the security held out to them, by **Government** becoming in a manner responsible for the payment of them, (a security they never have hitherto experienced), and pointing out to them the certainty that they will be paid, propose to them the relinquishment of interest upon their demands from the day of such adjustment, and **to** offer to them immediate payment, in proportion to their consent to compound for one half, one third &c. of their original debt—you **will, however,** observe that the debt due to Juggat Seat, being Rupees **5,25,000 is first to** be provided for, in monthly instalments of Rupees 8,750, **the remainder** after the appropriation of a part to be alloted to the payment **of the other** debts, according to their compromise first and next according to priority of debts. But as *the state* *of the Company's Finances* does not *at present* admit of any deviation from the Regulation of Government relative to the payment of salaries or other allowances exceeding 1000 Rupees per mensem, in certificates, all instalments exceeding that sum will be paid half in cash and half in certificates, **and you will transmit to the** Accountant-General **a copy** of the kistbundy **for his guidance in issuing** the certificates for these purposes.

So long a period having elapsed since Mr. Ives communicated his plan to the consideration of Government, the debts will probably have increased, at least, if not in the principal, in the amount of interest on it. The stoppages are, therefore, to continue until the whole be discharged. But as it appears, by the Nawab's own representations, that *the Debt has diminished,* the period for the continuation of the stoppage can only be considered an estimated period, and as far as concerns the fund for the dischage of the debts, will continue, until they be paid, and that for the Nawab's Family will remain, as hereafter more fully laid down.

It having been resolved that *a fund shall be provided from the stipend allowed to the Nizamut* for the maintenance of a future increasing family, the accompanying Paper, No. 2, transmitted to you, that you may observe that the whole amount set apart from the stipend, viz., **18,000 rupees,** is not for the Debt alone, but intended for both purposes, according to the terms laid down in it, but of the 18,000 rupees stopped monthly, 1,000 rupees per month is to be allotted for this Fund for the first year, 2,000 rupees per mensem for the second, and so on. An increase of 1,000 rupees per mensem to the Family Fund, and a decrease of 1,000 rupees per mensem from the discharge of the debts for the first nine years, when the sums, for the two purposes, so *stopped from the stipend,* will be equal.

As there will be a necessity, during *the above stated period of eighteen years,* for sundry **disbursements to** be made from the Family Fund, for the purposes of its institution, you will inform the Nawab that Government have determined that the sum directed to be stopped and appropriated to the purposes of this Fund as above described, remain under the name of an increasing Fund **to** defray **the** expenses of an **increasing family**, that it be, among the other amounts paid to His **Highness,** *left to his own disposal,* and that we conceive His Highness can have henceforward no cause to request the attention of the Company to his large family, as a provision for them increases in proportion. We enclose you, also, No. 4, those parts of the Articles proposed by Mr. Ives, which relate to the better carrying into effect the plan for payment of the debts, and *we direct that you shall use every argument in your power to persuade His Highness to adopt them.* They *probably may be objected to by His Highness* on the idea of an interference of a Court of Justice in His Highness' affairs; but the smallest reflection will fully point out to him that this interference is confined to the cases mentioned, and cannot have any tendency to depreciate the respect due to the **Nizamut,** which can be in no way effected, since the cases referred to are between individuals, and have no connection with the Nizamut itself.

You will explain to His Highness the tendency of the plan now laid down for the discharge of his debts, and for establishing a Fund for a future increasing family; and inform him that *his wish, that the sum to be alloted for the latter purpose should be a fixed sum instead of an increasing one*, would be incompatible with the important objection in view; since the proportion of the amount to be assigned for this purpose can only be regulated by the casual calls for it, and should be comparative with the urgency for the discharge of his debts, for which purpose the **period is** already very distant.

In **regard to the** reductions proposed **by this plan, should His Highness** make **any** objection to them, **you will inform him that we *have materially* considered on the *propriety of making reductions from the salaries of* pensioners, &c., dependent on the Nizamut Establishment, and** also in what proportion **such reductions should be made upon** the Nawab and his family, **and upon the pensioners, &c., and are** of opinion, **that so far as they may regard his own receipts,** respect for his own **credit and dignity ought to be an argument more** powerful in *favour of the present measure,* **than any other we could** use, and **a moment's reflection will** point **out to him,** *that his debts* paid, *these* reductions will be discontinued, and *he will secure his full amount at the end of the period proposed for these purposes;* and with respect to the proportion of the reduction, which will fall on the pensioners, &c., not only precedent, where relief to the Nawab and his family has been the object in view, justifies it, but every consideration of respect for him, from whose kindness **they** enjoy subsistence, every sentiment of the claims by which **they enjoy it, which** in many have arisen **from** the service and **attachment of their ancestors, from** ties of consanguinity and from **means of private interests, and,** above all, **that, as many of them have demands on** part of the **heavy debt due from the Nizamu**t, *the sacrifice of a small sum from* **a pension, which,** *let their claims be however just, it is still at the option of His Highness to withdraw,* **prevent its being considered an injustice, or even a hardship, when it is to furnish a resource for the payment** of an amount they **are entitled to; and still less so when the different** callings which many **of** them follow, and **the many other means of** subsistence which several of them enjoy, **come to be considered; all contribute to confirm** the *propriety* of making them.

We have approved of the sum allotted **by Mr. Ives as a salary for** His Highness' eldest son, namely, **2,000 rupees per mensem.** *Should His Highness continue his objection to this point,* as he made it to Mr. Ives, you will inform him that, as long **as the present system of** affection and duty subsists between the father **and son,** *the amount will be entrusted to His Highness' disposal*, and this appears only a nominal separation from other sums appropriated for His Excellency's own disbursement, and that only an absolute necessity which Government will, when occasion may require, determine, will it be separated from him.

In regard **to the salary** allowed to His Highness's son-in-law, **Mirza Kuleel, viz., 1000 Rs.** per mensem, we conceive it quite sufficient while he **holds the office of Dewan,** to which the salary **of** 2,500 Rs. **per** mensem is affixed, **and in the** event of his not holding that office, any addition to his salary **of 1000 Rs per mensem** must rest with His Highness.

We enclose for your guidance (No. 1) an account showing the several monthly sums disbursed in the Nizamut, with the reductions to be made from them, and refer you for particulars to Mr Ives' report and appendix, and to No 3 being the present appropriation of the stipend allowed by the Company to the support of the Nizamut of Moorshedabad, in which you will observe that there is the provision of 1800 Rupees per mensem for the purposes above explained.

Having already informed you that we wish that the Nawab Mobarukud-Dowlah should be considered in all matters concerning his own debts as the acting person, and determining also, *upon the same principle upon which Government left His Highness the free choice of his own Dewan* (when although they insisted on the dismission of Rajah Sunder Sing, they urged nothing further than that the choice of his successor should fall on a man of good character) *to contribute towards His Highness' satisfaction in a wish he has expressed to be the uncontrolled master of the stipend allowed him by the Company*, as much as may be consistent with our conviction that *the good intention of the Company towards him cannot be frustrated*, and in order to assure him that the preservation of his dignity has formed a material part of our consideration in digesting the plan proposed by Mr. Ives, *we have resolved* that a certain sum of the stipend shall be left to his own management as mentioned in the 3rd resolution before written.

The whole stipend, viz., 16,00,000 Rupees per annum or 1,33,333-5-6 per mensem, may be considered as divided, in the future appropriation of it, into two heads.

The first, being the sum to be actually disbursed for the use of the Nizamut amounting per mensem to Rupees 1.15,333-5-6¾.

The second being the sum stopped for the uses before defined, amounting to 18,000 Rupees per mensem.

The first of the sums is comprised from articles exhibited in account.

No 1. Rupees 1,13,043-13-10
The salary for the eldest son 2000-0-0
Surplus sum, Rupees 289-7-8¾.

and contains among other articles the pensions allowed to the Munnee Begum 25,000 Rupees per mensem. This last amount deducted leaves 90,333-5-6¾ *Rupees which is the sum we have determined shall be left to His Highness' management, uncontrolled in the disbursement of its part*, except as far as it shall be subject to a correspondence with the Governor-General, on any intimation, or representation, of any deficiency in the due discharge of the allowances and salaries which this sum includes; but as some of the pensioners may hereafter have cause to complain, and those, perhaps, persons whose claims to the pension rest upon grounds which, while Government think proper to give their opinion that they ought to continue, will fully authorize indeed call upon Government to see paid with regularity, *you will therefore inform His Highness that the pensions* (included in part of the Behalah, being the first part of No 3 in the Appendix to Mr. Ives' plan,) *amounting to* 1782 *Rupees, and the pensions to the Nawab's relations*, (being No. 1 of the same Appendix,) *amounting to* 5,917 *Rupees, making in the whole* 7699 *Rupees, are to be paid by you*, so that *the sum to be at His Highness's uncontrolled management*, but subject to the correspondence of the Governor-General, will be 82,634-4-5-6¾.

Upon the second sum you have already received full instructions, and it requires at present no further remark.

Having thus given you full and explicit instructions *in what manner the intentions of Government are to be executed, as far as concerns the future appropriation of the stipend* allowed by the Company for the support of the Nizamut, and having enclosed such account and statements as can tend to your more perfect comprehension of these Instructions, we have only to direct that you will urge to His Highness the necessity that, from the state of his affairs, exists for the most frugal management of those sums which Government have left to his own authority, not doubting but he will find the amount fully sufficient for all necessary disbursements, and even for others which the customs of the country, and his own wish to follow them, may induce him to make. You will also remind him that he has a large family to support, and that it is incumbent on him to devise means to render the Fund we have suggested in the above Instructions beneficial to them, by increasing it, when it may be in his power, from the abolition of such pensions as may be at his disposal by the demise of the present incumbents. We have considered that the numerous dependants on the Nizamut who receive pensions from causes which arose with their ancestors, from a heavy weight on the establishment, by being conceived as much due to the heirs and descendants of those to whom they were first granted, as to themselves; and upon mature deliberation on the subject, we have determined to divide them into two heads, *the first consisting of the relations and descendants of former Soubahs whose pensions cannot consistently with the dictates of affection, or with the just sentiments of the ties of relationship, be changed from the present system of hereditary continuance;* but the second is formed of pensions to people who cannot, whatever claims their ancestors may have had, be considered to have any themselves, or at least not of sufficient justice to descend to their heirs. *The pensions, therefore, to the relations and descendants of the former Soubahs,* and to those of His Highness Mobaruck-ud-Dowlah, amounting to, as appears by Mr. Ives's Report,

No. 1 to . . . . . Rs. 5,917
„   3 to . . . . . „   1,782
                                        ─────
                                        Rs. 7,699

shall be considered hereditary, and descend to their heirs. Those to servants, &c., shall be continued to the present incumbents, and on their demise *it shall rest with His Highness to continue them in toto or in part to their heirs.* But at the same time, in order to prevent the misappropriation of the sums that His Highness will have the disposal of at the demise of the present possessors, you will, on communicating this part of the plan to His Highness, request he will notify to the Paymaster of the Nizamut Stipends, such deaths as may occur, and *whether he wishes the heirs of the deceased to have the whole or any part of the pension* enjoyed by the deceased; and, in order further to induce him further to communicate such occurrence, you will point out to him the *benefit* intended by Government in leaving to himself the removal or continuance of a burthen on his stipend, and that *the wish of Government is that such pensions, or parts of them, as may, by his own determination, be unappropriated on the demise of the present incumbents, be one-half* added to *His Tosha Khana, and the other to the Funds for the* discharge *of his debts.* These sums, thus subject to his determination, appear by Mr. Ives's Report to be :—

   No. 4 to . . . . Rs. 3,327
   ,, 3 to . . . . ,, 948

     Per mensem Rs. 4,275

The accompanying account, No. 5. will more fully elucidate the future distribution of the Stipends, as it states the appropriation of it in such parts as are subject to His Highness' management, including those liable to exchange on the demise of the present incumbents with those declared *hereditary*, and the amount totally independent of His Highness.

The enclosed letter from the Governor-General to the Nawab Mobaruck-ud-Dowla, is forwarded to you, that you may deliver it on communicating these Instructions to him, and we trust that His Highness will not only discern *the attention of Government to whatever affects his happiness and dignity,* but add his exertions to yours to carry into execution a plan for his relief from heavy incumbrances, for the support of his own dignity and the respect of the Nizamut, and for the maintenance of an increasing family.

      We are, Sir,
     Your most obedient humble servants,
    (Signed)   CORNWALLIS,
     ,,   C. STUART,
     .,   PETER SPEKE.

Fort William, 30th September, 1790.

Though the proposals made by Lord Cornwallis are at variance with social etiquette, under which people of every description are allowed to disburse their own stipends whether for their own benefit or for the members of their family, yet as the object of them is clearly set forth, the *good intentions* of the Government might have been supported if the premises had been correct, that *sixteen lacs* was the full amount of the Nizamut Annuity assigned by the Agreement of 1770, or that the Company had any right to interfere with the *personal* allowance of the Nawab, but as the Nizamut had already been *illegally* deprived of the State Allowances, or nearly half its annuity, all the claims alluded to ought in justice to have been paid out of the money *withheld by the Company,* and no new measures ought to have been framed until all the arrears of the annuity had been paid away to meet the liabilities *unavoidably incurred in consequence of the curtailment* of it.

It will be further observable from a perusal of the letter to the Paymaster of the Nizamut Stipends, (which contains the five Resolutions adopted) that besides paying the Nawab's debts, a large reserve fund was set aside for *future exigencies,* and also for providing incomes for his eldest son and other members of his family, and *the Nawab was left entirely his own master over his affairs and Civil List,* in accordance with his request under the Agreement of 1770. Again from the body of the same letter it may also be noticed that *the choice of his Dewan was altogether vested in His Highness without control; that certain stipends paid from his annuity were declared hereditary; and that other stipends were to revert to His Highness in part on the decease of the holders, or altogether when his debts were paid;* but none of the suggestions for increasing the comfort and independence of His Highness were acted up to, and the future proceedings of the Government of India were invariably directed to further curtailment of the moiety of the annuity paid to the Nizamut.

The interests of the Nizamut which the Company had bound themselves by solemn engagements to protect and respect were thus set aside, and this act of injustice gave birth to all the unjust measures that have since been introduced, by which the Civil List, which should have been paid to all succeeding Nawabs Nazim has been gradually reduced, and consequently their social as well as political status has been lowered—notwithstanding their numerous and earnest appeals to the Government of India for justice.

We now turn to the consideration of the relations between the Government of India and the Nawabs Nazim, who have succeeded to the throne as "Soubahdars of the three Provinces of Bengal, Behar, and Orissa," since the time of Nawab Mobaruck-ul-dowlah, under the last Treaty of 1770, and of whom history does not give us any account, because they had ceded all their power to the East India Company for *certain considerations*, and though Princes of the Blood Royal, could only thereafter be looked upon as Titled Annuitants, having no voice in the Executive Administration of the country.

After the death of Nawab Mobaruck-ul-dowlah, his son, Nawab Bubber Jung, was, according to established custom, proclaimed Nazim and Soubahdar of the three Provinces, under the style and title of Nasir-ul-Moolk, Aiz-ul-Dowlah, Syud Bubber Ali Khan Bahadur, Delair Jung, and received from the Governor-General, Marquis Wellesley, the following assurance of faithful attachment, &c.:—

Extract from Translation of Persian Letter.

From the MARQUIS OF WELLESLEY *to the "Pillar of State and Defender of the Realm,"* AZOOD DOWLA NASIR-UL-MOLK, *my good brother* SYUD BUBBER ALI KHAN BEHADOOR, *surnamed* DELAIR JUNG.

Your Highness may be assured that this friend has Your welfare at heart, and will be ready at all times and happy to exert his utmost to promote the peace and comfort of the Nizamut, and *to maintain the splendour and uphold the interests of Your Exalted Court*, and with this object this friendly communication has been framed.

(Signed)   WELLESLEY.

Soon after the accession of Nawab Bubber Jung (or Delair Jung), a Special Committee was again appointed to inquire into the pecuniary difficulties of the Nizamut, to relieve which Lord Cornwallis had adopted certain measures before alluded to, and which had in the first instance been brought about by the reduction of the allowance stipulated for in the Treaty and Agreement of 1770. This Committee acting in concert with Her Highness Munnee Begum (who was then well advanced in years) suggested, that on the death of that Princess, the Nizamut Annuity should be further reduced by appropriating her annual allowance of Rupees 1,44,000 (£14,400)—which would otherwise have reverted to the Nawabs Nazim as the heirs-at-law—for the payment of the Nizamut Debts, building expenses, &c. The cost of buildings, &c., had up to that time been paid, under the provisions of the Firmaun of the Emperor of Delhi, by the Government.

In the instructions issued to the Nizamut Committee, appointed under the orders of Government of 24th December, 1801, for the purpose of *devising measures* to meet the various objects of immediate and future exigencies, connected with the *appropriation* and management of the Funds of the Nizamut, the Committee, among other measures of reform, was requested to provide a surplus Fund for the repairs of the Palace and Imambarrah, and to meet contingencies; and the following extract from those instructions will show that the attention of **the Committee** was specially **directed to** *the source* from **which such a Fund** could be established.

" The pension of 12,000 Rs. per mensem, at present assigned to the
" **Munnee Begum,** may also **be** considered as a future additional re-
" source when the pension *shall lapse* into the Funds of the Nizamut
" *by the Begum's decease,* and may **be** brought into the calculation
" of the Funds to be provided for the **more** distant exigencies of the
" family and of the Nizamut."

" His Lordship is led to consider this arrangement to be particularly
" *expedient* by adverting to the necessity of providing for the future
" management of the affairs of the Nizamut, on the decease of the
" Begum, which may be *expected* to occur in the course of a few
" years."

And in the Report of the Nizamut Committee, which was submitted to Government on the 9th November, 1802, and recorded in 1806, the Committee observed as follows, in regard to the Fund proposed to be provided for the purposes above set forth.

" The succeeding clause of **our instructions** refers to establishing a
" **Fund for the gradual repayment** of the sums which will be advanced
" **by Government for repairing and** rebuilding the Palace, and in
" **Paragraph 10th we were advised to** expect information on this sub-
" ject from our President.

" Mr. Pattle has informed us, that up to this time no progress
" whatever has been made in the object in question, nor, has any plan
" or estimate been prepared, but that from information lately received,
" he expects some **Engineer Officer** will shortly be appointed to take
" the necessary steps for putting this matter in train of arrange-
" ment.

" The object, therefore, appears remote, and not such as presses
" for immediate determination. The Committee are, besides, well
" satisfied on a summary but general view of their means and of the
" calls thereon, that, *from the present stipend* **not** the smallest re-
" source can remain for this head of expenditure, if others **which** are
" immediately pressing are to be provided for, **and a** Fund set apart
" for the liquidation of the Nawab's debts within a moderate term of
" years. He, therefore, respectfully submits, that, considering this
" as a distant claim, we should be permitted to meet it with a remote
" resource, without suffering it, unnecessarily, to interrupt the course
" of present arrangements. It occurs, therefore, that on a general
" principle, *the* **Pension** *at* present enjoyed *by the Munnee Begum,*
" *Rs* 12,000 *per mensem, is, that which, of all others, appears most*
" *proper to be taken into calculation as an article of resource after her*
" *demise,* **for the gradual** repayment **of Government** advances for

" *building a Palace.* The event is stated to be expected to occur in
" the course of a few years, and we have been induced, in this place,
" to take up and reply to the 8th and 22nd Paragraphs of our instruc-
" tions, which appear to involve a question of some delicacy and
" reference to an object which does not offer any immediate available
" resource, and is further of a nature, which rejects the assumption
" of any definite period for its being brought into action, still, as it
" is but too evident that *there is a wide disproportion between the*
" *expenses of the Nizamut and its resources*, we have every reluctance
" to throw this article entirely out of the question, although, for the
" sake of clearness and perspicuity, we are disposed to keep it thus
" distinct and separate, the general subjects which are incorporated in
" the detailed account forming part of this report "

This economical suggestion, however, did not come into action until after the death of Munnee Begum, in 1813, and during the Soubahship of Nawab Zyn-oo-deen (or Ali Jah), who on the death of his father, Nawab Bubber Jung succeeded to the throne under the style and title of Shoojah-ul-Moolk, Mobaruck-ul-dowlah, Ali Jah, Syud Zyn-oo-deen, Ali Khan Bahadur, Feroze Jung, and who on his accession received the following assurance from the Governor-General, Lord Minto, and accepted the same as an additional sacred pledge of perpetual friendship between the East India Company and the successors of Nawab Meer Jaffier Ali Khan:—

From LORD MINTO *to* NAWAB NAZIM ZYNUDEEN ALI KHAN, *dated 26th May*, 1810.

Mr. Richard Roche, in charge of Nizamut affairs, has received instructions to attend at the Musnud of the Soobahdaree, in the Court of that friend, on the part of this Government, to invest Your Highness with the Soobahdaree of the three Soobahs aforesaid, and publicly to proclaim the auspicious event to the people; and in concert with Your Highness to fix a day for the ceremony.

The stipend fixed on the accession of Your august Father, by the Honourable East India Company, will be continued to Your Highness without any difference; *namely—the annual allowance of sixteen Laks of Rupees will be continued to Your Highness* in monthly issues as usual; *in the mode already prescribed, or that Your Highness may consider expedient hereafter to arrange in conjunction with the Members of this Government* for the distribution of the pensions suitably to the circumstances of the dependents of the Nizamut, and also for the liquidation of the debts of the Nizamut, the burden of the responsibility whereof has now naturally devolved on Your Highness.

Above all, be assured that this person will at all times and in all junctures, to the utmost of his power and the best of his ability, proffer his best counsel and exert his most friendly aid *in supporting the rank and dignity*, and promoting *the ease, comfort, happiness, and welfare* of that esteemed friend and all his family.

And that friend may be assured that the friendship and regard this Government showed his honored father will, without any difference, be freely and willingly transferred to Himself, and that all *the honours, consideration, and respect due to the exalted station of the family* whereof Your Highness is now the HEAD and Source of dignity, *will be kept in view and observed towards that friend.*

On other points I would refer You to the Gentleman above mentioned, Mr. Roche, in whose worth and ability I have entire confidence, and favoured by whom You will ever receive renewed proofs of regard and attachment to Yourself and family, and the interest I feel in their welfare. I hope that considering this person a real friend and well-wisher, You will ever gratify him with letters of Your health and prosperity. What can I say more?

(Signed)   MINTO.

But in 1813, after the death of Munnee Begum, the suggestion of the Select Committee of 1802 was put into operation by the Governor-General, and the Nawab began to see the true intent and object of the Government of India, and the hopelessness of extricating the Nizamut from debt, so long as that Government determined to carry out the Policy which had been instituted ostensibly for the purpose of releasing the family from pecuniary difficulties, but which was really producing the opposite result; *for the Funds set apart for paying Nizamut debts and building expenses were diverted into another channel*, and His Highness the Nawab was not only compelled to abandon his right as heir-at-law to the future annual allowance (£14,400) of Munnee Begum, which ought to have reverted to him after Her Highness's death, but was also deprived of other private property of enormous value and monies amounting to upwards of £20,000, which were found in Her Highness's Palace after her decease, and authoritatively taken possession of by the Government officials, notwithstanding the remonstrances of His Highness, and the wishes of the Governor-General, expressed in the instructions furnished to Mr. Monckton, wherein while ascertaining the available assets appertaining to the Nizamut that might be set apart for the purposes of the new appointment he was guarded against depriving His Highness of the private property of the deceased Begum to which he was the legitimate heir.

In thus curtailing the Nizamut Annuity by coercion, the East India Company exercised *might* against *right*, openly violating their Agreement under the Firmaun of the Emperor of Delhi, "to provide for the expenses of the Nizamut," besides departing from the solemn obligations expressed in the Sacred Treaty of 1770. By the first act of curtailment alone they had even during the lifetime of Nawab Mobaruck-ul-dowlah deprived the Nizamut of nearly half a million pounds sterling, (irrespective of the Fund set apart by Lord Cornwallis) which with many other monies pertaining to the family, has never been accounted for to the Nawabs who have patiently borne all the oppression and injustice that has been inflicted upon them, and have returned good for evil, by ever continuing faithful and loyal adherents of the British cause, even in times of temptation, trouble, and danger.

The continued pressure put upon the Nawabs by the Government of India, as before stated, began to tell to their prejudice, and in 1816 the Government accounts of the Nizamut got into such inextricable confusion, that Mr. Edmonstone, Foreign Secretary to the Government, proposed a minute for introducing a new system of management into the Financial Department of the Nizamut, by the establishment of the Nizamut Agency Fund, and by diverting the accumulations of Munnee Begum's Stipend from their intended object, which the Nawab was in a manner forced to give his reluctant assent to.

This Fund was established for the payment of the Salaries of the Governor-General's Agents at Moorshedabad and of their Office Establishments. On the proceedings of Poll. Corr., 23rd July, 1816, No. 118, will be found a minute with regard to the Senior Judge of the Court of Appeal at Moorshedabad, who, ex-officio, held the situation of Superintendent of Nizamut affairs:

"The impracticability of discharging the duties of both situations, "more especially under the exigent demand for a change of system and "an augmented degree of superintendence in the Department of the "Nizamut, must be sufficiently apparent. If any practical proof were "required of the evil and inconvenience of the existing system with "respect to the concerns of the Judicial branch, I might refer to the "frequent occasions to which the Senior Judge has founded an applica-"tion to be relieved from a Circuit on the exigencies of his duties in "his capacity of Superintendent of Nizamut affairs.

"In addition to the degree on which analogous objections might "oppose the transfer of the duties of Superintendent of Nizamut affairs "to the Collector of the district, or to any other Civil Officers actually "attached to the station, would be the relative inferiority of his official "rank and situation. I am indeed fully persuaded, after long and "mature deliberation, that the appointment of a district officer of high "rank in the Company's service to fulfil (perhaps under a different "designation) the duties of a Superintendent of Nizamut affairs is the "only arrangement calculated to provide efficiently for the objects which "the preceding discussion will probably have shown to be objects of "indispensable exigency.

"Invested with the dignity of a representative character, and enabled "to devote his time and attention exclusively to the duties of his situa-"tion, an officer of that class possessing the requisite qualifications would, "I am confident, accomplish, at no great distance of time, an effectual "reform in the system of the Nizamut. I have no doubt that the "arrangement would be followed by reductions to a very considerable

"amount, arising out of the detection of abuses and impositions, and the
"uniform operation of a vigilant control, whilst the practice of abuses
"and impositions would be restrained, and the future accumulation of
"debt would be prevented, and the adjustment of every point connected
"with the affairs of the Nizamut, would be expedited and facilitated

"As an officer, such as I have described, must, to possess the requisite
"efficiency, be held by a servant of high rank and peculiar qualifications,
"the salary of it must also be fixed on a high scale. But, *however bene-*
"*ficial may be an arrangement of this nature, I should not have ventured*
"*to propose it at the charge of the Company* It is the practicability of
"providing for the expense of the proposed establishment, *without im-*
"*posing any burthen on the finance of the Company, or diverting any of the*
"*appropriated resources of the Nizamut,* that induces me to submit the
"plan to the consideration of the Board. I am further urged to bring
"it forward at this particular time, because it appears to me that several
"of the unadjusted points, enumerated in the memoranda of the Super-
"intendent, already reverted to, involve questions between the Govern-
"ment and the Nawab of considerable importance in the general
"arrangements of the Nizamut, delicate in their nature and difficult of
"adjustment, and, consequently, requiring the application of a degree
"of time and attention on the part of the person to whom the negocia-
"tion of these points may be confided, which the Superintendent could
"not possibly devote to them without injuriously neglecting his capaci-
"ties of Senior Judge of the Provincial Court.

"I have already observed, that *the salary of the suggested officer*
"*should be on a high scale,* and I am of opinion that it should not be
"less than 36,000 Rupees per annum exclusive of a sum for house rent
"and establishment. As the Superintendent of the affairs of the Nizamut
"has always been exercised by the Chief Civil Authority of the station,
"I am of opinion that it should be classed, in point of salary, above the
"office of Magistrate; but there are other forcible reasons for assigning
"to it a liberal allowance.

"The Office of the Superintendent, such as is above described, would
"be a species of political appointment in its nature, distinct from any
"other, and leading to no higher post in the scale of official gradation,
"but the person possessing the requisite rank and qualification would
"have just claim to aspire to a situation of greater emolument than
"that of a Magistrate of a city or zillah, and would not, therefore, be
"contented to remain long on a salary not superior to the salary of the
"latter officer, especially at a station so expensive as Moorshedabad. and
"where he would be obliged to maintain a certain appearance. This
"*would occasion a frequent change of the person holding the office of*
"*Superintendent, which would be a great public inconvenience, because a*
"*very long time would elapse before a person, qualified in other respects,*
"*could become acquainted with the extensive and complicated details of*
"*the Nizamut, on a full knowledge of which, his efficiency would,* of
"course, *essentially depend,* moreover, in a situation like that proposed,
"where *illicit advantages* would be so abundantly held forth to view,
"and might be so securely enjoyed, *a liberal salary* should, on general
"principles, be assigned. It is not perhaps among the least of the
"defects of the present system, that the duties of Superintendent of
"Nizamut affairs is *is performed* gratuitously.

"If the question to be decided were whether or not consistently with Public Obligations, lapsed stipends could be restored to the resources of the State, or, in other words, whether or not the Company is bound permanently to apply the sum of sixteen lacs of Rupees per annum to the support and benefit of the Nizamut, some forcible arguments might, I think, be adduced on both sides. I should feel it to be a question of considerable delicacy and difficulty, and should advise much caution and mature deliberation in forming a decision upon it. But the actual question is whether, or not, funds, which by the death of parties, for whose personal support they were assigned, are set free, shall not be applied, not in the augmentation of the Revenue of the Company, but in support of an arrangement, the exclusive object of which is the prosperity and even pecuniary benefit of the Nizamut, an object unattainable by any other arrangement. All judgments must, I conceive, concur in the same decision of the question. No individual is deprived by such an appropriation of a pre-existing right. The party is by death withdrawn from the Fund, and not the Fund from the party.

"Assuming as a covering sum 42,000 per annum, I have reason to believe that assets justly available may be found to that extent. The annexed statement, marked D, contains an enumeration and a detailed explanation of assets derived from the stipend of deceased Stipendiaries, which apparently constitute an accumulation of Funds to the 31st January last, to the amount of upwards of five lakhs of Rupees, and the accumulation, is, of course, greater up to the present time.

"Making allowance for the gain which would be obtained by purchasing Company's Paper in this market, the sum required completely to cover monthly payments, amounting to the annual expenditure above suggested, would, however, be little short of seven lakhs of Rupees. The reservation, during a further period of time, of the sources of accumulation, described and explained in the statement last referred to, would, of course, create the additional capital necessary to supply the deficiency, but possibly, it may be deemed equally just and convenient to supply that deficiency by the monthly appropriation of a sufficient portion of the lapsed stipends. This might be subject of further consideration. In the meantime, if the plan now proposed be thought expedient, measures should, I conceive, be adopted to ascertain, with accuracy, the extent of the funds actually disposable. If this information be not attainable in the office of the Accountant-General, it must, of course, be sought at Moorshedabad. The Board will determine, whether or not, to suspend the suggested appointment until this information be obtained. There is another consideration which may also effect the period of making the appointment. It will, probably, be deemed proper, out of delicacy and respect towards the Nawab, and with reference to the peculiar interest which he has in the arrangement, especially as it involves the alienation of Funds, which he may consider as appertaining to the Nizamut, that it should be adopted in concert with him.

"I do not mean by this, that the adoption of this plan must absolutely depend on his consent to it, but that the arrangement, its motives, objects and expected benefits, should be communicated to His Highness in the first instance, his observations upon it heard and attended to, and his objections, if possible, removed.

"If any difficulty, or objections, should preclude the prosecution of
"this preliminary measure through the agency of the Superintendent
"of Nizamut affairs, and the adoption of it should be judged indispen-
"sable, a gentleman might be sent, in the first instance, on a special
"deputation to Moorshedabad on the part of the Governor-General;
"intimation being given to the Nawab, that he is deputed to confer
"with His Highness on some points of importance connected with the
"interest of the Nizamut. In that case, *it might be convenient to invest
"him with special powers for the adjustment of those points* of the Super-
"intendent's memoranda which are most urgent, and *which must, neces-
"sarily, form subjects of negociation and discussion* with His Highness,
"founding this delegation on the superior importance of the concerns
"to which it relates, and the impracticability of the Senior Judge de-
"voting to the discussion and arrangement of them, the requisite por-
"tion of time and attention, consistently with other avocations of his
"Judicial affairs, supposing the general objects of the foregoing discus-
"sion to meet with the concurrence of the Right Honourable the
"Governor-General and my colleagues, the Board will determine
"whether, on the whole, it be most expedient to adopt any preliminary
"proceeding of the nature above described, or, at once, to establish the
"proposed appointment."

The Governor-General in Council fully concurred in the sentiments and opinions of Mr. Edmonstone, and deputed Mr. Monckton, the Persian Secretary to Government, to Moorshedabad, upon the special duty of conferring with the Nawab Nazim, as to the plan proposed by Mr. Edmonstone. The following is an extract from the instructions given to Mr. Monckton—

"You will observe that Mr. Edmonstone in his minute has repre-
"sented the total inefficiency of the existing as well as former arrange-
"ments, for securing a due appropriation of the funds allotted for the
"support of the Nizamut, and has described, generally, the course of
"the measures, proper to be pursued, for introducing an improved
"system of management into that establishment.
"The specific objects of your deputation may be classed under three
"heads. 1st., the accomplishment, by means of negotiation with His
"Highness the Nawab, of the plan of forming a Fund, from the re-
"sources of the Nizamut, to defray the personal salary of a Superin-
"tendent, and the expense of his establishment; 2nd, the disposal of
"the Munnee Begum's property; and 3rd, the adjustment of all de-
"pending questions.
"With respect to the 1st point, namely, the provision of a fund for
"the expense of the proposed establishment of an European Superin-
"tendent of the Nizamut, I am directed to observe, that *Government
"would consider itself to be perfectly warranted*, under the Nawab's

"engagement, *in applying* to that purpose *a portion of the personal pro-
"perty of the late Munnee Begum*, but as it is practicable, without
"having recourse to that measure, to provide the requisite fund for
"other objects appertaining to the Nizamut, and as it is an object of
"considerable importance to secure, if possible, the cordial and zealous
"co-operation of the Nawab in the future reform of the Nizamut, *the
"Governor-General in Council is disposed to avoid the adoption of a
"measure which would interfere so materially with His Highness's per-
"sonal interest, as the appropriation of a considerable portion of the pro-
"perty to which His Highness considers himself to be the heir, and there-
"fore, rather than subject His Highness to that privation, His Excellency
"in Council has resolved to supply the fund from available assets apper-
"taining to the Nizamut.*

"You will take an early opportunity of ascertaining with accuracy
"the extent of the funds actually disposable, and of devising the best
"means of supplying any deficiency."

The following are extracts from Mr. Monckton's Report, furnished from Poll. Corr., 19th October, 1816, No. 58-65.

"On the 24th ultimo I had the honour of paying His Highness a
"visit at Farakbaug, when I opened the subject of my Commission.
"I said to His Highness, that he was no doubt prepared, by the
"Right Honourable the Governor-General's letter, regarding my depu-
"tation, to expect from me communications of considerable importance,
"and with His Highness' permission I would explain to him the views
"of Government, stating, at the same time, my persuasion that His
"Highness would cordially acquiesce in them, not merely from a regard
"to his former engagement, but from a conviction that they were
"essential to the *future prosperity* of the Nizamut, and to the support
"of His Highness' own dignity and honour.

"I proceeded to unfold to His Highness the project for the separation
"of the office of Superintendent of the affairs of the Nizamut from
"the office of Senior Judge of the Provincial Court of Appeal and
"Circuit for the Division of Moorshedabad, and for *the formation of a
"fund from the resources of the Nizamut* to defray the personal salary
"of a Superintendent, and the expenses of his establishment, *prefacing
"that communication by a full exposition of the motives, objects and bene-
"fits to be expected from that arrangement*, as described in Mr. Edmon-
"stone's minute of the 25th March last.

"His Highness listened to me with the utmost attention. He seemed
"fully to admit the existence of the evils and abuses of the present
"system of the Nizamut, and did not offer any objections whatever to
"the principle of the suggested arrangement, for providing for the dis-
"charge of the duties of a Superintendent at the expense of the
"Nizamut. *His Highness, however, manifested some degree of impa-
"tience to learn how funds could be raised* to the great extent of seven
"lakhs.

"Anticipating the *anxiety* which His Highness would feel on this

"point, I had already taken considerable pains to ascertain what funds
" were actually available for the purposes of forming the proposed new
" establishment, and although my information was still imperfect I was
" enabled to assure His Highness that there are assets appertaining to
" the Nizamut nearly, if not entirely, sufficient to form the requisite
" fund. With a view, however, to demonstrate to the Nawab the con-
" sideration of Government towards His Highness, I observed that
" under His Highness' engagement, *Government would be warranted in
" applying a portion of the Munnee Begum's Treasure to the purpose of
" forming the fund,* but that as the measure would materially affect His
" Highness' personal interest by imposing, in a manner, on His High-
" ness the burthen of the expense, Government proposed to provide
" the funds, if practicable, from unappropriated assets appertaining to
" the Nizamut, and that accordingly my anxious endeavours had been
" directed to the accomplishment of that object.

" His Highness received the communication apparently with great
" satisfaction, and expressed his sense of the consideration shown to
" him, with regard to the mode in which the funds were to be sup-
" plied, in the event of the proposed office being established. I ex-
" plained to His Highness, however, that in computing the assets
" available for the purpose of forming the fund of seven lakhs, *I
" calculated on certain sums being repaid to the Nizamut from the
" Munnee Begum's personal property*, observing also, that the repay-
" ment of those sums was entirely distinct from any consideration
" connected with the plan for the new establishment for the Superin-
" tendence of the Nizamut, and that they would be added to the fund
" for defraying the expense of that establishment, as forming a part of
" the actual resources of the Nizamut.

" His Highness, having heard these observations, *did not seem
" disposed to pursue the discussion further*. He said that he felt too
" unwell to admit of his bestowing on the several points, which had
" been brought up under discussion that day, the degree of considera-
" tion requisite to enable him to form any decision, and desired to be
" furnished with a written statement of the several sums which it was
" proposed to deduct from the amount of the late Munnee Begum's
" Treasure.

" I expressed concern at His Highness's indisposition, but requested
" permission to observe that the points which I had submitted to His
" Highness's consideration, had undergone a full discussion, and that
" I was not aware of the difficulty which opposed a declaration of His
" Highness's sentiments. I said that we had been closeted for three
" hours, and that *if my conference with His Highness led to no result,
" an opinion would go abroad that the views of His Highness were in
" opposition to those of Government, an opinion which I would greatly
" lament. I assured His Highness that I had hitherto preserved in-
" violable secrecy with respect to the views of Government; that I had
" not even disclosed them to any person of my own*, and that although
" I had called on the Officers of the Nizamut for several statements,
" no one comprehended the object of them, and that *the anxious wish
" of my heart was to negociate the proposed arrangements personally
" with His Highness, and without the intervention or even knowledge
" of any other person. I therefore expressed an earnest hope that His

" Highness would not think it necessary to consult any other judgment
" than his own, but *act at once* according to his own wisdom and dis-
" cernment, in which case, *I felt* assured, His Highness would not
" allow me to leave his house without the gratification of knowing that
" *he concurred in the proposed* arrangements. The Nawab, however,
" *still* urged his indisposition as an excuse for *suspending his judg-
" ment* on all points.

" On my reminding His Highness of all his engagements, he desired
" that he might not be understood as having decidedly objected to any
" part of the arrangement which had been proposed to him; but
" observed that *he conceived himself at* liberty to represent to the
" Right Honourable the Governor-General *any inconveniencies or em-
" barrassments which might occur to his mind as likely to result* from
" them, and following up that observation by asking, whether his
" reply to His Lordship's letter ought to be transmitted through me.
" I replied that His Highness was certainly at liberty to pursue this
" course which he had described, and that I should not fail to furnish
" him with the statement which he required of the sums proposed to
" be deducted from the Munnee Begum's Treasure.

" With respect to the transmission of His Highness' letter to the
" Governor-General, I merely explained, that *I considered myself to
" be the channel through which His Highness' letter should be trans-
" mitted, according to the* regular forms of *official intercourse between
" His Highness and Government*, on all points connected with my
" mission.

" I advised His Highness, however, before he proceeded to address
" the Governor-General, to consider well the contents of His Lord-
" ship's letter, when he would observe, that *His Lordship had confi-
" dently anticipated His Highness' cordial acquiescence in the proposi-
" tions to be communicated by me*, not merely with reference to His
" Highness' engagements, but *from a conviction that they were calcu-
" lated to promote the general prosperity of the Nizamut*. I was,
" therefore, particularly anxious, and said that His Highness should
" act up to his engagements, and **not** by any representation or
" remonstrances against arrangements so equitable and beneficial in
" themselves, impose upon His **Lordship** the necessity of reminding
" His Highness of the circumstance **in which** the engagements
" originated, but by fulfilling his promise, **avoid** such necessity which
" would only afflict both His Lordship and His Highness with pain.
" His Highness observed that, *according to the tenor of the Governor-
" General's letter,* **the** *points,* brought **forward** *by me, were to be*
" **matters of negociation** *and that, therefore, he did not conceive*
" *himself absolutely required to comply with the* propositions of Go-
" vernment.

" I replied, that although **His Lordship** *was fully satisfied of the
" justice and propriety of the propositions,* and confidently anticipated
" His Highness's acquiescence in them, yet, he certainly wished that
" the grounds of those propositions should be fully explained to His
" Highness, and that His Highness's observations upon them should
" be heard, and any objections which might possibly occur to his mind be
" removed, as *His Lordship would regret being thought by His Highness
" to take advantage of his engagements, to require from His Highness*

" any sacrifice *which* **might** *appear to be unreasonable, or not* **de-**
" **manded** *by considerations connected with the future welfare of* **the**
" *Nizamut.* I requested His Highness to consider, that, *although* **he**
" *should ultimately acquiesce in the views of Government after repre-*
" *sentation and remonstrance, yet, his acquiescence* **under such circum-**
" *stances would* **have** *no grace;* as His Highness's **sincere** friend,
" therefore, *I* ***advised*** *him to declare* **at once** *his acquiescence* **in the**
" *views of* **Government.** Such was my anxiety on the subject, I added,
" that *I would* ***take*** *upon myself the responsibility of exonerating* ***His***
" ***Highness from*** **the** *burthen of supporting* **any** *of the late Munnee*
" *Begum's dependents out of her property, for which purpose I had*
" *allotted a fund of a lakh of Rupees, if he* **would** *only yield* ***a cordial***
" *assent to the other deductions from* **the** *property,* and also **to the**
" arrangement for the new establishment for the Superintendence of
" the affairs of the Nizamut, and, **that,** *in* ***making*** *this offer,* ***I*** *was*
" *not sure that my conduct would be* ***approved.*** I concluded by **saying,**
" **that His** Highness would not fail **to** recognise **in** that, and **also in**
" **the whole** arrangement, *my anxious solicitude* **to** *combine* **with the**
" *attainments of the views of Government for the benefit of the Niza-*
" *mut, the utmost possible consideration for His Highness's personal*
" *interests relative to the disposal of the Munnee Begum's property.*
" *His Highness was, however, quite inflexible; he declared his inability*
" *to give me any definite answer, and at length I took my leave with*
" *the expression of my disappointment at the suspension of his judgment*
" *upon the arrangements which had been proposed to him, and* ***of my***
" *hope that,* **on** *reflection, His Highness would let me have the* ***gratifi-***
" ***cation*** *of reporting to Government that they* **have obtained his**
" *approbation.*

"The tenor of **His Highness's** conduct certainly impressed me with
" the belief, that ***he either meditated a*** *decided opposition to the views of*
" *Government,* **or had determined not to act** without the previous com-
" munication with his confidential advisers.

"I afterwards learnt that His Highness held secret consultation
" with his father-in-law, the Nawab Shumshere Jung, and with one or
" two others on that night and **the** night following. In this interval I
" had prepared the statement which His Highness had requested, and
" was on the point of sending it to Farrakbaug, when His Highness
" sent me a message, signifying his intention of visiting me on the fol-
" lowing morning. *His Highness, however, being unfortunately taken*
" *ill, sent his father-in-law to me with a letter, informing me of his in-*
" *disposition, and containing the gratifying intelligence of his cordial*
" *acquiescence in the views of Government.*

"Before I close the letter I beg to state that no part of the funds for
" the new establishment for the Superintendence of the Nizamut is in
" the hands of the Collector, excepting the arrears of the Munnee
" Begum's personal salary, amounting to Rupees 2,67,703. *That sum*
" *might be immediately invested in the public Securities of Government.*
" The remainder **of the** funds shall be paid into the Collector's Treasury
" with the least practicable delay."

The following is an **extract from the letters received by**
Mr. Monckton in reply.

"The successful issue of your proceedings in the execution of such
"parts of those instructions, as formed the subject of the despatch now
"acknowledged, has afforded much satisfaction to the Governor-General
"in Council, who considers your conduct to be marked with the charac-
"teristic zeal, address, temper, and ability, which formed the ground of
"His Lordship's selection of you for the performance of this delicate
"and important service.

"The tenor of your conference with the Nawab, and the general
"course of your proceedings, reported in that despatch, being in entire
"conformity with the spirit of your instructions and of the views of
"Government. I am directed to proceed at once to convey to you the
"sentiments and instructions of His Lordship in Council on those
"points on which the special expression of the opinions and sentiments
"of the Government are required.

"The statements of *the sums to be deducted from the treasure of the
"late Munnee Begum*, and of the assets available for the purpose of de-
"fraying the expense of the proposed new establishment, both of which
"have been recognized and accepted by the Nawab, are entirely ap-
"proved.

"The sum of 2,67,703 Rupees, being the amount of the arrears of
"the late Munnee Begum's stipend, which forms one item of these
"assets, and is actually in the hands of the Collector of Moorshedabad,
"*will be invested in the public funds* without delay. Instructions, of
"which a copy is enclosed, have accordingly been issued to the Ac-
"countant-General and the Government Agent, and you will be pleased
"to convey the necessary instructions on the subject to the Collector;
"you will be pleased to make early arrangements for the payment into
"the hands of the Collector, of the remaining sums described, for the
"same purpose, reporting the actual payment, that *the necessary measures
"may be taken for investing the whole amount.*"

Instructions were accordingly issued to the Accountant-General and the Sub-Treasurer, who were at that period the Government Agents.

"The Governor-General in Council having concerted an arrangement
"with His Highness the Nawab of Bengal, for the establishment of a
"fund for defraying the expense of a new establishment for the super-
"intendence of the affairs of the Nizamut, I am directed to transmit to
"you the enclosed statement of assets appertaining to the Nizamut,
"which have been ascertained to be available for this purpose.

"The only part of these assets actually in the hands of the Govern-
"ment is the first item, namely, the arrears of the stipends of the late
"Munnee Begum from the period of her death till the 31st of August,
"1816, amounting to 2,67,703 rupees, which is in the Treasury of the
"Collector of Moorshedabad.

"It is the desire of the Governor-General in Council, that *the above
"sum should be immediately invested in* public Securities towards the
"formation of the proposed Fund. His Lordship in Council is accordingly
"*pleased to empower and direct you,* in your character of Government Agent

"*to purchase Government Securities* to the amount above stated, which "will be placed at your disposal for that purpose. *The advantage arising* "*from the discount on paper will belong to the Nizamut, and it is to be* "*accounted for to His Highness the Nawab.*

"The remaining sums will be paid into the hands of the Collector at "Moorshedabad, with the least practicable delay, and are then to be "disposed of in the manner above stated.

"A copy of this letter will be transmitted to the Accountant-General, "who will be instructed to take the necessary measures for placing at "your disposal the sum above specified, as well as the remaining sums as "soon as they are realized."

The following letters from Mr. Monckton set forth the Assets from which the Agency Fund was formed, and to which the Nawab was entitled as the heir-at-law:—

To HENRY STONE, ESQ., *Sub-Treasurer, Fort William.*

Sir,

Under charge of Lieutenant George Moore I herewith dispatch to you, for the purpose of being sent to the Mint for coinage, treasure to the amount of 2,28,320 Rupees, of that sum Rs 2,18,820 are destined to form part of a Fund of Seven lacs for defraying the expenses of a new establishment for the superintendence of the affairs of the Nizamut, and the remainder, namely, 9,500 Rupees, are to constitute a Fund for defraying the expense of an establishment at the tomb of the late Munnee Begum.

3. As the treasure is in old Rupees of sorts, I request that you will be pleased to cause Rupees to be assigned with the least practicable delay, and inform me of the amount of any deficiency, when it shall be immediately made good from the stipend of the Nizamut.

3. You will be pleased to communicate the arrival of the treasure to the Accountant-General.

4. The treasure is put up in fifteen boxes, fourteen of which contain 16,000 Rupees each, and the other Rs. 4,320.

I have, &c.,
(Signed) J. MONCKTON.

Moorshedabad, 19th Dec., 1816.

To J. W. SHEEN, ESQ., *Accountant General, Fort William.*

Sir,

You are apprized of the arrangement which has been concerted by the Government in Council with His Highness the Nabob of Bengal for the establishment of a Fund for defraying the expenses of a new establishment for the superintendence of the affairs of the Nizamut, and you have been furnished with a statement of assets available for that purpose.

2. You were informed by a letter from Mr. Secretary Adam, dated 19th

October, that of those assets the sum of 4,67,703 Rupees, being the arrears of the Stipend of the late Munnee Begum from the period of her death till the 31st August, 1816, was in the hands of Government, I deem it regular to explain to you, however, that although the amount of the arrears of the late Munnee Begum was correctly stated, the precise sum was not in the hands of Government. The amount actually due from the Treasury of the Collector of Moorshedabad at that time was only Rs. 2,63,703, and the balance of Rs. 3,399-6 was in the hands of the late Munnee Begum's Dewan.

3. I have now the honour to inform you that, including the balance of Rs. 3999,6 above stated, I have since paid into the Collector's Treasury the sum of 2,17,476-6 Sicca Rupees, making a total sum of 4,81,180 Rupees, and I herewith enclose to you the Collector's receipts for the amount.

4. The remaining assets destined for the fund of the proposed new establishment have been furnished from the late Munnee Begum's Treasures, and is in old Rupees of various denominations. I have, therefore, this day despatched to the General Treasury under an escort of Sepoys, commanded by Lieutenant George Moore, the amount of these assets, namely, Rs. 2,18,820, for the purpose of being sent to the Mint, and have informed the Sub-Treasurer that whatever may be the deficiency of the old Rupees in weight and quality shall be immediately made good from the Munnee Begum's allowance which has accumulated in the Collector's Treasury since the 31st of August.

5. The *fund of seven lacs of rupees* for the proposed new establishment for the superintendence of the affairs of the Nizamut, may, therefore, be considered to be completed, and it only remains for you to produce at the disposal of the Government Agent the sums paid into the Collector's Treasury, in order that *the amount may be invested in Public Securities.*

6. I beg leave to inform you that a further sum of 9,500 Rupees has been taken from the Munnee Begum's Treasure, for the purpose of forming a fund to defray the expenses of an establishment at the Begum's tomb, and that as that money is likewise in old coin, and must consequently be sent to the Mint, I have taken the opportunity of dispatching it to the general Treasury with the other treasure, making the total amount of the remittance tolls Rs. 2,28,320.

7. As the sum of 9,500 Rupees is *to be invested in Government Securities,* you will shortly receive the instructions of the Governor-General in Council to place that sum also at the disposal of the Government Agent.

8. The deficiency in the Rupees comprising the latter item will be met in the same manner as the deficiency in the Rupees belonging to the other Fund, and I have only further to observe that as the interest of 9,500 Rupees will scarcely be sufficient to cover the expenses at the Establishment at the Tomb of the late Munnee Begum, which are ascertained to be 574 Rupees annually, any small addition to the capital by the purchase of Company's paper at a discount is desirable.

I have, &c.,
(Signed) J. MONCKTON.

Moorshedabad, 19th Dec., 1816.

To JOHN ADAM, ESQ., *Acting Chief Secretary to Government, Fort William.*

Sir,

I have the honour to acknowledge the receipt of your despatch of the 19th of October, from which I was happy to learn that my proceedings as detailed in my letter of the 20th of September, had received the entire approbation of Government.

2. My subsequent proceedings have suffered great interruption in consequence of Hindoo and Mussulman Festivals, and particularly by the long illness of His Highness the Nabob.

3. Previously to the Nabob's indisposition, His Highness had attended with me almost daily for three weeks at the late Munnee Begum's apartments, for the purpose of inspecting and examining Her late Highness's treasure and jewels, as also her other property, the extent and variety of which was very great.

4. The jewels may fairly be estimated at not less than six lacs of rupees, the gold and silver utensils amount in weight to Sicca Rupees one lac, two thousand and fifteen, and the property in goods consisting of rich velvets, Benares, gold and silver stuffs, shawls, muslins, silks, beautifully embroidered purdahs, and a countless variety of other articles cannot be estimated at less than one lac and a half of Rupees. The collection of articles of every description was prodigious, and I have great satisfaction in stating that the whole of the property was in the highest state of perfection, as there was reason to apprehend from the late Superintendent's Report that it was not the case.

5. The treasure in gold, silver, and copper coin amounted to 150,507-12 Rupees, but in taking an account of the money, a box containing 16,053 Rupees was pointed out to me as belonging to Zabunnissa Begum, who is grand-daughter of His Highness Nabob Jaffier Ali Khan, and also to her brother, and she is the lady who claimed the enormous sum of nearly two lacs and a half of Rupees out of the Munnee Begum's property.

6. As Mr. Brooke, on the occasion of his being ordered to ascertain the extent of the late Munnee Begum's Treasures, had informed the Government that no parcel, however insignificant, was left unexamined, and as he had not even mentioned the name of the Nowassy Begum in any of his reports, I asked why Mr. Brooke had not been told that the box in question belonged to the Nowassy Begum at the time when the inventory of the Munnee Begum's treasure and effects was prepared under his directions. I was assured that the box was pointed out to Mr. Brooke as being the Nowassy Begum's property, but that because the Munnee Begum's seal was found to be affixed to it, he refused to admit that lady's claim, and said that he considered the whole of the property without distinction as having belonged to Her late Highness.

7. On inquiry, however, it appeared that the Nowassy Begum had always been in the habit of receiving her stipend through the Munnee Begum, and on examining the box, it was found to contain a large collection of the receipts of that lady for a stipend which she enjoys as a Member of the Rajmehal Family. Moreover, Meab Bahar Ufzoon, the eunuch who had charge of the Tosha Khana, declared that the box in question was the treasure-chest of Nowassy Begum, and that the treasure which it contained was no other than the money of her stipend, and they fur-

ther signified their readiness to confirm their declaration, if necessary, by oath.

8. With such evidence in favour of the Nowassy Begum's claim, I could not possibly consider the simple fact of Her late Highness's seal being affixed to the box, to furnish a justifiable pretext for rejecting that claim. I therefore deemed it my bounden duty to represent to His Highness the Nabob the propriety and necessity of his making over the treasure to the Nowassy Begum. His Highness being *entirely unprepared for this fresh demand*, evinced the greatest reluctance to admit the equity of it. But I told His Highness that I felt it incumbent on me to press the point with peculiar earnestness, because it was one which equally concerned His Highness's own honour, and the justice of my proceedings, and that I had too high an opinion of his principles to suppose for a moment that he could desire to withhold from his cousin what was her indisputable right. His Highness, after some consideration, acknowledged that as the eunuch who had charge of the Tosha Khana was prepared to support the claim of the Nowassy Begum on oath, he could not, with propriety, withhold the treasure from her.

9. But while I considered it to be an indispensable obligation of my duty to secure to the Nowassy Begum her joint right, I could not help regarding the fresh demand against the property of the Munnee Begum, as affording to the Nawab a ground of discontent, since *it was on the faith of my assurance that the treasure of the Munnee Begum amounted to fifteen lacs that His Highness recognized and accepted the statement of deductions to be made from that treasure*. Any new circumstance occurring to diminish still further the amount of surplus which the Nabob has been taught to expect for his own personal benefit, could not fail to be regarded by His Highness with dissatisfaction.

10. I therefore anxiously sought to compensate to His Highness in some measure for this disappointment.

11. It occurred to me that among the proscribed deductions from the Munnee Begum's treasures, there was one item, the amount of which nearly corresponded with that of the money found to belong to the Nowassy Begum, and which appeared to be the least desirable of all the deductions, namely, the sum of 17,500 Rupees, awarded to the wife of Shemut-ud-Dowla, *on account of interest on the amount of stoppages of her stipend. I therefore resolved to charge the resources of the Nizamut with the payment of that sum.*

12. Accordingly, after providing the funds for that purpose, I told the Nawab that I was much gratified by his honorable conduct in regard to the treasure which had been ascertained to be the property of his cousin the Nowassy Begum, but that as I was sensible of the disappointment occasioned to him by that claim, I was very anxious to provide the means of satisfying it without exposing him to loss by a diminution of the amount of the surplus which his Highness had been led to expect from the Munnee Begum's treasure, and I then explained to him the arrangement which I had made for that purpose.

13. His Highness seemed extremely gratified, and expressed his sense of obligation to me for my kindness.

14. By this arrangement I was enabled to combine with the performance of an act of justice to the Nowassy Behum the disposal of the late Munnee Begum's property in a manner to afford entire satisfaction to His

Highness's mind, and I trust that the attainment of this object will be considered by the Right Honorable the Governor in Council to furnish a sufficient apology for my taking upon myself to relinquish an item of deduction from the late Munnee Begum's Treasure without His Lordship's in Council previous sanction.

15. The sum of 16,053 rupees being deducted from the property found in the late Munnee Begum's apartments, the treasure which actually belonged to Her Highness amounted to Rupees 14,85,454-12, *out of which has been deducted Rupees* 8,58,043-14-8, and a further sum of Rs. 44,650 reserved for the purpose of reducing jewels mortgaged on bond, to the amount of Rs. 50,000, *leaving a surplus of Rupees* 5,82,760-13-4, *which has been formally made over to His Highness*, together with the whole of the jewels, gold and silver utensils, and other property amounting collectively to about 8,50,000 rupees. Thus, by the death of Her Highness the Munnee Begum, the Nabob has acquired personal property to the extent of nearly fifteen lacs of rupees, besides the possession of lands and houses, and the Chowk adjoining the Palace, which alone yields a revenue of 12,000 rupees per annum.

16. The late illness of His Highness having rendered him incapable of attending to business, has prevented any arrangement for transferring to His Highness immediately the Chowk and its Dependencies, and as His Highness has now proceeded on an excursion to Monghr for change of air, the execution of any measures for that purpose must be delayed until His Highness's return.

17. On the 15th ultimo, I sent to the Collector's Treasury the money required to complete the Fund for defraying the expense of the proposed new establishment for the superintendence of the affairs of the Nizamut, and I only deferred the communication to Government of the payment until the Collector should acknowledge the receipt of the money

18. An unexpected but apparently unavoidable delay, however, has occurred in taking an account of the money in the Collector's Office, a considerable proportion of the money, having been taken from the Munnee Begum's treasure, was in old coin. This circumstance rendered it necessary for the Collector to assort and pay the money before he could make any entry of it in his books, and I was not aware of the length of time which would be required for that purpose.

19. I had waited nearly a month for the Collector's receipt, when I was informed that it had not been found practicable to do more than assort the old coin, which was of various denominations, and that it still remained to assay it. I was, moreover, informed that the assaying of the Rupees in the Collector's Office would not supersede the necessity of their undergoing a similar process at the Presidency on being sent to the Mint to be recoined.

20. In order, therefore, to prevent further loss of time, I resolved to dispatch the Rupees of sorts to the General Treasury without delay, confining the payment into the Collector's Treasury to the Sicca Rupees of the standard weight. I accordingly withdrew the old coin from the Collector's Office, and dispatched it to the Presidency on the 20th instant, under an escort commanded by Lieutenant George Moore. In adopting this measure, I hope my conduct will be approved.

21. I have the honour to transmit to you, for His Lordship in Council's information, a statement of assets which have been placed in

the hands of the Collector, and of those which have been remitted to the Treasury.

22. I have transmitted to the Accountant-General the Collector's Receipts for 4,81,180 Sic. Rupees, and I have apprized him of my having dispatched to the Presidency, for the purpose of being recoined, the sum of 2,18,820 old Rupees, being the number required to complete the Fund of 7 lacs, stating at the same time that whatever may be the deficiency of the old Rupees in weight and quality, it can be immediately made good from the late Munnee Begum's personal allowance of 12,000 Rupees, which has accumulated in the hands of the Collector since 31st August last.

23. It will be in the recollection of His Lordship in Council, that among the deductions from the Munnee Begum's treasure, is a sum of 9,500 Rupees for the purpose of forming a Fund to defray the expense of an establishment at the Tomb of the late Munnee Begum.

24. As that money is in old coin, and *the amount is intended to be invested in the Public Funds*, I have taken the opportunity of sending it to the Presidency with the other Treasure, making the total amount of the remittance 2,28,320 rupees. I have prepared the Accountant-General to expect orders from Government on the subject of placing the further sum of 9,500 Rupees at the disposal of the Government Agents, *for the purpose of being laid out in the purchase of Company's Paper*, and I have informed him that the deficiency in the Rupees, as soon as the extent of it shall be ascertained, will be met in the same manner as the deficiency in the other part of the treasure.

25. As the monthly and occasional expenses of the establishment maintained at Munnee Begum's tomb are ascertained to amount to 574 Rupees annually, which rather exceeds the interest of Rs. 9,500, I have intimated to the Accountant-General that *the amount which may be gained by the Discount on Company's Paper should be added to the capital for the purpose of rendering the Fund more adequate* to its object.

26. I am engaged in settling the debts of the Nabob's several uncles, and am endeavouring to adjust them in a manner most favourable to their interest.

27. I hope also in a few days to submit a detailed Report of the Establishment of the late Munnee Begum, of two casualties which have occurred in them since His Highness's demise, and of the reductions which have actually been effected, or which may appear practicable.

I have, &c.,
(Signed) J. MONCKTON.

Moorshedabad, 26th December, 1816.

The following extract is from the instructions sent to Mr. Monckton in reply:—

"The Governor-General in Council approves of your having despatched "to the Presidency that portion of the money required to form the "Fund for defraying the expense of the proposed new establishment "for the Superintendence of the affairs of the Nizamut, which consisted "of Rupees of sorts, and of your communication to the Accountant-

"General on the subject of that remittance, and on the other points adverted to in the 17th and following paragraphs of your letter. The necessary orders will be issued for *investing in Government securities such portions of the money intended to form the proposed Fund,* as had not already been so disposed of."

The following is an extract from the orders issued to the Government Agent subsequently:—

"In continuation of my letter of the 19th October last, I am directed to transmit to you the enclosed Statements of the Assets, which have been placed in the hands of the Collector of Moorshedabad, and of those which have been remitted to the Presidency, for the purpose of forming a Fund for defraying the expense of the proposed establishment of the Superintendence of the affairs of the Nizamut.

"Mr. Monckton has reported the transmission to the Accountant-General of the Collector's receipt for the portion of that sum paid into his Treasury, and his having apprized the Accountant-General of the remittance of the remainder to the Presidency in Rupees of sorts.

"It only remains, therefore, to desire that you will, in your character of Government Agents, proceed, in the manner pointed out in my letter of the 19th October, with regard to that part of the money in question, which may not have been already invested in Public Securities for the purpose stated, and which will be placed at your disposal by the Accountant-General."

Mr. Monckton, in consideration of the services he had rendered in carrying out the instructions of the Governor-General, was nominated to the appointment which he had been so instrumental in establishing by the following letter:—

To JOHN MONCKTON, ESQ.

Sir,

The principal object of your deputation to Moorshedabad having now been successfully accomplished and the fund for the establishment of the proposed system of control and superintendence over the affairs of the Nizamut having now been formed by the actual receipt into the Treasury of the money intended to be appropriated from the resources of the Nizamut for that purpose. *I am directed to inform you that you are to consider your mission at an end, and that His Excellency the Governor-General in Council has been pleased to appoint you to the permanent situation of Agent to the Governor-General at Moorshedabad.* At this capacity, in addition to the more immediate and special duty of superintendence over the affairs of the Nizamut, you will consider yourself to be the channel of communication with all natives of rank residing at or visiting the city of Moorshedabad, as well as with the descendants of the Nawab Ihteram-ud-Dowla a collateral branch of the Family of the Nabob of Bengal residing at Rajmehal and not strictly comprehended in the establishment of the Nizamut.

2. The Governor-General in Council has been pleased to fix *the salary of the office of Agent of the Governor-General at Moorshedabad at* 40,000 *sicca rupees per annum,* after providing for this charge, a sum of 2,000 Rupees per annum of the interest of the Fund in question will remain available for the expenses of the establishment of your office, which with the amount of the present monthly establishment of 213 Rupees, making an aggregate of Rs. 379-4 per mensem, which His Lordship in Council conceives be fully adequate for that purpose. You will accordingly prepare and submit for the approval and sanction of the Government the details of an establishment at an expense not exceeding the aggregate amount above stated.

You will be proposed to return to Moorshedabad, to assume the office to which you are now appointed, as soon as may be convenient.

I have, &c.,
(Signed). J. ADAM,
Acting Chief Secretary to Government.

Council Chambers, 22nd February, 1817.

P.S.—You will receive from the Persian Secretary a letter from the Governor-General to His Highness the Nabob, announcing the appointment.

On the proceedings (see Poll-Corr. 10th May. 1817, No. 20-25), is recorded a letter from the Government Agents, of which the following is a copy :—

" We have the honour to acknowledge the receipt of your letters, " bearing dates the 19th of October and 4th of January last, relative to " the Nizamut establishment, and to state, for the information of Govern- " ment, that in conformity with the instructions conveyed in those " letters, *we have invested the several sums received by us from the General " Treasury,* and have now the pleasure of submitting an account exhibit- " ing the whole of this transaction."

On receipt of the foregoing letter, and the accounts which accompanied it. from the Government Agents, further instructions. dated the 1st May, 1817, were issued to the Accountant-General, from which the following is an extract.

" The Government Agents have been directed to deliver over to you " the Government Securities to the amount of Rupees 7,10,600, which " have been purchased on account of the Nizamut.

" You will be pleased to take necessary measures for having *those " Securities invested as the property of the Nizamut,* the interest in them " being assigned for the payment of certain special charges as follows .

	Principal.	Interest per an.
" For paying the Salary " and of the Office Estab- " lishment of the Agent to " the Governor-General at " Moorshedabad, . . -	7,01,000	42,060

"For the charge of an
"Establishment at the Tomb
"of the Munnee Begum . 9,600 576

"The Collector of Moorshedabad has been authorized to pay the "Salary and Establishment of the Agent to the Governor-General at "Moorshedabad, and the charges of the Establishment of the Munnee "Begum's tomb, monthly, at the above rates.

"You will be pleased to transmit the Government Securities above "mentioned, to the Collector of Moorshedabad, *with instructions to "balance in his accounts, the interets due on them half-yearly*, against "the monthly payments which he has been authorized to make as speci-"fied in the foregoing paragraph."

A further charge was made by the Government against the Nizamut, in accordance with the instructions given in the following letter :—

To JOHN MONCKTON, ESQ., *Acting Agent to the Governor-General, Moorshedabad.*

Sir,

I am directed to acknowledge the receipt of your letter of the 7th inst., and to inform you that the Governor-General in Council has been pleased to sanction the establishment proposed by you for the office of Agent to the Governor-General at Moorshedabad. The payment of the establishment will commence from the date on which it may have been entertained.

2. Although *it was originally intended that a portion of the expense of the establishment of the Agent* equivalent to the expense of the establishment heretofore maintained for the superintendent of *Nizamut* affairs *should be charged to the Government*, the Governor-General in Council, on a reconsideration of the subject, is disposed to think that *it will be more consistent* with the principle on which the office was constituted *to make the whole chargeable on the funds of the Nizamut.*

3. His Lordship in Council, would, however, be reluctant to bring forward a fresh demand on this account, however inconsiderable the amount, did he not suppose that funds sufficient for the purpose will have already accumulated from the arrears of lapsed stipends yet unappropriated, and which may be considered properly applicable to this object, as one connected with the general benefit of the Nizamut.

4. The *interest* calculated from the 1st January to the 21st February *accruing on the Government Securities* purchased on account of the Nizamut, which have been assigned for the payment of the salary of the Agent, *will be available* for the same purpose; as will also the interest calculated from the 1st January to the date on which the office establishment now sanctioned may have been entertained, accruing on the Government Securities assigned for the payment of a portion of that establishment.

5. The Governor-General in Council desires that you will submit a

Statement of the amount of funds which may have accumulated from the source specified in the 3rd paragraph of this letter, which may be made available for defraying that portion of the expense of the Agent's Establishment not yet provided for from the funds of the Nizamut. On receiving this report, His Lordship in Council will determine on the expediency of making this expense a charge on the Nizamut.

6. The Collector of Moorshedabad has been authorised to pay monthly on the joint receipt of His Highness the Nabob and of the Agent, the allowance for an Establishment at the Tomb of the late Munnee Begum. The payment of this Establishment will commence from the 1st of January, the date from which interest is due on the Government Securities assigned for defraying it.

I have, &c.,
(Signed) J. ADAM,
Acting Chief Secretary to Government.

Fort William, 10th May, 1817.

On the proceedings of the Poll-Cor. 5th July, 1817, No. 41-45 is recorded a letter from Mr. Monckton, forwarding a letter to the address of the Governor-General, from His Highness the Nawab Nazim, in submitting which, Mr. Monckton observed thus:—

"The only point in His Highness's letter which appears to require "particular notice is, the solicitude which His Highness has expressed "to receive from the Governor-General an assurance, *that the Com-* "*pany's Papers which have been purchased with the Funds of the* "*Nizamut*, for the declared purpose of defraying the expense of the "newly constituted Office, *shall be considered as appertaining to the* "*Nizamut, and not liable, under any change of circumstances, to be* "*diverted to purposes foreign to the interest of the house of Jaffier* "*Alee Khan.* Such an assurance would not, perhaps, be inconsistent "with the principle on which the Fund has been formed, while, it "would be particularly gratifying to His Highness."

The Governor-General replied to the letter from His Highness the Nawab Nazim, and forwarded it through Mr. Monckton; it ran thus:—

"It was matter of satisfaction to me to be able to form the Fund "for the payment of the new establishment by appropriating to that "purpose the accumulations of different branches of the Nizamut not "expressly destined to other purposes and which could not have been "applied to any object so truly beneficial. The money forming *the* "*fund* thus obtained amounting to seven lacs of Rupees *is considered* "*and recognized as the inalienable property of Your Highness's* "*Family, over and above the Sixteen lacs of Rupees per annum* "assigned for its support."

The Agency Fund must clearly have been a distinct and separate Fund, when the Hon. W. L. Melville, Agent Governor-General, addressed Government on 28th May. 1836, in the following words:—

"There is at present a peculiar pressure of business in the English "Department of this office—
 "1. The accounts of the Munnee Begum's Deposit Fund.
 "2. The Pension Fund.
 "3. The Pension Deposit Fund.

"Temporary aid is therefore required. I beg I may be empowered "to entertain an 'additional writer at 100 Rupees per mensem, *to be* "*charged to the Agency Fund.*'"

In a letter dated 1st March, 1836, Sir W. Macnaughten alludes to the several funds which the Hon. W. L. Melville, in an official communication dated 5th July, 1837, proposed to amalgamate; but as the proposition required *grave consideration*, the Accountant-General was referred to, who reported to Government on the 16th December, 1837, that by a Government Order of the 1st March, 1836, *the Funds had been amalgamated*,' which, in his opinion, "rendered unnecessary "any exhibition of the Agency charges in the accounts of this Govern- "ment!" This was apparently an opinion derived from Para. II. of Sir W. Macnaughten's letter where he states: "The different sums "composing the Fund formerly set aside for the payment of the ex- "penses of the Agency for the superintendence of the Nizamut "affairs have lately been brought together in the hands of the "Government Agents, and you will hereafter draw upon them "monthly, for the expenses of the Agency including your own salary. "*The Government Agents will be instructed to furnish an annual* "*account of this Fund directed to this office*, instead of the circuitous "plan hitherto followed of sending it through the Agent of Moor- "shedabad."

In a letter from the Civil Auditor to the Agent Governor-General dated 4th July, 1837, with reference to the charges for Agent's salary, office establishment, and rent, he states:—

"These charges are defrayable out of the interest of the Nizamut "Fund, called the *Agency Deposit Fund*, reserved in the Treasury of "Government under Order of Government of the 22nd February, "1817, and *which is declared to be quite distinct* from that denomi- "nated the *Nizamut Deposit Fund*, which is available for general "purposes connected with the welfare of the Nizamut Family."

As this Fund was thus declared distinct, it only remains to consider its condition at different periods.

In Para. 5 of General Raper's letter to the Government of Bengal, dated 17th April, 1843, after entering generally upon the subject of the Fund, he states—

"The different sums set aside for the payment of this Agency were, "under Government Order of the 1st March, 1836, finally brought "together in the hands of the Government Agents, and on reference "to their account current made up to the 30th April, 1842, a copy of "which was transmitted to me in Mr. (Officiating Secretary) Bushby's "letter of the 10th August last, I observe that the state of the "Nizamut Fund is adequate to the payment, not only of the entire "charge of the Agency, but *an annual accumulating balance of about* "*Rupees 24,000 is created in favour of the Fund by a surplus of* "*Interest over Expenditure*, as shown in the accompanying state- "ment *of the Government Securities composing the Nizamut Agency* "*Fund.*"

Again, Mr. H. Torrens, Agent Governor-General, when addressing the Government of Bengal on the 1st of February, 1848, on the subject of the Agency Fund, states:—

"It appeared that there were Sic. Rupees 12,29,645, yielding a sur- "plusage annually of Interest over Expenditure."

And by the Agent Governor-General's letter of 27th January, 1853, it further appeared that on the 30th April, 1852, the returns showed an accumulation of Rupees 16,47,044-10-5.

When Sir George MacGregor applied to the Accountant-General on the 12th February, 1857, after the Agency was abolished, for information as to the future custody of the Government Securities and cash pertaining to the Agency Fund, he received a reply from the Secretary and Treasurer of the Bank of Bengal, enclosing a Power of Attorney, afterwards executed by the Secretary of the Government of Bengal and the Agent Governor-General, *authorizing him* (the Secretary and Treasurer) *to realise the Interest on the Government Securities*, amounting to Rupees 18,39,100, made over to him by the Government Agent on account of the Agency (Nizamut) Fund. And a letter from the Government of Bengal, No. 2,675, dated 30th May, 1857, *ordered the consolidation of all such securities and directed that "the interest on these papers may be invested "from time to time, as it accrues, in the open Government Loan "of the day:"* thus the numbers and amounts of the Papers were altered.

In the Sub-Treasurer's letter to the Government of Bengal, No. 680, dated 19th November, 1860, the following return is given of the Agency Fund :—

Assets in Cash on this date, 19th November, 1860, Company's Rupees, 33,969-1-2

In Government Promissory Notes.

1 Note of	1824-25	Sa. Rs.	1,000		
2 „	1828-29	„	13,300		
3 „	1832-33	„	7,35,000		
		Sa. Rs.	7,49,300	Cos. Rs.	7,99,253-5-4
1 Note of	1835-36	Cos. Rs.	1,58,500		
1 „	1842-43		7,88,100		
1 „	1854-55		1,00,900		
2 „	1856-57		92,990		
3 „	1859-60		64,800		
				„	12,05,200-0-0
			Total	„	20,38,422-6-6

At the beginning of 1862, this Fund must have amounted to over twenty-one lacs of Rupees, and at the end of 1868 to over twenty-four lacs, yielding an interest of at least 10,000 Rupees per mensem, which is far beyond the requirements of the Agency, for the support of which this Fund was established.

By this new arrangement, as before observed, *the funds set apart for relieving the Nawab from pecuniary difficulties were diverted* for the support of an official with a large salary, Sicca Rupees 40,000 (£4312-10) per annum, (Page 68), whose duty it would be to wait upon the Nawab, and *watch over the interests of the Nizamut*, thus relieving the Governor-General from a duty and responsibility which was by courtesy incumbent on him; this official was, therefore, designated the Agent Governor-General.

The Fund from which the Agent Governor-General was paid was styled the Agency Fund, and amounted in 1817, at the time of its formation, to over seven lacs of Rupees (£70,000) (*See* Para. 5 of Letter, Page 62), besides other monies, of which no proper account was rendered, and *this Fund invested in Government Securities*, continues to exist up to the present day. At the beginning of 1860 the Sub-Treasurer to the Government of Bengal rendered an account (Page 72) which shows that the Agency Fund had then increased to Rs. 20,38,422,6-6 (£203,842), the interest on which at 5 per cent. must have then yielded £10,192 per annum, a sum amounting to more than four times the present salary of the Agent; besides its accumulations since 1860 ought to be considerable, and, together with other surplus money, should, in honor and justice, be accounted for to the Nawab, according to the terms on which the Fund was originally formed (see Page 70), when His Highness's great-uncle protested against it, until he received the following assurance from the Governor-General: "*The money forming this Fund thus obtained, amounting to seven lacs of Rupees, is considered and recognized as the inalienable property of Your Highness's family, over and above the sixteen lacs of Rupees per annum assigned for its support.*" Mr. Monckton also assured that Prince (Page 70) "*that the Company's Papers, which were purchased with the Funds of the Nizamut, for the declared purpose of defraying the expense of the newly constituted office, would be considered as appertaining to the Nizamut, and not liable under any change of circumstances to be diverted to purposes foreign to the interests of the House of Jaffier Ali Khan,*" so it is reasonable to suppose that all surplus should be applied for the benefit of the Nawab and his family.

But as money misapplied seldom produces good results, so it is to these Officials that we might trace the many annoyances and difficulties that have been thrown in the way of the Nawabs Nazim since 1817, and brought about the estrangement that now exists between the present Nawab and the Government of India, which, feeling itself bound to follow the representations of its own officers, *whether right or wrong,* has been led to act on several occasions in the most arbitrary manner, and with cruel injustice towards the descendants and successors of our oldest and most faithful ally in Eastern India. It is to the clearing up of these and other differences that we wish to draw public inquiry, and as we desire only to do justice, we can but lay the several questions open for discussion, so that right-thinking men may have an opportunity of deciding whether the acts of the Government of India have conduced to impress the Princes of that country with the idea that we are a just and honorable Nation, and always support the cause of *right* against *might*, as expressed in Her Most Gracious

Majesty's Proclamation of 1858 to the Princes, Chiefs, and People of India, which we will introduce as our subject is continued.

When Nawab Zyn-oo-deen (or Ali Jah) died without legitimate male issue, *his brother*, Nawab Wallah Jah, **succeeded** to the *hereditary* rights, honours, dignity, and privileges of the Nizamut or **Soubahdarry, under the** style and title of Boorhan ul-Moolk, Ehtisham-ood-Dowlah, Wallah Jah, Syud Ahmud Ali Khan Bahadur, Mahabut Jung, and received the following assurance of good faith and friendship from the Marquis of Hastings:—

From the MARQUIS OF HASTINGS *to* NAWAB SYUD AHMAD ALI KHAN BAHADOOR, *Nawab Nazim of Bengal, Behar, and Orissa, dated* 10*th August*, 1821.

On the receipt of the mournful intelligence of the demise of the late NAWAB ZYNOODEEN ALI KHAN BAHADOOR, the elder brother of that friend, no time was lost in transmitting a letter of condolence expressing the grief and regret of this person, on the sad and important occasion. This person in council has now resolved to seat that friend, the dear brother of the deceased Nawab of Pious memory, on the Musnud of the *Soobahadaree* of the Soobahs of BENGAL, BEHAR, and ORISSA. Instructions have been accordingly issued to Mr. Francis Russell to repair to the Court where that friend presides, and on the part of this Government to invest Your Highness with the *Soubahdaree* of the *three Soobahs aforesaid*, and in concert with that friend, to fix a day for the ceremony, and to determine the style and title, and to report to this person.

The *fixed allowances* and *other mutually established points, will continue* and *endure* as approved and sanctioned by the Home authorities in the life-time of the late Nawab;—*namely*, sixteen Lacs of Rupees annually, according to mode and arrangement settled, and that friend, in unison with the members of this Government, may consider proper for the distribution of the pensions, and *each Sirkar may deem right* with advertance to the position and circumstances of the connections and dependents of the Nizamut, will be as usual remitted in monthly issues to that friend. And be assured, that the *Government* will to the utmost of its power afford its friendly counsel and aid *in promoting the honour and dignity, ease, comfort, happiness and welfare* of that good friend, personally, and of all members of this family.

And that friend may be assured that the friendship and goodwill evinced by the Government for the late Nawab, *without difference*, be joyfully and cheerfully continued to Himself. And that the *honours* and *distinctions due to the exalted rank* of Your Highness' family, whose *credit, consequence, dignity,* and *splendour are now combined in that friend,* will be *always paid* and *faithfully observed.*

(Signed) HASTINGS.

It was during the Soubahship of this Prince that the most iniquitous measures were introduced by the officers of the Government of India for depriving the Nawabs of much pecuniary support to which they were by right entitled. It was proposed that certain funds should be established out of the Nizamut Stipend, and be placed under the immediate control of the Government, which could apply them as it wished, or if it thought proper, absorb them altogether, and thus bring down the social position of the Nawabs Nazim by accomplishing the ruin of the family.

The following correspondence will give an idea of the coercive measures adopted for carrying out the views of the Government whereby two new Funds (*Munnee Begum's* and *Deposit Fund*) were formed, which were afterwards in 1836 amalgamated, and have since that time swallowed up all the available resources of the Nawabs Nazim, of which the Government has taken the absolute control in direct opposition to the terms upon which the Trusts were formed. The object of these Funds (apart from any desire on the part of the Company to reduce the social status of the Nawabs) was to make up the deficiency caused by the *misappropriation* of the sums before set apart, for meeting the extraordinary liabilities of the Nizamut incurred by the reduction of the Annuity, and also for the expenses of new buildings, &c., when (the same) Mr. Monckton suggested that those sums should be absorbed as an Agency Fund to meet the establishment of the office of Agent Governor-General, which post he himself was the first to enjoy. Such is the way in which officials in India have misled the Government and done injustice to both Princes and People, and to this source may in a great measure be attributed the several insurrections that have taken place in that country.

Mr. Monckton, who was deputed to Moorshedabad for the special purpose of reporting on the affairs of the Nizamut, in his report submitted a suggestion for the appropriation of accumulations from the Nizamut Fund as follows :—

"The unappropriated portion of the Nizamut Fund assets will "accumulate at the rate of Sicca Rupees 15,114 per mensem, or "1,81,368 Rs per annum. It appears to me extremely desirable, that "*advantage should be taken of the present condition of the Nizamut,* "*to employ these large accumulating resources, as far as practicable,* "*in the construction of a suitable palace for the Nazim,* in the erec- "tion of proper offices and store rooms, the rebuilding of the public "gateways, in the completion of the Emambarrah. in the construction "of pucka drains within the precincts of the Killah, in the removal "of the decayed buildings, and in the application of the materials for "the purpose of strengthening the bank in front of the Palace yard "and other places appertaining to the Killah. The works, of course, "must be undertaken in succession as the Funds become available for "prosecuting them, with regularity, to a completion."

The orders of Government on Mr. Monckton's proposition are contained in the following extract from a letter addressed to the Acting Agent :—

"After providing for all the objects above described, and after re- "serving 120,000 Rupees for re-building the late Munnee Begum's "apartments, and the construction of a house for the Nawab's brother "the unappropriated assets, it was expected, would amount to 50,000 "Rupees at the end of December, and continue to accumulate at the "rate of 15,114 Rupees per mensem, or 181,368 Rupees per annum.

"The objects for which these Funds are intended to provide, are "stated, generally, in the concluding paragraph of Mr. Monckton's "letter of the 30th December.

"The Vice President in Council, however, adverting to the small amount of the funds which are, at present available for the prosecution of those objects, deems it advisable to suspend the adoption of measures for commencing any other works, than those already authorized, until, by a further reservation of the sources of accumulation, they shall have increased to the extent necessary for prosecuting them regularly and without interruption."

On the Proceedings noted above, is a letter from the Agent at Moorshedabad, dated 31st December, 1822, proposing the grant of an allowance to the favourite wife of the Nazim and to other relations from lapsed stipends of Munnee Begum, and showing the flourishing state of the Nizamut Finances.

"The Nizamut accounts for 1226, 27, and 28 having been laid before Government, the Nizamut's cash transactions with Nawab Shumshere Jung being adjusted as to the principal sums, the bonds, &c., having been delivered up, and a general account given, though a detailed one is required, and is now in progress, and Ameeroonnissa Begum put in possession of the Deories, my attention was directed to the internal arrangement of the Nizamut, together with the probable claim on the Deposit Fund, and I have now the honour to submit the result of my inquiries relative to the situation of His Highness' family, as also such measures as appear, most likely, to prompt the continuance of the present flourishing state of the finances.

"With regard to the Funds from whence these several pensions are to be derived, I beg to suggest, that, there which will be an excess on the present expenditure (for those to the wife and son of the present Nazim are but reversion) being paid from the stipend of the Munnee Begum, by which means they will not touch upon such parts of the Deposit Fund which His Lordship in Council may please to appropriate to the building of the new Palace, &c. &c., and *still a large annual accumulation to the Fund will be effected, leaving an annual saving of Rupees* 1,02,600 *applicable to such purposes as Government may deem most expedient.*"

The following extract is taken from the letter addressed by the Governor-General to the Nawab Nazim, proposing to His Highness the investment in Government Securities of these and other accumulations in the Collector's Treasury for the benefit of the family :—

"You must be aware, that *this Government has been constantly
"*anxious to promote the welfare and splendour of your family*, with
"due advertence to the claims of its numerous connexions and depen-
"dents, and that several measures have, at different times, been
"instituted to effect this salutary object. Thus, in 1802, a Committee
"was appointed of several gentlemen for the purpose of examining the
"various heads of expenditure and introducing economical reforms in
"the Nizamut. *The arrangements suggested by that Committee were
"carried into execution with the approbation as well of His Highness
"the Nawab Babur Jung, then Nazim, as the British Government.*
"They comprehended a revision and fresh settlement of each Serishtah
"of the Establishment and of the allowances to be drawn by all the
"dependents. *The settlement introduced on that occasion has con-
"tinued to this day.* Again, after the death of the Munnee Begum,
"Mr. J. Monckton was deputed to Moorshedabad to settle some
"important matters, and he continued there some time. At his sug-
"gestion, the lapsed stipends of the Munnee Begum, with some items
"of the same kind, were set apart to accumulate, so as *to form a Fund
"applicable to the building of a suitable Palace for the Nazim, and to
"furnish marriage portions for the females of the family besides other
"assistance to the different members of the Nizamut.* This arrange-
"ment continued till the lamented death of your late brother, Syud
"Zynoodeen, in the year 1821.

"It appears that a portion of the savings and lapsed stipends, which
"have been appropriated for the exigencies of the Nizamut Tuhbeels,
"accumulate in the Nizamut after the entire monthly allowances are
"drawn from the Collector's Treasury, but the stipends of the late
"Munnee Begum, amounting to 12,000 Rupees per mensem, remain
"in deposit with the Collector, and has been accumulating there for
"some years.

"The accounts transmitted by the late Agent show, that the entire
"amount of the appropriations of this description was, in 1226, two
"lakhs and eighty thousand ; in 1820, about two lakhs and eighty ; and
"that in 1228, amounted to no less than three lakhs of Rupees per
"annum, and, had the whole been properly kept inviolate, that sum
"should have been forthcoming for the year.

"*With regard, however, to the future accumulation on
"account of the Deposit Fund, I propose that they should be
"kept wholly in the Collector's Treasury, and invested in
"Securities of the British Government as the funds may
"accrue,* and the present amount, which approaches to near
"three lakhs of Rupees per annum, seems unnecessarily
"large, on which account, should you agree to allow the ac-
"cumulation to proceed in the Collector's Treasury, I pro-
"pose to limit the amount to two lakhs, leaving you the
"remainder to meet the expense of the daughters of His late
"Highness and others which have been recently recommended
"by you, and all other charges heretofore allowed from the

"Fund, but with full liberty to appropriate any excess to
"purposes connected with the splendour and credit of your
"exalted station."

The following is a copy of the instructions issued to the Accountant-General:—

"I am directed by the Honorable the Governor-General in Council
"to transmit the enclosed extract from instructions this day addressed
"to the Governor-General's Agent at Moorshedabad, from which you
"will perceive that *it is the intention of Government to invest imme-
"diately in Company's Paper the sum of six lakhs of Rupees* of the
"amount accumulated in the Treasury of the Collector of Moorsheda-
"bad *on account of the stipend of the late Munnee Begum.*

"You will be pleased to issue the requisite instructions on the
"subject to the Collector, and desire that *he will hereafter keep the
"account of the deposit and of all further accumulations of the same
"stipend, entirely distinct from other deposits* made occasionally in his
"Treasury on account of Members of the Nizamut under temporary
"arrangements of various kinds.

"Eventually, the *Fund above alluded to will be increased,* when
"due intimation will, of course, be furnished to yourself and to the
"Collector.

"Instructions will be sent to the Government Agents at Calcutta to
"receive the amount to be transmitted from Moorshedabad, and to
"invest it in Government Securities."

The following is a copy of the instructions to the Government Agent above alluded to:—

"Government having determined *to invest in Public Securities the
"sum of six lakhs of Rupees,* now lying in deposit in the Treasury of
"the Collector of Moorshedabad *on account of the Nizamut, I am
"directed to instruct you* to receive the sum when remitted to Calcutta
"by that Officer, and *to purchase such Securities as you may deem
"most advantageous.* The propriety of making the purchases with
"as little delay as possible need not be pointed out to you.

"*The interest that may accumulate is to be re-invested* as received,
"and the Paper is to be at the disposal of Government, as it may be
"required *for purposes connected with the Nizamut.* The order for
"this purpose will be communicated from this department."

No further orders appear on record on the subject of this Fund. The accumulations from the lapsed stipends of Munnee Begum from the year 1823, when the six lakhs were ordered to be invested in Government Securities, were as proposed by Mr. Monckton, held in reserve for making the new Palace, the Imambarrah, and other buildings of the Nizamut. These buildings have now been completed, and the cost of their construction is said to have exceeded sixteen lacs of Rupees!

On the subject of future investment of the accumulations from the lapsed stipends of the late Munnee Begum, and *the re-investment of the interest* accruing upon all sums so invested in Government Securities for the Nizamut, the intentions of Government appear sufficiently clear from the extracts given above, particularly the one from the letter to the Accountant-General.

The following is an extract from the instructions issued to the Agent in reply, date 28th February, 1823, regarding the formatton of both Funds:—

From H. T. PRINSEP, ESQ., *Persian Secretary to Government, to the* AGENT GOVERNOR-GENERAL, *Moorshedabad.*

Fort William, 28th February, 1823.

22. It remains to notice the proposition contained in the 5th Paragraph of Mr. Rickett's letter of the 19th Dec., viz., that certain charges incurred by His late Highness amounting in the aggregate to 80,138 should similarly be defrayed from the Deposit Fund.

23. Upon examining the items it appears to the Governor-General in Council that they are all of a personal nature that must have been actually defrayed before the accession of His present Highness. None of them remain as debts now due by the Nizamut, and as none of them are entered in the Nizamut accounts the reason is apparent, viz., that His late Highness conceived them to be of that description of charges to be paid by himself, personally, either from his allowance under the head of privy purse, or from the wealth that had come to him by inheritance.

24. It seems to the Governor-General in Council that Government might with equal propriety be called upon to replace every item expended by His late Highness from his privy purse allowance, and to make over the accumulation of that allowance untouched as a sacred inheritance of the Nizamut, as to sanction the particular charges

G

claimed in this instance. Had debt been incurred to meet them, and had the Nizamut been made over to His present Highness with an empty Treasury, in consequence, or otherwise embarrassed by the extravagance of his predecessor, this claim to relief from the Fund provided for such exigencies might have been deserving of consideration; but in the present instance His Highness succeeded to an accumulated treasure, from which his predecessor might have appropriated as many lacs as the statement shows him to have done tens of thousands; and *Government would neither have felt itself interested in the expenditure*, nor called upon to replace the amount. You will be pleased to take an opportunity of explaining to His Highness the light in which these charges have been regarded by Government.

25. You will have gathered from the above observations and orders that the Governor-General in Council is not disposed to grant the lac of Rupees solicited for the Nizamut in the sixth Paragraph of Mr. Rickett's letter above alluded to for the purpose of enabling His Highness to renew his establishments. *The plan of reserving this Fund was adopted with a view to place in the hands of Government a means of relieving any exigencies in which the family might be involved, as well as of portioning the daughters, and providing buildings or other operations of the kind, involving a present sacrifice of capital.*

26. If the Nizamut were destitute of other resources, the claim to assistance for an outlay of the kind now suggested might be admissable; but *while it enjoys the advantage of inheriting the wealth of its dependents* and thus becomes enriched from means in which other branches of the family are debarred from participating, it seems just that the aid of the Fund shall rather be extended to assist those who have otherwise nothing besides their monthly stipend to look to. *This principle it will be right to explain to His Highness in order that he may not consider the refusal as an ungracious act dictated by a desire to avoid contributing to the restoration of the splendour of the Court of Moorshedabad than which nothing can be further from the intention of Government.*

27. It may at the same time *be hinted* that the wealth inherited by His Highness from his brother could not possibly be better bestowed than in restoring the equipages and other establishments of the Nizamut to creditable state. Considering the amount already known by Government to have come into His Highness' hands, it is, in the judgment of the Governor-General in Council, quite impossible that the whole should have been expended, and could he suppose this to be the case, the circumstance would lead to his witholding from His Highness that confidence in his discretion and prudence which alone would justify an advance of the kind solicited in the present instance.

28. It is to be remembered, moreover, that His Highness has very recently come into possession of the wealth of the late Valiida Begum and though the Debt due to the Nizamut by the Seits may not, perhaps, have been actually recovered, there can, it is presumed, be no doubt of its ultimate realization.

29. *The above instructions leave the accumulations of the Munnee Begum's stipend in the Treasury of the Collector entirely untouched, the whole will consequently be open to be appropriated in the manner Government may deem most equitable and proper for the benefit of the Nizamut.*

30. At the close of 1225 this fund is stated to have amounted to Rs. 3,17,573, but in this sundry deposits are included on account of *the pension of Khulee Coollah and the like, which cannot be considered as part of the Fund.* The accumulation of the Munnee Begum's stipend alone after that date seems to have been Rs. 3,14,500, add to that amount the accumulation during the three years 1226,—27—28, and there is *a fund of Rs. 7,46,503 actually forthcoming in the Collector's Treasury.* It remains to determine the mode of appropriating this sum.

31. You are, of course, aware that *Government are* in a manner *pledged to provide a suitable Palace for His Highness, and that a large portion of the above sum will be required for this purpose.* As the advances of the building will, however, require to be made gradually, and the same fund will go on accumulating as heretofore, it cannot be necessary to reserve the large floating balance suggested in the 8th Paragraph of Mr. Ricketts' letter; *but of the seven lacs and a half, six lacs may safely be invested in Public Securities for the benefit of the Nizamut,* the Governor-General in Council accordingly desires that that amount may be forthwith remitted to the Government Agents at the Presidency for the purpose of being invested to the best advantage. The requisite instructions will be sent to the Collector and other officers of the Territorial Department, and the paper will be held in deposit in the same manner as that provided for the payment of the expense of the establishment of your office.

32. It remains now to point out to you that the views of Government for the future regulation of the control to be exercised by you over the expenses of the Nizamut, and the footing on which it is proposed to place His Highness in this respect.

33. Nothing can be more vexatious and unsatisfactory than *the present system under which His Highness is compelled to furnish Annual Accounts for Government to audit.* The system owed its origin to the embarrassed state of the Nizamut, and to *the desire of Government to lend the weight of its authority to enforce certain economical reforms deemed at the time necessary for its relief. Now, however, that the same motive does not exist for interference,* it seems to the Governor-General in Council that *it would be very desirable to withdraw from any minute supervision,* and *to confine the Agent's duty to that of ascertaining that every Member of the Family receives his due.* It might, perhaps, be sufficient for this purpose that the Agent should be ready to receive and inquire into all complaints, *under a declaration to His Highness,* that in case the payment of any one's stipend should be delayed, or of any legitimate demand being withheld, the Government would separate the allowance, or a fair equivalent for it, if not a money allowance, and pay it from the Public Treasury direct. It seems, however, desirable that your office should possess the means of settling the dues of all the Members of the Nizamut in case of dispute, and therefore a registrar of the present distribution of the several heads of charge should be formed as expeditiously as possible, with a due regard to correctness. The preparation of this record is stated to be already in progress, and in case of any difficulty in procuring the information required to form it from the officers of the Nazim, the Governor-General in Council is aware of no objection to your calling on the parties in each instance to state their respective rights.

34. Upon the formation of the register in question, the Governor-General in Council is of opinion that *the requisition of Annual Accounts, in detail, may be wholly discontinued, and* an arrangement being made for *the adjustment* and *witholding of the* amount appropriated to *the Deposit Fund, that the remainder may safely be delivered to His Highness to be disbursed according to his pleasure under the responsibility above described.* It will then suffice to require His Highness to deliver in a statement of the gross expenditure arranged under the general heads according to the register, as an assurance that the appropriation has been made according to it, or is reserved for the purpose, but without exhibiting any detail. This will be of use to prevent the matter from falling wholly out of view, and will further enable Government to remove the requisition of more exact accounts, should circumstances render it expedient to do so.

35. *It is by no means the desire of Government to increase indefinitely the appropriations for the benefit of the Deposit Fund. Their net amounts seems at present to exceed two lacs of Rupees after allowing for all the augmentations and appropriations sanctioned. This is one eighth of the entire Nizamut Stipend, and the Governor-General in Council would not wish to make it larger. At the same time he conceives it will be unadvisable ever to reduce the Fund below one lac and a half, or at any rate to trench on the amount of the Munnee Begum's Stipend Rs. 1,41,000 which has for so long a time been set apart for the purpose.*

36. Mr. Ricketts, in his letter dated the 31st December, proposes to make the following permanent allowances out of the existing Fund.

	Per mensem.	Per annum.
To His Highness' son	Rs. 1500	Rs. 18,000
To his mother, the Begum	,, 2300	,, 27,600
To His late Highness' three daughters, twenty-five of each	,, 750	,, 9,000
To seven concubines of His late Highness	,, 700	,, 8,400
	Rs. 5,250	Rs. 63,000
		,, 27,600
		Rs. 35,400

37. Of these *the only one deserving special notice is that proposed for the Begum of His present Highness. It is quite unusual to make any public provision for the wife of the reigning Nazim*, and though this was done in the case of the Doolhin Begum as a special indulgence to His late Highness, the Governor-General thinks, nevertheless, that the point cannot be conceded in the present instance without establishing a very inconvenient precedent, *His Highness will be free to make any appropriation in the Begum's favour* that he may desire, and *it will be better that she should feel indebted to His Highness' bounty, and subject to his pleasure in regard to her provision*, rather than that it should be guaranteed to her independently of his will.

38. Deducting this stipend, therefore, the proposed annual appro-

priations will stand at Rs. 35,400, which the Governor-General in Council has no hesitation in sanctioning.

39. It remains to ascertain the actual amount that will remain disposable. In this, however, there is a difficulty from the want of any distinct report on the subject of the late Valida Begum and her establishments. Putting wholly out of this question any advantage to the fund that may eventually arise from the promotion of Ameeroonissa Begum to that dignity, it would seem from the accounts of 1228 that there exists a fund of Rs. 2,57,713, which by the addition of the stipend enjoyed by His Highness as presumptive heir, becomes Rs. 2,75,713. This again being charged with the payment of the Munnee Begum's establishment (Rs. 25074) and with succeeding authorised augmentation (9830) is reduced to Rs. 2,40,809 *from which amount the stipends above authorized being deducted, the available Fund will stand* at Rs. 2,05,409.

40. *In consideration of the British Government withdrawing from the interference now exercised in auditing the accounts of His Highness, the Governor-General in Council thinks it will be necessary and not too much to expect that His Highness should consent to allow the above entire sum of* Rs. 2,05,409, *or say two lacs of Rupees to accumulate in the Collector's Treasury.*

41. *The British Government will in that case undertake the payment in future from that fund of all charges for new buildings or other expenses legitimately claimable from it and further will relinquish all desire to increase the fund, pledging itself on the lapse of any future stipend, to consider the suggestions of His Highness as to its allotment,* and except under special circumstances which may demand a different appropriation *to assign the whole for the benefit of the family* and its dependents.

42. You will be pleased to take an early opportunity of ascertaining *the sentiments of His Highness on the subject of the above proposition.* Should the plan be adopted, His Highness will no longer have any interest in witholding information of the decease of any stipendiary from the fear that the occasion will be taken to effect a saving in the distribution of his allowances, *his patronage and influence amongst the members of the Nizamut will be strengthened by the knowledge that his recommendations in behalf of individuals will be sure of due attention.* On the other hand, *a security will be given to the Fund* which it did not possess while the accumulation of a large proportion of it was allowed to be made in the Nizamut Treasury, and *the confinement of the control of the Agent to the investigation of complaints for the non-payment of authorized stipends or other advantages, will remove the chief motive of difference between that officer and the Nazim.* The arrangement will thus promote a better understanding between them, besides saving an infinity of trouble to all parties.

43. You will be pleased to submit your own sentiments on the above propositions along with those of His Highness.

44. It only remains to notice a few suggestions of inferior importance. In the eleventh paragraph of Mr. Ricketts' letter, dated 31st December, it is proposed to pay to the Bhow Begum from the Deposit Fund 10,000 rupees in part of the accumulated arrears of an allowance of 300 rupees for Meer Samanee's expenses, which it is said was never paid.

45. On this point, the Governor-General in Council remarks that the Bhow Begum, if she did not receive the advantage provided for her either in the money allowance or in some other shape, was at liberty to have applied to the Governor-General's agent, who would, of course, have taken measures in the lifetime of His late Highness to enforce the provision made in her favour. If she has neglected to do so for so many years, that circumstance will give her no claim on the Deposit Fund; but, on the other hand, if she can show that the allowance has been actually accumulating in the Nizamut Treasury, Government will be prepared to enforce its restoration.

46. With respect to the suggestion contained in the 12th and following paragraphs of Mr. Rickett's letter above alluded to the Governor-General in Council is of opinion that it will be the most advantageous plan in every respect to maintain the existing arrangements under which Mir Ghalib Ali Khan is vested with the charge of the Treasuries of the Nizamut and Raic Gunga Dhar controls the offices of Accountant as Naib Dewan. In confirmation of these appointments, you will be pleased to confer Khilluts on both the above individuals, and charge the same in your Contingent Bill.

47. The Governor-General in Council does not think that the proposition of Mir Ghalib Ali to *the permanent situation of Dewan* should be encouraged; on the contrary, in conferring the Killuts above sanctioned, it may be advisable to be careful that both are of precisely the same degree.

48. With respect to the matter stated in the 15th paragraph of Mr. Rickett's letter, the Governor-General in Council conceives it by no means improbable that the opposition and jealousies excited by the elevation of Ameeroonissa Begum may be fomented under hand by the party heretofore so decidedly opposed to her. He trusts they will disappear when parties are convinced of the inefficiency of such intrigues to affect the determination of Government. It will, of course, be your duty to avoid encouraging the existing disunion by too readily listening to the disparaging communications regarding each other, which will be eagerly obtruded on your attention.

49. The Report promised by Mr. Ricketts on the arrangement of the Decrees consequent on the promotion of Ameeroonissa, will, of course, be anxiously expected.

50. It is the intention of the Governor-General to address a letter direct to His Highness on the subject of the arrangements proposed above. This will be prepared and forwarded to you for delivery in the course of a few days. In the meantime, you will have the opportunity of making yourself fully master of the intentions of Government, and it has hence not been thought necessary to delay the dispatch of this letter until the preparation of the Documents, &c. It will, of course, be proper to delay any direct communication with His Highness on the subject until its arrival.

I have, &c.,
(Signed) H. T. PRINSEP,
Persian Secretary to Government.

Fort William, 28th January, 1823.

From the above letter (Para. 28, 29, and 30), it will be observed that after the establishment of the Agency Fund in 1817 (Page 60), the allowance of Her Highness Munnee Begum (£14,400 per annum) had been allowed to accumulate in the Collector's Treasury without a fraction of the Nizamut debts having been paid therefrom, as originally intended—the amount immediately available was found to be Rupees 7,46,503 (£74,650), and of this amount £14,650 was set apart for building a new palace for His Highness, and the remainder, £60,000, *was invested in Government securities, bearing interest for the benefit of the Nizamut.* This fund was called Munnee Begum's Fund, and ought to have been accounted for with interest to His Highness the Nawab or his heirs-at-law, as well as all lapsed stipends which by the terms of Paras. 26, 30 and 41 of the above letter belonged to His Highness, but were never paid to him.

It may be noticed from Paras. 33 and 34 that after all the trouble and expense attendant on the appointment of the officer known as Agent Governor-General, for the purpose of adjusting the Nizamut accounts, those accounts appeared to be in still greater confusion than before, and accordingly, instead of economizing by abolishing the office of Agent, it was proposed by the Governor-General that a new plan of retrenchment should be adopted by which, instead of paying Munnee Begum's allowance of £14,400 into the Collector's Treasury at Moorshedabad, and allowing it to accumulate there for the benefit of the family; that amount should be retained by the Government, and absorbed as a sinking fund and in addition (Paras. 36, 37, 38, 39, and 40) it may be observed that further sums which before had been entirely at His Highness's disposal, were also set apart by the Government for the purpose of bringing up the amount to two lacs of Rupees (£20,000) per annum, which the Governor General suggested should be allowed by the Nawab to accumulate in the Collector's Treasury *"in consideration of the British Government withdrawing from the interference exercised in auditing the accounts of His Highness"* (Para. 41) the British Government undertook *"the payment in future from that fund of all charges for new buildings or other expenses legitimately claimable from it,"* and further agreed *" to relinquish all desire to increase the fund, pledging itself on the lapse of any future stipend to consider the suggestions of His Highness as to its allotment, and except under special circumstances, which might demand a different appropriation, to assign the whole for the benefit of the family and its dependents;"* how far this pledge has been acted up to, will appear hereafter.

This Fund, which like the others, was established by coercion (see Correspondence, Pages 56, 79, 82), was considered as "the Sacred Inheritance of the Nizamut Family," and styled the Deposit Fund. Its accumulations of £20,000 per annum from the time of its formation in 1823 must have rapidly amounted to a vast sum, for which the British Government as Trustees were responsible, and perhaps it was this fact that led the Governor-General, Lord Dalhousie, in 1854, to arbitrarily declare that *" no more of the Capital of the Deposit Fund should be invested, but that thenceforward it should be considered a mere book debt bearing no interest,"* with a view of reducing the liability of the Indian Government, which, having taken upon itself the entire control of the Fund, was responsible to the Nawab for all accumulations by interest or otherwise, " over and above the two lacs of rupees (£20,000) per annum," set apart for its purposes: for it was distinctly stated by the Governor-General, when the fund was formed, that His Highness would be at "*full liberty to appropriate any excess* (over and above " two lacs of rupees per annum) *to purposes connected* " *with the splendor and credit of His Exalted Station.*" (Page 80.)

No further pecuniary advantage was taken of the Nizamut by the Company during the lifetime of Nawab Wallah Jah, but after his death the work of spoliation was again proceeded with, and all the sacred pledges given to him were set aside without regard to the result— *the ultimate ruin of the Nawabs Nazim and their families.*

On the death of Nawab Wallah Jah, his son, Nawab Humayoon Jah (the father of the present Nawab) ascended the musnud, as the Nazim and Soubahdar of the three Provinces, under the style and title of Shoojah-ul-Moolk, Ihtisham-ood-Dowlah, Humayoon Jah, Syud Mobaruck Ali Khan Bahadur, Feroze Jung, and received the following assurances of devoted attachment and friendship from the several Governors-General who conducted the Government of the Provinces during his reign of thirteen years:—

From LORD AMHERST *to* NAWAB SYUD MOBARUCK ALI KHAN BEHADOOR FEROZE JUNG, NAWAB NAZIM *of Bengal, Behar, and Orissa, dated* 14*th January,* 1825.

" Truly, on the receiving of the joyful intelligence of the happy " installation of Your Highness on the *Chahar-balish* (throne) of "ancestral authority, the budding of joy of this friend so bloomed with delight, that to describe one of its thousand blossoms or to dress a single rose from the bough in just array, is beyond the flowers of rhetoric.

"May HE who is high and holy consecrate and prosper this auspicious event, so happily commenced, and completed to the credit and honour of Your Highness, and the dependents of Your exalted family, and long preserve You in health and felicity.

"Your Highness may be assured that the *regular fixed allowances*, and *other mutually settled points will remain*, and continue as approved and sanctioned by the Home Authorities in the time of the late NAWAB SYUD AHMED ALI KHAN BEHADOOR, that good friend's noble father :—*namely*, Sixteen Laks of Rupees per annum, in reference to the regulation and arrangement which have been fixed, and *Your Highness may in future consider proper to concert with the Members of this Government for the distribution of the pensions according to the judgment of both Sircars*, suitable to the condition of the dependents of the Nizamut, will be issued as usual in monthly portions, to that friend.

"And every mark of friendship and regard shewn by this Government to the late Nawab will, without difference, be cheerfully and joyfully continued to Your Highness, and *the respect due to the rank*, and the *honours*, and *distinctions appropriate to the high and eminent family of* Your Highness, whereof the elevation, splendour, conduct, and direction now centre in Your Highness, *will be always kept in view and observed*.

"(*Signed*)   AMHERST."

To His Highness NAWAB SHUJA-UL-MULK, EHTESHAM-UD-DOWLAH HUMAYOON JAH, SYYUD MOBARUCK ALEE KHAN BAHADUR FEROZE JUNG.

My honored and valued Friend,

Being desirous of returning to England, I some time since expressed my request to be relieved from the charge of the Supreme Government of the British possessions in India, and it is my intention to embark for Europe about the middle of next month.

I have not yet heard whether any individual has been appointed to succeed me from England, but should no one arrive in that capacity before my departure, Sir Charles Metcalfe, who has received a provisional appointment to that effect, will succeed me in the office of Governor-General, and will exercise, until further orders, the important functions of the high office.

In like manner, the Honorable Mr. Blunt will in that case exercise the powers of Governor of the Agra Presidency.

It is a source of great satisfaction for me to reflect that during my residence in India, *the intimate connection which happily subsists between Your Highness and the Honorable Company has been strengthened and confirmed*, and of no less gratification to know that in my successor Your Highness will experience the same disposition to cultivate and improve *the existing harmony and good understanding* between the two Governments, **and an** inviolate adherence to **the** engagements by which **Your Highness** and the Honorable Company are indissolubly connected.

Your Highness may be assured that no distance **of time,** nor local situation will impair the sentiments of personal respect and esteem which I entertain towards you, or diminish my solicitude for the continuance of **Your** Highness's prosperity, happiness and welfare.

In conclusion, I beg to express the high consideration I entertain for Your Highness, and to subscribe myself

Your Highness's sincere Friend,
(Signed)   G. W. BENTINCK.

Fort William, 24th February, 1835.

To His Highness NAWAB SHUJA-UL-MULK EHTESHAM-UD-DOWLAH, HUMAYOON JAH, SYYUD MOBARUCK ALEE KHANN BAHADOOR FEROZE JUNG.

My honoured and valued Friend,

Your Highness has no doubt been apprized through the ordinary sources of intelligence, of my nomination to the charge of the Honourable Company's possessions in India.

I have now the honour to inform Your Highness that I arrived at Fort William on the 4th of March, and that I have taken charge of the office of Governor-General of India.

Your Highness may be assured that *I am cordially disposed to maintain the relations of Harmony and Friendship subsisting between the two States,* to establish the utmost degree of individual friendship with Your Highness, **and to seek the** confidence of all the States and Chiefs **of** Hindostan **and the Deccan,** *by a scrupulous adherence to subsisting* **engagements** *and to the obligations of Public Faith and Honour.*

In conclusion, I beg to express the high consideration I entertain for Your Highness, and to subscribe myself

Your Highness's sincere Friend,
(Signed)   AUCKLAND.

Fort William, 7th March, 1836.

To His Highness NAWAB SHUJA-UL-MULK EHTESHAM-UD-DOWLAH, HUMAYOON JAH, SYYUD MOBARUCK ALEE KHAN BEHADUR FEROZE JUNG, G.C.H.

My honoured and valued Friend,

I have learned by Dispatches received overland from England the mournful intelligence of the death of His Most Gracious Majesty King William the Fourth, whom, after a happy and prosperous reign of seven years, it pleased the Almighty to call to his Mercy on the 20th of June, in the year of Our Lord, One thousand Eight hundred and Thirty-seven.

The late Sovereign, by his many excellent qualities, had greatly endeared himself to his subjects, who deeply and unanimously lament his loss.

By the demise of His late Majesty, the Imperial Crown of the United Kingdom of Great Britain and Ireland has solely and rightfully come to the High and Mighty Princess Alexandrina Victoria, niece of the late Sovereign, who has been duly proclaimed by the Grace of God, Queen of the United Kingdom of Great Britain and Ireland and Defender of the Faith. May Her reign be prosperous.

Considering Your Highness as a sincere friend of the British Government, I have deemed it necessary to communicate the above circumstance for Your information.

In conclusion, I beg to express the high consideration I entertain for Your Highness, and to subscribe myself

Your Highness's sincere friend,
(Signed)   AUCKLAND.

Fort William, 11th September, 1837.

To His Highness NAWAB SHUJA-UL-MULK EHTESHAM-UD-DOWLAH, HUMAYOON JAH, SYUD MOBARUCK ALEE KHAN BAHADUR FEROZE JUNG, G.C.H.

My honoured and valued Friend,

I am much concerned at being obliged to inform Your Highness, that I am unable to realize the pleasure I had anticipated of visiting you on my way up the country.

There is so little water in the River at this season of the year, that it has been found impracticable for my boats to proceed up the Bhagurathi, and I have, therefore, been compelled to go *viâ* the Soonderbunds. This is a great disappointment to me, but I trust that I may be more fortunate on my return, and that I shall then have leisure to converse with you fully on *all matters connected with Your interests.*

My Friend, I have received your letter on the subject of your recent misunderstanding with my Agent. To dwell upon such unpleasant topics can be attended with no benefit. I had dismissed the matter from my mind, and I trust that Your Highness will forget all that has happened. My Agent, I feel assured, from his recent communications, entertains for you the same friendly sentiments as before, and *my regard for Your Highness is undiminished.*

In conclusion, I beg to express the high consideration I entertain for Your Highness, and to subscribe myself

Your Highness's sincere friend,
(Signed)   AUCKLAND.

Fort William, 20th October, 1837.

From the first of the above letters, and the expressions used in the second and third of the " existing harmony and good understanding between the two Governments," and "the relations of Harmony and Friendship subsisting between the two States," it is evident that the Nawab was recognized as a Sovereign and Independent Prince, and again the further assurance contained in the second letter—"*the inviolate adherence to the engagements by which Your Highness and the Honourable Company are indissolubly connected*" together with the reasons adduced by the servants of the Company themselves in the subjoined letter, must lead all disinterested men to the conclusion that the Nawab had *the Right* to claim from the Company a full return of all that he and his ancestors had been deprived of by their servants, though he had not *the Power* to enforce his claims.

To H. PAULIN, ESQ., *Attorney to the Honorable Company.*

Sir,

"I am directed to acknowledge the receipt of your letter of "the 17th inst., forwarding copy of the Advocate-General's "opinion regarding the question of the liability of the Nawab "Nazim to the jurisdiction of the Supreme Court."

"2. In reply, I am desired to transmit for the information of "the Advocate-General, copy of a communication which has "been received on the same subject from the Governor-General's "Agent at Moorshedabad, and to state as follows:"

"3. His Honour in Council is decidedly of opinion that the "*Supreme Court has no right to exercise jurisdiction over the* "*Nawab Nazim of Bengal,* and should the attempt to move the "Court to adopt this course of proceeding be persisted in "*it is requested that the Advocate General will adopt every neces,* "*sary legal means for resisting it.*"

"4. It will be observed *from the Treaty,* 1770, of which a copy "is annexed, that *His Highness the Nawab has been recognized* "*by the British Government as an Independent Prince, and that* "*the National Faith is pledged, for nothing being proposed or* "*carried into execution derogating from his Honour.*"

"In order to prevent his being *liable to any indignity* from "subjecting his person, or property, to the process of the Zillah "Courts, Regulation 19 of 1825 was passed, *prescribing certain* "*rules under which* alone he could sue, or be sued, *in those Courts.* "With regard to the Supreme Court, the case is very different.

"As the Government has no power to regulate the proceedings of this Court towards persons acknowledged to come within its jurisdiction, *if the liability of the Nazim were to be admitted, there is no degree of indignity which might not be inflicted upon him* by its ordinary processes, *in contravention of the pledged National Faith*, and of *the respect which is obviously due to the Representative of our oldest Ally on this side of India.*"

"5. Without intending to limit the discretion of the Advocate-General, as to the grounds of objection which should be taken up, His Honour in Council would wish every possible exertion to be made to establish *the Right of the Nawab Nazim to be exempted from the jurisdiction of the Supreme Court.* Any further information which can be procured from the Government Records, here or at Moorshedabad, shall be furnished to you on your requisition and the Vakeel of His Highness the Nazim, stationed at the Presidency, will likewise be directed to place himself in communication with you.

"6. The case of Raja Hurreenauth Rae, referred to by the Advocate-General, does not appear to His Honour in Council to bear any analogy to the present. *Raja Hurreenauth Rae was a subject of this Government, from whose gift he derived his title, while the Nawab Nazim is a Prince, whose Independence has been recognized by a Treaty with one of his Predecessors,*

"I have, &c.,
(Signed) "C. E. TREVELYAN,
"Deputy-Secretary to the Government.

"Council Chambers, 20th February, 1834."

It now, therefore, rests with the British Government and Nation to redress the wrongs inflicted by the officers of the Government of India, and to support the cause of *justice* against *oppression* by restoring to the descendants of our faithful Allies whatever privileges they may on inquiry be lawfully entitled to.

Nawab Humayoon Jah was, in consequence of his devoted attachment to the British cause, honored by His Majesty, King William the Fourth with the distinguished insignia of the Order of the Grand Cross of Hanover, and being of an independent disposition, was for a time treated with much more consideration by the

Government of India than his Predecessors. In 1834 a special Agreement was drawn up with him, which restored to him the absolute right of controlling his servants and exchequer without the interference of the Government, and further guaranteed to him that in future the Nizamut allowances should not be reduced but that all stipends which lapsed by the death of relatives or dependents should revert to the reigning Nawab's Treasury.

To HIS HIGHNESS NAWAB SHUJAA-OOL-MOOLK, EHTE-SHAM-OOD-DOWLAH, HUMAYOON JAH, SYUD MOBARUCK ALLEE KHAN BEHADOOR, FEROZE JUNG.

MY HONOURED AND VALUED FRIEND,—I have had the pleasure of receiving your Highness's letter, dated the 17th February last, announcing your acquiescence in the agreement concluded between yourself and Captain Thoresby, for the better regulation of the future expenditure of the Nizamut.

As the Articles of this Agreement appear to me to be conducive to Your Highness's welfare, *I also acquiesce in it, and the Governor-General's Agent has been directed to consider it as the rule under which Nizamut affairs are hereafter to be administered.*

By the 4th and 5th Articles, *Your Highness is now vested with the entire management of the Nizamut Establishment*, and the savings which you may be able to effect by prudent economy and careful attention to business, will remain to be disposed of by yourself, as you may consider most for your own advantage; but Your Highness must clearly understand that this discretion has been vested in you, on the condition expressed in the Agreement, "*that no just dues or debts remain unsatisfied.*" The principle of the new arrangement, therefore, so far as these two important Articles are concerned, consists in *Your Highness being solely responsible for the management of the fund set apart for the Nizamut Establishment;* and should any debt be hereafter contracted which that fund is unable to bear, the Agreement will become annulled, and the British Government will be at liberty to adopt whatever measures may be considered expedient and proper at the time without reference to it.

It is hoped, however, that such a contingency may never occur. Your Highness will now be in possession of ample funds to meet every necessary expense, and as *any balance which may remain at the end of the year will be at the disposal of Your Highness,* you will also have a manifest interest in the observance of a strict economy.

In conclusion, I beg to express the high consideration which I entertain for Your Highness, and to suscribe myself,

Your Highness's sincere Friend,
(Signed)   C. T. METCALFE.

Copy of Agreement proposed in 1834.

The form in which the Nizamut accounts are rendered through the Agent to the Government being unsatisfactory and productive of no good, and the present Nizamut system causing considerable inconvenience, a new arrangement, agreeably to the terms of the following paragraphs, has been devised with the full concurrence of the Nawab Nazim, Humayoon Jah, by the advice of the Agent to the Governor-General, and is approved and sanctioned by His Excellency the Right Honourable the Governor-General in Council, to have effect from the commencement of the Bengal year 1241, after the settlement of all former accounts, when a brief abstract of the Nizamut expenditure, according to a form approved by the Nazim and Agent, will be furnished, generally, for the information of Government in lieu of detailed accounts.

I. All customary perquisites comprehended under the names, Mamoolat, Zumistanee, &c., granted to the Uqrooba besides their respective pensions, shall be commuted to cash payments from the beginning of the above year, after the decease of the receivers of the compensation allowances, *if there are no heirs entitled to succeed to it, the reversion shall be to the Nizamut Treasury.*

II. The stipendiary account shall be kept distinct from all others, and the monies on account of pensions shall be deposited in a separate chest appropriated to that purpose. The Khazanchee or Darogah appointed to the charge of it, and to make the disbursements and keep the accounts, *shall be answerable to the Agent, as well as to the Nawab Nazim, for the correctness of his issues* and the existence of the balance.

III. It is earnestly recommended to his Highness to introduce a more simple and effective mode of keeping the Nizamut accounts, and to make such arrangements as may ensure the final settlement of the current expenses of the preceding month in the course of the following month, including the salaries and wages of every description of servants, so that there may be no debts incurred, and no dissatisfaction occasioned in consequence; such regularity will tend to the security of His Highness's interests, as well as ease and comfort.

IV. Such reductions and modifications of the different establishments in the Nizamut as shall be thought desirable and proper by the Nawab Nazim, either at the present time, or hereafter, shall be executed by him, and *with regard to the salaries of his servants and the entertaining and discharging them, he is at liberty to act as he pleases without any interference.*

V. Pensions, which have been or may hereafter be assigned to servants and dependents, *shall revert to the Nizamut Treasury as casualties occur, and shall, with other savings effected by retrenchments, be at the entire disposal of His Highness*, provided that no just dues or debts remain unsatisfied.

VI. The intent of the foregoing arrangements is, that by the introduction of method and order into the affairs of the Nizamut, which shall provide for the full efficiency of all departments and prevent the recurrence of pecuniary embarrassments and debts, His Highness the Nawab Nazim may enjoy an increase of ease and Happiness.

(Signed) C. THORESBY,
Acting Agent Governor-General.

The 15th February, 1834.

It will here be necessary to explain the circumstances which led to the drawing up of the above Agreement; and to do this, we must draw attention to the correspondence that took place before the arrangement was made.

The following extract was taken from a note by the late Mr. Stirling, dated in 1830, and placed upon record in 1833, containing his remarks on the Nizamut accounts for the years 1233 to 1235 B.S., or A.D., 1226-29.

" There ought indeed to be large sums forthcoming in the Nizamut
" Treasury, on account of certain lapsed stipends which are supposed
" to accumulate there, as part of the Deposit Fund, but Mr. Dale
" explains that the greater part of that money has been long ago
" irrecoverably disposed of by the present Nawab's father, and that
" the Treasury is in fact empty. It is hopeless, therefore, to look to that
" source for any material relief. The above consideration leads me to
" submit one or two observations on the expediency of simplifying our
" dealings with the Nizamut, and the mode of keeping the accounts, *by*
" *relinquishing all demands on account of lapsed Pensions,* supposed to
" accumulate in the Nizamut Treasury, and *making over the whole of*
" *the Nizamut Stipend to the Nawab,* subject to the payment of the
" established allowances, with exception to the sum of Rs. 1,44,000,
" which remains in the Collector's hands, **to form the annual increase-**
" **ment of the Deposit Fund, and Rs. 60,000 paid to Nawab Mustapha**
" Khan. *I imagine that that amount is adequate for the legitimate*
" *purposes of the Fund,* viz., the construction of buildings and *the*
" *occasional relief and benefit of the different members of the family,*
" *including His Highness himself,* and *I do not see that we have any*
" *right to keep back from the Nazim's receipt a larger portion of the*
" *sixteen lacs,* which is assigned by Treaty, for the support of the
" establishment, than suffices for the above objects. According to the
" present system, the accounts sent up to Government are involved in
" the utmost intricacy and confusion, and exhibits no view at all of the
" real state of affairs. They are prepared on the supposition, that *the*
" *Nizamut expenditure is regulated according to scale fixed by the*
" *Committee of* 1802, and that the portion of the stipend in excess
" thereof, and not otherwise formally appropriated, is forthcoming in
" the Nizamut Treasury: but in practice the Regulations of the Com-
" mittee have been widely and constantly departed from. As might

"have been expected, there is a continued tending to increase of
"outlay, and year after year a large excess appears which it has been
"seen for three years *under our own arrangement* averaged nearly
"Rs. 50,000 per mensem. The Court of Directors seem to think that
"*an addition* of Rs. 56,000 per annum *might be made to the Deposit*
"*Fund by the appropriation of lapsed stipends*, and no doubt the
"Nizamut Treasury is answerable for a part of that amount; but as it
"is always in point of fact disbursed to cover the excess of current
"expenditure, it seems useless to retain such a nominal demand.
"Indeed, if the thing is looked closely into, it shall be found that
"much of these nominal lapses have been reassigned under the
"authority of Government to different pensioners, and is therefore not
"really available for the increase of the Deposit Fund.

"Mr. Dale is distinctly of opinion, that, *it would not be advisable*
"*to increase the Deposit Fund by requiring the Nazim to repay into*
"*the Collector's Treasury any part of the stipend which now passes*
"*into his hand*. What, then, is the use of keeping up a nominal
"demand under this head in account? He has given me a statement*
"by which it appears, that, the Nawab receives from the Collector's
"Treasury Rs. 1,16,333 per mensem, and the actual current expen-
"diture of the Nizamut is Rs. 1,14,616, The benefit conferred on
"the Nawab, therefore, by the adoption of the principle which I

* Annual Stipend	16,00,000	0	0	0
Retained in the Collector's Office on account of Munnee Begum	1,44,000	0	0	0
Paid to Nawab Mustapha Khan 5,000 per mensem	60,000	0	0	0
	13,96,000	0	0	0
Or Monthly	1,16,333	5	6	3
Present Monthly expenses for 1236 B. S.				
Sheristah Nizamut.	35,692	0	0	0
Bahala	31,407	13	9	2
Moolazaman	0	0	0	0
Deoree	0	0	0	0
Nawab Bubboo Begum	1,867	0	0	0
Kullumdan Khanah	12,000	0	0	0
Ashoor Khanah	1,500	0	0	0
Imarut	1,500	0	0	0
Moossiffadenay	152	8	0	0
Sheristah Agentee	16,022	13	0	0
	1,14,616	2	17	2
Balance	1,717	2	9	1
	1,16,333	5	6	3

"advocate, would average at about Rs. 1,717 per mensem, or Rs.
"20,600 per annum. His Highness spends the money as it is, or, at
"least his accounts exhibit extra charges to that amount; but, at
"present the excess might be debited to what is called the Privy
"Purse, or *Kullumdan Khanah*, and occasionally orders have been
"issued to that effect.

"Mr. Dale, at the same time, suggests, that, *there are certain
"stipends*, such as those drawn by the Ameeroon Nissa, Nujeebun
"Nissa, and Bhow Begums, *which would very properly lapse, if re-
"quired, to the Deposit Fund* on the demise of the present incum-
"bents, and this may be a point for consideration hereafter, with
"reference to the state of the Fund and the demands upon it at the
"time of each lapse."

The following extract from a note recorded by the late Mr. (afterwards Sir William) MacNaghten is in continuation of Mr. Stirling's
note:—

"I beg leave to bring to the notice of Government, accompanying
"draft of a note by the late Mr. Stirling, and a draft of a letter
"founded thereon, relative to the Moorshedabad Nizamut affairs,
"which I found in the office shortly after taking charge, but which do
"not appear to have been acted upon.

"No accounts have been furnished since the period referred to in
'these documents, and if the Governor-General in Council is aware of
"no objections, I would propose to require the Accountant-General
"and the Acting Agent immediately to report the existing state of
"the *three* Funds, *viz.*, the Nizamut Fund, the Deposit Fund, and the
"Agency Establishment Fund.

"There is a part of Mr. Stirling's proposition I think might be
"modified, or rather of which I do not exactly see the use. Alluding
"to the confusion of accounts which prevails, he suggested that *the
"Nazim should be exempted from the necessity of furnishing any
"account of Lapsed Pensions*, except in the instance of one or two
"individuals who are at present living and in the enjoyment of large
"stipends. It might certainly be as well to dispense with an account,
"particularly, of the various disbursements, which do not, and are
"not, required to correspond with the rates laid down in 1802; but
"there seems no great probability of *inconvenience resulting* from
"the practice of requiring a report to be made on the death of
"each Pensioner, whose pension it may be proposed to assign to
"another."

The following extract is taken from the instructions issued to the
Agent on the occasion:—

"In regard to the sums which ought to be forthcoming in the
"Nizamut Treasury, on account of certain lapsed stipends, supposed
"to accumulate there as part of the General Deposit Fund, it appears
"from the late Acting Agent's statement that the greater part of that
"money has been long ago irrecoverably disposed of by the present
"Nawab's father, and that the Treasury is in fact empty.

"Referring to this fact, and anxious, if possible, to simplify our
"dealings with the Nizamut and the mode of keeping accounts, the
"Governor-General in Council is of opinion, that, *it is expedient to
"relinquish all demands on account of Lapsed Pensions* supposed to

"have accumulated in the Nizamut, but which have mostly, by the authority of the Nawab, been re-assigned to different Pensions, and are, therefore, not available for the increase of the Deposit Fund.

"According to the present system, the accounts sent up are involved in the utmost intricacy and confusion, and exhibit no view at all of the real state of affairs. They are prepared on the supposition that the Nizamut expenditure is regulated according to *a scale fixed by the Committee* in 1803, and that the portion of the stipend in excess thereof, and not otherwise formerly appropriated, is forthcoming in the Nizamut Treasury, but in practice the Regulations of the Committee have been widely and constantly departed from.

"At the same time, however, the Governor-General in Council would have it understood, that the Lapsed Stipends which it is proposed to make over to His Highness are those which have nominally lapsed and nominally accumulated. In regard to other stipends which may lapse in future, they shall be regularly reported as heretofore."

The above correspondence resulted in the determination of the Governor-General to come to some definite understanding with the Nawab, who, naturally solicitous about the welfare of the Nizamut, had frequently applied to him for the restoration of the lapsed stipends and also the control of his own affairs, which the Government had before deprived him of, but at last conceded to him by the Agreement of 1834.

But the Agreement of 1834, like all others, was doomed to be set aside by the Government of India, for in 1836, Mr. (now Sir Charles) Trevelyan recorded the following minute on Nizamut affairs, which was eagerly taken up and acted upon in spite of the remonstrances of the Nawab, who in a private letter to the Agent Governor-General remarked, "This is a strange arrangement, and an odd way of fulfilling promises."

"I now proceed to notice the accounts which have been furnished of the *three* Deposit Funds, namely, the Deposit Fund in the Collector's Treasury, the Deposit Fund which has hitherto been kept in the Nawab's Treasury, and the Deposit Fund for the payment of the Agency for the Superintendence of the Nizamut kept by the Government Agent at Calcutta.

"The Deposit Fund lately kept in the Nawab Nazim's Treasury, generally called *the Nizamut Deposit Fund, consists of the savings realized by lapses in Fund of about seven lacs of Rupees a year* appropriated for the payment of the Nawab's relations. By the order of 11th July, 1833, all demand was relinquished on account of the savings from this Fund up to that date. The Nawab has informed Colonel Cobbe, that, about Rs. 90,000 have accumulated since that period, and that the present monthly addition is as high as Rs. 5,220

"*The large sum of about seven lacs of Rupees a year, which forms the basis of this Fund,* has hitherto been disbursed by the Nawab from his own Treasury as pensions to the different Members of the Nizamut family. Although the Nawab was the immediate Agent in the business, his proceedings were strictly controlled by the Agent, and he was expected to account for the balance which remained after paying the pensions. This balance, *i. e.* up to Rs. 56,000, to make up two lacs, was intended to swell the general Deposit Fund, but as yet nothing has ever been realized.

"The monthly addition to Munnee Begum's Deposit Fund is 12,000 Sicca Rupees, and to the Pension Deposit Fund Rs. 5,220, and *the latter will be continually on the increase owing to the lapse of pensions* of which only a portion is generally continued to relatives.

"It is believed that *of the above aggregate sum* of Rs. 7,03,365 a year, appropriated to the payment of the collateral branches of the Nizamut Family, Rs 62,640 *have already lapsed. The annual sum will form the foundation of another Deposit Fund, which will receive continual accessions from the decease of the different stipendiaries.* This Deposit Fund hitherto had only a nominal existence in the Nazim's Treasury, but it will hereafter have a real one in the Collector's.

"*Supposing these calculations to be correct,* Rs. 9,36,660 *a year will hereafter be retained in the Collector's Treasury, of which Rs.* 2,06,640 *will form the increasement of the Deposit Fund, and the remaining Rs.* 7,30,020 *will be disbursed to different members of the Nizamut Family. The sum reserved for the Deposit Fund will,* as before stated, *increase every year.*"

The following is an extract from the instructions issued to the Agent in consideration of the suggestion contained in Sir Charles Trevelyan's note.

Dated 1st March, 1836.

"The Deposit Fund lately kept in the Nawab Nazim's Treasury (generally called *the Nizamut Deposit Fund) consists of the savings realized by lapses in a Fund of about seven lacs of Rupees a year* appropriated for the payment of the Nawab's relations. By the orders of the 11th July, 1833, all demand was relinquished on account of the savings from this Fund up to that date. The Nawab is stated by Colonel Cobbe to have informed him that about Rs. 90,000 has accumulated since that period, and that the present monthly addition is as high as Rs. 5,220.

"*You will therefore call upon the Nawab to pay* in the Collector's Treasury *the Rs.* 90,000 *above mentioned,* which will be carried to *the credit of the Pension Deposit Fund,* the name which may here-

" after be *most conveniently* given to this Fund, as *this sum of about
" seven lacs of Rupees a year, which forms the basis of the Fund, will
" hereafter be retained* in the Collector's Treasury, and the Pension
" due out of it to the Junior Members of the Nizamut Family will be
" disbursed direct from thence. The savings will, of course, accumulate
" in the same place. It is requested that you will make a special re-
" port on the Pension Fund and the Pension Deposit Fund as soon
" as sufficient time has elapsed subsequent to the adoption of the
" arrangement by which these Funds have been transferred to the
" Collector's Treasury, to enable you to ascertain the exact amount of
" each."

With reference to the foregoing instructions, the Agent at Moor-shedabad reported as follows:—

" Agreeably to the 5th paragraph of your letter I beg to inclose a
" statement of the Munnee Begum Deposit Fund, prepared in the
" Collector's Office, and, exhibiting a balance in favour of the Fund,
" Rs. 4,43,681, on the 30th of April last. To this is to be added Rs.
" 90,000, which will be paid in a few days on account of the Lapsed
" Stipends Deposit Fund, and which would have been realized ere
" now, had not His Highness, from circumstances already before
" Government, abstained from drawing his allowances, a total of
" assets amounting to Rs. 5,33,681. This appears at credit, and de-
" ducting the sum of Rs 3,31,442, as above specified, (Nizamut Debts)
" a balance of Rs. 2,02,239 in favour of the Deposit Fund will remain.
" The sum now carried to credit in this office, on account of Lapsed
" Stipends in the new Deposit Fund, is Rupees 6,567 per mensem,
" and something more of accumulation may, perhaps, be received from
" His Highness after we have received the Rs. 90,000. The detailed
" accounts, however, I have not yet received from His Highness."

A careful perusal of the documents relating to the formation of the several Funds (pages 38, 60, 79, 82 and 85) will at once bring to the reader's notice, by comparison, the discrepancies that exist in the minute of Mr. (Secretary) Trevelyan above quoted. The Nizamut Deposit Fund which is vaguely alluded to as consisting of "the savings by lapses in a Fund of about seven lacs of rupees a year appropriated for the payment of the Nawab's relations, &c.," was as the Governor-General expressly stated (page 85) to consist of two lacs of rupees (£20,000) annually, and no more; of which Munnee Begum's stipend of Rupees 1,44,000 (£14,400) was to form a part, and the balance Rs. 56,000 (£5,600) was to be made up by the Nawab depositing that sum annually in the Collector's Treasury, and further in consideration of the Nawab agreeing to the establishment of this Fund, *the British Government undertook the cost of all buildings and other expenses* (such as marriage portions, debts, &c.,) *legitimately claimable from it, and relinquished all desire to increase the Fund,* " *pledging itself on the lapse of any future stipend, to consider the suggestions of His Highness as to its allotment.*" But the British Faith, pledged by the Governor-General, was violated by the adoption of Mr. Trevelyan's suggestion that the sum of Rs. 62,640 (£6,264) per annum, which had already lapsed, would "*form the foundation of another Deposit Fund, which will receive continual accessions from the decease of the different stipendiaries,*" (Page 101) because the Governor-General had limited the amount to be contributed by the Nawab to make up the two lacs to Rs. 56,000 (£5,600), which was a part of the Rs. 62,640 (£6,264) alluded to by the writer. Again, in the last Para. the sum said to be set apart Rs. 2,06,640 (£20,664) to form the increasement of the Deposit Fund is inaccurate, for the Governor-General had limited the amount to Rs. 2,00,000 (£20,000), as before stated. Of the sum of Rs. 7,30,020 (£73,002) reserved for the "different members of the Nizamut Family," barely one half has been disbursed to them by the Government! The Nawab naturally asks, Where has the balance gone?

From the instructions issued to the Agent Governor-General for carrying out of this new coercive measure, the result may easily be conceived, for the whole of the Rs. 7,30,020 (£73,002) reserved for pensions to different members of the Family will when they are all dead *remain to the credit of the Government,* as also any other pensions future Nawabs might wish to set apart for their relatives, so that eventually the Nizamut Civil List, which by the Treaty of 1770 was fixed at £318,000 per annum, will be reduced to a mere pittance!

Thus, by absorbing the lapsed stipends into the Nizamut Deposit Fund, instead of restoring them to the Nizamut Treasury, the Government has gradually reduced the Civil List of the Nawab Nazim; and the ultimate result of the measure will assuredly be the entire ruin of the Nizamut which the British Government had pledged itself *to support for ever.* A further proof of the injustice of the above arrangement may be found in the fact that before the Nawab attained his majority, when the Government itself, through the Agent Governor-General, managed his affairs for him, "*the sum considered applicable to the "Nazim's own household was quite insufficient to maintain "it on the scale fixed by the Committee of* 1802," and which was the standard appointed by the Government for the guidance of the Agent; if, therefore, the Agent Governor-General himself was unable out of the annual allowance to meet all the requirements of the Nizamut, how then was it possible for the Nawab himself, with a reduced Civil List, to avoid getting entangled in pecuniary difficulties?

But another singular act soon followed the formation of the "Lapsed Stipend Fund." In the year 1837, the Honourable W. L. Melville, who held the appointment of Agent Governor-General, found that the system of keeping five separate accounts of the Nizamut Family, Agency, Munnee Begum's, Deposit and Lapsed Stipend Funds, entailed a large amount of extra trouble and expense in the office of the Collectorate at Moorshedabad, and proposed (in an official communication, dated 6th July, 1837) that the Funds should be amalgamated as one common Fund since they all belonged to the same family and were similarly invested in Government Securities. This proposition required *grave consideration*, so the matter was referred to the Accountant-General, to be disposed of as he thought best, and he, on the 16th December, 1836, reported to the Government that " the Funds had been amalgamated," under the common name of the " Nizamut Deposit Fund."

The surplus of interest on the Government Securities forming this Fund, over and above the two lacs of rupees annually set apart by the Government for the objects of the Fund (Page 85), after even deducting the amount required for the expenses of the Agency, ought, according to the Governor-General's promise (Page 79), to have been made over to the Nawab "*for purposes connected with the splendour and credit of His Exalted Station,*" as also (by the Agreement of 1834, Page 96 and the Order of Lord Cornwallis, Page 38) all pensions that might lapse by the decease of relatives and dependents; but instead of this being done, every fraction has been absorbed into the Nizamut Deposit Fund, and retained by the Government; and even *the allowances* that should have been made to the Nawab and his relatives out of that Fund in accordance with the terms of the Trust, *were frequently denied* to them, and many sums out of the Fund were " *diverted to purposes foreign to the interests of the House* " *of Meer Jaffier Ali Khan.*" But the work of spoliation did not stop here, for even the pensions of men-servants and others were absorbed under the following instructions.

PROPOSAL THAT LAPSED STIPENDS SHOULD REVERT TO DEPOSIT FUND.

To Colonel J. CAULFIELD, C.B., *Agent Governor-General,* 18*th July,* 1838.

Sir,

I am directed by the Honourable the Deputy-Governor of Bengal to acknowledge the receipt of your letters, dated the 12th and 18th instant. reporting the death of Wazaree Begum, *alias* Fatimah Begum, on the 14th December, 1836, and of her sister on the 3rd of the same month, who enjoyed a pension of 35 rupees, which His Highness the Nawab Nazim recommends being continued to Syuds Bahir and Ahmed Ali, sons of Shahibzadi Begum. In reply, *I am desired to state that the principle* which His Honour *the Deputy Governor desires to see observed* in cases of this description, is the following:—

Pensions enjoyed by men-servants being as ordinary life-pensions, *should be resumed wholly on the death of incumbents, and annexed to the Deposit Fund,* except in very especial cases. Stipends enjoyed by relations of the Nawab Nazim should, as heretofore, be ordinarily continued to their heirs, and when divided amongst several heirs, one or more of whom may die without descendants, the portions of such should also lapse to the Deposit Fund, unless there are dependants of the deceased, the support of whom would be a duty incumbent upon the surviving heir, in which case so much of the lapsed portions as may be necessary to cover their additional expenses may be continued to their survivors who undertake this obligation.

The *Deputy-Governor is of opinion that through the Deposit Fund,* and by occasional grants in the manner usual, *more good will result to the members of the Nizamut* than if the whole amount set apart for that family were frittered away in petty allowances to impoverished dependents. It is on this account His Honour inclines ordinarily to favour the Deposit Fund, and not from any unwillingness to listen to His Highness's recommendations in favour of individuals.

I have, &c.,

(Signed) H. T. PRINSEP,
Secretary to Government.

Thus step by step the officers of the Government of India carried out their Policy with the ultimate view of shaking off the responsibility of the Nizamut, which no doubt they looked upon as an incubus, forgetting that it was to the family of Meer Jaffier alone that they owed their own position and all that they had acquired. Such was the gratitude and consideration shown to the descendants of our faithful Ally by the *servants* of the East India Company! But the Court of Directors did not altogether forget the duty they owed to the Nizamut under the conditions of the Firmaun by virtue of which alone they held office as the Collectors of the Revenues of the Provinces—for although they tacitly sanctioned the work of spoliation which was being carried out by their servants in India after the present Nawab (of whom we will now speak) ascended the throne, by coinciding with the views expressed by the Deputy-Governor of Bengal in respect of Lapsed Stipends of dependents reverting to the Nizamut Deposit Fund; yet they boldly declared that "*the Deposit Fund was not public money, but a part of the assignment by Treaty of the family.*"

Extract from Despatch No. 17, dated 24th April, 1840, from the Honourable, the Court of Directors to the Governor-General of India.

"*The principles which have been laid down by the Deputy-Governor* "*for the disposal of stipends on the death of Stipendiaries have our* "*concurrence.* We think with him that the stipends of mere "dependents should never, without strong special reasons, be con-"tinued to their descendants, and *that when the members of the* "*Family itself die without direct heirs, their stipends should lapse to* "*the Deposit Fund rather than pass to the nearest relations*, unless "they have left dependents whose support would naturally devolve "upon some other Members of the Family, to whom, in that case, an "increase may be granted adequate to the burthen so imposed upon "them. It is very correctly stated by the Deputy-Governor, in Mr. "Prinsep's letter to Colonel Caulfield, dated the 18th July, 1838, that "through the Deposit Fund and by occasional grants in the manner "usual, more good will result to the Members of the Nizamut, than "if the whole amount set apart for that family were frittered away in "petty allowances to impoverished dependents.

"It appears, however, to us that these views require a more liberal "application of the Deposit Fund to the relief of individuals, whose "distress are not produced by misconduct, than are at present prac-"tised. For example, when an inundation laid a great part of the "City of Moorshedabad and of the surrounding country under water, "and the Agent reported that among the sufferers were many of the "Nizamut Family, who would require assistance to enable them to "repair the damage their houses have sustained by the inundation, "*the Deputy-Governor* returned for answer, that he *did not think the* "*public money* could advantageously be employed in relieving the "distress occasioned by the inundation. *The Deposit Fund, however,*

"is not public money, but a part of the assignment by Treaty of the
"Family, which part is allowed to accumulate for its general benefit.
"The accumulation already proceeds at a more rapid rate than the
"demands on it, and will proceed still more rapidly now that the
"Fund is to derive the benefit of all lapses which may take place.
"We think, therefore, that not only grants in favour of the depen-
"dents on the Nizamut should be freely made from the Fund in cases
"of general calamity like that just alluded to, but that a revision of
"the general allowances of the family should occasionally take place
"with a view of increasing the provision for those of its members,
"whose stipends, from sub-division or other cause, *are not adequate
"to their rank* or to the claims on them, or whose conduct entitles
"them to a mark of approbation from Government.

"Thus administered, the Fund might be made in some measure an
"instrument of moral discipline, which appears to be much required,
"and for which no other *obvious expedient* presents itself."

Since the Court of Directors particularly impressed upon their officers in India that "*the Nizamut Deposit Fund is not Public money, but a part of the Assignment by Treaty of the Family,*" a clear argument is thus established, viz.: There must be an existing Treaty; the Treaty of 1770 is the last and only one that can be said to exist, and therefore the assignment of the Family therein specified must be a *legitimate* demand as there is an *acknowledged claim* under a Treaty. Thus apart from all other documentary evidence, the *right* of the Nawab Nazim and his successors to the assignment set forth in the Treaty of 1770 is clearly established by the Court of Directors themselves; we will, therefore, leave this question for a time, and proceed to introduce to our readers the measures introduced by the Government of India for controlling the Nizamut together with other coincidences that have transpired during the lifetime of the present Nawab Nazim.

Nawab Humayoon Jah died on the 3rd October, 1838, and his son, the present Nawab Nazim Syud Munsoor Ullee, succeeded to "*the hereditary honours and dignities of the Nizamut and Soubahdarry of Bengal, Behar, and Orissa,"* and was publicly acknowledged as such by the following Proclamation :—

Extract from page 925 of the Calcutta Gazette of Wednesday, 19th December, 1838, No. 101. Fort William.

POLITICAL DEPARTMENT,, 19*th December,* 1838.

PROCLAMATION.

By order of the Governor of India, the Deputy-Governor of Bengal notifies to the Public and to the Allies of the British Government, and to all friendly Powers, that the Nawab Shoojah-ool-Moolk, Ihtisham-ood-Dowlah, **Humayoon Jah,** Syud Mobaruek Ullee Khan Bahadoor, **Feeroz Jung,** having departed this life at Moorshedabad, on the 3rd October, 1838, his son the Nawab Syud Munsoor Ullee Khan, *has succeeded to the hereditary honours and dignities* of the Nizamut and Soobahdarry of Bengal, Behar and Orissa, and His Highness *is hereby declared,* under the authority of the Government of India, *to be the Nazim and Soobahdar of Bengal, Behar and Orissa,* and *to have assumed and to exercise the authority, dignities, and privileges thereof,* under the **style and** title of Mootizum-ool-Moolk, Mohsen-ood-Dowlah, Fureedoon **Jah,** Syud Munsoor Ullee Khan Bahadoor, Nusrut Jung.

Published and proclaimed by His Honour the Deputy-Governor of Bengal.

H. T. PRINSEP,
Secretary to the Government of Bengal.

General Order by the Honourable the Deputy-Governor of Bengal, under date the 19*th December,* 1838.

The Honourable the Deputy-Governor of Bengal has been pleased to direct, that a salute of 19 guns be fired from the ramparts of Fort William at 12 o'clock this day, *in honour of the accession* of His Highness Syud Munsoor Ullee Khan *to the Musnud* of the Provinces of **Bengal,** Behar and Orissa, *and that the above Proclamation be read at the head of all the Troops* in Garrison at sunset this evening under **a salute of** three **volley** of Musketry.

H. T. PRINSEP,
Secretary to the Government of Bengal.

Calcutta Gazette : Wednesday, Dec. 19th, 1838.

Soon after his accession to the throne, His Highness received the following *comforting assurance* from the

Acting Governor-General on behalf of the Government of India :—

To His Highness the NAWAB MOOTIZUM-OOL-MOOLK, MOHSEN-OOD-DOWLAH, FUREEDOON JAH, SYUD MUNSOOR ALEE KHAN BAHADOOR, NUSRUT JUNG.

My Honoured and valued Friend,

I have been highly gratified by the receipt of your letter, announcing the intelligence of your having ascended the Musnud of your ancestors on the day of the Eedool Fitr.

I sincerely congratulate Your Highness and your connections on this most happy event, and pray the Almighty may long preserve Your Highness in the enjoyment of *this exalted Dignity.*

Your Highness may rest assured that the same degree of consideration and attention as were shown to the late Nawab by the British Government, will be equally experienced by your Highness, and *the Dignity and honour of the illustrious House which you now represent will ever be an object of care and solicitude to this Government.*

I hope Your Highness will gratify me with letters conveying the intelligence of Your Health and Welfare.

In conclusion, I beg to express the high consideration I entertain for Your Highness, and to subscribe myself

Your Highness' sincere Friend,

W. MORISSON.

When the present Nawab Nazim ascended the throne of ancestral dignity he was only nine years of age, and his affairs were therefore managed for him by the Government through the Agents Governor-General. Having no family to provide for then, his expenses were but small, and consequently much of the personal allowance of seven lacs allotted to him during his minority accumulated in the hands of the Agent Governor-General who, on the part of the Government as a Trustee, invested *a portion* of the savings in Government Securities while *another portion* was withheld by the Government itself. Of these savings, the part withheld by the Government has not yet been paid to the Nawab because he claims interest thereon (to which business men will surely consider he is justly entitled), but, unfortunately for the Nawab, the Government has the money and the power in its hands, and will not accept his release for the principal unless he foregoes all claim to the interest! Such is the manner in which justice is being administered in India by the Government at the present moment!

As to the other portion of the savings of His Highness's stipend during his minority which was invested in Government Securities by the Agent Governor-General as the legally constituted Representative of the Government for and on behalf of His Highness, we blush for the credit of Englishmen to bring the subject to public notice; but as the Government of India has not yet made amends to the Nawab for the acts of its Agent, and the Nawab has been constrained to appeal for public redress, we must, in justice to His Highness, set the whole matter before our readers and leave them to judge of the enormity of the wrong done to the Nawab by the Government of India, first, in the person of its Agent, and again in respect of the reply given by Lord Canning to this portion of His Highness's Memorial in Para. 10 of the Letter from the Officiating Secretary to the Government of India, which will be quoted hereafter.

The Agents Governor-General have always been *appointed by the Government to watch over the interests of the Nawab*, and the Government must therefore be responsible to the Nawab for their acts, whether profitable or otherwise. When advantage to the Government was secured by the Agents Governor-General (Mr. Monckton and others), their acts were invariably supported; but in the instance of Mr. Torrens, where the Nawab had a just claim against the Government for £250,000, he was told, " *it does not appear to the Governor-General in Council that any good object can be gained by further inquiry.*" " *The matter may, therefore, be allowed to drop.*" Such is the consoling information the Nawab received as compensation for the heavy loss he suffered during Mr. Torrens' incumbency as Agent Governor-General; the character of which and the parties concerned, we will leave our readers to ascertain for themselves from the following correspondence.

SUMMARY *of the extraordinary Transactions of* MR. HENRY TORRENS, *the Officiating Agent to the Governor-General at* MOORSHEDABAD, *in wasting a large Sum of Money belonging to* HIS HIGHNESS *the* NAWAB NAZIM *of* BENGAL, BEHAR, *and* ORISSA.

His Highness the Nawab Nazim of Bengal, &c., was waited on by Mr. H. Torrens, the then Officiating Agent to the Governor-General at Moorshedabad, who induced him, under pain of the Governor-General's displeasure, to sign a document authorising the sale of the Government Securities belonging to His Highness. These Securities were the savings accumulated during His Highness's minority, and amounted to Rs. 19,81,300. This sum was afterwards increased, by the result of reinvestments, to Rs. 27,40,700, the amount mentioned in paragraph 29 of His Highness's letter to Her Majesty's Secretary of State for India in Council under date 8th April, 1860. The excuse brought forward by Mr. Torrens for requiring the Nawab Nazim to place so large an accumulation of funds at his disposal, was, that the Government were desirous of seeing the money judiciously laid out in the purchase of landed estates for the benefit of His Highness. On thus obtaining the Nawab Nazim's sanction for their sale, Mr. Torrens appointed the firm of Messrs. Mackenzie, Lyall, and Co., Auctioneers of Calcutta, Financial Agents to His Highness, and instructed them to dispose of the securities; which this firm accordingly did, under the Agent's supervision and instructions. Previously, however, to obtaining a power to sell the papers, Mr. Torrens had attempted to do so on his own responsibility. Under date 13th February, 1848, he addressed the following letter to the Government Agent, Treasury, without any previous communication whatever with the Nawab Nazim :—

To THE GOVERNMENT AGENT, *Treasury.*

Calcutta, **Feb. 13th,** 1848.

SIR,—Please deliver to Messrs. Mackenzie, Lyall, and Co., the **Government** Securities belonging to His Highness the Nawab Nazim, **Bengal, standing** in the name of the Governor-General's Agent at **Moorshedabad.**

I have the honour, &c.,
(Signed) H. TORRENS,
Officiating Governor-General's Agent.

This letter was not acted on, as it was deemed necessary that **the Agent should obtain the signature of** His Highness **to enable the Government Agent, at** the Treasury, **to** endorse them to him as *Officiating Agent to the Governor-General at Moorshedabad,* and hold them subject to his instructions. The following is His Highness's letter to the Government Agent :—

To the GOVERNMENT AGENT *for the time being.*

"SIR,—With reference to my Power of Attorney in your favour, dated the 18th instant, I request you will be good enough to endorse **to H.** Torrens, Esquire, *Officiating Agent to the Governor-General at Moorshedabad, for the time being,* or order, **the** Government Securities remaining in your possession belonging to me, holding them subject **to** his instructions.

" I have the honour to be, &c.,
" (Signed) SYUD MUNSOOR ULLEE.
" Calcutta, 22nd Feb., 1848."

On the *very day* that Mr. Torrens obtained the signature of His Highness to **this letter he wrote the subjoined to the Government Agent, and delivered it to Messrs. Mackenzie, Lyall, and Co., for** presentation :—

To the GOVERNMENT AGENT *for the time* **being.**

" Calcutta, 22nd Feb., 1848.

" SIR,—Be pleased to hand over to Messrs. Mackenzie, Lyall, and **Co., the Government Securities remaining in your custody belonging to His** Highness the Nawab Nazim of Bengal, endorsed to me **as** directed.

" I have the honour, **&c.,**
" (Signed) H. TORRENS,
" Officiating Governor-General's Agent at Moorshedabad."

At this time **His Highness was only eighteen years old, and had** but recently attained that age. The *natural respect* with which he had been taught to regard the Agent **to the Governor-General, together**

I

with *his youth and inexperience,* precluded him from *suspecting* the motives of the Agent, more especially as he was made to believe that by conceding to Mr. Torrens' request, he would be meeting the wishes of the Government which that gentleman represented, and even supposing His Highness to have entertained a doubt of Mr. Torrens' good faith in entrusting so large a sum of money to a comparatively unknown firm, *there was no one* with whom he could advise on so delicate a subject, or *with whom he could consult in matters affecting so high and trusted an official* as the Agent to the Governor-General.

As soon as the funds of His Highness were placed in Messrs. Mackenzie, Lyall, and Co's. hands, Mr. Torrens not only permitted others to draw on them, but proceeded to pass orders on them, *not as a private individual,* but invariably *in his public capacity* as *Agent* to the Governor-General at His Highness's Court. One of his first acts was to enter into Articles of Agreement with a Mr. Robinson, in March, 1848, for the building of a Steam Boat at a cost of Rupees 65,000, to be paid for out of the funds in the hands of the so-called Financial Agents to His Highness. It certainly seems to have been a stretch of authority on the part of Mr. Torrens, to have entered into any such agreement, or to have given directions for the disbursement of monies, which could only be considered as *the private funds* of the Nawab Nazim. Some light is, however, thrown on this subject by a passage which occurs in a letter which will be found *in extenso* elsewhere. Mr. Torrens in this passage observes—

"*The Steamer, as you will learn, is abandoned. From the first I thought it a shadowy scheme, a* HENLEY *humbug, but it locked up Funds.*"

The steamer, however, was not abandoned until large sums had been advanced, and His Highness had also, subsequently, to sustain a lawsuit on this account.

Mr. Torrens, besides personally *disregarding* the interests of His Highness, *failed altogether to exercise a proper supervision over the monies* of which he had obtained the disposal.

There was, at the time when the Government Securities were transferred to the custody of Messrs. Mackenzie, Lyall, and Co., a man named Lewis Tiery, who was employed in the Palace of His Highness as a *Mechanic* and *Writer*. This man's position did not entitle him to receive orders personally from the Nawab Nazim, *nor* to represent His Highness in any way whatever. He was, in fact, employed under the Dewan in the capacity mentioned, yet on and after the 21st June, 1848, we find him opening a correspondence with Messrs. Mackenzie, Lyall, and Co. His first letter is as follows:—

"To Messrs. MACKENZIE. LYALL, and Co.

"Berhampore, 21st June, 1848.

"DEAR GENTLEMEN,—I am directed by His Highness the Nawab Nazim of Bengal to request you will be good enough to arrange to put aside Co.'s Rupees 25,200, and place the same to His Highness's account, to meet the several orders His Highness intends drawing in favour of Mr. **F. C. Lewis.**

"Yours faithfully,
"(Signed)   L. TIERY."

On receipt of this letter, Messrs. Mackenzie, Lyall, and Co., who had hitherto *only received instructions from the Agent direct*, very properly sent a copy of it to that officer for verification and explanation. For reply, Mr. Torrens returned the copy, with the following memo. written across it :—

"His Highness the **Nawab** Nazim's order to this **effect** *was given to my knowledge.*

"(Signed)   H. TORRENS,
"Officiating Agent Governor-General.

"Berhampore,
"June, 26th, 1848."

About a fortnight later L. Tiery again wrote **to Messrs. Mackenzie,** Lyall, and Co. as follows :—

"Messrs. MACKENZIE, LYALL, and Co.,

"Exchange.

"DEAR GENTLEMEN,—I beg to advise, by the order of His Highness the Nawab Nazim of Bengal, that, I have drawn on you, payable at sight, in favour of Saduck Ally Khan, the Aruzbagee, Co.'s Rupees 10,000, being the amount available on account of His Highness.

"Yours faithfully,
"(Signed)   L. TIERY.

"Berhampore,
"14th July, 1848."

On the same **day he also** sent the following letter to the same Firm :—

"Messrs. MACKENZIE, LYALL, and CO.,

"Exchange.

"DEAR GENTLEMEN,—I beg to enclose an order in favour of Meer Saduck Aly Khan the Aruzbagee, endorsed over to you, and request you will be good enough to credit the same in that gentleman's account till **further** instructions.

"Yours faithfully,
"(Signed)   L. TIERY.

"Berhampore,
"14th July, 1848."

Messrs. Mackenzie, **Lyall, and Co. sent a** copy of these two letters to Mr. Torrens, who **returned them with** a memorandum, of which the subjoined is a copy :—

"I have been informed by Mr. Tiery that this order has been given, and that personally to him by the Nazim, and *I believe the statement to be true.*

"(Signed) H. TORRENS,
"Officiating Governor-General's Agent.

"July 21st, 1848."

In the first of these Memoranda, the Agent speaks of the order to Mr. Tiery as being given *to his knowledge;* in the second he expresses *his belief* in the truth of Mr. Tiery's statement. The result was that Messrs. Mackenzie, Lyall, and Co., not only attended to the orders conveyed in the above letters, but from that time accepted L. Tiery as a confidential Agent of His Highness—a position he never occupied. In this transaction it is difficult to tell which to reprehend the most—the carelessness and negligence of the Agent, or the easy faith of the Financial Agents he had selected for His Highness. On receiving a copy of Lewis Tiery's first letter, the Agent's plain duty was to have satisfied himself, by some communication with His Highness, as to the position the writer held in His Highness's Establishment. This he neglected to do, even when a second opportunity was offered him. Nay, in this last instance, he in a manner pledged his faith for that of L. Tiery. The facts are that, Tiery was never authorized to act on the part of His Highness, and that, as far as His Highness's orders are concerned, the letters of that individual are barefaced forgeries. Moreover, Messrs. Mackenzie, Lyall, and Co., finding him supported by the Agent, afterwards invariably acted on his letters without reference and without question. The consequences need not be detailed.

Meer Saduck Ally Khan, the Aruzbagee, mentioned in the letters of Lewis Tiery quoted above, was a person high in the confidence of the Agent, but a man originally of no standing or position, and one who *could neither read nor write.* That he enjoyed the fullest confidence of the Agent is shown from the fact that when the Nawab Nazim proceeded to Calcutta early in 1848 to pay a visit to the Governor-General, Lord Dalhousie, Mr. Torrens selected Meer Saduck Ally Khan to accompany His Highness, and at the same time he ordered Messrs. Mackenzie, Lyall, and Co., to pay to Meer Saduck Ally Khan large sums of money of which the Meer was entrusted with the expenditure. The favouritism here shown by Mr. Torrens will be obvious when it is known that in selecting the Aruzbagee—an officer answering to the Chief Usher—to accompany His Highness—he forbade the two highest Officers of His Highness's Court, *viz.,* the Dewan Rajah Seetanath Bose Bahadoor, and the Nawab Nazir Darab Ally Khan Bahadoor to leave Moorshedabad. Again, the importance of Meer Saduck Ally seems to have sprung up about the time the papers were made over to Messrs. Mackenzie, Lyall, and Co., as within a fortnight from that time Mr. Torrens had ordered them to make over to the Meer, more than *two and a half lakhs* of Rupees (£25,000). Saduck Ally Khan died shortly after His Highness's visit to Calcutta, but in the meantime upwards of *six lakhs* (£60,000) had been made over to him by Messrs. Mackenzie, Lyall, and Co., either by the order of Mr. Torrens direct, or in compliance with the orders of Lewis Tiery: and when he died he was found to be worth *several lakhs!* His importance in the transactions with Messrs. Mackenzie, Lyall, and Co., will, however, be rendered still more obvious by a perusal of Mr. Torrens' own letter quoted elsewhere.

Before referring to these documents, it may, perhaps, be advisable to mention the circumstances connected with the purchase of the Midnapore Estate. It may also be well to state here, that although the ostensible reason brought forward by Mr. Torrens to induce His Highness to consent to his having the control of the savings of His Highness's minority was the desirability of so large a sum being expended in the purchase of landed Estates, yet of the whole sum of Rupees 19,81,300, (£198,130) only *five lakhs and a half* (£55,000) were expended in buying the Estate in Midnapore and nineteen grants in the Soonderbuns. The last was anything but a profitable investment, seeing that the grants had mostly to be cleared of jungle, &c., before they could be expected to attract settlers, and even then their only crop for several years would have been an inferior sort of rice. To return, however, to the Midnapore Estate, Mr. Torrens of his own authority had appointed a manager of the landed estate of His Highness in the person of a Mr. Alexander McArthur. This person was to receive in return for his services Rupees 1,300 (£130) per mensem, salary, together with a commission of 10 per cent., and he was further to have an office found him *next* to the *Exchange*, the business establishment of Messrs. Mackenzie, Lyall, and Co., and was to have all his travelling and other expenses paid. The Midnapore Estate was about this time put up for sale by the Authorities *for arrears of Revenue* —a sale which transferred the Estate *free of all encumbrances* which existed after the permanent settlement of 1793. This Estate was bought in his own name by Mr. McArthur, on account of His Highness, for Rupees 86,000 (£8,600) at the Collector's auction. By a private arrangement, however, entered into between Mr. McArthur and a person named John Campton Abbott, who was, or pretended to be, the owner of the Estate, the difference between the price of the Estate at the Collector's sale, and Rupees 3,00,000 (£30,000), or Rupees 2,14,000 (£21,400), was paid to Mr. Abbott in satisfaction of his presumed claim, and out of this sum Mr. McArthur received, as his share, under the name of commission, no less than Rupees 30,000 (£3,000); that Mr. Torrens was aware of this, may be gathered from the deposition of Mr. McArthur, and from Mr. Torrens' own letters. Mr. McArthur, in his reply to His Highness's suit, says, " And this deponent further saith that at the time of the said sale of the said Estate for *arrears of Revenue*, the said Estate was the property of Mr. John Campton Abbott, and that by an agreement in writing, made between the said John Campton Abbott and this deponent, so authorized and acting as aforesaid under such instruction as aforesaid, and with the *full knowledge and consent of the said Governor-General's Agent,* and as this deponent *believes, of the said complainant himself,* previous to the said sale, it was agreed that the price of the said Estate should be three lakhs (£30,000)."

Mr. Torrens, in his letter of 11th May, 1848, wrote as follows :—" The Midnapore Zemindaries, in the district of that name, was, after much deliberation, taken of its owner, Mr. Abbott, for *three lakhs of* Rupees (£30,000), under the stipulations duly set forth in a deed of settlement between Mr. McArthur and himself. It was finally purchased by Mr. McArthur, at the Midnapore Collector's sale, on 29th April, in his name for the Nazim." Mr. McArthur states that he *believed* himself to be acting with the consent **and** knowledge "of the said complainant himself," a statement for which he had no foundation whatever, as *he was appointed by Mr. Torrens*, and conducted his business entirely with that gentleman. At that time the account of His Highness's funds, in the hands of Messrs. Mackenzie, Lyall, and Co., stood in their books in the name of "H. Torrens, Officiating Agent to the Governor-General, Moorshedabad," and on the 29th April, 1848, that account was debited with the sum of *three lakhs* "cash (£30,000) paid for the Midnapore Estate;" as might be expected from the extract given above from Mr Torrens' letter, that item was passed in the account as correct. There can be no difficulty in determining the character of the part played by Mr. McArthur in the purchase of this Midnapore Estate, and it is scarcely to be doubted that if he were not directly aided by the Agent, that officer showed an utter disregard of all business etiquette, which it is difficult to account for on any other supposition. Mr. McArthur in his deposition stated that he believed the Estate to be worth rather more than 40,000 Rupees (£4,000) *per annum* after paying the Government revenue. If this were the case, or if the Estate were even worth *three lakhs* (£30,000), it may be asked, whether in so rich a district as Midnapore, it is likely that the surrounding Zemindars would have allowed so valuable an estate to be sold to a stranger for £8,600, little more than two years purchase, or one-third of what they knew to be its real value. The facts and circumstances adduced above are sufficiently important in themselves to cast grave doubts on the motives and conduct of Mr. Torrens in disposing of the large sums over which he had obtained command, but there is documentary evidence which will, as it were, convict Mr. Torrens out of his own mouth, and which will bring the blame to him, of all that His Highness has ever urged against him. That this evidence only transpired after Mr. Torrens' death, frees His Highness from all imputations of bringing a charge against a man who has gone to his long account; **and it** should rather be regarded as a misfortune, that His Highness should be unable to place certain questions in their proper light, without, at the same time, being compelled to bring grave charges against the character **of a** deceased Agent. Luckily, Mr. Torrens has written letters which, in themselves, are a sufficient accusation against himself These letters, which have been alluded to above, are now given in full. On the 19th July, 1848, Messrs. Mackenzie, Lyall, and Co., rendered their accounts to Mr. Torrens as *Agent to the Governor-General* entrusted with the management of His Highness's funds. The accounts, as they stood, appear not to have been satisfactory to the Agent, as about a month after their receipt, he penned the following letter to Mr. Donald McCullum, a member of the firm of Mackenzie Lyall, and Company:—

"Berhampore, August 23rd.

"MY DEAR SIR,—Yours of the 9th July came to hand with the account. Mr. Tiery, the Accountant here, suggests it as expedient *not to put the paper in yet*, although **I have** looked over the items and found them *unexceptionable*. The fact is, that the account as it stands would not be understood by the Meer and the Eunuchs, and would *purposely* be misundertood by the Rajah. I must, I fear, induct you into *the muck of our intrigues;* the R.'s shares in which, and object, is best shown by his depreciation of our Government Securities, to get the papers indorsed **to him of an** Estate in Ceylon (nice investment) belonging to a high personage mortgaged to us. He is at the bottom of a great deal of mischief, and has been unceasing in his efforts to discredit me at head-quarters, as I side with no one, and am well with all, which does not suit his books, as the Agent should be, he thinks, in his hands, as old Raper was through his own creatures, against whom he carried on a farce of bitter enmity for three years, while these rascals pillaged the Nizamut and underhand gave half **to the** honest Rajah. He is at the bottom of a sea of villany, besides **being** now in that stage of a Bengali's life when he **is** morally trading on **his** capital, *i. e.*, making money by roguery on a previous good character.

"*The entry 'paid to Meer Saduck Alli by order of H. Torrens,' a plain and simple matter as we understand it, is enough in the hands of a rogue to bring me into the Supreme Court on a charge of collusion with that person to enrich ourselves with the Nazim's money. It is not as H. Torrens, but as the Governor-General's Agent, in whose name the paper stood, that I interfered in the matter*, and the sums transferred to the Meer were by the **Nazim's** order communicated through the Governor-General's Agent. **It** was only as such (professionally) that *I interposed to protect the young man's interests*, and this was a bit of *moral* courage, that **I do** not think many of my Service would have ventured on. Will you prepense this matter please, and let me hear from you? You understand that I am indulging the vindictiveness of a Bengali disappointed of the use of nineteen lakhs of Rupees, which he has for years been looking forward for, and that I must walk very warily, for the fellow **is** a type of his race for cunning. *Could you enter 'to Meer S. A. by order of the Nazim as per accounts rendered.'* I have nothing to do **in** the matter, and the mention of my name is really calculated to do **me** injury in the way in which it stands. Whereas the monies paid **to the** Meer as His Highness's *managing man*, were all **as** per account rendered **to the** Rajah, **or** to Mr. Tiery, **the** Accountant, or for goods **with your knowledge, and** extricate me, please, from the difficulty I stand in. **Or if you cannot alter your** books, I must address Government. The imputation **of** mixing **myself up** *with the missing money* for the Nazim would be just Maclean's **case** at Madras over again, *and the imputation only would suffice to lose* **me** *this appointment*.

"Let me have a note of the costs of remittance to Carter, as it is **made** not on my own, but a public account, and I must get reimbursed.

"*Pardon me, but I have missed noting the important point of the heading. Why not 'His Highness the Nawab Nazim in account, &c., &c.?' He is a man, a major in years, and my trust charge of his affairs ceases*

"*The steamer, as you will learn, is abandoned. From the first I thought it a shadowy scheme—a* HENLEY *humbug—but it locked up funds*.

"Between ourselves, **the** Government, I fancy, expect the Nazim not to press them **for two lakhs** of Rupees granted for building purposes, *and he must build what is to* be done?

"I hope all's **well with you** at home; **my babes are** well, but wife poorly.

"Yours very truly,
"H. TORRENS."

Five days later, Mr. Torrens wrote again to Mr. McCallum as under:—

"Berhampore, August 28th.

"MY DEAR SIR,—I should not, perhaps, have quoted Mr. Tiery, whose suggestion simply was that I should not put these accounts in the hands of the Rajah, *till the balance was a little square*, knowing as he does the sort of things that are said in the Nizamut as to the expending of money.

"*I am glad you can alter the heading and entries.*

"I need not say, that in all financial transactions for and on account of the Nizamut, I have the most implicit confidence in your *skill* and *judgment*, having so long had experience of the *mode* in which your firm does business.

"Yours, &c.,
"H. TORRENS."

The more important passages in the above letters were underlined for obvious reasons. In the interval which elapsed between them, Mr. Torrens would seem to have received an intimation from Mr. McCullum, that he would comply with the Agent's wishes. In reading the first of these letters one is struck with the manner in which Mr. Torrens, whilst pleading his own cause, does so in a way to frighten the firm into his views. He fears the effect of certain items in the accounts in the hands of "a rogue." But he had previously indicated who that *rogue* was likely to be, and given him such a character as to make him an object of fear in the eyes of Messrs. Mackenzie, Lyall and Co. Mr. Torrens further remarks, that if the firm cannot alter their books, he "must address the Government," and that "the imputation *would be sufficient to lose him his appointment.*" And, of course, in either case, the firm would lose their post of financial agents. All these reasons, combined, induced them at once *to alter* not *only* the *heading* of their accounts, but the *entries* in these accounts. The effect of these alterations would be, of course, to remove the responsibility from the Agent to His Highness the Nawab Nazim. Mr. Torrens was aware that the entries relating to Meer Saduck Ally Khan were sufficient to bring him into the Supreme Court, and hence, in order to persuade Messrs. Mackenzie, Lyall, and Co., to consent to alter their books, he asserted what was not true, that "the sums transferred to the Meer were by the Nazim's order." He also mentions the Meer as "His Highness's managing man." The fact being, as before stated, that His Highness's managing man was the *Dewan* Nizamut, Rajah Seetanath Bose Bahadoor, and that the Meer occupied a post answering only to that of *Chief Usher.*

These letters, besides throwing some light on Mr. Torrens' relations with Meer Saduck Ally Khan, reveal also the position of Mr. Tiery, who is called the Accountant, and who appears as the confidential adviser of Mr. Torrens, in pointing out to him the necessity of withholding the accounts from "the hands of the Rajah *till the balance was a little square.*" It may possibly excite some surprise that the accounts should be rendered to the Rajah, considering that Meer Saduck Ally Khan was the managing man of His Highness.

The subject of the contract for the purchase of a steamer has been already touched upon; but it may be useful to place the sentences, "it locked up funds," and he "must build," as seeming to show that Mr. Torrens had an object in dissipating His Highness's funds.

Mr. Torrens speaks of "the *missing money for the Nazim*." What this *missing money* was Mr. Torrens never informed His Highness, nor has His Highness ever had in his possession letters or accounts which could directly enlighten him on this point.

The only evidence which appears to bear on this subject is the following letter, addressed to Messrs. Mackenzie, Lyall, and Co., by the Agent to the Governor-General at Moorshedabad:—

"Allipore, April 20th, 1848.

"Messrs. MACKENZIE, LYALL, AND CO.

"DEAR SIRS,—From the amount of funds belonging to His Highness, the Nawab Nazim of Bengal, now in your hands for investment, have the goodness to assign, by His Highness's desire, the sum of two lakhs (rupees 2,00,000) *to the credit of Meer Saduck Ally Khan*, to enable him to discharge obligations *now incurred*, or *to be incurred*, under instructions by them for the Nazim.

"You will be good enough to adjust payments to Meer Saduck Ally Khan in such a way as may best serve the interests of His Highness, while at the same time satisfying the Meer, and, at your leisure, inform me of your arrangements for His Highness's information.

"I am, yours faithfully,
"H. TORRENS,
"Offg. G. G.'s Agent for G. G. the
"N. N. of Bengal."

Under the date of this letter the following entry appeared in the original accounts of Messrs. Mackenzie, Lyall and Co.:—

"20th April, 1848. To cash paid, third instalment assigned to Meer Saduck Ally Khan, Aruzbagee, as directed by H. Torrens, Esq., in his letter of this day, rupees 2,00,000." There is nothing whatever on record to show what became of the large amount thus paid away by order of Mr. Torrens. It is important, however, to observe that although Mr. Torrens only received authority to dispose of the savings of His Highness's minority on the 22nd of February, 1848, yet this sum of rupees 2,00,000 paid to Meer Saduck Ally Khan on the 20th of April, 1848, was not the *third* "instalment," but the *third* "amount," for a purpose which now here appears. It only remains to remark that a knowledge of these transactions, revealed in these letters, only came out in the trial of the suit which His Highness instituted in 1854 against Messrs. Mackenzie, Lyall, and Co.

All that has been mentioned above as reflecting on the conduct of Mr. Torrens has been taken from the records of that trial; nothing has been advanced which cannot be supported by documentary evidence, if not by the papers filed in the suit. The force of the facts now brought forward compelled the late Governor-General to acknowledge that **the facts of the case, as** judged by the evidence of his own letters, was ***most condemnatory* of** the conduct of Mr. Torrens. No allusion has been made in this narrative to Mr. Torrens' interference in creating new posts in the Nizamut Service, and in inducting men of his own into situations without His Highness's permission; nor to the case of *jewels*, which he suggested *should be presented to* Lady Dalhousie. His letters show that he **acted** independently of His Highness, whom *he never condescended to* consult, and that he invariably acted, as he phrases it, "professionally" as *Agent* to the *Governor-General at Moorshedabad*.

Can it be doubted that in obtaining the unchallenged use of so large a sum as nearly twenty lacs of Rupees (£200,000), he was actuated by a desire to enrich himself at the expense of His Highness, and that in furtherance of this object, he acted *in collusion* with Meer Saduck Ally Khan and Lewis Tiery? The result was, that funds which, rightly applied, might have materially ministered to the honour and dignity of His Highness the Nawab Nazim, and which might have secured him from pecuniary difficulties **and** embarrassments during his life, and which being at his own sole disposal, might have enabled him to provide for his family in a manner suitable to their rank and expectations, without seriously encroaching on other funds of the Nizamut in the hands of the Government; these funds so vast, and so capable of benefiting His Highness, of securing the increased ease and happiness of his family, *were squandered without His Highness's knowledge*, and in defiance of all principles of *honesty, and official propriety*, by the man, who, on all occasions, was presumed to be His Highness's *best friend*, and who, invariably, asserted that all he did was as the *trusted representative* of the BRITISH GOVERNMENT.

(Copy.)

No. 46 of 1853.

From the AGENT GOVERNOR-GENERAL AT MOORSHEDABAD *to* CECIL BEADON, ESQ., SECRETARY *to the* GOVERNMENT *of* BENGAL.

Fort William,
Dated Berhampore, 12th April, 1853.

SIR,—I have the honour to transmit for the information of the Most Noble the Governor of Bengal copies of the documents noted in the margin, and beg to offer the following observations:—

2. My predecessor, Mr. Money, in his despatch to Government regarding the accounts of the minority of His Highness the Nawab Nazim, states, "on the 1st of September, 1847, there were in the possession of the Government Agent, Government securities appertaining to the Nawab Nazim to the amount of Company's Rupees 19,81,300, and in cash Rupees 31,334-10-1, and that in the months of February and March, 1849, the whole of those securities were under the instructions from the late Agent, Mr. Torrens, delivered to Messrs. Mackenzie, Lyall, and Co., leaving in the hands of the Govern-

ment Agent on the **30th of** April, 1852, a balance only of Rupees 415-8-2.

"The accounts submitted to His Highness by Mackenzie, Lyall, and Co., show a **most** profuse expenditure of the large fortune that had been laid by **so** carefully during his minority. Seventeen lacs were expended **in** less than two months, and the entire capital was dissipated in less than two years, leaving the Nawab Nazim a debtor in their books.

"His Highness is anxious that the accounts should **be** carefully sifted, and if any sums have been improperly **expended, or** paid **away** without due authority, measures **may be taken for their** recovery."

3. Mr. Money, at the **Nawab Nazim's request,** called upon Messrs. Mackenzie, Lyall, and Co., **in his letter dated the** 14th September, 1862, for authenticated **copies of all the** vouchers **in their** possession by which they had paid **away monies** on His Highness's **account,** specifying the **names of the** persons **who** drew on them **for the** different sums **charged in their** account current, and the names **of the** parties to whom **the** money was actually paid.

4. Messrs. Mackenzie, Lyall, and Co., in reply, refer Mr. Money **to the** detailed **accounts** rendered by them to the Nizamut alleging **that** they **contain the** information called **for,** and offering to prepare **the** voluminous vouchers for the inspection in their office of **any** party duly authorised to examine them.

5. By desire of the Nawab Nazim, Mr. Money wrote to **Messrs.** Mackenzie, Lyall, and Co., informing them that His Highness had given full authority to Mr. R. D. Turnbull, a gentleman residing in Calcutta, of high character, and **an** excellent accountant, to examine all His Highness's **accounts, and** requesting them **to** furnish Mr. Turnbull with all **the vouchers** connected with the accounts submitted **by them to His Highness, through** the late Agent, **Mr.** Torrens.

6. In reply **Messrs. Mackenzie, Lyall, and Co., inform Mr. Turnbull** in a letter dated **the 10th November, 1852, that they are quite pre**dared to submit for **his** inspection, **in** their **office, all the vouchers** for the accounts rendered by them to His Highness on **the** *understanding that in so far as they are concerned no attempt* **is** *contemplated of re-opening these accounts* which they allege **were so long ago** furnished by them. and which were subsequently **deliberately audited, settled, and passed by His Highness, and further that some valid reason** must be assigned for the re-examination **of** accounts **which have** been deliberately closed, before they can consent to the re-opening of **them.**

7 Mr. Turnbull **then** requested Messrs. Mackenzie, Lyall, and Co. to let **him know who** had examined the vouchers relating to the accounts **which His Highness** the Nawab Nazim had handed over to him for **examination, and** which vouchers they object to **produce** unless it is **distinctly understood** that no attempt is **to** be **made to** re-open their "**settled accounts**;" Mr. Turnbull further **requested** them to furnish **him with a** copy **of the letter in** which His Highness's satisfaction of the correctness of **the accounts is expressed.**

8. Messrs. Mackenzie, Lyall, and **Co., in reply, refer Mr. Turn**bull to their former communication to **him dated the 10th instant.**

9. It will be observed that Messrs. Mackenzie, Lyall, and Co., will not produce the vouchers for Mr. Turnbull's inspection except under the distinct understanding that no attempt should be made to re-open their "settled accounts;" a proviso to which His Highness would not give his consent, having no recollection whatever that he had ever seen or approved the accounts, or in any way given his sanction to their being settled and passed. I then placed myself, at His Highness's request, in communication with Messrs. Allan and Thomas, Attorneys-at-Law, and directed them to write to Messrs. Mackenzie, Lyall. and Co requesting them to furnish either Mr. Turnbull or myself with such proofs as might be at hand in verification of the accounts submitted by them to the Nawab, embracing transactions from February, 1818, to 30th of April, 1849, during which time they had acted as His Highness's Agents.

10. I, at the same time, told Messrs. Allan and Thomas to intimate to Messrs. Mackenzie, Lyall, and Co., that in seeking for information about the accounts, His Highness had no desire or intention to assail the accounts with any view to cause them trouble, loss, or injury, on the contrary, that His Highness will, as far as he possibly can do so, facilitate the means of proof which they may have to offer, and will approve and allow all such items as in justice and fairness belong to His Highness's accounts.

11. Messrs. Mackenzie, Lyall, and Co., in their note date 17th Jan., 1853, in reply stated, that the death of their book-keeper, who compiled the accounts in question, the indisposition of Mr. McCallum (one of the partners), from which he was just recovering, the years that have passed away since the transactions alluded to were closed, will occasion a search among records long since put aside, and necessarily cause a considerable delay in laying their hands on the voluminous papers appertaining to these operations.

12. That they will, however, have the task set about forthwith, and when the documents are in train, Messrs. Allan and Co. will be again communicated with, but much time will be required for the purpose, as the present is their busy season, and it would be most inconvenient to have their current business interrupted.

13. In consequence of the circumstances disclosed in evidence at the recent trial for perjury against Mr. Tiery, and particularly adverting to the evidence of Mr. D. McCallum, one of the members of the firm of Mackenzie, Lyall, and Co. (a witness for the defence), it appeared to His Highness the Nawab Nazim to be necessary for the protection of His Highness's interests, that suits should be immediately commenced against Mackenzie, Lyall, and Co., and Mr. Tiery, for an account and reimbursement of the various sums received, and applied by them.

14. The evidence at the trial shows that the greatest irregularity, and even *fraud*, had in many instances been practised on the Nawab in the application of the enormous sums alleged to have been disbursed on his account, and Mr. McCallum's own evidence establishes that what he did was under Mr. Tiery's authority, and without the sanction or approval of His Highness, therefore it became evident that the sooner the extent and liability incurred by these parties can be ascertained, the sooner will the amount improperly applied, and disbursed, be recovered.

15. His Highness seeing that no time should be lost in adopting legal steps against both Messrs. Mackenzie, Lyall, and Co., and Mr. Tiery, signed two Retainers, empowering Messrs. Allan and Thomas, attorneys-at-law, to prosecute in the Supreme Court the above suits.

16. Before the trial of Mr. Tiery, a General Retainer, on behalf of His Highness, had been given to Mr. Ritchie, as senior counsel, and Mr. Cowie, as junior counsel, and since the trial Mr. Peterson has been added, as it was through his means that such important information was obtained on the trial as to the merits of the Nawab's claims.

17. His Highness hopes shortly to learn that bills have been filed on his behalf against Messrs. Mackenzie, Lyall, and Co and Mr Tiery.

18. Meanwhile, it is desirable that the fact of the intended suits should be kept secret until the suits have been actually instituted.

19. His Highness would be glad to learn that these proceedings had met with the approval of the Most Noble the Governor of Bengal.

I have, &c.,
(Signed) G. H MACGREGOR.
Agent Governor-General.

Office of **A. G. G.**, Moorshedabad,
12th April, 1853.

The action instituted by the Nawab against the mercantile firm in Calcutta, the agents of Mr. Torrens, for the recovery in part or altogether of the sums they held for him having been afterwards stopped at the instigation of the Government, the Nawab was hopelessly debarred from obtaining his rights either in his political or his social position, and has ever since waited patiently to appeal to British Justice for the recovery of this and others of his lawful dues, which should long since have been accorded to him in full by the Government of India.

In 1848, the Governor-General, the Earl of Dalhousie, on his arrival in India, addressed His Highness in the following terms:—

From the **EARL OF** DALHOUSIE, K.T., *to* NAWAB SYUD MUNSOOR ALI KHAN BEHADOOR, **NUSRUT JUNG** (*the present* NAWAB **NAZIM** *of Bengal, Behar, and Orissa*), *dated* 12*th January*, 1848.

" Nawab Sahib, of high worth and exalted station, my good brother, may peace be with you.

"After expressing wishes words cannot describe for a joyful meeting what I have now the pleasure officially to announce, You will have heard through the ordinary channel, my appointment of Governor-General of India; I arrived at Calcutta and assumed the duties of my office on the 12th January, 1848.

"Your Highness may be assured that this friend is desirous, and *bent heart and soul to do all he can to knit the ties of attachment and friendship, and to connect the bonds of harmony and concord between the Honourable East India Company and Your Highness,* and that personal sentiments of the highest regard and esteem should confirm the Relations between us, while zealously striving to promote the interest, establish the authority and maintain the best understanding between all the states and Sirdars of Hind, and the Deccan, and this High and Paramount power *by strict observance of word and bond, and enduring fulfilment of Compact and Treaty in terms of existing conditions, stipulations and articles* arranged and concerted.

"You have my hearty good will, and wish You well,

"(Signed)   DALHOUSIE."

The name of Lord Dalhousie is well known to readers of Indian history as connected with the policy of annexation and spoliation which carried out in India during his administration, notwithstanding the remonstrances of the Home Government and of the Native Princes who suffered by it. The Policy of unscrupulously setting aside all sense of Public faith and honour, and openly violating treaties and engagements of the most solemn kind under the most slender pretexts, and without mature consideration, cannot possibly be justified. There can be but little doubt that the annexation of Oude and other arbitrary acts committed by Lord Dalhousie caused His Lordship to be looked upon as the despoiler of Indian Princes, and set on foot that feeling of disaffection amongst the allies and tributaries of the British Government in India, which eventually led to the dreadful crisis in 1857 know as the Indian Mutiny or Sepoy Rebellion. The present Nawab Nazim did not escape the general spoliation, for he was also treated with gross injustice by the Noble

Lord, yet he quietly bore up against the indignities offered him, and in 1857 was found one of the few faithful allies of the British in India, as will hereafter be shown.

From 1848, the year in which Lord Dalhousie entered upon his duties as the head of the Administration in India, till 1854, he had in vain sought for some pretext whereupon to assault the hereditary rank, privileges, and dignity of the Nawab Nazim and Soubahdar of Bengal, Behar, and Orissa; but in 1854 an accident suggested to the Noble Lord a favourable opportunity for breaking the pledges given by the British Government to support this Prince and his family for ever, and to observe an inviolate adherence to the obligations of Public Faith and Honour. His Lordship at once took advantage of this accident for inflicting upon His Highness summary injustice, by depriving him and his family at once of their rights and privileges, and the immunities and protection which they before possessed of carrying on all legal proceedings through their Attorney or the Agent Governor-General. The Regulations of 1805, 1806, and 1823 were repealed, and Act XXVII of 1854 was arbitrarily framed. His Lordship having ignored the rights and claims of His Highness which were secured by Treaty — reduced his salute from nineteen to thirteen guns, and prevented his going on future shooting excursions except under Police Surveillance, withholding at the same time the sums of money set apart for his expenses on those occasions. With regard to the several Trusts or Funds that had been established out of the Nawab's money and styled by the Court of Directors "*the Sacred In-*

heritance of the Nizamut Family," His Lordship declared *they were all public money,* and proposed that they should be converted into *" a Book Debt bearing no Interest,"* although the money was or ought to have been invested in Government Securities, bearing interest, *" which was to be accounted for to the Nawab "* (Pages 61 and 79). But what was the accident which led to all this injustice ? The following correspondence will show. His Lordship seemed determined to carry out certain ends, and with this object held the Nawab responsible for a criminal act committed in his camp while on a shooting excursion, of which he neither knew anything at the time nor heard of for a long time afterwards, and of which His Highness's servants even, who were accused of complicity, were declared innocent after a threefold trial. Several English gentlemen (Mr. Garrett, Judge of Bhurboom, and the Honourable Ashly Eden, Secretary to the Government of Bengal, and others) were present with His Highness in the Camp. Yet neither they nor His Highness heard a word about the affair till some months afterwards, when suspicion was awakened that something wrong had been done by somebody. This led to an inquiry into the affair by His Highness, and afterwards to the public trials, first by Native and then by English Judges. The principal actor in the tragedy, a stranger in the Camp, was never caught, he having made his escape before the Camp returned.

To gentlemen of the legal profession this case will furnish much interest, and exhibit the arbitrary power exerted by the Governor-General of India, not only against a Native Prince, but also against the patient investigatious of Courts of **Justice** presided over by English Judges!

MURDER CASE.

From the Secretary to the Government of **Bengal**, *to the Governor-General's Agent,* MOORSHEDABAD.

Dated Fort William, 15th Nov., 1853.

Sir,

I am directed by the Most Noble the Governor of Bengal to forward for your information, and for the purpose hereinafter mentioned, copy of a letter from Mr. E. T. Trevor, who was entrusted with the prosecution of Aman Ali Khan and others, on a charge of wilful murder, together with two printed copies of the judgments of the Sessions and Nizamut Courts on the case.

2. Whatever view may be taken *of the judicial decision of the lower tribunal* as regards Aman Ali Khan, and the other criminals, who have been acquitted on all the counts of the charge, the fact is established by the conviction of five of the prisoners, that a gross and horrible act of cruelty extending over several days, commencing with the torture of two suspected persons, and ending with their death, was committed in the camp of the Nawab Nazim by persons either in his service, or under his authority, and within fifty yards of His Highness's own tent; Aman Ali Khan the chief eunuch, by his own admission, was cognizant of the outrage, he heard in his tent the cries of the victims, though his tent was pitched on the opposite side of the Nawab Nazim's tent to that near which the torture was inflicted, and it is in evidence that the same cries were heard by others in the camp. Though this atrocious crime was committed in the district of Malda, during the first five days of April, no information of its occurrence was given to the police of that district, or to any other public officer. On the contrary, it was given out, *apparently on authority,* that the men died of cholera, and it was not until the 1st of May, after the return of the camp to Moorshedabad, that a report of the real circumstances reached the magistrate of the district, and led to the inquiry which terminated in the trial.

3. The Governor of Bengal *cannot consent to permit this matter to rest at the point to which the judicial decision of the Sudder Court has left it.* It is quite necessary, in his Lordship's opinion, that the Nawab Nazim, in whose camp, and under whose very eyes this monstrous outrage upon humanity has been perpetrated, should be required to give an explanation of his conduct in the matter; that measures should be taken to mark the sense entertained by the Government of such proceedings, and that safeguards should be provided against repetition of them in future.

4. The history of the case, as it affects the Nawab Nazim and the eunuchs, his servants, is as follows:—

K

5. His Highness, during his late shooting excursion in the district of Malda, pitched his camp, on the 30th March at the village of Ranpoor. the murdered men, Hingoo, a Fakeer, and Muddee, the son of a Golah in the service of the Nazim, accompanied the camp. The persons named in the margin formed part of His Highness suite, and of these, Syud Iman Ali was Urzbegy of the Palace, and Aman Ali Khan, the chief and confidential eunuch, having the general control over all His Highness's arrangements during the excursion.

6. The principal tents in the camp belonged to the Nawab Nazim, to Aman Ali Khan, and to the other eunuchs. His Highness occupied the centre tent, one side of which was the tent of Aman Ali Khan, and on the other the tent of the other eunuchs. They are *generally pitched* at a short distance, about fifty yards, from each other.

7. On the morning of the 31st March, while His Highness, with the greater part of his suite, was out shooting, a box containing property, belonging to one Meah Arzoomun, was found missing. Hingoo and Muddee were seized on suspicion of having stolen the box, and throughout that day, both *before*, and after His Highness's return from shooting, were beaten and tortured for the purpose of inducing them to confess, and point out the property. The torture was inflicted in the verandah of the eunuch's tent, and in a pal pitched within two yards of it. It was inflicted by servants of the Nawab Nazim, under the direction of the Urzbegy, and in the presence of all the eunuchs, except, perhaps, Aman Ali Khan himself, and Aman Ali Khan was, on his own admission, cognizant of what was going on, and *sent messages to stop it*. The beating and torture appear to have been continued under the same circumstances during the 1st and 2nd April. On the 3rd of April, the camp moved to Allal, and the tortured men being unable to walk, were carried with the camp. There *they were attended by the native doctor to the camp*, who applied ointment and poultices to the wounds. On the 5th, the camp moved to Gujoli, and there the tortured men were seen by George Shapcott, the coachman, and others in the camp, in the same pal as before, with their bodies raw and swollen, and the native doctor ineffectually applying remedies. Hingoo died on that day, and Muddee the day after, both from the effect of their wounds. Certain persons in the service of the Nawab Nazim were summoned by a Hurkara to wash the bodies previous to burial, and these persons saw the state of the bodies, and *knew* that death had been caused by beating. The bodies were then buried at a short distance from the tents, and it was given out that the men had died of cholera. During the whole of this time, from the 31st March to the 6th April. Aman Ali Khan, and the other eunuchs dined with the Nawab.

8. Although the evidence adduced on the trial was not sufficient to satisfy the Court of Nizamut, Adawluth, that Aman Ali Khan and other **eunuchs** were guilty of the *legal* crime of being accessory, **or** privy, **to** the culpable homicide of which the other prisoners were most deservedly convicted, and *though the judicial sentence of acquittal passed by the Court is final, and respects the liability of these men to criminal punishment, yet the effect of that sentence is by no means to relieve the* **eunuchs** *of the least degree of responsibility for their conduct*

to their master, the Nawab Nazim, and still less to relieve His Highness from the least degree of responsibility for his own acts, and those of his servants to the Government under which he lives, and upon which he depends.

9. His Lordship **has read** the judgment of the Zillah and Sudder Courts, and **the** arguments of the Council on both sides with great attention, **and** *he rises from the perusal of them satisfied beyond* **all** *reasonable doubt,* not only that Aman Ali Khan and the other **eunuchs were** cognizant of **the** torture of the murdered men, **of** their **death in consequence** of the torture, and of the falseness of **the rumour which** ascribed their death to cholera, **but** *that the former failed to use the influence he had to prevent the crime, and that the latter took an active part in its perpetration.*

10. In the absence of any explanation on the part **of the Nawab** Nazim, *it must also be inferred* from the circumstances stated on **the** trial, that His Highness, **whose** *tent was pitched about fifty yards from the place where the men were tortured, and who dined daily with the eunuchs,* **was** himself **cognizant of** the torture, of the death that ensued from the **torture, and of the** falseness of the rumour which ascribed the **death of these men to** cholera. And, *if this be so,* His Highness has failed in his duty to the Government in not causing information of the **crime to be given to** the proper authorities, and *has rendered himself liable* to a **very serious** responsibility.

11. Under the circumstances above detailed, **I am** directed by **the Government to request** that **you** will call upon **the** Nawab Nazim to **state fully and exactly, in writing,** what was his knowledge of the events **connected with the torture and** death of Hingoo and Muddee, **both during and after their occurrence,** and to explain *why he failed to* **exert his authority to prevent the** *perpetration of so outrageous a crime, almost in* **his very presence;** *why he has continued, and still continues, to* **show** *favour and* **countenance to** *those who were concerned in, and cognizant of it;* **and** why, after **the** death of **the murdered** men, he did not **either inform** you of what had occurred, **or cause information** thereof to **be** given to **the** Officers of Justice.

12. You will request a formal interview **with** His Highness for the purpose of delivering to him **in person a copy of** this letter, and you will take the occasion of impressing upon **His** Highness *the extreme gravity of the position in which he has placed himself.*

13. His Lordship expects an early reply to this communication.

I have, &c.,
(Signed) CECIL BEADON, ESQ.,
Secretary to the Government of Bengal.

Fort William, the 21st Oct., 1853.

From E. TREVOR, ESQ., *to* CECIL BEADON, ESQ. *Secretary to the Government of Bengal.*

SIR,—
I have the honour *to submit* **the** *following remarks upon the judgment of the Sudder Nizamut,* in the case of Government *v.* Aman Ali Khan,

and others. I am induced to do so, as *I consider* that the parties released, were all committed to the Sessions on a charge *which has been fully proved against every one of them* (I allude to the charge of privity), by the evidence relied on by the Judges, *by evidence*, allowed in its full force as it stands, and *by the facts* of the case as allowed by all.

2. The evidence against Aman Ali Khan is somewhat different from that against the other released dependents, and his case I would consider separately. I propose, in the first place, to offer a few remarks upon the reasons assigned by the Judges—for the rejection of all the evidence adduced for the prosecution, which speaks of the active perpetration of any of the released persons in the torture of the deceased. In the next place, I would consider how (irrespective of this rejected evidence) *the charge of privity is fully proved* against all the inmates of the eunuchs' tent; and lastly, how the same charge is fully proved against Aman Ali Khan.

3. First I would draw attention to the reasons assigned by the Judges for the rejection of four of the witnesses for the prosecution in these remarks and, indeed, in *all the remarks which I may consider it my duty to make* on this case. I trust it will not appear that *they are offered in the spirit of a disappointed advocate*, but of one, who entrusted with the conduct of the case, only after the committal of the accused to the Sessions (and, therefore, in no way responsible for the evidence offered in support of the charges), has really some good resources to assign for his belief, that some of the guilty parties have escaped the punishment due to the crime proved against them.

4. Four witnesses have been rejected *in toto*, Hossainee, Denoo, Hurgun, and Rabaruali. The first-named, was the servant of the person whose box was said to have been stolen, and in whose charge it then was, so that, as stated by the Court, *he is the party upon whom suspicion would naturally fall;* but it is to be observed, that it does not appear, that suspicion did at any time attach itself to this man up to the very day of his giving evidence, he continued in the service of his former master, and it is to be observed, in the next place, that the torture of the deceased took place at the end of March and beginning of April, and this man's evidence was taken not until the beginning of May, and then, no inquiry into any theft was being instituted, so that *I do not see why he should then be anxious to bring the charge of ill-treating the deceased home to the defendants.* I am not certain that I fully understand the remarks of the Court relative to this man, but after giving them all the consideration in my power, I refer to the authentical manner in which the argument is put, that the evidence of an approver is to be considered as entitled to more credit than that of an ordinary witness, as the former is under a special obligation to disclose the whole truth. I always thought that every witness was under the obligation of an oath to do so, and should think that an ordinary witness under the obligation of an oath, was more likely to tell the truth than an approver—a party to the crime, under the special obligation to tell the truth, on the pain of being placed again in the felon's dock—*with regard to the improbabilities in this man's evidence.* I can only say, that *I am credulous enough to believe them all;* and with regard to *the gross contradictions*, the Court do not say, whether the man contradicted himself or other witnesses. Even the learned counsel, for some of the

defendants, Mr. Clarke, does not accuse him of the former, and the points on which he contradicts the other witnesses, as given by Mr. Clarke, to which tent the parties accused of the theft were first taken on the return of His Highness from hunting on the day of the theft, the position in which they were bound, the medicine applied to the wounds, and the manner in which they were conveyed from one halting place to another. In my humble opinion, *contradictions upon these immediate points, rather make for the truth of the material points deposed to*, particularly when it is borne in mind, that his evidence before the Judge was much more detailed than that before the Magistrate, and that his evidence upon nearly all the above points was elicited by questions from the Court or the counsel for the prisoner. For instance, when this man said, the men were bound hand and foot, he was called on by the Court to show the position they were in, which he did. However, this person was not a mere "casual observer"—as the other three rejected witnesses were, and if his evidence is contradicted by them on minor points, it is entitled to be believed in preference. It no where is asserted, to the best of my knowledge, that the evidence of this man is contradicted by evidence considered trustworthy by the Court.

5. The other three witnesses are rejected, because their evidence is contradicted by other evidence better entitled to credit. This is conclusive. But I must be allowed to observe, that in their remarks upon the evidence of these men, the Judges have thrown doubts on a point, which was not denied by the accused themselves, viz., the presence of these men in the camp. It would appear that the Judges have overlooked a petition presented to the Magistrate by the defendants, in which they allege that two of the five witnesses I withdrew, were not present in the camp at all, and ask permission to prove they were not there. Now surely had the three witnesses, rejected by the Court, not been there, a similar petition would have been given them before the Magistrate, and as surely, evidence would have been offered by the learned counsel for Aman Ali Khan to show that the very witnesses who deposed to his client "having instigated and participated in the outrage," were not in the camp at all.

6. Another point calling for remark is, that these witnesses being "casual observers," were not likely to be able to depose to particulars after such a lapse of time, but with all deference I would submit that the death of the parties, whom these persons depose to having seen beaten, very shortly after the ill-treatment, being, as allowed by the Judges themselves, "a matter of notoriety ;" and these three witnesses having, according to their own uncontradicted statement, accompanied the camp for more than two months from first to last, it is very probable, nay, I may say certain, that the subject would be frequently discussed, and those things which would not have been remembered, perhaps, by a mere passer-by, became fixed in their memory ; should not the same objection apply to some of the evidence relied on by the Court, especially to that of Hadjee Monnah ?

7. Allowing, however, that the evidence of these four witnesses is unworthy of any or the least credit, and putting it aside altogether, I do maintain, as I said before, that *there is evidence sufficient to bring the charge of privity home to all the parties who have been released*. I would consider first the case made out against the defendants, excepting Aman Ali Khan.

8. The charge which I maintain to be fully proved against these persons is thus defined by the Court of Sudder Nizamut, in a Circular, No. 8, dated 7th June, 1857.—" The act which constitutes ' privity' in this country, corresponds with the misprision of felony in English law, viz., the concealment of a felony which a man knows, but never assented to, or the observing silently the commission of a felony without using any endeavours to apprehend the offender; it is, therefore, strictly an offence of a negative kind—consisting in the concealment of something that ought to be revealed;' and again, a little lower down. "The one (viz., privity) is in its kind negative, and requires nothing but silent, passive acquiescence in the commission of a felony to constitute it."

9. Now, I submit that to prove a crime of this "negative" nature, circumstantial evidence is the species of evidence most to be relied on; by circumstantial evidence, I mean direct evidence of certain minor facts, which, if unexplained by any other evidence, proves that it is impossible, but that the parties should have known of the felony. Now the facts of this nature in the present case, as either allowed by all, or fully proved by evidence considered trustworthy by the Court, are these: In the camp of His Highness, there were three tents, and three only; these were pitched in a line, in the centre was the tent of the Nawab, on the one side that of Aman Ali Khan, on the other that of the defendants who have been released, and of two of the defendants who have been punished, close outside this tent (" two or four cubits distant," one witness, Mahomed Ameen, calls it), was pitched a pale, in that pale for some days, the deceased were, in it *they received medical treatment for their wounds*, and in it they died. Their bodies, frightfully lacerated, and "raw all the way down," as the witness, George Shapcott, deposes. Now, with all this array of facts against all the inmates of the tent, and in the absence of any attempt to explain them, the Court have declared them not guilty of *privity*, or, in other words, *it is not proved* that these men "concealed anything that ought to be revealed."

10. But there is evidence against them. The eunuch, Mahomed Ameen, whose testimony has been considered trustworthy by the Sudder Court, went to the tent of the Meahs on two occasions, when the deceased were being ill-treated on the first day, and the day after. This witness had been out shooting with the Nawab on the morning of the day of the alleged theft, and had returned with the retinue, so that the Meahs were in the camp at this time, and in the absence of any attempt to prove that they were not in their own tent, it is a fair presumption, that they were there. This witness went there and saw Burra Sahib and Mogul Jan beating the deceased, one of whom was bound, and both were in the tent of the Meahs. He does not say he saw any of these latter; but as I said in my written reply, this man was a most unwilling witness for the prosecution, and had evidently a wish to screen his fellow-eunuchs. He went the next day to the Meahs' tent a second time; this time he did not go inside, but he saw the deceased in the verandah of the tent; the hands of one of them tied to the tent-pegs. Some of the Meahs at this time were inside, and some were outside the tent, but this man could not remember any of their names; he could only

remember that he saw the Urzbegy Syud Eman Ali and his servant. Now surely, it can hardly be said, that all this beating and binding could take place inside the tent, in the verandah of the tent, and the inmates thereof know nothing about it. But so it has been held by the Sudder Court. Neither the evidence from the acknowledged facts of the case, nor that borne by Mahomed Ameen has been considered sufficient to make out even a *primâ facie* case against these men, for it must be remembered that (with the exception of Afreen) they have only called evidence to character. I repeat, that *with all due reference to the Judges of the Sudder Court, every inmate of the Meahs' tent has been proved to be guilty of privity.* I say, that to **suppose** they knew nothing of the torture and subsequent death of **the deceased, is to suppose something more extraordinary than any inconsistency apparent in the evidence of the four rejected witnesses. That they concealed whatever they knew from the proper authorities is evident** from the whole case.

11. But *although I believe these men all to have been guilty of concealing the felony, I think that the ends of justice would have been fully answered by a slight fine,* for I consider them to have been completely **under the** orders of the chief eunuch, Aman Ali Khan. I make this observation *on the supposition that privity alone is proved.* The Court having rejected the evidence that proved an active participation.

12. I come now to consider how Aman Ali Khan is *affected by the evidence as to the charge of privity.* The Court have recorded the following "as regards the charge of privity to the crime, we would remark that there is no direct evidence to the fact of the prisoner, Aman Ali Khan, (37) taking any part, or being directly or indirectly concerned, either in the burying of the bodies, **or in** giving currency to the report **of the** thieves having died of cholera. *The mere possibility* that the rumour **of the** death of **these men** reached **the ears of** the prisoner (37), **is not** in itself sufficient **to** bring home **to him the** charge of concealing, **or procuring** the concealment, of the **felony;** *to establish such a charge,* **there need** *be some* **proof** *that,* **though not** *consenting, he was personally cognisant of* **the crime, and, though able,** *refrained from preventing it,* **or** *neglected* **to use any endeavour for the apprehension of the offenders.** Now, **I** am **quite** prepared **to** allow, that there is *no evidence* direct or indirect **to** show that Aman Ali Khan took any part in the burial of the deceased, or in spreading the report of their death from cholera. But surely, the charge of **privity** may be brought home to him by evidence **in** other points than **these.** I maintain there is abundance of proof **to** show that he was personally cognisant of the ill-treatment of the deceased—in fact, he confesses it—he allows that *on two occasions, he sent persons to forbid it;* as **to** his neglecting to use any endeavours for the apprehension of the offenders, it **is** patent on the record that he never did so. It must **be borne in** mind that this man produced no evidence to explain anything, **he** merely produced evidence **to** character, which evidence has **had no share** in producing his acquittal, as it is not alluded to in the judgment. It follows, then, **that *in*** *the opinion of the Court, there is **not** sufficient **evidence direct, indirect,** or presumptive to warrant this man having **been put upon his trial.*** What that evidence is, I will now endeavour **to show.**

13. First, I would call attention to the facts as either allowed or deposed to. This man was the Dewan of the Nawab, he was consequently the second in rank in the camp; he had a tent of his own. on the other side of the Nawab's tent, from that of the Meahs' tent; they were all pitched in the immediate vicinity of one another. This man had *the general superintendence* of all matters during this hunting excursion, to him it would appear all matters were referred. At Nowguriah, for instance, when the defendant, Fureed Khan, was about to carry off a driver of one of the game-carts. Shapcott interfered, saying, "You shall do nothing until the Khan Sahib comes." This being an appellation of Aman Ali. Again, *when the deceased are being ill-treated on two occasions*, the matter is reported to Aman Ali Khan, and *he sends orders to the parties to desist.* This man *every day, from the date of the seizure of the deceased to the day of their death accompanies His Highness out shooting*, his companions on these occasions being some of the inmates of the eunuchs' tent, added to this, "the notoriety" of the events, for as the Judges say in another part of their judgment, "The notoriety of the events, which form the grounds of this case must have made them known to many who were present with the Nawab's camp." Yet with all this, *it is not allowable to presume that Aman Ali Khan knew of the death of the deceased in consequence of the treatment they had received.* I submit, that in the absence of all evidence to explain the above circumstances consistently with his own innocence, there arises a strong natural presumption of Aman Ali's guilt. I maintain that to suppose this person *ignorant of the cause of death* of the deceased, is to make a supposition inconsistent with the admitted circumstances of the case, *I say, that we have direct evidence to show that Aman Ali Khan is guilty of privity.* By which I mean, that *we have direct evidence of some facts which render it impossible to believe that this man never knew that a felony had been committed.*

14. Did the evidence go no further than this? I should, with all deference, think it "sufficient to convince the minds of all reasonable men beyond all reasonable doubt," but the evidence goes much further. In my opinion, there are two facts which bring the guilt of *privity* home to the accused, without the least doubt. These facts are : 1st. that he *knew* of the beating on the first and second day, proved by his own admission and by the evidence relied on by the Court. 2nd. That *he gave orders to the camel-drivers to go to the Burra Sahib for orders*, and *his* orders were to take one of the deceased to Nowguriah. To take them in order.

15. It appears, as given in the judgment, that the deceased were beaten for several days in succession, between the 31st March, the date of the alleged charge, and the 5th of April, the date of the death of Hingoo. The ill-treatment did not apparently continue for more than three or four days, as it would appear from the evidence of Bhughabun Ghose, the apprentice, that *the deceased were under medical treatment*, while the encampment was at Allal, *in fact, they were not beaten after they left Puranpore.* Now the time the encampment was at Puranpore *was four days;* and we have the admission of Aman Ali Khan, that *he knew of the beating on the first and second days. Now suppose there had been evidence to implicate* one *of the defendants, as participating in*

the ill-treatment, only on these two occasions, would he have been released by the Court, and acquitted of all share in the homicide? Would not the Court have said, in a case of this nature, where the ill-treatment extended over four days, *it is impossible to say at what particular time these poor wretches met with the injuries that were actually fatal to life?* It is proved that *you ill-treated them two days out of the four, and therefore you are as guilty as an accessory in the culpable homicide of the parties.* Apply this to Aman Ali; he knew that the parties were beaten two days out of the four, (but how far the ill-treatment had proceeded it is impossible to say, for within *a week from the last occasion the parties died*), having been in the interior within a few paces of the tent occupied by this man's daily companions, and yet the Judges say, *"It is an unfair construction of the acts of Aman Ali to presume that he was necessarily aware that death was the consequence of such ill-treatment."* I submit, that *it is a most fair presumption to suppose, that, as the ill-treatment was twice reported to this person,* subsequent occurrences were reported too, and that in the absence of the least attempt to explain anything whatever, *"Enough has been proved to warrant a reasonable and just conclusion against him."*

16. I am not sure that I understand the meaning of the expression, "an unfair construction of the acts of Aman Ali," &c. *As far as I understand the matter, I put no construction upon his acts, in any way different from that put upon them by the Court.* What I do is *to draw inferences* from those acts, *to show that he must have known of the death of the deceased,* having confessedly, on two occasions, heard of their ill-treatment.

17. I proceed now to consider the evidence affecting **Aman Ali Khan** given by the two witnesses of the defendant, Fureed **Khan**. I maintained as mentioned by the Court, and do maintain, that this evidence *implicated* Aman Ali Khan most seriously, and I infer from the strenuous efforts made by Mr. Longueville Clarke, the learned Counsel for Aman Ali, to throw discredit upon it, that that was his opinion also, yet the Court says, "*that taken as it stands, it does not go far enough to show that the prisoner* (37) *was aware for what purpose the camels were required.*' *The Court are not quite correct* in saying that from the third witness nothing was elicited. The witnesses were four in number, from the first nothing was elicited inculpating Aman Ali, from the second and third evidence inculpatory was elicited, and the evidence of the remaining one was not taken at the desire of the defendant—calling him. It appears from the evidence of these and other witnesses, that it had been at one time the Nawab's intention to go to a place called Nowguriah from Purranpore, and to that place Shapcott, with others, had gone in advance. His Highness afterwards changed his mind, and determined not to go to Nowguriah, but to Allal instead; it therefore became necessary to recall the advance camp to Purranpore; *for this purpose, partly, at about eleven o'clock at night, two camels were ordered to be got ready.* **The drivers went to Aman Ali's tent to ascertain whether the order they received was correct or not. They received for answer, from himself, that they were to go to the Burra Sahib and do what he told them. They went, and were ordered to take a letter** to the Mooshieff Jeehun Lal at Nowguriah, and to take a man who was put in charge of Furreed Khan, one of the camel drivers. Now it is

admitted that *the person called the Burra Sahib is not one of the Nawab's retinue at all,* why, then, should he be the person to give any direction about the change in the Nawab's plans? *But he was, by all accounts, the most active instrument in the torture of the two deceased, he was the first to arrest Muddee.* **On every** *occasion of ill-treatment he was present;* **he saw them die, and ordered their** *burial.* When, then, we find persons referred to this man, by name, for directions, when we find one of the deceased immediately given into their charge, is it not a fair presumption, in the absence of any explanation, that the person referring these parties to such a man knew what would be the consequence of their going to the Burra Sahib for orders? As for the assent of Aman Ali Khan to what took place at Nowguriah, the Judges quite misunderstood me if they thought that I inferred such assent from what was deposed to by the witnesses whose evidence I am now considering. Assent would have made him an accessory. Privity, as defined by the Court, is " the concealing a felony which a man knows, *but never assented to.*" To bring the charge of privity home to Aman Ali Khan, it is not necessary that he should be responsible in any way for the ill-usage at Nowguriah; what I maintain is, that there is every *presumption* that he knew why the camels were sent to Nowguriah. There would be no weak presumption that *he knew it from the very situation that he held in the camp of the Nawab;* to this is added the testimony of the two witnesses, that *he ordered them to go to the Burra Sahib for orders,* a man *not connected with the Nawab's household, but the most active in the torture of the deceased,* these facts, I submit, induce a strong suspicion of guilt, and where " the accused might, if he were innocent, explain those circumstances consistently with his own innocence, and yet does not offer such explanation, a strong natural presumption arises that he is guilty, and in general when a party has the means of rebutting and explaining the evidence adduced against him, if it tends to the truth, the omission to do so furnishes a forcible inference against him."

18. Surely the facts deposed to by these witnesses do bear me **out in the opinion that** Aman Ali Khan is seriously implicated thereby. **No explanation** whatever is offered. None could be offered, I presume, for the efforts of the learned Counsel were mainly directed to throw discredit on the testimony, and in that he has been successful; but, *taken as it stands, the Judges say, it is not sufficient to bring the charge of privity, even home to Aman Ali Khan. They cannot draw any conclusion from it condemnatory of the accused, for he had no motive for ill-using the thieves, and it is in evidence, that he endeavoured to prevent their ill-usage.*

19. With *respect to motives*—I think that considering the position held by the accused, *he may be thought to have been interested in the discovery of the theft* said to have taken place in the camp, where he managed everything, **and in the** immediate vicinity of his own tent, and he certainly **knew** on two occasions, by his own admission, that the persons accused were ill-treated to make them point out the property. So that even allowing that *he had no personal motive for ill-treating them,* it is admitted, that he knew they were ill-treated, and as for his endeavours *to prevent their ill-treatment,* is it to be believed, that the notoriously powerful Aman Ali Khan, the favorite eunuch and Dewan of the Nawab, could not have put a stop to the

ill-usage, had he been really in earnest? Even had he not been able to do so, there were the police in the very village, whom he might have called to his aid. I do maintain that to allow this man knew of the ill-usage on two occasions, and knew no more, that he told the camel-drivers to go to the Burra Sahib for orders, and did not know what those orders were to be, is to suppose something far more improbable than anything deposed to by the rejected witnesses.

20. I would again call attention to the definition of privity, as given above in Para. 8, to prove a crime of this negative nature, the crime of concealing something known. Evidence tending to prove such knowledge is, of course, necessary, and if there is no evidence to prove that the person charged confessed his knowledge of the felony, *the evidence from facts tending to prove that he must have known it, is of peculiar value.* Such evidence, I maintain, **we have in this case.** The acknowledged facts of this case, independent of direct testimony, do, in my opinion, bring home to Aman Ali Khan, and the other eunuchs, the guilt of privity. For it must be borne in mind that no explanation whatever is offered of anything. Surely in the absence of any explanation or contradiction, enough has been proved to warrant a just and reasonable conclusion against the accused. Surely the evidence is of such a nature as to exclude to a moral certainty, every hypothesis, but that of their guilt of the offence imputed to them.

21. I have now, in conclusion, to express a hope, that *I have said nothing in these remarks at all showing a want of respect towards the Judges who have released the accused.* Should there be *anything at all approaching to disrespect,* I can only say, it is unintentional, *it is the judgment I attack, not the Judges.*

22. I trust I may be allowed to express my opinion that the Magistrate, Mr. Carns, in the preparation of this case generally has evinced great care, and he was of essential service to me in the conduct of it, from his intimate acquaintance with all the circumstances as deposed.

I have, &c.,
E. J. TREVOR,
(True copy)
Under-Secretary to the Government of Bengal.

PROCEEDINGS *before* the *Sessions-Judge,* MR. D. J. MONEY, *containing the Speeches of* LONGUEVILLE CLARKE, ESQ., *Barrister-at-Law, and* W. A. MONTRIOU, ESQ., *Barrister-at-Law, Counsels for the Defence, and the Reply of* E. J. TREVOR, ESQ., C.S., *Prosecutor on behalf of the Government; together with the Report submitted by the Sessions-Judge, and the Judgment of the* **Nizamut Adawlut.**

September 7th, 1853.

Mr. Longueville Clarke addressed the Court to the following effect:—

"I have the honour of appearing before the Court on behalf of five of the thirteen prisoners now under trial.

"The names of my clients are Aman Ali Khan, Jowaher Ali Khan, Mussurut Ali Khan, Meah Bellal, and Meah Ekbal, and they are arraigned on six counts; but against the first only there is a seventh count.

"The first and second counts charge them all with being principals and accessories to the murder of Hingoo and Muddee. The third charges them with being privy to the crime, but what legal offence this count is intended to describe, my experience is too limited to enable me to determine, for the language is defective, and the object is vague. The fourth count accuses them of torturing and beating, which only amounts to aggravated assault, as it does not allege that death was the result. The fifth count alleges that they were accessories to the crime charged in the fourth. To the sixth count, the observations I have made on the third are equally applicable, and the seventh, which charges Aman Ali Khan alone with issuing orders for the beating and torturing is as regards him a mere repetition of the fifth count.

"Having analyzed the charges, I cannot enter on the merits of the cause without gratifying myself by expressing to the Court my deep feeling of obligation for the manner in which this trial has been conducted, a conduct which has been alike beneficial to my clients, and to me of the most important assistance, and while the tone which has prevailed, and the aid which has been rendered have equally supported the dignity of Court, and evinced its humanity, I shall have to comment on the course which Mr. Trevor has adopted in regard to some of the witnesses, of which I will now merely say that it was alike honourable to the prosecution as it was considerate towards the prisoners, while both he and Sumbhoonauth Pundit have in the kindest manner rendered me valuable service by their interpretations, and allowing me the inspection of the documents.

"I am anxious to call the attention of the Court in the first instance, to the leading points of the case on which the prosecution must rest.

"*Every concomitant by which atrocious murders are characterized, is not only wanting, but has actually been reversed in the story which the Court must believe before a verdict of guilty can be pronounced.* Suddenness, solitude, and secrecy are the distinguishing marks of the worst murder: but this murder, according to the evidence, has been the most prolonged, the most public, and the easiest of detection and conviction that the annals of *perjury* can show has ever been attempted to be proved.

"About eight days was the time that this flogging, burning, and torturing was said to have occupied. It began at Purranpore, it was repeated at Nowguriah, then again at Purranpore, from which the victims were carried to Alall, and the scene closes at Gajotee.

"There was no secrecy, for the passers-by and all the camp could see, and the camp contained about four thousand persons.

"But as if all this was not sufficiently monstrous, one witness swears that the wretched men were brought into His Highness's tent, whose permission was solicited to blow them away from a gun; others swear that during the whole time they were kept tied within twelve cubits of the Nawab's tent, and that he must have heard their nightly screams. All this is represented to have been done by the orders of my client, Aman Ali Khan, yet *it is not contended that he could have had any motive* for such unheard of cruelty. The stolen property did not belong to him nor does it appear that the accused had in any way given him offence. He is the favourite of the Nawab, the Head of the Palace, that is known, and that I admit; for it constitutes the first step in my defence, it is the key which unlocks the mysteries of this case. Was there ever a favourite yet, was there ever a successful courtier, who had not in the Palace a hundred implacable enemies, who considered his honours to be a robbery of their rights?

"I say that this is the case here, and *it is palpable to common sense* The details of the story are too monstrous for belief.

"Aman Ali Khan had *neither object nor motive*, he had not anything to gain but all to lose; the abhorrence of *a humane master* the vengeance of a vigilant Government, the detective qualities of a talented European neighbourhood—can it be believed that devoid of motive, without loss to annoy, or insult to provoke, he would have braved this array and dared the gallows?

"If then I prove that Aman Ali Khan is not guilty, from the absence of all motive, the certainty of detention, and the dread result which must have followed, *it is a much more easy task to prove why the charge has been made which so reeks with conspiracy and perjury* I ask a question of the Court, is it not true that Mr. Carnac, the magistrate, has been taxed, overwhelmed, and oppressed with having sixty-eight witnesses vomited on him, as I allege, by the plotters in the palace? It is true, the Calendar proves that. Is it not true, that of these sixty-eight witnesses, only about twenty have been called by the Government prosecutors, and the rest abandoned? It is true, the record of the Court proves that. *It is not true that of the twenty examined, five of them were declared by Mr. Trevor to be unworthy of belief, and one of the five was committed by the Judge for perjury?* The records of the Court will again prove that that is true.

"Whence then has all this scene of perjured iniquity arisen? Not from Aman Ali Khan, whose innocence is his best defence, but from the plotters in the palace, whose success depended on the ruin which they hoped by conspiracy and perjury to effect

"I now proceed to remark on the evidence in detail, and will commence by observing that I shall not detain the Court with any comments on the statements of the five witnesses who were rejected by the prosecutor, namely, Shaik Methoo, Khyrattee, Subzeeferosh Joomuck Doctor, and Jeebun Pattan. What they said cannot affect my clients, but must damage the general credit of the case which they have attempted to support.

"The first witness put into the box was Dhunnoo Shaik, and the account he gives of himself, independent of discrepancies, must taint the whole of his evidence. He admits that twelve years ago he was, in consequence of the Darogah's report, discharged from the Police of which he had been a burkundaz: since that time he has been a wanderer, and without any employment, subsisting by begging and being an itinerant vendor of smoke, that he had delayed giving information at other thannahs, but hearing, as he says, that the Darogah was inquiring for him, he voluntarily came forward in the hope of earning a good name, and becoming an oomedwar. Having clothed himself with these qualifications, he would have the Court believe that he went to the door of the Nawab's tent, stood within a cubit and a half of His Highness's person, heard him deliver his directions, yet none of the body-guard or numerous attendants drove him from the place or even ordered him to retire. In his statements, Dhunnoo Shaik alleges that the Nawab returned on the day of the alleged theft at one o'clock, and that the arrest of the suspected parties took place about an hour before, yet it is proved by witnesses far more creditable that it was the custom of His Highness to remain out until four, five, and six o'clock, that on this day he returned about five, and that the arrest of the suspected parties was about nine in the morning. Now these mistakes are too palpable to admit of any other solution than that the witness could not have been in the camp at the time to which he deposes.

"This witness stated before the magistrate, that Aman Ali Khan had said to His Highness, if you will give the order, I will have the thieves blown from a gun; but in this Court he never mentioned that such a request had been preferred to the Nawab; on the contrary, he represents it as a direct threat to the thieves from Aman Ali Khan, and when asked to reconcile this discrepancy, he attributes it to a blunder of the magistrate's writer. But I will not detain the Court with further comment on such evidence.

"The second witness, Hingoo Khan, was a beggar in a pitiable state of frightful leprosy, and he admitted that the Darogah had sent for him at the instigation of the discarded burkundaz and aspiring oomedwar. The offspring was worthy of the accoucheur, and if possible surpassed him in improbabilities and discrepancies He alleges that as early as twelve o'clock in the day, he saw Aman Ali Khan cutting a bamboo and beating the thieves at the tent of the Meahs, yet before the magistrate *he swore that he did not see anyone beat*, but heard the Khan give orders to beat, whereon he was frightened and ran away. It will also be observed that this witness does not depose to either of my clients, Mussurut Ali Khan or Meah Bellal, beating, or ordering, or taking any part in the alleged transaction. It has been distinctly proved by George Shapcott, who has been nine years in His Highness's service, that it would have been inconsistent with the rank of Aman Ali to have gone to the tent of the Meahs; and is it then possible to believe that he would still further have degraded himself by personally chastising a thief? I pass over such evidence.

"The *next witness* comes forward under circumstances of grave suspicion. The stolen property had been under his care, and stealing or negligence might be imputed to him. He was personally interested in warding off imputation, or detecting the thief, and it must, therefore, all throughout have been his anxious object to achieve them; accordingly we find him immediately accusing Burra Shaib and Mogul Jhan of having practised a joke on him, which they deny. He never suspected Muddee or Hingoo, nor mentioned their names, yet within a quarter of an hour, Burra Shaib produces Muddee as the thief, but on what ground, or for what reason, no explanation has been given. As far as the Court knows, Burra Shaib may have pounced upon the first man he met with for good reasons of his own, and lost no time in administering punishment, as if the guilt of his victim were beyond a doubt. The Court will not forget that *Burra Shaib is in the service of some Begum, and fled on inquiry being instituted.* It will also be found that Hossainee in no one respect whatsoever inculpates his master Urjoomund. If this be **false**, it taints all his evidence; **but if it be** true, as I believe it strictly **is, then can it** be credited that **Aman Ali,** who had sustained no loss, **should** cause a cruel murder **to be** committed while **the** man who **was** plundered was forbearing **and for**giving.

"This **witness will be found to** contradict the two former witnesses, Dhunnoo **Shaik and** Hingun Khan, for he states that on the return of **the** hunting party, His Highness retired to his tent, Aman Ali to his own, and the Meahs **to** theirs, from which the Meahs proceeded to Aman Ali Khan's tent **to** inform him of the theft, and it was then he gave the orders to beat. How can this be reconciled with the evidence which represents the thieves having been taken by Aman Ali to the tent of the Nawab, and Aman Ali having gone to the Meah's tent, and **with** his own hand inflicted punishment? Of the three stories two must be false, or is it not more probable that all three are untrue? Yet these men are the three first witnesses for the prosecution, and is it on such evidence that men are to be hanged?

"Here let me solemnly declare, that in regard to my five clients, **as I** view the case **on the one hand, and** weigh the evidence on the other, the eternal and undeviating principles of mercy and of justice demand from the Court an entire acquittal, or capital punishment. Mercy will always free those against whom perjury may have conjured up suspicion, but justice will administer the worst of punishment to the miscreants **who murder by torture.**

"**The language is as true as it is bold, but such is my confidence in** my case, **that I should have ill discharged my duties had I employed** expressions less decisive.

"Again, the statements by this witness of the position of the thieves, **with arms and legs** stretched out, laid on their backs, their feet held up, **and** beaten **on** the **soles of** the feet, and above all, the brandy which the doctor gave them to **drink,** and also applied to their bodies —and mixed with their poultices—are inconsistent with, or are contradicted by the evidence of all the other witnesses, and I may here shorten the matter by concluding these remarks with calling the attention of the Court to the statement of the various vehicles which this witness and also each of the other witnesses, describe to have been the means of conveyance by which the accused were transported from one spot to another. No two of them agree.

"**And now passing** over Methoo and Khyrattee, who were rejected **by the prosecutor, it is my province** to introduce and point the consideration of the Court **to the merits** of Shaik Ruheem Ali, the cook. **He had** never been employed **in** the Nawab's service, nor ever joined the camp before, but he swears in the commencement of his evidence that he made jugy soup for His Highness. This is modified afterwards to pounding the ingredients, and finally dwindles down to watching the boiling of the pot. When His Highness eschews jugy soup, the favourite courtier takes to curry, and more unaccountably, he takes to the ticca cook to make it. Now, if I could believe this story, and if it were proved that the Khan had disapproved of ticca cook's curry, then I could be tempted to believe that the ticca cook, being an injured individual, and having more prudence than courage, sought reparation for the insult by the safer course of the law and the rope, than by cookery or the hazardous experiment of a sop in the pan.

"I implore the pardon of the Court for the lightness of these observations, but I am uncontrollably overcome by the immeasurable absurdity of our ticca cook's history of himself, the exploits he performed, and the evidence which he has dished up, and which he believes the Court will swallow. But let me point out a few of his inconsistencies. Look to his answer to the Court about the orders of the 9th of May and the 14th of June; look to what he says that the theft was discovered at half-past six o'clock a.m. precisely, whereas Shaik Hossaince, who lost the property, did not discover the robbery till nine This cook told the magistrate that Aman Ali and the Meahs lived in the same tent; he describes what Affreen and Meer Ekbal did, yet he could not see from the Karkhannah what was going on, and he swore in contradiction to every witness that His Highness and Aman Ali rode on the same elephant. I ask the Court is this man to be believed? Was he ever in the camp at all, or has he been recruited as the leper was by Dhunnoo Shaik, that Alpha of the prosecution and the Darogah's domdeen?

"The seventh witness sworn was Shaik Aman Ali. I pass him over as he was merely called for as a matter of form.

"The eighth witness only, Jingoo, speaks of one of my clients, Mussurut Ali, and all the offence he proves against him is, that from the distance of an arrow's flight, he saw Mussurut following a crowd. It were idle to detain the Court with commenting on evidence which does not support any of the charges preferred.

"The ninth witness, George Shapcott, gave in my humble judgment, evidence alike unquestionable as to probability of fact and honesty of motive. I will not comment on his statements, I leave them to the judgment of the Court; but if they obtain the credit I think they deserve, they must disprove the leading points of the case for prosecution, and secure the acquittal of my clients. I would particularly point to the character he has given of Aman Ali Khan, and which I will incontrovertibly confirm by other evidence

"The tenth witness, Dhoolob Hurkaru, saw blows given, but cannot name who gave them I have not denied, nor will I deny, the savage treatment which these unfortunate victims suffered from Burra Shaib, and the camel-driver, and others. My case is, that my clients were neither act nor part in these cruelties, and I pass over the evidence of this witness as not impugning them in the least.

"The eleventh witness, Gousee Chobdar, speaks only to one of my clients beating, that is Meah Bellal. I ask the Court to turn to his evidence, it amounts to an improbable story. He says that in the morning he **saw the thieves** taken towards the Mangoe Tope. He recognised ten **persons with the** thieves, all of whom he names, and adds there were **many** others; of these he singles out seven as inflicting blows, and **one of** them Ekbal, he particularizes as not beating. This is absurd **on the** face of it, as a man after a lapse of five months could **not possibly pick** out seven men from a large crowd who were **beating, and one** who was not. Such evidence is palpably **the offspring not of fact, but of** fancy, and the Hall of Justice is not the nest in which fancy can **be** permitted to breed.

"The twelfth witness who **was sworn, Shaik** Shoobuter, is one of rejected of **the** prosecution.

"The thirteenth witness, Shaik Jaylee, **the Gharreewan,** in no way affects my clients, and the fourteenth **witness, Hajee Newmash,** comes under the same class.

"Ameer Alie **was** the fifteenth witness who was called before the Court, and if **this** person, who was produced for the prosecution, is believed, there is an end of the story of Dhunnoo Shaik and Hingun Khan, as to Aman Ali having gone **to the tent of** the Meahs, for he says, 'I did not see Aman Ali **go to the tent of** the Meahs; but they used to go to him, and whenever he gave any orders he used to send for them.' This fully corroborates George Shapcott's statement regarding the position and rank of Aman Ali in the camp. Again Ameer Ali contradicts all the witnesses who allege that Meah Bellal was one of the party who took the thieves to the river, and who joined in beating them. He states that there were five persons who did it, and he named them all, and pointed them out, and Meah Bellal was not among them; but Shaik Hossainee the approver was, and in this he is confirmed by the eleventh witness, Gousee Chobdar. This fact is not more important than probable. It not only throws a doubt on all Hossanie's evidence, **but is also a positive contradiction ; and can any**thing be more probable than that the man to whom blame, if not suspicion, attached, **as the stolen property had been in his charge, should** join in the **beating which was inflicted to compel its restoration.**

"The sixteenth **witness, Mahomed Ameer, confirmed Ameer Alie re**garding Aman Ali Khan not **having gone to the tent of the Meahs,** and distinctly states that had **he gone there, or beaten the thieves, or** taken them to His Highness's tent, **or asked permission to blow them** from a gun, he must have seen and **heard of it.**

"I would particularly point the attention **of the Court to** a most important statement made by this witness, that on the day of the robbery he had been out with the hunt, and on their return they were **informed** of what had taken place, and that the thieves had been captured. His Highness and Aman Ali Khan each retired to their own tents, and **the witness** proceeded to where the thieves were kept. He returned **to Aman Ali,** and stated that **the** men had been beaten, who immediately despatched a servant with orders to prevent it. The next morning it was reported that the thieves had been again beaten, and Aman Ali despatched another **servant** with similar orders. This man gave his evidence **in a fair and distinct manner**; there was no discrepancy in his evidence before **the magistrate** and the Court. His position in the **household is respectable,** for he draws a salary of one hundred a **month, and being produced** by the prosecution I have a

L

right to demand that he should be credited. I doubt that my friend Sumboonauth Pundit can find zeal enough to solicit the Court to disbelieve this most respectable of his witnesses, and fix its faith on the evidence of the Oomedwar, the leper and approver

"The seventeenth witness, Joomuck Doctor, is another of the discarded of the prosecution, and the eighteenth and nineteenth, Shaik Khagattee and Shaik Shakwee, do not affect my clients, but merely prove that one of the unfortunate victims was washed and buried.

"The twentieth witness is the fifth and last of the discarded ones; and the twenty-first, Bhugobun Ghose, the apprentice of the Doctor, does not name one of my clients, and with him the case closes.

"I shall content myself with merely calling a few witnesses to the character of my clients, for, as I can conscientiously affirm, that in my humble judgment I cannot find anything in the case against my clients which is not either too monstrous for even credulity to credit, or else has been contradicted by evidence for the prosecution. It has been often and truly said, that the besetting difficulty attendant on every case which is tried in an Indian Court, is the mass of falsehood with which the truth is invariably involved, which leads to convictions, by depriving prisoners of the benefit of doubts that in England would prove their palladium. But this can never be the case when the doubts are only reasonable but unanswerable, and can any one affirm that the revenge or intrigues which have undeniably polluted this trial with the five perjured and discarded witnesses, have not only also corrupted others whose evidence although received, is of a character that is similar. I will conclude in the language of the Nizamut Adawlut, in a case of murder and affray, decided by Sir Robert Barlow and Mr. Raikes on the 15th of last month, in which they said :—

"'In these depositions the Sessions Judge has placed implicit faith, and taken together as they stand in the record they would afford, if trustworthy, a mass of evidence quite sufficient for the conviction of the prisoners. But it is impossible to allow oral evidence of this description to pass into proof in this country, without testing its fidelity in some way, and judged by the proofs to which we have subjected it, much of this testimony becomes valueless in our estimation.'"

Mr. Montriou appeared in defence of Meah Urjoomund, Hajee Tamas, Meah Affreen, Mean Emaum Ali (Urzbegy) Mirza Mahomed Hosain *alias* Mogul Jann (Naib Meer Moonshee) read in the Court of the Sessions Judge of Moorshedabad, 7th September, 1853.

The learned gentleman spoke as follows :—

"The charges against these prisoners embrace several alternatives.— They are first charged with actually killing two persons named Hingoo and Muddee, under circumstances which constitute either murder, or culpable homicide. They are next charged as being implicated in the same crime which others have actually committed, so as to bring them within one of the descriptions.

"The prisoners are next charged with inhuman treatment or torture and beating of the same persons, without reference to their death, and the alternatives of Aânut and Razdareere added, in case their concern in the torture or beating be proved to come more properly under one of those descriptions.

"The last Count it is unnecessary for me to notice.

"In the first place, I beg to note an important rule or precaution which, the peculiar form of the record, or nutthee, in the Courts of the East India Company, makes necessary, on the same account it is perhaps difficult for this Court strictly to observe. It is this:—The only evidence which can be taken at all into consideration against the prisoners, is that which has been orally given in the face of this Court. What has been deposed to before the magistrate, or as it is called in the Foujdarree, has been used and must still be used, to rebut and contradict, or in any way to discredit what the same witness has said here; but no claim in the Foujdarree deposition can legally, or justly be treated as in evidence here against these prisoners. They must be convicted, if convicted at all, upon statements sworn to upon this trial and in this place. Nothing in those depositions becomes evidence for the prosecution unless it be in the same words repeated by the witness upon his examination here. All else must be entirely dismissed from the mind of the Court.

"The following is a short narrative or outline of the state of facts which the Government of this country, through their able and specially delegated representatives here present have endeavoured (as far as it can collect their intentions from the evidence offered), to exhibit, by proof to the judgment of this Court in this case.

"Towards the close of the month of March last, His Highness the titular Nawab Nazim of Bengal attended by a numerous establishment and suite, computed to be upwards of 2000 persons, was on a sporting excursion in the Maldah district. It would appear that all His Highness' household, all the officers and Mohurrirs of the numerous departments necessary, or usual for the state or the wants of His Highness accompanied him. In a word, the whole of the Court, household and officers of the Nawab Nazim were transferred into the Lushkar or camp to which we have now to direct our attention, and of course a numerous tribe of Omedwars, fakeers, mendicants, and vagabonds of every class followed in the train, and mingled among the crowd of this courtly, but motley assemblage. Immediately attendant upon His Highness, and filling the principal offices, were the Meahs of whom the chief in dignity was Aman Ali Khan, who appears to have been the General Naib, or Lieutenant of His Highness. Under him, in various gradations were the others, including the Darogah, or superintendent of the Elephants, and of the kitchen department, also the Urzbegy (who is not a Meah). The main business of the expedition being sport, it was the custom of His Highness to quit the camp in the early morning of each day, accompanied by his more favoured associates and attendants, and to return to his camp in the afternoon or evening usually about four or five o'clock. There were three principal tents, or Kheemas: viz., one for His Highness personally, one for Aman Ali Khan, and one for the other Meahs, with whom also dwelt the Urzbegy, Meer Emam Ali, and Mirza Mahomed Hosain, known as Mogul Jaun, and described to be Naib Meer Moonshee. One morning, somewhere about eight or nine o'clock, and while His Highness and his usual suite were out sporting on their elephants away from the camp a small box containing money and other valuables was missed from the Meah's tent; the box being in the special custody of one Hosainee, a slave or domestic Khavas of the prisoner Meah Ur' joomund. Muddee the lad, the son of one Etwarree, Khavas of the Nizamut, was seized upon some ground of suspicion, and-accused of the theft; fear or remorse, or both, combined, induced Muddee to assert that he could and would produce the missing property. He named an accomplice Hingoo Fakeer, who was thereupon also arrested.

" Information given by Muddee to discover or trace the stolen property proved to be mere pretext, and this experiment was repeated several times. Nothing whatever was discovered or found. In the meanwhile, those who were in charge of the supposed thieves, as a means of extorting the truth, and exasperated at the repeated deceptions practised upon them, and the trouble given to them by their captives, punished the latter severely, and subjected them to cruel usage, which at the end of six or seven days caused the death of both Muddee and Hingoo. They were secretly buried in the jungle. The local police would appear to have connived at the crime, for it remained (notwithstanding its notoriety in the camp of His Highness) uninvestigated and unnoticed by authority of any kind until the return of His Highness from his sporting expedition at the close of April, when, the rumours coming to the ears of the Shanuggur Darogah, steps were taken to bring the criminals to justice, which have finally led to, and ended in this trial. The persons who are said to have committed such barbarity against the helpless slave boy and mendicant, and who are now upon their trial, are the whole of the principal officers, the entire body of courtiers and dignitaries (so to speak) of the household of His Highness the Nawab Nazim; to whom are added, not as the mere servants' agents, but as companions and helpers of the other defendants in their alleged cruelty, a Mahout and a camel-driver, making in the whole thirteen accused.

" Such seems to be an outline of the case supposed or intended to be made by the evidence which has been heard. I say intended, because I do not believe that the Government Prosecutors themselves can suppose they have supported the more serious class of charges—I mean those which assume that a criminal homicide has been committed—with even *primâ facie* proof. And here I take leave to advert to what I believe to be a fundamental maxim and a guide in every Court of Criminal justice where a British judge presides ;—I may say in every country of civilized and educated men. Every man is presumed, and believed (judicially) to be innocent of a crime imputed to him until he is proved to be guilty ; and by proof here is meant complete proof —evidence which leaves no rational doubt. In merely Civil complaints, a case of suspicion is enough, if it be not met by answer and by counter-evidence, to warrant condemnation ; but not so with charges of crime. Who ever heard of a British tribunal being satisfied with *primâ facie* proof against an alleged murderer ? How infinitely various are the cases which may be supposed, where to prove innocence of crime would be impossible ; but where to impute or prove ground of suspicion is an easy task ! But I am well assured that the maxim I have noticed will not be doubted here. If the evidence of guilt has not been satisfactory, and led to an undoubted conclusion in the minds of the Court, I know that my clients will be, as they ought to be, fully acquitted. It does not, however, require the aid of this universal and well-established rule to clear the ground of the most serious crimes (as respects consequences) charged in this calendar, of which, as I have observed, a *primâ facie* case or basis of proof has not been offered. To establish homicide, the first essential and indispensable ingredient of proof is the cause of death. What pretence of proof has there been of the **cause** of death? Were it even possible that the Court could form any *definite* idea, from the whole body of the evidence, of the nature of the injuries inflicted or **said to** be inflicted, still they have no data whatever from which they can connect those injuries with the death, as cause and effect. It would, indeed, be an awful responsibility were they called upon to do so. It is for the prosecutor, by his proofs, to connect them directly and irresistibly ; and **not to leave the matter to** guess or conjecture, or possible **inference.** We have no *sooruthal,* no testimony whatever, medical or otherwise, **of the state of the** bodies of either when they died (for the miserable equivocations **of the** bheestees, Kangally and Shikhadee, throw **no** intelligent light **on this** subject), no intelligible **testimony** of the commencement, progress, or termination of any mortal **disease, nor even** of any injuries **or** ill-treatment from any particular person or persons which must have produced a mortal disease. However, it is enough for my present purpose that *the cause of death is left in doubt.* This fact alone precludes the possibility of a conviction upon the first class of counts ; and I infer from the fairness and honourable candour with which the prosecution **upon** this trial **has** been conducted throughout, that had such a course **been** allowed by **the** practice and procedure **of** this Court, those **counts** would have **been altogether** abandoned upon the **close** of the **case. As** it is I **think it** unnecessary, and that it would **be trifling with the** Court to say **more** in refutation of them than I **have said.**

"There **remains the** charge of torturing and **beating the slave-boy, Muddee, and the fukeer,** Hingoo, and of being act **and part in our conniving at that torturing and** beating. Against this **charge or series of** charges it is my **duty to defend** five of the prisoners :—1, Meah Urjoomund ; 2, Hajee Tamas ; 3, Meah Afreen ; 4, Moer Emam Ali Urzbeggy ; and 5, Mirza Mahomed Hosain, **called also Mogul Jaun. As** regards the first and second, I think **the evidence already in** proof sufficient for their exculpation. For **the others I shall** produce some testimony of collateral facts, which **will assist** the Court **in** coming to a conclusion in their individual cases respectively. The constant and **uniform** duties of the Urzbeggy upon the person of His Highness the Nawab Nazim during this hunting expedition, extending as that attendance did regularly **to** a late period of each night, rendered his commission of the offences charged against him so nearly an impossibility **as to be,** I submit, a sufficient refutation of whatever part of the charge might **otherwise** be considered proved. This attendance can, I believe, be **satisfactorily** proved, although the best evidence of the fact is obviously **not** procurable ; it **is** either **above our** reach, or at the bar of this Court. The **Meah** Afreen, it **is** already **in** evidence (but from one witness only), although attached **to** the Nizamut household, is not connected with the personal establishment of His Highness the Nawab Nazim, and formed no part of His Highness's suite in this hunting excursion. He was accidentally present with the lushkar at Hyatpoor and Purranpoor, but no further; having gone with a message and condolences of the Begum upon an occasion of an accidental hurt which occurred to His Highness. This will be proved, and will assist in refutation of the attempt to implicate Meah Afreen. The Moghul Mirza Mahomed Hosain, against whom so much has been positively and recklessly sworn, is a person of great respectability, whose father and grandfather held office under the ancestors of His Highness. His duties are of a literary and confidential character, and upon this journey it was his particular business to be in attendance upon the Khan Sahib, Aman Ali. The nature and times of that attendance will be shown, as in the case of the Urzbeggy, to be wholly inconsistent with the reckless and unmeaning conduct which the witnesses have charged him with.

"Witnesses to general character will be called, especially to that of Meah Urjoomund, whose known benevolence of heart and conduct is such and so universally attested as to place him beyond the reach of calumny; except, indeed, from persons of the station and ignorance of those who are the pillars of this unfortunate though memorable prosecution. He has ever been as much admired by the gentry and the wealthy who have been brought in contact with him, as he has been a friend to the poor and to the unfortunate. It is a remarkable feature in the mass of contradictory testimony which has been heard upon this trial, that although the witnesses have thought it necessary (for an obvious but short-sighted reason) to attempt in some way to implicate this prisoner in the facts which they came here to detail, they felt the influence of his general character sufficiently to qualify their falsehoods in various ways; and the same witness variously, at different times, in favour of Meah Urjoomund, and in favour of him alone. The most bitter of them has thus reluctantly defeated his own object: for, I believe, that even taking each witness separately untested by the damning experiment of comparison with his fellows no criminal mind can fairly be imputed to Meah Urjoomund, and all Courts have adopted the axiom of the Roman Law, *Nullus reus nisi mens sit rea.*—A criminal act cannot proceed from a harmless mind or intention.

"Before proceeding to review the evidence in detail, it will be useful to consider the kind of proof by which a charge of this nature might be expected to be supported, so as to give it at least the semblance of truth; which consideration will involve other probabilities and suppositions that will be found to bear most materially upon the case. The English Law says, (and I neither know, nor can I suppose, that either the Mahomedan *Shurrah* or the precedents of the Company's Nizamut Adawlut say otherwise), that every fact put in issue in a Court of Justice must be proved by the *best* evidence, of which, according to its nature and character, it is capable. The fact or chain of facts in issue here is, whether the highest officials and intimate associates of His Highness the Nawab Nazim, have, or have not, been guilty of murderous and wanton cruelty, not as a general charge, but in a particular specified instance; not for any purpose of ambition, revenge for personal dishonour or disgrace, from no motive of policy, but in wanton and palpably useless torture to extort a confession of the theft of the private property of the only one of them who is not shown (I am sure it will be admitted), or pretended to have taken an active part, by will or act, in the alleged torture. Again, the torture was not in secret, nor under any precautions whatever (as far as has appeared) against detection and punishment. It was in open day, in presence of some 2000, many hundreds of whom were strangers to all parties concerned; and a still larger number, by station, habits, fears and hopes, much more likely to sympathize with the sufferers than to screen the evil-doers. On the other hand, this barefaced cruelty would appear to have been unusual and isolated. Not only is this the first criminal charge brought against the associates and officers of the Nizamut, since that name became a title merely, and ceased to administer justice (because they have ceased to have subjects); and placed as they are in the trying and difficult, nay, invidious position, of possessing the pageantry, the state, the outward homage of sovereign princes, but with the rights and the responsibility of the meanest subject, with no prerogative, no *real* privilege—it is matter of surprise that, in such a position, the household, the Court of the Nizamut, should not have become amenable to the visitations of British Justice. Yet so it is. The crime now charged against them by the Government of this country is an isolated instance—one little to be expected, and said to be perpetrated by the acts and sanction of a class of men of proverbially gentle and peaceable habits, and demeanor, of whom the chief (so called) criminals have already received, out of the mouths of witnesses for the prosecution, unhesitatingly, a character for integrity and humanity. Nor can it be collected or conjectured from the evidence, that any of these, during the long interval between the commission of the alleged crime and the first official notice of it, viz., the information of the Darogah of this city, on the 30th April, acted in any way as a guilty man, especially as one possessed of means and powers would act: however, fortunately for the cause of truth, the testimony offered contains intrinsic proof that no apprehension could have existed in the minds of any of the prisoners who had the power to influence, to corrupt, or to place out of reach the witnesses of the crime. No one witness has pretended that any such attempt has been made either with regard to himself or any other person. A vague remark not amounting to evidence was, I believe, made by one of the witnesses, imputing receipt of a bribe to the local police of the Maldah District, and I do not doubt that any of the others who came here prepared to testify to the presence of the police at the scene of the crime (which was certainly the easiest mode of disposing of an obvious difficulty in the credibility of their general story) would have thought it fitting to guess at a like conclusion. This circumstance, therefore, cannot be taken to form an exception to the proposition which I have inferred and stated, and in its favour we have the presence of and remarkable deposition of the approver, the servant of Meah Urjoomund. We have, too, the khas servants of His Highness over whose affairs and household be it remembered the accused Aman Ali Khan had undisputed sway, he being, to use the significant language of the herald, Hajee Nunha. From these considerations, from these facts, are we not justified in making, are we not bound and compelled to make, the following deduction? Before men of the character and position of the principal defendants, including all for whom I appear, *can be fairly, or consistently with sound policy and good government,* placed upon their trial for offences such as those here charged against them, respectable, consistent and probable testimony must be adduced (because there exists no obstacle to its production, and it must undoubtedly exist) worthy of belief from its own intrinsic weight, irrespective of the chances or possibility of refutation, and further corroborated by the probable certainty, that, if the testimony be false or exaggerated, undoubted means exist of exculpation, without let or hindrance.

"That this deduction, this axiom I may say, is the more imperative to guide our judgment in this case, because we are wholly dependent upon that most frail, most dangerous of instruments in this country, that will-o'-the-wisp to the administrators of justice—oral evidence. We are wholly without circumstantial evidence of any kind. For even the geography of localities, for every fact, for every link of every fact which is to be the part of the chain, I do not say of condemnation, but of suspicion against the prisoners, we must look to and depend upon fleeting words, and still more fleeting memory; to them alone, without any other aid, any circumstances or *indicia*, which cannot lie whatever. We are told the men are dead; we are told of rumours why they died; we are told, in many and various and strange descriptions, of their treatment and conduct some few days preceding the alleged date of their alleged decease; we are told of the supposed reasons and motives of that treatment; but who in this Court knows (putting aside admissions of the prisoners, of which none are in evidence here) that such men ever even existed? Assaults and personal injuries to the living are proved in Courts of Justice by those who suffered them; homicide and death are proved by the production and judicial inspection of the body. I do not say that this normal rule can never be with safety departed from; far less do I intend to base the defence of my clients upon any denial of the existence or the death of either Muddee or Hingoo. It is wholly unnecessary, and therefore inexpedient, that I should do so. A great English criminal judge and lawyer, Sir Matthew Hale, is well known to have made and adhered to the rule, never to permit a conviction of murder where the body, as the best proof of the *corpus delicti*, was not forthcoming. This rule has since, in especial cases, been departed from by the English Courts, as well as by the Company's Nizamut Adawlut. My object in now alluding to this defect in the present evidence is, to illustrate the great difficulty that the Court must necessarily have in satisfying their conscience even upon the broader, notorious, and easily tested facts of the case, without other guide than oral evidence. But how much greater and more serious is the difficulty when the facts to be proved are dependent upon not merely honest and minute and careful observation and attention, upon not merely honest and unbiased, but sure and intelligent recollection!

"Let us, then, make some inquiry into the intelligence, the respectability, the consistency, and title to this great confidence (which they must be entitled to in order, not only to attach even suspicion of guilt to my clients, but *to divest this remarkable prosecution of a character of rashness and impolicy unexampled even in the history of British India*) of the persons from whose mouths the oral evidence proceeds.

And first, who are the witnesses relied on (we need not now refer to those precious *morceaux*, those examples, remarkable not for their rarity, but for their perfection as examples of audacious and seemingly unconscious mendacity, whom the Public Prosecutor has not less judiciously than honourably rejected from his proofs) in support of this prosecution? They are fifteen in the whole, viz.:—

"Two Fakeers, or beggars, one of them a leper.

"One approver, the Khawas, or slave, from whose custody the yet missing property (which Muddec and Hingoo were accused of stealing) was lost.

"One Teckâ scullion.

"Five menial attendants of His Highness the Nawab Nazim, viz., a batta burdar, a peon, a tailor, a chokedar, and a nukub, or herald.

"Then, one Christian, and certainly respectable witness, His Highness's coachman.

"A Toekâ grave-cart driver, employed under the coachman.

"Two of the camp bhistees.

"An ignorant helper to a person said to be employed as the koberaj of the camp; and lastly,

"A Meah, who is the deputy and mosahib of Aman Ali Khan. He completely exculpates the latter, and shows no disposition to affect any of the Meah's by his evidence; but he is evidently called because he is not unwilling to make a scapegoat of the Moghul prisoner.

"Now, it is not an unimportant fact, that these fifteen are selected from an enormous mass of lengthy depositions in the Foujdarry, comprising more than one hundred witnesses, of whom sixty-eight are in the calendar. They are the cream of the collection—a collection made, of course, by the efforts, or under the auspices, of that Darogah who distinguished himself by his report of the "Bazar Rumours," on the 30th April—rumours which, as he then said, accused no one, and had no definite form, but which, between that date and the commitment for trial, some six weeks hence, have ripened into the definite and intelligent testimony of these fifteen witnesses. And what have these witnesses told us? Have we heard from them one consistent tale, or one tale with unimportant narrations? Do they all, or any fair proportion of them who profess to have witnessed the same evil deeds—above all, do they inculpate the same persons as the doers of those deeds, or do they vary in this respect in a manner impossible for honesty to vary. Is there mixed up with possible truth impossible falschoods, or inconsistent statements as to matters for which the witness was unprepared? Has or has not each witness his evident bias, even on comparatively unimportant parts of his story, showing the danger of confiding in his meditated account of what actually affects the questions at issue? To the presiding Judge, and to the Muftee, I might with propriety and confidence put these suggestive questions, without actual reference to the details of that evidence which they have both so carefully noted, and have, doubtless, already most attentively weighed; but I proceed to note and compare a few of these details.

"Dhunnoo Shaik, the beggar, who carries the hookah, and who leads the race of the elect fifteen, saw, at noon of the first day, the two victims tied by their feet to separate tent-pegs, on their backs, with their hands bound behind. At this time, the Meahs, Afreen, Bellal, Ekball, Hajee Tamas, and the Moghul (whom he confounds with Meer Emam Ali, the Urzbeggy), the Mahoot, and the mysterious Burra Sahib (whom all implicate, perhaps because he is absent), were present, and in some way encouraging the Zulen. He next sees the young Khawas taken to the river by Sepoys After the return from the river, His Highness returned, viz., about 1 p.m. The suspected thieves are summoned before, and are taken to His Highness by Aman Ali Khan personally. His Highness interrogates them. The Khan Aman Ali threatened their lives before His Highness, *who ordered their release:* which order is countermanded by the Khan. Witness, on the second day, saw Muldee tied on his back as before, but Hingoo was sitting, torn and bleeding. The day after, the boy was seen to have been burnt all over his body. They were taken in two majholoe garries to Allal. Witness helped to dig the grave of the boy. Who were present at the burial, besides the two Bhestees and this witness? Burra Sahib and Shere Ali Fakeer. This witness saw all the Meahs engaged in beating.

"Hingun Khan, the leper, saw the two men tied to the tent-pegs, not of the Meah's tent, but of Aman Ali Khan, three or four ghuries before the Khan returned with His Highness from Shikar. The Meahs and a great crowd were there. The only beating which this man professes to have witnessed was inflicted by the Khan personally, at his own tent, and he evidently implies that the victims had not been beaten at all until then.

"Hossainee Shaik, the approver, gives his version of the loss of his master's box. He, of course, disclaims the slightest interference in, or encouragement of, the maltreatment of the suspected men. This slave represents the Naib Meer Monshi and Burra Sahib, men who were the companions and equals of his master, as being so terrified with his (witness's) insinuations and accusations, when he awoke and discovered his loss, that they forthwith set about hunting the camp for a thief, whom (as he now professes to believe) they falsely accused. He represents himself as paralysed with fear, and either wholly unwilling or unable (from his state of utter prostration) to take any steps to render any assistance whatever. Yet this trusty menial acknowledges, that during his eight or nine years' service with the Meah Urjoomund, he has not known or heard of his master being guilty of a single act of violence; and although he received not a single reproof from his master at Purranpore, his state of head-kawas continued to Allal, which he gives as a reason for not having seen the suspected men, or knowing anything about them at that place. He alone remained inactive; he, who knew and felt how much his own izzut at least was concerned in recovery of the property (to say nothing of his duty or gratitude to his master), he alone was tender-hearted and silent! According to this man's account, Muddee (after Hingoo being brought) was taken, before the return of the Meahs and His Highness on the first day, to the river to the Modee's shop. After His Highness's return they were taken to a garden or plantation, on which occasion the Mehter is first introduced. *He denies that they were taken to the tent of His Highness or of Aman Ali Khan.* He describes them as having been bastinadoed whilst tied with their feet up and head downwards. In his evidence here he distinctly implicates his master as approving of the beating. On the journey to Allal, according to his account, one thief was taken in a palkee, the other in a cart

Perhaps the most remarkable feature in this wretch's evidence is the mean attempt to implicate his master, who he distinctly exculpated before the Magistrate ; but he was probably not aware, when he made his Foujdarry deposition, of his master having told the Magistrate, as the truth was, that this very man, his own servant, informed him, upon his arrival in camp, of the loss of the box, and of the capture of the suspected men (one of them, Hingoo, by Hossainee himself) ; whereupon *the Meah Urjoomund,* upon hearing the ineffectual attempts to trace his property, *ordered the release of the prisoners* This man's testimony bears upon its face, to my mind the consciousness of guilt, and that his only hope of escape is by corroborating the case, made, or supposed to be made, against all the prisoners.

" Ruheem Ali, the teeka cook, or scullion, is a travelled man, who has studied divers arts in divers climes ; and it would appear that we are indebted to his former master, Mr. Porter (whom this witness asserts to be in his debt for all he earned, besides money advanced during his two months' service), for the haphazard testimony of this extra cook's-mate or scullion. According to this man's account, Aman Ali Khan was with Urjoomund when they jointly inquired, " What Tamasha is this ?" And then (*i.e.* immediately on alighting from their elephants) the former gave the order to beat. The suspected men were then (*i.e.* after the return of His Highness) taken to the river, and from the river to the Bazar, where they were beaten in the presence of a crowd, and ordered to be dragged by their feet His account proceeds, that on the second day the men were taken to a kudam-tree. It is this man who describes an occurrence, contradicted by all the others nigh, that Aman Ali Khan, before going to Shikar in the morning, stayed back, suffering the Nawab Nazim to proceed alone, whilst he went to the tent of the Meahs to give orders for beating the captives ; who thereupon were beaten by Joomun, by Peeroo Mahout, and by the Mehter (By the way, where is this Mehter, who has been several times referred to, although at different times by different persons ?) He describes a search and diving process in a small boat, not spoken to, that I am aware, by any other witness. This was on the third day, at Puranpore. It was just after this description that the witness added, " Teen duffa ya haluth hooa ;" which would appear to have been the index, in his own mind, of the several searchings and bringings back to which he had to depose, and accordingly had deposed.

" The pert and over-zealous manner of this man in the witness-box must be in the recollection of all who were present : how he overlooked the Sheristadar when writing his words ; and how, on one occasion, when he had delivered himself of what he considered a telling fact or opinion, in his anxiety to proceed he asked of the writer, ' Lieka ap ?' The manifest and important discrepancies between his Foujdarry deposition and his evidence being pointed out to him, he unhesitatingly disavowed them, and ascribed them to the writer. I request of the Court, whilst considering their judgment, not to omit making this comparison, which will alone remove all doubt (should any remain in their minds) of the utter worthlessness of this teeka vagabond's testimony. He was on the look-out for a teeka job, and he has found one doubtless as well suited to his antecedents as to his taste.

"We next have Hingoo Khan, His Highness's pandish-bearer, who must often have attended the Meahs, or at least in their presence, as the constant guests and companions of His Highness. Little could they, or indeed any of His Highness's household now at the bar of this Court, have expected to see this familiar attendant arrayed against them. But so far has the ingenuity of those enemies who have continued and originated this baseless prosecution (who will, I fervently trust, as I believe they will, ere long, be discovered, and meet with at least a portion of their deserts) triumphed. The old familiar faces, not indeed of persons of station or respectability (I use this word rather in its conventional Bengalee than European meaning and sense), but the menials who have obeyed their slightest nod, are brought here. There is something unusual and remarkable in this. One inference from it I have already drawn; another is scarcely less obvious. *These men must have been taught, and lately taught too, that the sun of these nobles of the Shahnuggur has set; that they have nothing to fear from their frowns or to hope from their good-will. But little acquaintance with the Asiatic mind is needed to trace and deduce how it is that these men are found, at the bidding of the British Sircar (through that strong arm of its power, not always righteously used, the Mofussul Police, the herd of nazirs, darogahs wogherah), bearing testimony, unthought of and unsuspected, against persons whom their young prince and master certainly does not, because he cannot with truth, accuse; but whom he, as certainly, may not assume to protect, although I do not and cannot doubt that he sympathises with them in the strait in which they are now, I venture to say, most unjustly reduced.* This man, Hingoo Khan, relates the visit to the indigo factory between the hours of nine and ten in the morning of the second day, when he particularizes the Moonshee Moghul Jan, Burra Sahib, and Joomun, as the conductors of the elephant upon which Muddee was bound, and the Meahs, Mussurut Ali and Afreen, as following at the distance of an arrow's flight, a fanciful measurement, but not difficult of comprehension as a watching distance. A remarkable statement by this man, both in the Foujdarry and here, and quite inconsistent with all other testimony to the same circumstance, is, that Muddee was brought back from Nowghurrea on an elephant, not on a camel. In the Foujdarry he added that Moghul Jan and Burra Sahib were seated on the same elephant—a still more serious discrepancy. The two depositions otherwise materially differ; and after his former deposition was read to him, this witness, nothing loth to abide by the fuller statement, declared, "What I said before the magistrate was true." But he nevertheless admitted, that what he said respecting the cause of death was *from rumour* only.

"Next is the evidence of George Shapcott, a witness, to my mind, undoubtedly credible, as far as integrity and absence of corrupt motive is concerned. Indeed, I by no means object to this man's testimony being used as a lever, a touchstone, to raise and to test the mass of incongruous statements with which the prosecutor's tale is incumbered.

How much doubt, exaggeration, and falsehood will thus be dissipated, although Shapcott's experience travels but a part of the weary journey of the alleged seven days' cruelty! From him, then, we learn that a *bonâ fide* search for stolen property was made at Nowghurrea; that the lad Muddee was taken there; that upon his apparently false information the witness Jungloo was seized, and would have shared the fate of Muddee but for the interference of Shapcott; that this interference was nothing more than the use of Aman Ali Khan's name, which effectually stayed the meditated injustice of punishing before proof or sufficient inquiry. We hear of no retort from the camel-driver that the Khan had ordered the boy to be beaten; we learn also from this witness—and it is an important fact as bearing upon the testimony of others—that the boy Muddee retracted his accusation of Jungloo at Nowghurrea and transferred all ground of suspicion to two lezes or Nautch-girls, at Purranpore; we learn that no person of authority (and Moghul Jan and Burra Sahib would have been such) were present with the boy there; that *the camel-driver was the only one of the prisoners whom he saw beat*: and considering the station, ignorance, and habits of this camel-driver, he surely cannot be very harshly judged for administering some correction to a boy who had admitted himself a thief of valuable property, and was palpably trifling with and imposing upon the servants' great and useful labour in an apparent spirit of wantonness (for I know not what rational motive to ascribe). Which of us would expect his jemadar or syces to act with leniency or philosophical forbearance in a similar position? The jemadar accused by Shapcott is, for some unexplained reason, not here. Shapcott proves that all this happened on the morning of the 28th March, viz, the seizure and release of Jungloo (for he distinctly says the boy's accusation of the latter was after, or at least during the beating), and as I understand him, the arrival at Nowgurrea of the camel which brought the boy; we are assured from his evidence that the boy did not return to Purranpore on an elephant, as insisted on by the pandish-bearer. From a subsequent part of his evidence we find that the kooberaj Joomuck and the Mehter were for some time administering remedies to the captured men; that no one of the prisoners at this bar (excepting the camel-driver in the manner mentioned) took any part or concerned themselves in the matter, so far as this witness knows (and is it possible he should not have known, if a tithe or a modicum of the stream of testimony from others were not false, and wilfully false?), that both men were buried under a cotton tree in the Maidan, within view of the stables, early in the afternoon of two consecutive days. Although the evidence of this witness not only does not implicate, but, upon the whole, is clearly exculpatory of my clients from any share in, or conduct, or sanction, of any ill-treatment whatever; for the circumstance that the accused men, with the Khawas Etwaree, were living in a pal or mat-shed three or four yards off (such is his evidence) from the Meah's tent, can surely warrant no conclusion against the innocence of the Meahs, that they were necessarily act and part in any injuries sustained by or inflicted on those men. I must yet comment on that part of Shapcott's testimony which shows the condition of the bodies of Hingoo and Muddee when he saw them under the pal. He describes the skin being off different parts of their bodies, also swelling ; no injuries to the face or head ; no wales or cutting up of the flesh ; no ulcerous openings : no pouring out of blood or matter from wounds. Now, what must be the deduction from this evidence in a judicial mind ?

" I submit they are :—

" 1. That injuries of a more serious and less superficial character than those seen and described by the witness could not then have existed.

" 3. That much of the appearances described may have been the result of unskilful medical or surgical treatment.

" And how much are these positive and necessary inferences, corroborated by comparison with the deliberate testimony of some of the others ? The teeka cook's mate, says, ' Only the eyes were visible, all the rest was one bruise.' By some their hands are described to have been frightfully lacerated, and they were burnt with hot gools. Are then the accounts of the cruel beating and torturing, and their effects, supported and contradicted by Shapeott's description ? He shows no disposition to keep back or to hesitate in describing, or to soften down his recollection of the state in which he saw them. He speaks of it as any humane man would, upon whom what he saw made a strong impression, and who would therefore be likely to give a somewhat coloured and unintentionally biased view of the object seen. He in effect disproves the circumstantial description of wounds and ill-treatment, variously and in contradictory terms certainly, but generally spoken to by the low native witnesses.

" The hurkara or peon, Doodall, returned with Muddee on the camel from Nowghurrea to Purranpore. He speaks to a carrying to the river side on (I think) the second day. He describes the two to have been tied by the tent, with their hands tied together, but the feet at liberty ; he saw them slapped and kicked, not beaten with sticks, by the Urzbeggy, by the Moonshee, Burra Sahib, Joomun and the Mahooth.

" This man's evidence needs no comment : it would seem to be an indifferently selected portion of the camp rumours ; and he does as little for the cause which he is called to support as he well can : indeed, his silence as to much which is said to have been notorious and manifest to all would be unaccountable, upon the hypothesis that either the gravamen of the charge itself, or of the varying circumstantial statements in its support, is or are mainly true as stated.

" That the Chobdar Ghassoo has belied himself, and come forward also with his portion of the camp rumours, or that Ameer Ali, the Nukub, is a pretended witness of what might or might not have happened, is an obvious and an insuperable inference from a simple list, for which neither of them were prepared. Ghassoo relates a plausible story of his accidental presence under the kudum-tree, near the tent of the Aman Ali Khan. He was sick, he bathed there, and was openly and continuously there during the day.

" The Nukub had his bester also under the same tree, but he knows nothing of the chobdar : indeed he positively denies that he was there during the intervals when he came home for his meals and rest, and when not parading the camp or the bazar. At all events, they each speak to the taking to the river-side circumstantially. This fixes the time of the presence of each under the tree ? Can there be any doubt that if several native servants had their besters at that tree, and were simultaneously looking on at such a scene as they describe, each would have been able to speak to the presence of the other, especially as there was something especial in the **presence** of the chobdar, also in his condition and occupation ? The fact I believe to be, that the Nuzub hazarded the answer that he was under the tree, little thinking why he was asked. I may almost say, *Utrum horum mavis accipe*. In truth it is impossible (without looking to other discrepancies or objections to their evidence) that either of these men can be judicially relied on. It would indeed be a hazardous responsibility to have to guess or to calculate which is to be rejected, which is the real Simon Pure.

"The only remarkable feature in the evidence of the carter Junglee Shaikh is, that it materially contradicts the trustworthy George Shapcott as to the occurrences at Nowghurrea ; a fact which must be in the recollection of the Court. This testimony, therefore, needs no comment from me. The same objection applies, but not so strongly, to the deposition of Hajee Nunha. This man implicates a new asamee, the Mooshieff Jehun Lall. He recollects the remonstrances of the wounded Meah Hajee Tamas. At Gujol, he deposes that Muddee complained to his father that his body was burning—that Muddee was attended by the Koberaj and a Brahmin, who gave him, not plaster, or ointment, or poultice, but internal medicine—something to drink, and pills.

"This man says that on the road to Allal, Hingoo travelled in a meeana, Muddee on a ruth. He describes the marks on Muddee's body at Gujol to be those which we had seen at Purranpore, viz., marks of korah and caning. Statements as of fact made by this witness in the Foujdarry he now acknowledges to be hearsay.

"The evidence of Meah Ameen shows, *inter alia*, that there was nothing remarkable in Etwarree's having a pal pitched in the neighbourhood of the Meah's tent. He distinctly contradicts those who implicate Aman Ali Khan, or the other Meahs, or the Urzbeggy, and he speaks as others do to the prevalence of cholera in the Lushkar. I think it quite unnecessary to remark upon the evidence of the bheestees and of the Khoberaj's servant, Bugghobun Ghose; feeling satisfied that no impartial mind can build condemnatory conclusions against my clients upon anything that those three have said,·collectively or individually.

"Such, then, is a cursory review of the proofs, or of *what are subsituted for proofs*, in this most serious and most extraordinary case ! In the name of justice and of common sense, what definite or intelligible tale of guilt do they reveal, or can there be extracted from them ? Are these miserable equivocators, these paupers and menials, the select from the 2000 of the camp, from the mass of the Foujdarry deponents, the "best evidence" procurable in support of charges of this nature ? If the public prosecutor thinks that they are, I call upon him to show how and why they are. It is a scandal and a shame, it is a grievous wrong to *the aimiable young prince* whose servants and companions these are, that my clients should be called upon to undergo the disgraceful ordeal of a public trial—should have suffered months of anxious incarceration—should (for their necessary self-protection) have been put to great charges upon such paltry, contradictory, inconclusive, such impossible testimony as this. To suppose that they can be convicted upon it would be monstrous. Not one of them (Meah Urjoomund, Hajee Tumas, the Urzbeggy, Meah Afreen, or Moghul Jan Moonshee) denies that the two men were, or rather might have been, for all they know, beaten (but by no means to the extent pretended): *not one of them saw or sanctioned that beating—not one of them had any cause or assignable motive for doing so; neither of them made inquiry about the deaths of these men, or had reason to do so.* Such information as they subsequently obtained was from the *rumours* of the camp or from the mouth of the accomplished, the rejected Doctor Joomuck. And here I would digress to observe, that the discrepancies and contradictions which have proved fatal in the eye of the public prosecutor to the credit of five of his selected witnesses, by no means betray an anxiety to defeat the prosecution. Those men have not served or answered the purpose as expected; they have proved their own worthlessness, that they have deliberately sworn falsely, either here or in the Foujdarry, or in both places; but their evidence here as conclusively proves that they are hostile, in thought and intention, to the prisoners at the bar. The inference is irresistible, that they are members of a conspiracy; they have only been less skilful or less fortunate than some of their companions. What more need I say upon the general complexion of the case? I have endeavoured to insist upon and to argue the general rules which should be brought to bear upon its consideration; and I have curiously adverted to some, but only some, of *the palpable defects and discrepancies* (the public prosecutor will in vain strive to show them to be *honest* discrepancies) in the details of the evidence. One remarkable head of discrepancy, showing the gross carelessness as well as untruthfulness of the witnesses, one which must have made a deep impression upon the minds of the Court, I do not think I have specially noticed; I allude to the description of the manner in which the men, Hingoo and Muddee, were conveyed from Purranpore to Allal

" I have also yet to observe upon one very prominent and remarkable fact, or rather *an omission which involves many facts*, in what I may call the forensic history of this prosecution. Etwarree, the father of the deceased boy, Muddee, who attended his dying moments, who nursed him during his mortal sickness, who procured medicine for his child, and was found weeping at the entrance of the pal; this man has not been examined, nor has his absence been in any manner accounted for. We have heard from the witness that, with one exception (mentioned, I think, by the slave Hossaince), *no complaint or remonstrance was made by Etwarree at any time—not a word is breathed of his attributing Muddee's mortal sickness to maltreatment of any kind,* although he was the khas khawas of His Highness. We hear of no *coaxing, no threats, no presents, which, if they existed or occurred, must or might have been proved here.* The court, surely, are not to be asked, on such a trial as this, to have intuitive knowledge of facts; and nothing but the existence of some collateral independent facts not before the Court, and which have no reference to or connexion with anything in proof, can render this man's absence, and still more his proved silence and *unmurmuring submission to the calamity which befel his child*, other than unanswerable and incurable defects in the affirmative proof by which alone the case for the prosecution must stand or fall.

"*Guesses and conjectures cannot, legally or justly, by any juridical principle at all, be admitted or stand in the place of any part of that affirmative proof.* Of course it may be said (as a prosecutor in such a dilemma always must say), 'Oh, if Etwarree considers or knows that his son was not ill-treated, why do you not call him in your defence?' The principles upon which I have already insisted are a sufficient answer to any such query. I am not here on behalf of either of my clients to prove innocence, but to show that you have not proved guilt. You have not produced that sort of evidence, either in character or in detail, which can lead the mind of a Judge to a safe conclusion. You may have given enough to suspect something against somebody, but not to condemn any particular person or persons—certainly not against those whom I defend—of any defined misconduct. In no Court of Criminal Justice where an English Judge presides, is the Judge obliged to arrive at any conclusion. The panel may be guilty or innocent. The Judge has merely to do with the proofs of ascertained and defined guilt. Moreover, in this case each of the principal defendants is deprived of what would be the most likely and the most credible evidence of his not being amenable to the charge preferred. His bhaebunds, his companions, those with whom he lives, who know his way and habits; because they are all by his side, suspected criminals like himself; *with how much more reason and intelligible ground of suspicion might several of the witnesses have been substituted in their place!* The Fakeer, who virtuously declined the invitation to beat, which the other 300 Fakeers accepted; the tender-hearted slave, who made no effort to recover the treasure so unaccountably spirited away whilst he was sleeping—at a time, by-the-bye, when, if at any time, he should have been awake, viz., immediately after his night's rest.

"Where, under such circumstances, would be the wisdom or the discretion of attempting, by testimony, to disprove what is not proved?

"As to Etwarree, I know nothing and wish to know nothing of him. I am told he was examined in the Mofussil; if so, his deposition will be with the nutthee; and I do not object, nor do I suppose the learned defender of other persons will object, to that deposition being looked at. Had its contents fitted the case for the prosecution, doubtless the deponent would have been, like the others, committed to the care of the Police Nazir, one of whose duties throughout the Mofussil of India I understand to be, to act as the whipper-in and custodian of witnesses!

"I would add a few words with reference to the Naib-Meer-Moonshee, the Moghul prisoner. This man's case is peculiarly hard. Neither from caste, kindred, or occupation, has he the sympathy of those classed with him. It must have been observed by all who listened to the evidence that each of the witnesses had a disposition to screen or to tread lightly upon the reputation of some one—each, I mean, of those attached to the Nizamut; and doubtless had the Meer

M

Moonshee himself, Mirza Mahomed Hosain, been on my friend the public prosecutor's list, he would have some reluctance, with whatever impressions, recollections, or disposition otherwise he might have come here, to represent his deputy not merely as a thief taker, but as the servant, tool, and executioner of thief-takers.

"As it is, he has been recklessly named; and he, together with the absent Burra Sahib, of whom I know and can say nothing) have been, as it were by common consent, brought in on different occasions *as scapegoats*, or, at least, as useful adjuncts to make the case complete. As regards the Meahs themselves, I can be at no loss, when I see the favours and distinctions heaped upon them by their princely master and benefactor, to understand, why and how they have been so wickedly implicated in a transaction, which if it occurred, and whatever its character, was the work either of their drudges and menials, or of the thousand vagabonds, fakeers (doubtless always ready for excitement or tomasha of any kind), with which the camp was infested. I am not bound to define, because it is not, as I humbly but earnestly submit, within the province, much less the duty, of this Court—if they are not perfectly and conclusively satisfied that the guilt of any or either of my clients has been legally proved—to define in their own minds any conclusions or probabilities whatever. *The certain knowledge of truth is not given to man.* The rules by which the Courts of enlightened nations endeavour, if not to arrive at truth, at least never to come to a mischievous as well as untruthful conclusion, are defined. Forensic judgment is a science, and it is indispensable that it should be so. But were I asked what moral and extra-judicial conclusion my mind arrived at from this evidence, I should say—*Those two men have been maltreated by some persons who believed themselves justified, in consequence of the suspicions attached to them, and of their conduct under these suspicions: the subject formed the common topic and rumour among the fakeers, menials, and followers of the Lushkar, and the accounts given here amount to evidence of those rumours merely, and not of any facts at all.* No one witness (excepting always the Christian coachman, whom I accuse only of involuntary exaggeration) has been an eye-witness of what he pretends; but some may have seen enough to sketch or picture a tale upon sufficient encouragement, the outline being filled up and the picture coloured by the guess of his fellows during the safer, and perhaps, yet more, during the dangerous proximity to his co-witness enforced by the system of the Mofussil police. I consider that the treatment, the wounds, the conduct, have been all palpably and grossly misdescribed—not merely exaggerated. As to the deaths, there is at least a strong moral probability that the rumour of the death by cholera may be correct as to one, if not of both: if it be otherwise, I should say no man can draw any conscientious conclusions whatever from the evidence. All is vague. It is lamentable that it should be so; but how much more lamentable would it be that, in order to arrive at any affirmative judgment, we should venture to condemn even the meanest of our brother-men upon conjecture?"

The following is the reply put in by Mr. Trevor and Shumbo Nauth Pundit, conducting the prosecution on the part of Government:—

"Sept. 7th, 1853.

"Before proceeding to offer the remarks we may consider it our duty to make upon the case in general, we would wish to express publicly the satisfaction we have received from the testimony borne by both the learned counsels for the defence to the manner in which the prosecution has been conducted by us. It has been our endeavour to conduct the case with the spirit of fairness towards the accused, and it is a pleasure to us to learn that in this attempt we have not been unsuccessful. We also beg to be allowed to add our testimony to that of the learned counsel for the defence, to the great consideration that has been evinced through the course of this trial by the Court towards the accused. Mr. Clarke, the learned counsel for five of the accused, Aman Ali Khan, Musserut Ali Khan, Jowahir Ali Khan, Meah Ekbal, and Meah Belal, has contented himself with calling witnesses to character. We have, therefore, only to beg the Court to bear in mind that where *the point at issue is, whether the accused have committed a particular act,* evidence of their general good character is obviously entitled to little weight unless some reasonable doubt exist as to their guilt. There are one or two facts given in Mr. Clarke's defence which do not exactly correspond with the evidence as taken down by us. For the clearing up of these discrepancies we shall have to ask you to refer to your notes after we have finished this reply. The other learned counsel, Mr. Montriou, defends five of the accused, Meah Urjoomund, Hajee Tamas, Meah Afreen, the Urzbeggy Imam Ali, and Mirza Mahomed Hossain, *alias* Moghul Jan. For the two first-named the evidence given in defence is evidence to character. The defence for Meah Afreen is, that *he was not the servant of the Nawab at all*, but of the Nawab Begum, and sent by that lady to His Highness with a letter of condolence after the occurrence of some injury to His Highness's person. The defence of Meer Imam Ali, the Urzbeggy, is, that his duties were of such a nature as to keep him so late of a night with the Nawab as to render his participation in the perpetration of a crime charged nearly an impossibilty. The defence for Mirza Mahomed Hossain is, that his particular business was to be in attendance upon the Khan Sahib, Aman Ali; that the nature and times of that attendance were such as to be wholly inconsistent with the conduct attributed to him by the witness for the prosecution. The defendant, Fureed Khan, denies the charge of having beaten one of the deceased, and calls witness to prove his defence. The defendant, Joomun Shaik, sets up an *alibi* as his defence, but calls no witness to prove it. The defendant, Peer Khan, who confessed before the magistrate, denies before this Court, but calls no witnesses.

"Before proceeding to notice how far the several defendants have substantiated their respective defences, we have a few remarks to offer upon the case generally. *The first thing is, that the matter was first reported by the Shahnuggur Daroga as a rumour: we submit that it was natural it should be so.* The crime was not committed in the Moorshedabad district at all. On the return of His Highness from the hunting expedition the rumour naturally began to be rife in the city, and it was strictly the Daroga's duty, as laid down in Section iv., Clause i., Regulation xx. of 1817, to make the report he did. Another point requiring notice is the retinue that accompanied

His Highness upon this occasion. The learned counsel for the defendant Urjoomund, and others, would seem to suppose that the whole Court of the Nawab accompanied him in this expedition; but this nowhere appears in the record, nor is it natural that it should be the fact It is more natural to suppose that on these occasions His Highness would lay aside some of his usual state; indeed, one witness, Mahomed Amrru, distinctly deposes to a not unimportant fact, viz., that all the Meahs, except Aman Ali, dined with His Highness every day, Aman Ali doing so occasionally.

"The next point to be noticed is the evidence adduced for the prosecution. The witnesses we have considered our duty to produce have, some of them, been subjected to a cross-examination as, we will venture to assert, has seldom been heard in our native courts of justice. They have been questioned not only on points bearing on the case, but on matters quite irrelevant They have been in the box, some of them a whole day, one man a day and a half; and, after all, what contradictions have been elicited from them? Very few, we maintain, on any material point; and all the contradictions are of such a nature as to prove rather the truth of the main story, than that *these men have hanged together to bring punishment and disgrace on the heads of the accused* We appeal to the demeanour of the principal witnesses in the box as a proof that what they deposed to was, in the main, true.

"The counsel for the defence, Mr. Montriou, admits the cool demeanour of one, and attributes it to pertness and over-zeal. We assert that it is ridiculous to suppose that these fakeers and menials should have stood the cross-examination they did, and in the manner they did, had their evidence been founded on a lie. The leper, the itinerant vendor of smoke, the 'ticca,' scullion (also called the 'beea' vagabond), the tailor, to have in a great measure, if not entirely, baffled the efforts of two Supreme Court Barristers, is a proof to our mind, not of the want of talent in the counsel, but of the support the witnesses had in the knowledge that they were in the main speaking the truth. They differ as to the time of the several occurrences; it is only natural that they should Months have elapsed since the occurrence took place, and had they all agreed as to time we should have heard that such 'unanimity was wonderful.' They differ as to the mode in which the two deceased persons were conveyed from one place to another. Of what consequence is a discrepancy on such a point as this? We are told of conspiracy. Where are the conspirators? Would not any one conspiring have brought forward witnesses of a superior walk of life to those adduced for the prosecution? *Would His Highness have continued in his service up to the present time* (as he has several of the witnesses) *parties conspiring to bring ruin and disgrace upon a man high in his favour and service?* The poverty and low state of the witnesses for the prosecution have been much insisted on by the learned counsel for the defence. We glory in them—they are our strength. It is stated by the learned counsel for Urjoomund, and others, that in all cases the best evidence is to be given. To this axiom we assent; but venture to think, that in his application of it the learned counsel is in error. The axiom refers to the evidence best in quality, not best in strength. We assert that in quality no evidence can be better than that produced for the prosecution, being as it is the evidence of those who profess to have seen with their own eyes the facts they depose to.

"The next point calling for notice is the non-appearance of the father of the deceased, Muddee. This is a thing of frequent occurrence in this country—so frequent, that, as long ago as 1822, a regulation was necessary to authorise the punishment of parties when, in cases of murder, the heir of the slain refuses to prosecute. We are confident that to this fact no weight will be attached by the Court, especially when the accused are, as one of them in the present case is, men of wealth and influence. The next point to be noticed is the evidence of the English coachman in the service of His Highness, George Shapcott. Both the learned counsel for the defence mention in terms of commendation the manner in which this evidence was given, and we are also ready to agree with those gentlemen. *This witness implicated only one of the defendants as actually beating;* but his evidence is very strong as to the state of the bodies of the deceased shortly before death at Gujol—the only place he saw them after he had seen one of them at Newgurriah; as at Purranpore he was encamped on the other side of an indigo factory, away from the rest of the lushkur, and at Allal on the other side of the river. His description is borne out as to one of the deceased, Hinaoo, by the two Bhistees, who brought water to wash the body, and whose evidence, with due deference to the learned counsel, Mr. Montriou, we consider in every way trustworthy. This evidence has, we presume, put an end to the defence set before the magistrate, that the deceased died of cholera, and we moreover beg to remark, that not one single witness deposes to the prevalence of cholera in the camp, as stated by Mr. Montriou. The number of persons in the camp were, as far as appears, about 2,000, and during the two months the hunting party lasted, not a single witness deposes to the deaths amounting to one dozen!—a very different state of things from what would have been had cholera been prevalent. The inferences to be drawn from the evidence as to the state of the bodies a short time before and immediately after the death, as deposed to by George Shapcott, the two Bhistees, and the apprentice who attended them, that is, from some cause or other, the bodies were in a dreadful state of laceration; and connecting their appearance with the beating and torture as deposed to by the other witnesses, we have, in the absence of any attempt to prove how their bodies became in such a state, a right to connect the two as cause and effect. Besides the English coachman, there is another witness, whom we suppose the learned counsel for the defence will allow to be respectable—we refer to Mahomed Amrru, the Emmuck, the Darogah of the tents, the sharer of Aman Ali's tent. The Court will doubtless bear in mind the very unwilling manner in which this man gave his testimony—the explanation he offered relative to the pal being pitched so near the Meah's tent; and how he admitted that all the Meahs dined every day with His Highness; but it has been attempted to be proved that it would be derogatory to the dignity and high position of Aman Ali Khan even to go to their tent. The servant degraded by entering the tent of those his master delighteth to honour ! ! !

"We now proceed to remark on the defence set up by the defendants, who have called evidence besides that to character. For the defence of Meah Afreen two witnesses are called. We grant that *this defendant is not a servant of the Nizamut*, but it is proved that he was at Purranpore the day the camp arrived, and the following night, by both his witnesses; and one of them, Hossain Bur, would have the Court believe that this man, who accompanied His Highness of a day out hunting, was at night fain to sleep under a tree with the servants. The parties who were charitable enough to have a pal put up for a dying Fakeer and the son of a Khawas within a few paces of the Meah's tent, had not hospitality sufficient to offer the shelter of a tent at night to Meah Afreen, the companion all day in hunting of His Highness. Further comment on such evidence as this is quite unnecessary. For the defence of the Urzbeggy Emam Ali, one witness alone appears, and all that he says is that the defendant used to go to His Highness when called for, but that there was no exact time for attending. This falls far short of the defence set up and requires no comment from us. For the defendant Mirza Mahomed Hossain, *alias* Moghul Jan, two witnesses are called. It would appear that this man is a sort of Perunneah, or Robokarnuvees; the office he bears being that of Naib Meer Moonshee, certainly nothing of a confidential nature, although it may be called in one sense literary. The defendant Fureed Khan calls witnesses to prove that he never beat at Nowgurriah the the deceased Muddee. His witnesses were four in number; three were examined. Of these two were camel-drivers, and one was a mate Mahouth. These men came prepared to swear through thick and thin, that they accompanied Fureed Khan on the occasion in question to Nowgurriah, that they were with him all the time he was there, and that he did not on that occasion beat anybody. The first witness was duly cross-examined, and nothing was elicited inculpating any of the defendants. Mukhoo, was the mate Mahouth, and went on foot to Nowgurriah while the others rode on camels. He had been cross-examined by Mr. Trevor, and he had sat down, when the Court asked him by whose orders the camels were sent to Nowgurriah He then mentioned Aman Ali's name, and was soon after cross-examined at great length by Mr. Clarke, the learned council for Aman Ali, but *nothing was elicited from him at all contradictory* He said that he remained with the camels at the tent of the Meahs, while the three camel-drivers went to the Khan's tent. He was asked if he heard the Khan give the order, he said "No," but that *he had heard* from the three camel-drivers who had gone to the Khan's tent, that he had given the orders for them to go to the Burra Sahib and do what he told them. His account was perfectly natural. There was a crowd at the place where he was, but that he could swear he h ard from the camel-drivers that they had received orders from Aman Ali Khan. Of course he could. These three men men alone, as far as he knew, went to the Khan's tent for orders. The next witness was Bakeer Ali, one of the three camel-drivers who went to Nowgurriah with Fureed Khan, and who were stated by the witness last referred to to have gone to the tent of Aman Ali. It was elicited by a question from the Mohie, that the two camels were taken, by Aman Ali's order, to Nowgurriah ; that he told the drivers to go to the

Burrah Sahib for orders; that they went; that the Burra Sahib gave them a chit to one Jechunal at Nowgurriah, and told them to take Muddee (one of the deceased) there. That they did so. He also swore distinctly that Fureed Khan did not hit any one at Nowgurriah. Now *we allow that what these men said* about Fureed Khan *is totally false* but that does not taint all their evidence. We affirm that there is hardly ever a case in which influential parties are concerned, in which the principle of rejecting part **and** adopting part of a witness's evidence is not called into play. In affray cases especially, we may remark, there is always an attempt **to** inculpate either the Zemindars themselves, on whose behalf the affray took place, as being actually present; or, if they are not named, their principal **servants** are. In numberless instances the evidence of the same witness is considered as worthy of belief, *quoad* the latteals, and rejected *quoad* the Zemindars or their servants. It is a satisfaction to us to be able to state that the principle we contend for is recognised in England. The rule is thus laid down in 'Taylor on Evidence,' pages 949-950:—' Where a party being surprised by a statement of one of his witnesses calls other persons to contradict in a particular fact, the Judge is not on that account **authorised in** rejecting the entire testimony of the contradicted witness. The discrepancy may, indeed, form a fair topic for counsel as to the degree of credit to which the witness is entitled, but the whole evidence must go to the jury, who may be perfectly justified in believing **one part** of it **and** rejecting the other.' If this is applicable to England, **where** the sanction of an oath is much regarded, how much more applicable is it to *India, where* unfortunately, *an oath is no guarantee for truth!* That principle we apply here. We would *reject* the evidence of these men as to Fureed Khan's innocence, contradicted as it is by that of George Shapcott, and *adopt* it **as to** Aman Ali. The Court will doubtless remember the manner **in which the facts inculpating** Aman Ali were elicited from **these witnesses, the manner in which they** gave their evidence, and the **vain attempts of the learned counsel to** make them contradict themselves. **We have no doubt that the evidence** of these two men **will** have due weight with **the Court.**

"Before finally dismissing this defendant **Fureed Khan, we beg to direct** the attention of the Court to his defence. In two points he corroborates the evidence of the prosecution He says that on the day **of the** theft His Highness returned from hunting at one o'clock, and he also states that Muddee started from Nowgurriah on a camel. That **on** the road they met Moghul Jan and Buara Sahib, who took him on an elephant. The fact deposed to by one of the witnesses for the prosecution, that he did return on an elephant, has been much insisted on as a serious discrepancy by Mr. Montriou.

" It only remains for us to notice a point relative to one of the charges which has been **animadverted** upon by the learned counsel for the defendant **Aman Ali Khan**—we allude to the third account, which charges the defendants **with 'privity;'** the meaning **of** this term is thus explained in C.O., **No. 8 of vol. iv.** (page xxiii. of the Addenda of Beaufort's Guide, 132a) : ' The **act** which constitutes what is called "privity" in this country corresponds with "misprision of felony" in English Law, **viz**, the concealment of a felony which a man knows **but never** assented to, or the observing silently *the commission of a* *felony* without using any endeavours to apprehend the offender. It is, therefore, strictly an offence of a negative kind, consisting in the concealment of something that ought to be revealed.'

"Accessoryship, on the other hand, is an offence of a positive kind and of a higher degree of criminality, implying an active preparation, either by procuring, counselling, commanding, or abetting another to commit a felony, or with a knowledge that a felony has been committed by another, by receiving, relieving, comforting, or assisting the felon. The distinction between the two offences is marked—the one is a misdemeanour in English Law, the other is a felony; the one is in its kind negative, requiring nothing but silent, passive acquiescence; in the commission of a felony, either by counsel and command before the act, or by relief and assistance given to the felon after the fact. It appears then, that to have made this charge intelligible to the learned counsel for the defence we must have used the term 'misprision of felony,' which would not have been allowed by the Court to remain in the calendar. We now conclude this reply, leving the result with all confidence in the hands of the Court, *feeling sure that every justice will be done* in the matter.

"(Signed)   E. TREVOR.
(,,)   SHUMBONAUTH PUNDIT,
"Conducting the prosecution on the part of Government·

"7th September, 1853."

The following is the report by Mr. Money, the Sessions Judge of Moorshedabad, to the Sudder Nizamut Adawlut, at Calcutta :—

To the REGISTRAR *of the* SUDDER NIZAMUT ADAWLUT.

"Fort William.

"SIR,—I have the honour to submit, for the purpose of being laid before the Court of Nizamut Adawlut, the proceedings on the trial noted below, held at the station of Moorshedabad on the 22nd, 23rd, 24th, 25th, 26th, 27th, 29th, 30th, and 31st August, and 5th and 7th September, 1853.

"2. The prisoner pleaded Not Guilty.

"Court of the Sessions Judge for the City of Moorshedabad.

"Trial, No. 1, of the Sessions Judge for the month of September, 1853.

"Case, No. 7, of the Magistrate of Moorshedabad for the month of July, 1853.

GOVERNMENT PROSECUTOR

versus

"37. Aman Ali Khan (father's name not known), aged 33 years;

date of apprehension, 6th June, 1853, or 25th Jeyt, 1260; date of commitment, 30th July, 1853, or 16th Srahem, 1260.—*Acquitted.*

"38. Musserut Ali Khan, son of Abdoola, aged 35 years; date of apprehension, 6th June, 1853, or 25th Jeyt, 1260; date of commitment, 30th July, 1853, or 16th Srahem, 1260.—*Acquitted.*

"39. Syud Emaun Ali, son of Syud Buher Ali, aged 52 years; date of apprehension, 6th June, 1853, or 25th Jeyt, 1260; date of commitment, 30th July, 1853, or 16th Srahem, 1260.—*Fourteen years' labour in irons.*

"40. Joahir Ali Khan (father's name not known), aged 60 years; date of apprehension, 6th June, 1853, or 25th Jeyt, 1260; date of commitment, 30th July, 1853, or 16th Srahem, 1260.—*Acquitted.*

"41. Meah Urjoomund, son of Abdoola, aged 30 years; date of apprehension, 6th June, 1853, or 25th Jeyt, 1260; date of commitment, 30th July, 1853, or 16th Srahem, 1260.—*Acquitted*

"42. Meah Afreen (father's name not known), aged 30 years; date of apprehension, 6th June, 1853, or 25th Jeyt, 1260; date of commitment, 30th July, 1853, or 16th Sahrem, 1260.—*Acquitted.*

"43. Meah Belal (father's name not known), aged 27 years; date of apprehension, 6th June, 1853, or 25th Jeyt, 1260; date of commitment, 30th July, 1853, or 16th Srahem, 1260.—*Acquitted.*

"44. Meah Ekbal (father's name not known), aged 25 years; date of apprehension, 6th June, 1853, or 25th Jeyt, 1260; date of commitment, 30th July, 1853, or 16th Srahem, 1260.—*Acquitted.*

"45. Hajee Tamash, son of Abdoola, aged 50 years; date of apprehension, 6th June, 1853, or 25th Jeyt, 1260; date of commitment, 30th July, 1853, or 16th Srahem, 1260.—*Acquitted.*

"46. Mahomed Fureed, son of Bahoo, aged 26 years; date of apprehension, 6th June, 1853, or 25th Jeyt, 1260; date of commitment, 30th July, 1853, or 16th Srahem, 1260.—*Fourteen years' labour in irons.*

"47. Mirza Mahomed Hossain, *alias* Moghul Jan, son of Mirza Ali Khan, aged 30 years; date of apprehension, 15th June, 1853, or 2nd Assar, 1260; date of commitment, 30th July, 1853, or 16th Srahem, 1260.—*Acquitted.*

"48. Joomun Shaik, son of Akaloo Shaik, aged 40 years; date of apprehension, 17th June, 1853, or 4th Assar, 1260; date of commitment, 30th July, 1853, or 16th Srahem, 1260.—*Fourteen years' labour in irons.*

"49. Peer Khan, son of Shanduth Khan, aged 50 years; date of apprehension, 21st June, 1853, or 8th Assar, 1260; date of commitment, 30th July, 1853, or 16th Srahem, 1260.—*Fourteen years' labour in irons.*

Charge.

"The prisoners charged, on the first count, with the wilful murder of Hingoo and Muddee.

"On the second count, with being accessories before and after the fact.

"On the third count, with privity to the said crime.

"On the fourth count, with torturing and beating the said Hingoo and Muddee, deceased.

"On the fifth count, with aiding and abetting in the said torture and beating.

"On the sixth count, with privity to the said torture and beating.

"On the seventh count the prisoner, No. 37, is charged with having issued orders for the said torture and beating.

"Date of the deceased being seized, 31st March, 1853, corresponding 19th Cheyt, 1259.

"Dates of their deaths, 5th and 6th April, 1853, corresponding with 24th and 25th Cheyt, 1259, respectively. The prisoners have been in jail from 7th July, 1853.

"3. The history of this painful case is briefly told. The time occupied does not extend over more than five or six days. His Highness the Nawab Nazim of Moorshedabad, during a shooting excursion in the district of Maldah, pitched his camp on the 30th March last at a village called Purranpore. On the 3rd April the camp proceeded to Allal, and from thence on the 5th April to Gujol, both villages in the same district.

"4. Two men—Hingoo, a fakeer, and Muddee, whose father is a gholam in the service of the Nizamut—accompanied the camp.

"5. The prisoners, 37, Aman Ali Khan; 38, Musserut Ali Khan; 39, Syud Imam Ali; 40, Joahir Ali Khan; 41, Meah Urjoomund; 43, Meah Belal; 44, Meah Ekbal; 45, Hajee Tamash; and 47, Mirza Mahomed Hossain, *alias* Moghul Jan, formed a part of His Highness's suite: 42, Meah Afreen, had joined the camp, having been sent on a special errand by the Nawab Begum Sahib: 46, Mahomed Fureed was a camel-driver; and 49, Peer Khan, a mahouth in His Highness's service: and 48, Joomun Shaik, was the servant of 37, who was the Urzbeggy of His Highness; the prisoner 38 holding also a high office in the Nizamut; and the prisoner 37 was the chief and confidential eunuch, having the general control over all His Highness's arrangements during this excursion.

"6. The principal tents in the camp belonged to His Highness, Aman Ali Khan, and the eunuchs. His Highness occupied the centre tent, on one side of which was the tent of Aman Ali Khan, and on the other the tent of the eunuchs. They were generally pitched at a short distance from each other.

"7. On the morning of the 31st March, while His Highness, with the greater part of his suite, was out shooting at Purranpore, a tin box containing property to the value of above rupees 700, belonging to the prisoner 41, was missing. Hingoo and Muddee were seized on suspicion of having stolen the box, and throughout the day, before and after His Highness's return, it would appear were tortured and beaten for the purpose of inducing them to confess and point out the property.

"8. The same night Muddee was conveyed on a camel to a place called Nowgurriah, about eight or nine miles from Purranpore, that he might point out a ghareewan to whom, he said, he had given the property. He was then unmercifully beaten, when he declared he had not given the property to the ghareewan, but to two Nautch girls at Purranpore; upon which he was again placed upon the camel and brought back, part of the way on camel, and part on an elephant, to the camp at Purranpore.

"9. On the 3rd **April** the two men were taken, with **the camp, to** Allal; and again, on the 5th, from Allal **to Gujol, where the same** day Hingoo died, and Muddee the day after.

"10. It was given out in the camp **that these** men had died **of** cholera, and it was not until the 1st May following that the Daroga of Shahuugger, **in** the city of Moorshedabad, reported to the magis**trate** that he had heard that a murder had been **committed in** the camp, but that no one came forward to prosecute.

"11. The order which he received from the magistate led **to inquiry, and** inquiry led to disclosures which formed grounds for **the trial before** the magistrate, terminating in the commitment of **the** prisoners **to** the Sessions Court on the charge of murder, and other lesser **counts.**

"12. Having given a brief outline of **the case,** I will **revert to the** evidence upon record.

"13. The witness who enters more fully into detail regarding the **tortures to** which Hingoo and Muddee were subjected is Hossainee Shaik, witness 5 on the calendar. He was the personal servant of the prisoner 41, and was permitted to turn Queen's evidence. His statement before the Sessions Court is to the following effect:—I am **a** servant of Meah Urjoomund (prisoner 41). I had a tin box under my charge belonging to my master. One morning I was asleep. Burra Sahib (absent) and Moghul Jan (prisoner 47) were sitting inside my master's tent. About eight or nine a.m. I awoke and missed the box, and asked them about it. They said they did not know where it **was.** I told them I was sure they had hidden **it.** They denied this, and said, **as I** had given them a bad name I should be punished when the **thieves were** caught. Burra Sahib and prisoner 47 went out and brought in **Muddee.** I did not go with them. Muddee was questioned about the theft, but would **not confess. He was then** taken and tied inside the **tent;** and **because he would not** give up the property, Burrah Sahib and prisoner **47 beat him with a corah.** They continued beating him till he promised, **if they left off, he would** show **where** the property was. He then said it was **with** Hingoo, and he **would** show them where Hingoo was. They loosened him and took him **to** the indigo factory, where the fakeers lived. Not finding Hingoo there, they brought Muddee back to the tent, and again beat him till he told them Hingoo was under a tree near the kitchen tent. They went out, and I saw them bring Hingoo to their **tent.** They said they had found him sleeping under the tree near the kitchen. Muddee told him to confess about the property, as they were taking away his life. Hingoo denied having taken the property. They then tied Hingoo and began to beat both Muddee entreated them not to beat him more, and **said he** would show them where the property was placed. They took Hingoo and Muddee to the river-side, and, not finding the property, brought them back, beating them, **and** began again, to beat them in the tent. Muddee then said he would show them the property at Purranpore, near which Hingoo had concealed it under some grass. Not finding it there, they again brought them back, beating them. Muddee said he would show it near the indigo factory They took them there while I remained in the tent. They again brought them back, beating them. Muddee then said he would show it under the sand near the river amongst some thorn-bushes. They took them there, and were searching when His Highness returned from hunting. I saw them searching. The river was about one or one-half russee from the tent. His Highness went into his tent, and Aman Ali Khan (prisoner 37) into his, and the Meahs into theirs. My master (prisoner 41) saw me crying, and asked me what was the matter He called out 'Hossainee' three times. I mentioned about theft, and upon his asking where the thieves were, I pointed out where Burra Sahib and prisoner 47 were bringing them. The Meahs said to the thieves, 'Why do you suffer yourselves to be beaten? Give up the property.' They would not confess The Meahs then went to the tent of prisoner 37, and I went with them. Prisoner 37 ordered them to be beaten till they produced the property. He called out, 'Beat them! Never mind if they die. One is a Chelah in His Highness's service, and the other a Fakeer; if they die, we can say they died of cholera.' The Meahs then went to their tent, and Meah Emam Ali (prisoner 32), Meah Ekbal (prisoner 44), Meah Belal (prisoner 43), Meah Afreen (prisoner 42), and Mussuruth Ali Khan (prisoner 38), began together to beat them. By the order of prisoner 37, Peer Khan (prisoner 49) brought a cutcha beyt with thorns in it, and they tied the thieves inside the Meah's tent and beat them. Muddee then said the property was in a garden. They took them to the garden and there searched, but found nothing, and took them back to the tent and beat them. They tied their hands and feet and beat them with the beyt and the coruh. The prisoner 39 again took them to the garden, and afterwards Joomun Shaik (prisoner 48) servant of prisoner 39, and prisoner 49, kicked them, and prisoner 39 took them with the Mehter, and told them they should be beaten with his jharoo if they did not give up the property. Not finding it in the garden, they brought them back and tied them to the tent-pins of the Meah's tent, and began to beat them. Burra Sahib and prisoner 47 made sharp wedges and drove them through their fingers, their hands being tied. The feet and hands were tied to separate tent-pins. (The witness showed in Court the way in which they were fastened.) They loosened them after a while, when they cried out for water. The prisoner 37 said they should have urine for water. About 2 p.m. they tied them again and took them inside the tent. The Meahs told them, if they would point out where the tin box was they would give them water and heal their wounds. Hingoo declared that he knew nothing about the property. Muddee said he had given it to Hingoo. They again tied them up to the two tent-poles, with their heads downwards and their feet uppermost, and beat them with the kutcha thorned beyt. They all beat them. The witness pointed out the prisoners 47, 44, 43, 42, 39, 38, 49, and 48. Prisoner 41 was there threatening, but not beating. Hajee Tamas (prisoner 45) was there, but did not beat I did not see Mahomed Fureed (prisoner 46). I saw Meer Ali Khan (prisoner 40) there, but he did not beat. They were beaten all along in the same tent. The prisoner 41 and the Meahs lived in the same tent. On the fourth day the camp left Purranpore and proceeded to

Allal. They took the thieves with the camp, one in a meana and the other in a Suggur-garre. They beat them again there. Muddee said that Hingoo had informed him that the property would be found under a certain tree at Purranpore. Burra Sahib and prisoner 48 went there on an elephant Muddee was conveyed in a meanah. God knows what they did there. They went early and returned late in the evening. Burra Sahib and prisoner 48 said they had been worn out by searching for the property, and could find nothing. Then Burra Sahib, in the tent, trod with his feet upon Hingoo's chest. Hingoo begged him to cut his throat, but not to tread upon him. Burra Sahib, with prisoners 39 and 47, said, that until he showed the property they would beat him to death. They then brought Joomuck Doctor, and prisoner 39 told him to give them some brandy to drink, and to use some as an application. I saw a little mixed with a poultice and a little drunk by them. They were then inside a pal on one side of the Meahs' tent, near the bottle khana. After staying four days at Allal the camp proceeded to Gujol. About noon of the day which they reached Gujol, Hingoo died, The prisoner and the rest threatened Muddee with the same fate unless he disclosed where the property was, telling him that he was a Chelah of the Huzoor, and the other only a Fakeer; that they would not take him back again, but cut his throat and bury him there. During the night he was very weak, and died in the morning. They buried Hingoo about 3 p.m., near a bamboo jungle. They buried Muddee about 8 or 9 a.m., near a gallows. Muddee's father was a Gholam (slave) in His Highness's service, and Muddee a Chelah. Burra Sahib and prisoner 47 said Muddee had once come to the Meahs' tent, and therefore suspected that he had stolen the property. Hingoo's left hand was broken and the skin of both feet torn off. The thieves died from the violence of the beating. Hingoo was about forty or fifty years old, and Muddee about twenty years old. No property was ever found. My mas'er still retains me in his service. I saw prisoner 37 come one evening to the Meahs' tent and threaten the prisoners, but he did not order them to be beaten.

"14. The most rigid cross-examination by the counsel for the defence did not shake this witness's evidence.

"15. How far it is corroborated by the testimony of other witnesses, will appear from a brief abstract of what they deposed to from their own knowledge.

"16. Shaik Dhunnoo, witness No. 1 on the calendar, stated that one afternoon, about 9th Cheyt, he saw Muddee and Hingoo tied up at the end of the Meahs, with their hands bound behind them and their feet fastened with separate cords to the tent-ropes in front of the tent. That on Muddee's declaring the property was near the river (which he did because he was thirsty and wanted to drink) both the men were taken there and brought back, as nothing was found. That information was sent to His Highness, who was out shooting, and who returned about 1 p.m. and sent for them, and questioned them regarding the theft. That prisoner 37 threatened to have them shot if they did not give up the property, and that when His Highness ordered them to be released, he ordered them to be tied up. The next morning the witness saw Muddee's hands and feet torn by tent-pins, and bleeding, and he was burnt all over his left arm and shoulders, and from the knees to the feet. He saw marks of beating on Hingoo when they were leaving Purranpore for Allal. They tried to place the thieves in Suggur-Garrees, but could not manage it, they cried out so much, and were obliged to put them in Majhola-Garrees. After staying two days at Allal the camp proceeded to Gujol, where he heard Hingoo was dead. Muddee died the same night. Next morning saw Jeeboo Shohada burying some one, and helped to dig; saw the corpse of Muddee. Burra Sahib (not present) was there; he brought the burial clothes to be put upon the body. Shere Ali, Fakeer, and two bhistees, were there; witness took off the clothes that were on Muddee, put the other clothes on, and they buried him. He saw Hingoo's grave. Muddee was buried one russee distant from the encampment, and Hingoo one half russee off, in a bamboo jungle. When he saw Muddee and Hingoo tied up at the Meahs' tent, he saw there the prisoners 42, 43, 45, 44, 47, 39, 41, 40, 37, and 49, as well as Burra Sahib: all the Meahs beat them, and the prisoner 47 gave orders. The witness did not know the names of the prisoners 43 and 44, but recognised them from having seen them before, and pointed them out.

"17. Hingun Khan Cooria, Fakeer, witness 2 on the calendar, saw two thieves tied near the tent of prisoner 37 for stealing the property of the Daroga of Bhilt Ebana, and the prisoner 37 pare a bamboo and beat them both: their feet were tied to the tent-pins and their hands behind them. This was a little after (12) noon. One was Hingoo; did not know the other. Hingoo was much older. Two days after, at Allal Ghaut, he saw both of them tied up near the cooking-tent, and marks of burning on one of Hingoo's hands. On the fourth day the camp reached Gujol, where he heard both were dead. When the prisoner 37 beat the thieves, His Highness was in his own tent, and all the Meahs in theirs. It was about one hour after their return from shooting.

"18. Ruhum Ali Shaik, witness 9 on the calendar, states that one morning in the month of Cheyt, at Purranpore, a theft occurred in the tent of the prisoner 41, and soon after there was a noise, and he went with others and saw two thieves tied up in front of the Meahs' tent. Presently a crowd collected, and the people of the tent began to call out 'Maro banchootko,' and to beat. He returned to his own duties. About 2 P.M. His Highness returned from shooting. There was a great uproar, and people running about. The prisoners 37 and 41, returning at the time, asked what the tamasha was: the people at the tent told them that a box had been stolen; 37 called out 'Banchootko khoob maro,'—Make them confess where the property is. The thieves begged them not to beat them, and said they had concealed the property in the sand, and would point it out. They took them to the sand and searched, but did not find it. They then called out 'Banchoot, humlogko dhoopme dooraya,' and beat them with a cane and a thorny branch of a babool tree, and the corah and the mehter beat them with a jharoo, and they took them near the bazaar, to the sand by the river. They then beat them excessively, and when they fell from weakness they ordered them to be tied by the feet and dragged; after which they took them back to the tent and witness went to his work. During the night he heard cries of 'Dohay Company! Dohay Nawab Sahib!' The next day His Highness went out shooting. They brought the thieves out of the tent; they begged not to be beaten, and said the property was under a kudum gatch towards the west, and they would show it. They took them there to a ditch, and witness went with them. The witness saw them beaten there and again brought back. The next morning, when His Highness was going out shooting, the prisoner 37 ordered the thieves to be well beaten. Witness saw the thieves to be brought out and beaten severely. They entreated them not to beat them, and told them there was a sunken boat in the river where the property was, and they would show it. They went to the boat, and as the thieves were searching for the property they called out 'Look! they are not searching, they are drinking water;' upon which they were taken to the dry ground and beaten with the corah, beyt, and jharoo, all the way back to the tent, where they were tied up again inside. The witness saw the prisoners 42, 43, 44, 47, 48 and 49, beat the thieves when they were taken to the kuddum gatch. The prisoner 37 went with them. The witness saw the thieves taken in separate doolies from Purranpore to Allal, and from Allal to Gujol. They belonged to the Nizamut as well as the bearers. The witness describes the bodies of the men as being quite raw and coloured from the beating and the fingers without any skin on The eyes only escaped. The prisoner 41 as well as 37 gave orders for the beating. The witness was also cross-examined at great length

"19. Hingoo Khan, buttah burdah in the service of His Highness, witness 7 on the calendar, saw Muddee and Hingoo bound one evening at Purranpore, between 7 and 8 p.m. Prisoner 49 tied their hands behind them very tight, and on their calling out, prisoner 41 told them to tie them looser. A camel-driver took Muddee away on a camel to Nowgurriah, and brought him back to Purranpore the next morning on an elephant. Saw the prisoners 47, 48, and Burra Sahib with the prisoners 38 and 42, following behind, take Hingoo and Muddee to the factory, where he believes they were beaten. Heard cries one night, either from Hingoo or Muddee, of 'Dohay Darogah Sahib! Dohay Darogah Sahib!' From Purranpore to Allal, Muddee was sitting in a garee belonging to the Nizamut; his body was covered, but he saw his foot, which was exposed: it was swollen. The prisoners 47, 49, and Burra Sahib were on the elephant with Muddee, when he returned from Nowgurriah. States his belief that the thieves died from the beating. The treatment of the thieves was spoken of in the camp, bazaar, roads, and everywhere. Saw clothes in the hands of Burra Sahib for the bodies of the men.

"20. George Shapcott, coachman to His Highness's service, witness 20 on the calendar, was eye-witness to the treatment of Muddee by the prisoner 46 at Nowgurriah. He states that Muddee was brought there on a camel by the prisoner 46, a camel-driver, to enable him to point out the ghareewan to whom he said he had given the property. He pointed out Junghee gareewan, who was about to be tied up, when the witness interfered in his behalf, and he was released. But Muddee, in his presence, for 15 minutes, was unmercifully beaten by the prisoner 46. He did not see Muddee again till he saw him and Hingoo at Gujol Hath. They were in the same pal, and attended by Joomuck Doctor, who, with the aid of the Mehter was applying turpentine and sweet-oil to their legs, and getting ready poultices Hingoo then was dying, and Muddee was calling out to the people outside to bring water for him. The Burra Sahib was there all the time. The next morning he went again towards the pal, and saw Muddee in a dying state. From his own tent he saw them both buried. The witness describes the appearance of Hingoo's body when he saw him in the pal, that he was raw from the knee to the foot—raw in parts from the neck to below the waist; the skin was off, and the body very much swollen. He describes Muddee also as being in the same state, 'raw all the way down,' when he saw him dying. When he last saw Muddee and Hingoo there were no appearances of cholera.

"21. Doolal Hurkara, witness 12 on the calendar in the service of His Highness, was an eye-witness to the prisoners 39, 47, 48, 40, and Burra Sahib, taking the two thieves with their hands bound to the river and back, and beating them both going and returning.

"22. Ghasoo Chobdar, witness 11 on the calendar, in His Highness's service, heard the noise of beating in the Meahs' tent the day the two thieves were apprehended, and cries of 'Meah Sahib hy!'—I will show them all. Saw the Burra Sahib and the prisoners 46, 47, 48, 49, with 39, 42, 43, taking the two thieves to the mango grove, and beating them, and bringing them back the same way, not having found the property, to the tent. Does not know what occurred in the tent. Saw them again at noon taken to the river-side, and brought back the same way. He did not see 42, 43, beat, and is not positive as to 39, though he saw a beyt or some instrument in his hand, and believes he was beating. He went with the advanced tents to Allal, and about 3 P.M. saw the thieves brought in a Nizamut Suggur Garre near the tents. Their feet were bound with bandages Prisoner 37 gave all the orders, and had all the arrangements about the garres, tents, &c. When he witnessed the beating, he saw the thieves taken to the Meah's tent. The thieves always remained here.

"23. Junghoo Shaik, the Gharrewan, witness 16 on the calendar, confirms the evidence of George Shapcott regarding his interference in the witness's behalf, when Muddee was beaten at Nowgurriah. The prisoner only struck Muddee twice in the presence of the witness; but, from his statement it would appear that Muddee had been beaten elsewhere. He saw marks upon his arms. He saw prisoner 46 tie Muddee, and put him on a camel before him, and take him to Purranpore This witness states that prisoner 46 took the two thieves to Allal in two Nizamut meanahs.

"24. Hajee Nunha, witness 19 on the calendar, tailor in His Highness's service, confirms G. Shapcott's testimony regarding the beating of Muddee at Nowgurriah, when he could not point out the Gharrewan to whom he said he had given the property. The Moonshief, who was comparing the Gharrewan's name with the list in his hand, called out to Muddee, 'You have told a lie, you rascal!' 'Maro Hurumzadko!' Prisoner 46 began to beat him, and he kept calling out, 'Dohay Jonab Alie!' 'Dohay Sahibka!' 'Humko nahuk marta!' The prisoner, seeing the beating, ran away. The next morning he saw prisoner 46 take Muddee with his arms and legs, bound on a camel, to the factory at Rogonauthpore. One day, at Purranpore, went to the tent of the prisoner 49, where all the Meahs lived There was only Burra Sahib there; Muddee had told him that he had given the property to the fakeers. Burra Sahib sent for them all, and by his directions they beat Muddee. Saw on his body blows of runchus and corahs. On the fifth day proceeded to Allal; remained there **two** days; and on the 4th reached Gujol. The next morning went to **the** Meah's tent; saw Muddee sitting there, and his father Etwarree; and heard Muddee say to his father, 'My body is burning; give me **some** medicine to cool it.' He also called out. 'Meah Sahib! give me some medicine to cool my body! Khan Sahib! give me **some** medicine to cool my body!' The Doctor came, and the Bhatjee, and gave the father some medicine for his son, saying it would cool him. About 4 P.M. heard that Muddee was dead. The witness saw Hingoo with Muddee in a talka-pal, near the tent of prisoner 39. Saw Hingoo on the road going to Gujol in a meanah. Muddee was on a ruth at the time. Both belonged to the Nizamut. Points out prisoner 48 as **present** in the Meahs' tent, when the fakeers beat Muddee. Saw on **the bodies of** Hingoo and Muddee marks of the corah and beyt.

"25. Ameer Alie, witness 21 on the calendar, employed as a Moojrayee **in** His Highness's service; one day at noon at Purranpore saw prisoners 47, 48, 49, and Burra Sahib, beat Hingoo and Muddee some with a stick and some with their hands. They took them in this way to the river, and then brought them back, and took them to the Meah's tent. What occurred there he does not know.

"26. Mohammed Ameen, witness 22 on the calendar, **a** eunuch in the service of His Highness, states that **one day** at Purranpore he **went** shooting with His Highness, and returned **with** him. A man came and gave information that the box of prisoner 41 **was** lost. On this His Highness went to his tent, and prisoner 37 **to** his. Witness heard the thieves were caught, and went to see them in the Meahs' tent. He saw Hingoo tied, and another, whose name **he** does not know, but his father's name is Etwarree, sitting near him. Burra Sahib and prisoner 47 were beating them with **a** stick or beyt—cannot say which, and threatening them; Hingoo was saying, 'You are beating me unjustly, let me go' Witness went and told prisoner 37. He sent Amanut Hurkaru to Urzbeggy (prisoner 39), to inquire who was beating them, and to let them go. Witness saw nothing more that day. He remained in the tent of prisoner 37. The next morning early some one came—Ramjebun or some one—and said they were still beating the thieves and had not let them go. Prisoner 37 **sent** Ramjan Assarburdar, and desired him to go and see if the thieves were still there, and if so, to let them go. This witness, in reply to a question by the Court, stated that when he went to the Meah's tent to see the thieves, he saw there prisoners 39 and 48, and that some of the Meahs were inside and some outside the tent. He could only remember the prisoners 39 and 48. He did not go inside the tent. He saw the thieves in the verandah of the Meahs' tent. Hingoo's hands were tied to one of the tent-pins. He did not mention to prisoner 37 that prisoner 39 was in the tent when he saw the beating. Prisoner 39 knew that he was there. Ramjan went to the Meahs' tent, but witness does not know what information he gave on his return to prisoner 37. He does not know if the thieves were released according to his orders. They died seven or eight days after at Gujol. Witness gets 116 rupees per mensem from His Highness for different offices. On being questioned by the Counsel for the prosecutor he stated, that the camp went from Purranpore to Allal and from Allal to Gujol. There were three tents in the camp, one belonging to His Highness, one to prisoner 37, and one to the Meahs. Witness lived in the tent of prisoner 37. In the Meahs' tent there were the prisoners 39, 41, 38, 47, 40, 44, 45, 43, 42, and Burra Sahib, and servants. His Highness's tent is always pitched in the centre, that of the prisoner 37 on one side, and that of the Meahs' on the other. There was a kanat between His Highness's and the Meahs' tent; the distance between the two tents about 100 haths; the distance between His Highness's and the tent of prisoner 37 about 80 or 90 haths. The two men died in the pal near the Meahs' tent. Witness saw the pal. It was two or four haths from the Meahs' tent. The pals were in charge of the darogah of the Farashkhanah. Witness is the darogah of the Farashkhanah. No one came to him for the pal for the two thieves. Etwarree used to live in that pal, and the two men were brought there, and died there. Etwaree Khawas and other Khawasses occupied the pal. Generally the pal these men occupied was placed two or more haths from the Meahs' tent, more or less, according to the nature of the ground. The pal was standing near where he first saw the men beaten. On being cross-examined by Mr. Montriou, the witness stated that prisoner 39 used always to dine with His Highness, and prisoner 47 occasionally. Excepting prisoner 45 and prisoner 47, whose hand was broken, all the Meahs dined every evening with His Highness.

"27. Kangalu Sheikh Bhistee, in the service of His Highness, witness No 27 on the calendar at Purranpore, one day saw one of the thieves—does not know his name—brought there on a camel. Went from Purranpore to Allal, and from Allal to Gujol, where the thief died. The hurkaru told him to bring some water, and come along with him. Went and washed the body of the thief before it was buried. Describes the injuries upon it. The skin was off all over, from the back and different parts. The wounds appeared to have been caused by beating. It was about 3 p m. He was buried in a bamboo jungle, near a tank. He was buried immediately after the washing. The grave was dug before witness came there. He was called by the hurkaru about 3 p.m.

"28. Shaik Shekardee, witness 28 on the calendar, went with His Highness's camp from Purranpore to Allal, and from Allal to Gujol. After Hingoo's death, a hurkaru called witness, and he went with water to where the body was, near a grave. Saw marks of beating all over the body, arms, legs, &c, long marks. Did not notice whether there were injuries about the feet. Did not observe whether there were marks of burning. Washed the body and came away. The grave was ready when he arrived there. Did not know Hingoo. Does not know the Hurkara's name. He was a servant of the Nizamut. Witness is also. Knew the Hurkara was a Nizamut servant by his stick and chauprass. Did not know him before. Points out the grave as being two or three russees distant from the tents. On being questioned by Mr. Montriou he stated that Kangali went with him, and they both washed the body.

"29. Bhozwan Ghose, witness 29 on the calendar, applied ointment upon the arms and feet of the two thieves at Allal. Prisoner 48 told him it was ordered by prisoner 41 and prisoner 39. They were under a tent pal near the tent of the prisoner 41. There were long scars upon the feet, hands, and arms The back was swollen, but he did not see marks. Saw marks of beating, and suspects there were marks of burning. Marks of beating, are long; and of burning, round Saw round marks upon the shoulders. The wounds did not heal from the applications. The man died. The applications, or poultices, were made of atta (meal), milk, and ghee. Gave them for five days at Allal. The thieves were in a tent put near the Mealhs' tent. Prisoner 48 first called him. Prisoner 41 gave him orders to put the poultices on. Used to apply them every morning at 6 a.m. Witness arrived at Gujol after the camp at nine that night. Heard next morning the thieves were dead. On a question being put by Mr. Montriou, the witness stated that he thinks the men must have died from beating. Heard they had been beaten, because a box had been stolen; but judges they died from beating from the wounds he saw. The wounds, when he last saw the men, were better, but the men died

"30. Khasinath Roy and Ahaloolla, two witnesess, proved the confession of prisoner 49, taken before the magistrate."

This closed for the prosecution.

"31. Mr Clarke put in a written defence for his client's prisoners No. 37, 38, 40, 43, and 44, and Mr. Montriou the same for his clients, prisoners No. 39, 41, 42, 45, and 47. Prisoners No. 46, 48, 49, defended themselves.

"32. Out of thirty-eight witnesses for the defence named by the prisoners in the Magistrate's Court, Mr Montriou only called four, and the prisoner 46 called three. Fresh witnesses to character only were called by both the counsel in behalf of their respective claims; and their testimony, though not exculpatory with reference to the facts proved in evidence was very favourable to them.

"33. The following are the witnesses called on behalf of the prisoners Nos. 42 and 46 :—

"34. Kahoolan, witness 92 of the calendar, a mallee in the Nawab Begum's service, went with prisoner No 42 to the camp on an errand from the Begum at Purranpore. Lived under any tree they could find. Left the camp at Purranpore Were at Purranpore a night and a day. Arrived the same day His Highness arrived there.

"35. Hossain Bur, witness No. 91 on the calendar, in the Nawab Begum's service, went with prisoner No. 42 and Hawo and Kahoolan to His Highness's camp. They left it at Purranpore. Prisoner 42 used to remain, sometimes with witness sometimes with His Highness. Remained with him under a tree at Hyathpore. Prisoner 42 lived two days in His Highness's tent.

"36. Mehengoo Shaik, witness 98 on the calendar, camel-driver in the service of His Highness, was with the prisoner No. 46 in the journey; was with him when he went from Purranpore to Nowgurriah, and when he returned; did not beat any one before him, or quarrel with any one.

"*Cross-examined by Mr. Trevor.* Went from Nowgurriah to Purranpore with prisoner 46 on a camel. There were four persons. Bakur and himself went on one camel, and prisoner No 46 with somebody else—does not know who—on another camel. Does not know whether he was in the service or not. Went to bring Ashab by the order of prisoner 37. The prisoner 46 made the man who was with him over to Jechun Lal; never asked the prisoner 46 who the man was or anything about him. Nowgurriah is five coss from Purranpore. The man returned with them. Never asked about him.

"*By the Court.* The prisoner 37 sent the camels for the Ashab.

"Mookoo Shootisban, witness 99 on the calendar, examined by the prisoner 46. The prisoner 46 went with the camp. Was with him when he went from Purranpore to Nowgurriah, and when he returned, made no disturbance on the way. Afterwards went to Raj Mehal. For five years never saw him quarrel with anybody. *Cross-examined by Mr. Trevor.* Witness went on foot to Nowgurriah. There were two camels, and four persons on them,—on one prisoner 46, and the man who had been caught—does not know his name; and on the other Mehengoo and Bakur. The man who had been caught was given over to Jechun Lal Bahoo.

"*By the Court.* A box had been stolen, and he was, therefore, taken at night to Nowgurriah to point out the property. He was taken by order of the prisoner 37. On his return he was taken to the Meahs' tent. The witness states he saw nobody beat the man at Nowgurriah, and saw no marks of beating.

Cross-examined by Mr. Clarke. They were all close to the tent with the camels; heard prisoner 37 give orders to take Muddee and the order for the camels. Witness stood by the the Meahs' tent, and the prisoner 46 and the other driver went to the tent of prisoner.

"37. Did not hear the order. They all told him prisoner 37 had given the order. Does not remember who first told him, or who secondly, or who thirdly told him. A hurkara came first and conveyed the orders. They did not believe him, and went to make sure. Left Purranpore at eleven at night, and about 3 a.m. reached Nowgurriah. It was morning when they returned.

"38. Bakir Ali, witness 100 in the calender, examined by prisoner 46. Is a Nizamut camel-driver! was with prisoner 46 in the camp; went with him from Purranpore to Nowgurriah. Did not see him oppress any one in the way. Went from Purranpore to Raj Mehal, and then to Maldah. Considers prisoner a good man.

"Mr. Montriou declined to put any question to the witness, on the ground that nothing said by any of the witnesses for prisoner 46 could affect his own clients.

"*Examined by the Court.* Prisoner 46 and a man he does not know went upon one camel. He (witness) and Mehengoo went upon another. Left Purranpore at ten or eleven at night. Went with a letter. The letter was from Burra Sahib to Jechun Lal. Next morning they returned about 8 or 9 A.M. to Purranpore. On the way, one quarter coss from Purranpore, they met Burra Sahib on an elephant, and gave up the man to him.

"*Examined by the Mohir.* The camels left Purranpore by the orders of prisoner 37. They went first to his tent, and he gave the order to take the letter and the camels to Nowgurriah. He said 'Whatever Burra Sahib orders, let that be done.' On their return they had no communication with prisoner 37. Jechul Lal gave no reply, but only ordered the men to be taken back. Burra Sahib gave the letter and the man for them to take to Jechun Lal.

"*Cross-examined by Mr. Clarke.* Three of them went to the tent of the prisoner 37. The two camels were left near the Meahs' tent. Witness, Mehengoo, and prisoner 46, went and stood at the door of the tent. Prisoner 37 was in the tent; his bed was near the door. Did not see anybody else there; the servants may have been. It was night. They were all three together. Does not know who spoke first. The hurkara called them. They asked what orders he had to give. Prisoner 37 said that Burra Sahib would give the letters. Cannot say if prisoner 37 was lying or sitting: only heard him speak, and knew he was there. The other two were Nizamut camel-drivers. Can swear they went for orders. Cannot remember who spoke first. The hurkara ordered them to take the two camels to the tent of the prisoner 37. They took the two camels and left them at the Meahs' tent, and went for orders to the tent of the prisoner 37. They were servants, there was no Jemadar, and they went for orders. They went to the tent of the prisoner 37, because all orders were given by him; they did not, therefore, go to the Meahs' tent. Yes, swears to all that he has stated. Does not remember what they said to prisoner 37. Remembers his orders. It was 'Go to the Burra Sahib, and do what he directs.' Prisoner 37 did not say anything about Muddee. Burra Sahib only pointed out the man. Did not speak about Muddee. Told them to take this man and the letter to Nowgurriah. This witness adds that he never saw Muddee beaten, and did not see George Shapcott at Nowgurriah, nor any marks on Muddee.

"39. The prisoner 46 declined to call any more witnesses.

"40. Having given an abstract of the principal parts of the evidence upon the record, it will be necessary to examine some of the objections raised by the Counsel for the defence, to the credibility of the testimony adduced in behalf of the prosecution.

"41. The Counsel for the prisoner 37 and others considers the evidence of Dhunnoo as disentitled to credit, because he has stated that on the day on which he witnessed the beating at Purranpore, His Highness with the Meahs returned from shooting about 1 p.m., and that the thieves had been arrested an hour before; whereas more credible witnesses state that it was His Highness's custom to stay out till 4, 5, and 6 p.m.; and that on that particular day he returned at 5 p.m., and the arrest took place about 9 a.m.

"42. It is unfortunate for the argument of the learned Counsel that the prisoner 37, his client, when examined by Mr. Lock, the officiating magistrate, on the 16th of May, 1853, admitted that he returned from shooting on that day about 1 p.m. or 2 p.m. That it was the same day on which Dhunnoo witnessed the beating is clear, because the prisoner 37 also admitted in that examination that on the return from shooting at that time he heard that a small box belonging to the prisoner 41, darogah of the Phul Khana, was missing, and that two men were arrested on suspicion. That the prisoners 37 and 47, with their servants, prisoner 48 and witness No. 5 and others, beat them, and that he sent three or four times to prevent the beating; and he distinguishes that day from the day following by stating further that the next day they were also beaten by the prisoners 39 and 48, the prisoner 47, Burra Sahib, witness No. 5, and others being present in the tent, and that he again prevented the beating; and when asked what persons were acquainted with these circumstances, he mentions the names of Meah Ameen and prisoners 38 and 41, 44, 42, 45, and 47, as being present.

"43. The return of the shooting-party in the middle of the day is also admitted by the prisoner 39 in his examination before the Magistrate on the same date, the 16th May, 1853, and by the prisoner 46 in his defence, and the prisoner 49 in his confession.

"44. The Counsel for the prisoner 41 and others, in his written defence states that the admissions of the prisoners before the Magistrate are not admissible as evidence in the Sessions Court.

"45. The Magistrate took the examinations of the prisoners, and put the same into writing, and they formed part of the judicial inquiry. Such examinations, when reduced into writing, and attested by the prisoners and signed by the Magistrate, and placed upon the record, are admissible as evidence; that is, such weight will be given to them as the Court may consider them entitled to with reference to other parts of the examination, the circumstances of the case, and the evidence generally. This has been the practice of the Court, and the Court is not aware that such practice is opposed to the principles of English Law or inconsistent with the requirements of justice.

"46. A written examination taken in conformity with the regulations, which are the Magistrate's guide, is the best possible evidence of the prisoner having made a declaration of all that is contained in that examination. If the objection should be, that a part of it has been elicited by the questions put by the Magistrate, the objection would not hold good so long as the Magistrate does not put the questions in such a way as to extract a confession, but for the purpose of elucidating or explaining what the prisoner may be willing to state with reference to the charge. It only would hold good where the prisoner by such questions might be entrapped into making statements that would be used against him on his trial, which, but for those questions, he would not have made. It surely was incumbent on the learned Counsel to prove, in behalf of his clients, that there was some omission or irregularity in the taking of the examination in order to prevent its being used against them, instead of simply asserting that such evidence was inadmissible.

"47. The witness Dhunnoo, No. 1, does not state that the thieves were arrested an hour before the return of the party from shooting, but that it was one hour before their return that he first saw them bound and beaten. He did not (he states in the beginning of his deposition) hear of the theft till twelve at noon.

"48. The discrepancy which the Counsel for the prisoner No. 37 has pointed out between what the witness stated at the Sessions Court and before the Magistrate regarding the threat used by prisoner 37 to the two thieves is capable of being explained. It would seem from his answer, when questioned, that his statements before the Magistrate were true, only that the words 'If you do not give the property' were omitted, meaning that the prisoner 37 asked for the order and gave it.

"49. The evidence of Hingun Khan, butta burdar. The points which the Counsel for the prisoner 41 has laid stress on as rendering his evidence totally inadmissible, because he considers it inconsistent with all other testimony to the same circumstances, viz, that part of his evidence in the Sessions Court, in which he states that Muddee was brought back from Nowgurriah on an elephant, and not on a camel, and that part of his evidence before the Magistrate, in which he states that Burra Sahib and prisoner 47 were seated on the same elephant, are points which, being incidentally confirmed by the defence of the prisoner 46, and other evidence on the record, would dispose the Court to give that evidence greater credit.

"50 With reference to the evidence of Hingun Khan, butta burdar, the points which the Counsel for the prisoner 41 has laid stress on as rendering his evidence totally inadmissible, because he considers it inconsistent with all other testimony to the same circumstance, viz., that part of his evidence in the Sessions Court in which he states that Muddee was brought back from Nowgurriah on an *elephant*, and not on a camel, and that part of his evidence before the Magistrate in which he states that Burra Sahib and prisoner were seated on the same *elephant*, are points which, being incidentally confirmed by the defence of the prisoner 46 and other evidence on the record, would dispose the Court to give that evidence greater credit.

"51. With regard to the objections urged by the Counsel for the prisoner 37 to the statement of Hossainee Sheikh, No. 5, there is no doubt that he was *personally* interested; but the personal interest he must have felt in the proceedings and the result of the trial can form no legal ground for the rejection of any part of his testimony that can be borne out by other evidence. He was put upon his defence at first by the Magistrate; and after his examination was taken he was made Queen's evidence. He distinctly states Burra Sahib and prisoner 47 arrested Muddee because he had once come to the Meahs' tent, and they suspected him of the theft. He states that his master, prisoner 41, was present; and though he did not beat he threatened. This is not an entire exculpation of his master. There is no contradiction of his evidence by Dhunnoo to render it unworthy of credit. *All* he has stated relative to the beating, and *what* he stated regarding the brandy, may appear inconsistent with the evidence of other witnesses, because they have not stated the *same*; but their not having stated what he states is no proof that he may not have seen what he related. There is a difference in the statements of the witnesses regarding the conveyances in which Muddee and Hingoo were taken from one place to another; but it may be accounted for by the presumption that they saw them at *different* times, since it is shown that they were carried first from Purranpore to Allal, and then one of them from Allal to Purranpore and back again, and then both of them from Allal to Gujol, and also by the *length* of time that has elapsed since these occurrences. Hossainee Sheikh deposes that they were taken sometimes in one conveyance and sometimes in another.

"52. Ruhm Khan, witness No. 9, has spoken of the theft as happening at 6 a.m. This was upon cross-examination by Mr. Clarke. He appears to have associated it with the fact that His Highness and his party had gone shooting *when* he heard of the theft; and it is possible, from this association in his mind, that he had miscalculated the time. The other discrepancies are not sufficient to affect the credibility of his general testimony.

"53. Both the learned Counsel for the defence consider George Shapcott's evidence as entitled to the *fullest credit*. His evidence convicts *only* the prisoner 47 (camel-driver), who maltreated Muddee at Nowgurriah.

"54. The same meed of praise for *truthfulness* of testimony is liberally given by both the Counsel to Mahomed Ameen, witness 22. His evidence convicts the prisoner 47 and Burra Sahib of beating Muddee and Hingoo at the Meahs' tent,. and prisoners 39 and 48 of being present. He states that *some* of the Meahs were inside the tent and some out. These two witnesses have, the Court has no doubt, spoken the *truth in as far* as they have deposed: but their *silence* regarding transactions to which other witnesses have sworn is no proof that these transactions did not take place.

"55. The prisoner 49 confessed before the Magistrate, and it has been proved by the attesting witnesses that the confession was *voluntary*, and that no *undue influence* was exercised over the prisoner.

"56. The confession is to the following effect: 'I did not murder Hingoo and Muddee. Last Falgoon I rode on an elephant, and went with His Highness on his expedition. I am in his service. On arriving at Purranpoor I heard one day that a theft had taken place in the tent of prisoner 41, and that the thieves were arrested and were being beaten. On hearing this I went to the tent to see the thieves, and saw Burra Sahib, prisoner 47, Hossainee, witness 5, and Joomun beating Hingoo and Muddee in the tent of the prisoner No 41. Some were beating with a rattan and some with a corah, and the two thieves were crying and calling out for His Highness's and the Company's help, "Dohaee Nawab Sahib,"—"Dohaee Company!" Seeing this I returned to my elephant. On *that* day His Highness came back from his hunting excursion at *noon*, and in the absence of the Peadahs I went and placed a ladder against the elephant, by which His Highness descended and went to his tent. Prisoner No. 37 and the other Meahs, whose names I do not know, but I can point them out if I saw them, asked where the thieves were, and Hossainee Khavas said they were in the tent. Then all the Meahs, including prisoner 37, went to the tent and began to beat the two thieves, and they tried to run away in consequence of the torture; but prisoner 47 and Burra Sahib, abusing me, called out to me to go and catch them, and I caught them. They ordered me afterwards to tie them, but I refused, as I have children (bal butcha), on which they threatened to beat me if I did not tie them up. I was therefore obliged from fear to tie both Hingoo's hands with a tent rope, and then ran away. What happened afterwards I do not know. I went with the *advance* tents, and do not know if they were subsequently beaten. On reaching Gujol I heard the two thieves were dead. I saw the corpse of Muddee when he was buried, but not that of Hingoo. There were wounds upon Muddee's body. In some places the skin was torn off, and in some there were bruises. Some said they died of beating, some of cholera—the doctor knows. I only saw them on the day they were beaten and the day they died.'

"57. **This confession, of** course, is only evidence against the prisoner himself, and not against the other prisoners. The *whole* of this confession must be considered, although *all* the parts of it may not be entitled to *equal* credit. The same rule applies to this confession as to the admission in the examination of the prisoner 37, to which the Court has adverted. The *whole* must be considered, and **if there is any part** in favour of the prisoner, which is not disproved **by the evidence for the prosecution**, and is not improbable in itself, **it should be weighed and judged of by** *all* the circumstances **of the case** The reason of such a **course,** both as a maxim in law and **as a practice** in Court, **is obvious,** because it is most probable that **what a** prisoner admits may be **true, as** he could have no motive to criminate himself, but **it is** still left **to the** Court to weigh the *whole* with all the circumstances **of the case as they** appear in evidence.

"58. The law officer, **after a very prolonged and patient** trial, during which the prisoners at **the bar have had the benefits, most of** them, of the services of able Counsel from Calcutta to conduct their defence, has given his Futwah, which convicts by Tazeer, prisoners 38, 39, 42, 43, 44, 47, 48, 49, and 46, of aggravated, culpable homicide as principals; prisoners 40, 41, and 45 of privity (41 being besides the *owner* of the property, and on violent presumption the *instigator* of the above crimes), and Aman Ali Khan, No. 37, of instigating and giving orders, and beating on **violent presumption,** and of privity to the above crimes on full proof.

"59. I have maturely weighed the whole of the evidence for and against the prisoner, taking into consideration such discrepancies as in my mind affected the credibility of any part of the evidence, and adopting **only as the** grounds **for** my judgment such parts **as** I considered trustworthy, and on which safe **reliance could** be placed.

"60. I will briefly touch upon one or two points **as they have presented** themselves successively **to my** consideration.

"1st. Whether **the two men, Hingoo** and **Muddee, actually died** about the time **they are said to have died in His** Highness's camp?

"On this point there can be no **doubt upon the evidence.**

"61. 2nd. Whether they died a natural **death or by** accident, or whether it was the result of an unlawful act, **deliberately** committed by others?

"62. It was given out that these men died of the cholera, but there **is** not the shadow of a proof to support the rumour. **On the contrary,** there is sufficient evidence to show that they had previous to their death been repeatedly, and, as one of the witnesses expressed himself, unmercifully, beaten. It was a continuous beating, a protracted, **cruel torture,** at different times and in different places, making it difficult **after** so long a lapse of time for the witnesses to the cruel acts to depose with minute exactness to *all* the circumstances attending each separate transaction. I lay aside all *general* presumptions in a case of so serious a nature. From the evidence, however, a violent presumption arises, **that** when the beating had told upon these poor wretches, when **their skins had** been taken off them, as one witness said, and their flesh was, **as** another described it, *raw, like raw beef,* and sores covered their bodies, that *then,* and not till then, the cruel torturing ceased, and **native** doctors were sent for to give their aid in the last extremity. **A veil has** been thrown over the last scenes of the painful tragedy, but enough of evidence has been produced, amounting to legal presumption, *to unite cause and effect*, and, in the absence of any proof whatever to the contrary, to show that the men died from the maltreatment they received, and that their bodies were buried not far from His Highness's camp at Gujol. The learned Counsel for the prisoner 41 has referred to the rule of that great and merciful judge, Sir M. Hale, against the conviction of murder, where the body, as the best proof of the *corpus delicti*, is not forthcoming. This is of imperative force in cases where the evidence is circumstantial, and there is the slightest doubt of the death of the party. In this case the evidence is principally that of eye-witnesses, and the death of the parties has never been denied by the prisoners.

"63. The next point to consider is, whether these unlawful acts, this continuous and cruel maltreatment, terminating so fatally, constitute the crime of murder, or culpable homicide, or any other crime of less degree.

"64. The English Law has laid down generally a clear distinction between the crime of murder and that of manslaughter. Any unlawful act which deprives another of life, in the commission of which there is no *malice* expressed or implied, is manslaughter. But what is this malice, and in what manner is it to be ascertained? Blackstone, with his usual clearness and penetration, attempts to define it. He states, that the malice necessary to constitute the crime of murder is not confined to an *intention* to take away the life of another, but that an intent to do an unlawful act, which may probably end in depriving another of life, is *included in it;* that the malice prepense essential to murder is not so properly malevolent to the individual as evil design generally arising from a bad heart, which may be expressed or implied

"65. So that if a man, not having in his heart a positive purpose to take life, should entertain a purpose to do another some very grievous bodily injury, and carry out that purpose, and in the prosecution of it death ensue, although the death may ensue *beside* the original intention, the act would be murder.

"66. There might therefore be, in the painful case before the Court, some grounds on the general principles of the law, which would rule such cases for considering the crime one of murder; but after giving this point the deepest attention, I am constrained, with reference to all the facts of the case as elicited by the evidence, to regard it as culpable homicide under very aggravated circumstances. I am borne out in this view by the Kasi Mahomed, v z , Byjonauth and others, decided by the Court of Nizamut Adawlut on the 29th March, 1825. A case of excessive cruel and savage torture, for the purpose of compelling a confession of theft and production of property, which ended in the death of the person abused. The Law Officer of the Circuit Court acquitted the prisoners, while the Judge convicted them of *wilful murder*. The Judges of the Court of Nizamut Adawlut, C. Smith, H. Shakespeare, and W. B. Martin, convicted the prisoners of culpable homicide with aggravating circumstances.

"67. Mr. Clarke observes that every concomitant by which murders are characterised has been reversed in this case; that suddenness, solitude, and secrecy are the distinguishing marks of the worst murders: but this was the most prolonged, the most public, and the easiest of detection; and Mr. Montriou takes the same view, and from the *openness* of the acts doubts the possibility of their commission,

" 68. The *publicity* of the acts; that is, of such acts as were committed *outside* of the Meahs' tent, is no ground for discrediting the joint testimony of so many witnesses, though to some extent it may be ground for believing that those who committed them did not in the commission of them *intend* to take life, but to go to the extremest length *short* of taking it. The *publicity* may be attributed to the *presumption* under which the prisoners appear to have acted, that as members of His Highness's household they had *within* his camp the power to apprehend and punish for theft, and to the *gratification* which some of them, peculiarly circumstanced as they are, might naturally feel in openly displaying that power, and to the *hope* that in the event anything untoward happening the ægis of the Nizamut might be extended over them to shelter them.

" 69. The motive of the crime is clear. It was the discovery of the stolen property, and the men were maltreated to the death on the suspicion that they were the thieves, and with the view of making them confess. The *exact* time when each separate act was committed is not so important in a case like this, where the crime has *continuance;* nor is it so necessary, where *so many* were concerned at different times, to specify distinctly the *exact share* which each took in each different transaction, or to particularize distinctly the *exact instrument* which was used by each in the beating It is not necessary to prove by whom the *fatal* blow was given; all who were present aiding and abetting the acts would be principals; all who were present and assisting at the beating would be guilty of the death of the parties, though they themselves did not beat *providing death* ensued from the beating.

" 70. I disagree with the Futwa in the conviction of the prisoners on the different counts. I would convict the prisoners Nos. 39, 46, 47, 48, and 49, as principals in the culpable homicide of Muddee and Hingoo, attended with very aggravated circumstances, and with reference to the precedent of Byjnauth and others already alluded to; I would recommend them to be sentenced to 14 years' imprisonment, with hard labour in irons, in banishment; and the prisoners Nos. 40, 42, 43, 44, as aiding and abetting in the aforesaid crime, to 10 years' imprisonment, with labour in irons; and the prisoners 41, 45, on the same count, but as less culpable, and with reference to their previous good and inoffensive character, to 6 years' imprisonment, with labour without irons; and prisoner No. 38, against whom only *one* witness, Hossainee, deposes as to beating, another, Jinghoo Khan, deposing only to his *following* the party who took the deceased to the Factory, as privy to the crime, to 3 years' imprisonment with labour, commutable to a fine of 100 rupees.

" 71. With regard to prisoner No. 37, I must say I am not satisfied with that part of it which would implicate him as the instigntor, which he would be if it was satisfactorily proved that he gave orders for the two men to be beaten. It is true that a number of presumptions may by their accumulation become important, and it has been held a good maxim in weighing evidence. ' *Possunt diversa genera ita conjungi ut quæ singula non nocerent, ea universa tanquam grande reum opprimant.*' There is a presumption that the witnesses spoke the truth in what they stated regarding the orders the prisoner 37 gave, when Muddee at night was taken on a camel by the prisoner No. 46, with a letter from the Burra Sahib, to Nowgurriah. His directions may have extended to the conveying of Muddee under surveillance to Nowgurriah, for the purpose of discovering the property which he was accused of having stolen; this does not amount to *legal* presumption. The statements of the witnesses regarding their having heard him give the orders for beating, from the manner in which their evidences are given, are not sufficient for conviction. The Council for No. 37 has called the attention of the Court to the number of enemies who are likely to have plotted against his client. The accumulative presumption, arising from the whole of the evidence, affords full legal proof of his being an accessory after the fact, both in harbouring the principals and in concealing the crime, and I would recommend him to be sentenced to one year's imprisonment, with labour.

(Signed)   J. D. MONEY.
Sessions Judge.

The 22nd September, 1853.   Moorshedabad.

JUDGMENT OF THE SUDDER NIZAMUT.

Present MR. MILLS *and* MR. RAIKES.

"This case is referred for the orders of the Court on two grounds; firstly, because the Sessions Judge disagrees with the futwa of the law officer in regard to the degree of criminality of some of the prisoners: and secondly, because he is of opinion that the principal prisoners are deserving of a higher punishment than it is within his competence to award.

"It would appear that the Nawab Nazim of Bengal, attended by a large retinue, went towards the end of March last on a shooting expedition in the Maldah district, and that on the morning of the 31st March, while he was out sporting, a box containing money and some valuables was missed from the tent of the Meahs, which at the time was occupied by the prisoners, No. 38, 39, 40, 41, 43, 44, 45, and 47. The box belonged to the prisoner No. 41, and was in charge of the approver Hossainee. It would further appear that a lad, by name Muddee, was arrested on some vague suspicion; that he was severely beaten, as a means to induce him to deliver up the stolen property; that he inculpated Hingoo, who was subjected to similar ill-usage; that this ill-treatment was continued for several days in succession; and that it caused the death of Muddee on the 5th, and that of Hingoo on the 6th of April. The above is a brief outline of the facts of the case, which are established by general evidence, and are admitted by the Counsel who represented the prisoners 37, 38, and 40 before the Court. The Sessions Judge has convicted the prisoners 39, 46, 47, 48, and 49, as principals; No. 40, 41, 42, 43, 44 and 45, as aiders and abettors; 33 as privy to the crime; and 37 as accessory after the fact.

"As the crime was for some time concealed from the authorities, no inquest was held, and no medical evidence is forthcoming as to the state of the bodies after death; but the evidence of Mr. Shapcott, the two bheestees who washed the bodies, and the apprentice who applied remedies before death, as to their condition a short time before and immediately after death, fully justifies the Court in the belief, or violent presumption, that the deaths of the deceased were in consequence of the cruel maltreatment they had received. The question for the determination of the Court, therefore, is, whether the accused parties before the Court took any, and what part, in this ill-treatment, or are in any way connected with the crimes charged against them.

"Mr. Clarke and Mr. Waller, for the prisoners, having strongly pointed the consideration of the Court to the worthlessness of the evidence in general, urging that the charge against their clients originated in a foul conspiracy, got up by plotters in the palace to criminate and ruin the prisoner No. 37, who is the favourite of the Nawab Nazim, and the head man of his household.

"The notoriety of the events which form the grounds of this case must have made them known to so many who were present with the Nawab's camp, that we are not surprised to find that a large number of witnesses was, in the first instance, brought forward to tender evidence against any accused party; but of these the Government Prosecutor selected twenty; and in consequence of contradictions and discrepancies in the depositions of five of these witnesses before the Sessions Court, he rejected their testimony as unworthy of credit. The testimony of the remaining witnesses on which the leading points of the case must rest, and on which the Sessions Judge has based his verdict against the prisoners, has, under the above circumstances, been narrowly scrutinized as regards its truth, and carefully weighed with reference to its respectability, its general consistency, and the probabilities suggested to our minds in considering all the circumstances of the case. Before coming into Court we had attentively considered the evidence, the written defence put in by Counsel at the Sessions Court, and the remarks of the Sessions Judge in refutation of the objections raised therein to the credibility of the testimony of each witness, and had come to the conclusion that the statements of Hossainee Sheikh, the approver, Dhunoo Khan, Raheem Ali, and Hingun, were open to grave suspicion. This suspicion the arguments of the Counsel for the prosecution have failed to diminish.

"The Counsel for the defence have strongly animadverted upon the testimony of the above-named witnesses in particular. They have directed attention to their want of respectability, the circumstance under which they came forward to give their evidence, the general improbabilities and contradictions involved in the statements, and the difficulty of believing that they were ever allowed to be spectators of the events they describe.

"The Court will first remark on the evidence of the approver, Hossainee. This man was first arrested as implicated in the statement of his master, Urjoomund, prisoner No. 44. His defence was taken down by the magistrate, and as that defence exculpated himself from all participation in the crime, and directly inculpated the other prisoners, the magistrates at once released him and made him a witness in the case, proceeding at the same time to record his testimony on the part of the prosecution. He is thus called an *approver*, and his statement is relied upon as carrying with it all the weight attached to evidence of this character when properly supported. This man had special charge of the missing property, and is the person, therefore, on whom blame, if not suspicion, would naturally fall. He was interested in the discovery of the thief, or in removing the suspicions of his master from himself; and nothing can be more probable than that he both knew and participated in the ill-treatment of the deceased. In fact two credible witnesses deposed that he was aiding and abetting those who inflicted the torture on the thieves; yet he refrains from disclosing any such participation, and in no way implicates himself. To have rendered his evidence effective, the magistrate should have, in conformity with the provisions of Regulation X. of 1824, tendered to him a conditional pardon; this was not done: he was, therefore, placed under no special obligation to disclose the whole truth, as in the case of an admitted approver: and taking his evidence as that of an ordinary witness, it appears to us to have been dictated by a wish to exculpate himself at the expense of his fellow-criminals, and *to teem with improbabilities and gross contradictions, which compel the Court to set it aside altogether.*

"As respects the witnesses Dhunoo, Hingun Khan, and Sheikh Raheem Ali, we observe that the first is a discarded Burkundaz of Police, who was the first person who came forward and volunteered evidence, as he himself states, in the hope of earning a good name, and procuring employment; the second is a lame mendicant, who was indicated by Dhunoo as able to give information in this case; and the third describes himself as a cook, temporarily employed in the Nawab's service during this hunting expedition.

"It is impossible to ascertain whether these persons were present at the Nawab's camp as represented; the way in which they account for their presence there does not impress the Court with any reliance on that point, and the occurrences which they relate as taking place daily, from the commencement to the close of this affair, must have taken hold on their memories in an unusual manner, to enable them, after so long an interval, to depose to particulars of which they then conceived themselves to be mere casual observers. The Court observe that Hingun Khan made such palpable contradiction before the sessions that the Judge has recorded his opinion that *the discrepancies are irreconcileable, and the evidence is not entitled to much credit.* We also remark that these witnesses are the only persons who depose to the prisoner No. 37 having instigated and participated in the outrage: one deposing that he threatened to blow the thieves from a gun, and countermanded the Nawab's order for their release; while another alleges that No. 37 trimmed a bamboo, and chastised a thief with it; statements apparently so exaggerated could hardly be relied upon unless made by persons of undoubted veracity, and, in the present instance, totally fail to convince us of their truth, being in direct opposition to the testimony of far more credible persons. Moreover, we observe that the Sessions Judge himself discredited such part of the evidence of these witnesses affecting the above prisoners as instigating the assault. Under these circumstances, we cannot but regard the general character of *the evidence of these witnesses as doubtful and suspicious, and we feel therefore constrained to discard it in toto.*

"The remaining witnesses seem to the Court to have given a connected and probable account of what took place within their own observation and knowledge.

"They are all servants of the Nawab, and their occupation accounts for their presence on the spot. Mr. Shapcott's evidence is in no way impeached, and that of Ameer Ali and Mahomed Ameen has been scarcely called in question: and the Court, after duly considering the exceptions taken to the remaining witnesses by Mr. Montriou in his elaborate review of their depositions, are of opinion that the contradictions elicited on cross-examination are on points so immaterial as in no way to shake the confidence of the Court in their general credibility and trustworthiness. Applying, therefore, this proof to the case of the prisoners, we find there is nothing in it to bring home to the prisoners Nos. 37, 38, 40, 41, 44, and 45, any of the charges on which they stand committed; and only one witness speaks to the presence of No. 42, and another to that of No. 43, on the occasion of the thieves being taken to the river-side, but they even do not implicate them as taking any part in maltreating or encouraging the maltreatment of the prisoners.

It has been argued by Ramapersaud Raj, that the presumption naturally arising from all the facts of the case is sufficiently strong to **convict** the prisoner No. 37 of accessoryship after the fact to the murder, and of privity to the same. The Sessions Judge has found the prisoner guilty of the first charge, inasmuch as he harboured the criminals and concealed the crime. On this point we have to observe, that to justify a conviction on this charge there must be **some act** proved to have been done to assist the felons personally. The evidence discloses no proof of any overt act, nor of any other act on the part of the prisoner, **from** which such an inference can fairly be deduced. As regards the charge of privity to the crime, we would remark that there is no direct evidence to the fact of the prisoner No. 37 taking any part, or being directly or indirectly concerned, either in the burying of the bodies or in giving currency to the report of the thieves having died of cholera. The mere *possibility* that the *rumour* of the death of these men by torture had reached the ears of prisoner No. 37, is not in itself sufficient to bring home to him the charge of concealing or procuring the concealment of the felony; to establish such a charge there must be some proof that, though not consenting, he was personally cognizant of the crime, and, though able, refrained from preventing it, or neglected to use any endeavours for the apprehension of the offenders. An admission was made in the Foujdarry by prisoner No. 37, which is corroborated by the most respectable witness **examined, to the** fact that the prisoner, when he heard the thieves were subjected **to** ill-treatment, sent persons to forbid it on two different occasions, and to release them. Thus there is evidence of an attempt to prevent the offence, and though death subsequently ensued some days afterwards, it would be, I think, an unfair construction of his acts to presume that he was necessarily aware that death was the consequence of such ill-treatment.

"Much stress has been laid by Mr. **Trevor**, both in his written defence and in his arguments before the Court, on the evidence of the three witnesses cited by **Furreed Khan**, No. 46, as inculpating the prisoner No. 37. On their cross-examination they stated that the camels, on one of which the deceased Muddee was conveyed, bound to Nowgurriah, were sent by the orders of the prisoner No. 37, and that he was therefore assenting to the ill-treatment inflicted on the deceased. These witnesses have palpably perjured themselves as regards **Fureed Khan** never having beaten Muddee, as their evidence is directly contradicted by that of George Shapcott; and Mr. Trevor would wish us to reject that part of the testimony and adopt it as to **Aman Ali.** Evidence so tainted must be received with extreme caution: but taken as it stands, we are of opinion that it does not even go far enough to show that the prisoner No. 37 was aware for what purpose the camels were required. One witness states that he *heard* from the three camel-drivers that they had received orders from Aman Ali Khan to take Muddee to Nowgurriah, and another swears that the two camels were taken by Aman Ali's orders to Nowgurriah, and that he desired the drivers to go to the Burra Sahib for instructions. From the third witness nothing inculpatory of the prisoner was elicited. Considering that the prisoner had no motive for ill-using the thieves, that it is in evidence he endeavoured to prevent their ill-usage, we cannot, from this evidence, draw any conclusions condemnatory of this prisoner.

"By the evidence of the witnesses relied on by the Court, it is satisfactorily established that the prisoner, No. 39, who lived in the Meahs' tent, took a part in the ill-treatment of the deceased. The witness No. 11 deposed to his taking, with others, the thieves to the river-side, and to his beating them going and returning. No. 12 confirms the fact, with this qualification, that he did not see the prisoner himself beat them, and No. 22 speaks to the prisoner being in the tent and present when the thieves were being chastised by others; and to the prisoner No. 37 sending orders to this prisoner to stop the maltreatment.

The prisoners, Nos. 46, 47, 48, and 49, together with Burra Sahib, who has evaded justice, are identified by the witnesses generally as taking the most prominent part in the gross maltreatment, ending in death, of the deceased persons; and Mr. Shapcott's evidence especially identified **No. 46, the** camel-driver, as on one occasion beating the deceased Muddee in the most unmerciful manner for the space of **15 minutes.** There is also the clear and well-attested confession of the prisoner No. 49 before the magistrate. We, therefore, in concurrence with the Sessions Judge and Law Officer, convict the prisoners Nos. **39, 46, 47, 48, and** 49, as principals in the culpable homicide of **Muddee and Hingoo.** The case is attended with circumstances of such aggravation and deliberate cruelty, deducible from the evidence generally, as to render the crime scarcely distinguishable from wilful murder; but adopting the principle generally inculcated by the precedents of this Court, that unless the intention of the criminal to take life is fairly inferable from the nature and circumstances of the case, a conviction of wilful murder cannot pass, we convict them of the minor offence of culpable homicide, and sentence them, as proposed by the Sessions Judge, to fourteen years' imprisonment with labour in irons.

"The Court have noticed in its place the irregular manner in which the magistrate has admitted Hossainee to be an approver. The Court further notice, with censure, the unfairness and impropriety of the magistrate's proceedings as regards the prisoner Urjoomund, in first taking his defence, then converting him into a witness and examining him on oath, and then, because he considered that he had *not spoken the whole truth*, re-arraigning him on the original charge and committing him for trial."

In whatever light we view the course taken by Lord Dalhousie against the Nawab Nazim in connection with the above unfortunate affair, we cannot but consider it most unjustifiable; for even admitting that His Lordship had a right to differ in opinion from the Judges of the Court of Nizamut Adawlut as to the culpability of the ssrvants of the Nawab, there was certainly not the least ground for implicating the Nawab himself, or holding him responsible for the acts of his servants. Besides, there were present in the camp with His Highness several European gentlemen of high standing in the Company's civil service, and it is surprising to think that none of those gentlemen (one of whom was a Judge) were called to account by His Lordship for the same reasons adduced against the Nawab. Again, if His Lordship was dissatisfied with the judgment of the highest Court of Justice in the land, he might have ordered another trial to be proceeded with, before jumping to a hasty conclusion as to the guilt of the Nawab's servants (who had been thrice tried and acquitted), and then, without any just cause punishing their master for their supposed act on a mere assumption that he must have been cognizant of whatever occurred in his camp, even while he was away from it. We feel assured that every right thinking Englishman will with us disagree with His Lordship's opinion and ill-judged conclusions.

The action taken by Lord Dalhousie is fully set out in His Highness' Memorial to the Secretary of State for India, and also in the Narrative of the Nizamut Affairs by the Agent Governor-General, to which we would refer our readers for further information, leaving it to them and an enlightened public to distinguish the right, and to exercise the power in their hands, by doing justice to the Prince who has suffered so much from the effects of such arbitrary measures!

Lord Dalhousie's term of office ceased soon after this, but the result of his arbitrary acts and the annexation policy, by which solemn treaties and engagements with Indian Princes were set aside, soon after broke out in the terrible Mutiny of 1857, when Lord Canning held the reins of Government in India.

In 1856, Lord Canning, who was afterwards the first Viceroy of Her Most Gracious Majesty, gave His Highness the following assurance of "*consideration, respect, and friendly interest &c.;*" of the British Government :—

From LORD CANNING TO NAWAB SYUD MUNSOOR ALI, KHAN, BEHADOOR, (*the present* NAWAB NAZIM *of Bengal, Behar, and Orissa,*) *dated* 11*th March,* 1856.

"Nawab Sahib, of high worth and exalted station, my good brother,
"I wish you peace.
"After expressing devoted desire beyond description for a happy
"interview, I would announce what You will have gleaned from
"the newspapers of the 29th February last, that this friend has been
"appointed to succeed the Most Noble the Marquis of Dalhousie K.T.
"as Governor-General of India.
"Permit me to add, this friend entered Calcutta, the seat of
"Government, and assumed the duties of this high office on the 26th
"February, 1856, corresponding to the 22nd Jumadee-ul-Sanee,
"1272, H.
"Your Highness may be assured *the consideration, respect, and*
"*friendly interest* in the prosperous administration *of your affairs,*
"and *just regard to the honours and dignities* due to *your hereditary*
"*rank and the prescriptive privileges of your high station, guaranteed*
"*by the stipulations of subsisting Treaties and long established Rela-*

" tions, observed and cherished by former Governors-General, will on
" the part, also, of this sincere friend, be fervently fostered and punc-
" tually fulfilled.

" Assured of this friend's interest in your welfare, I hope you will
" not fail to favour him with letters that may cheer him with the
" welcome intelligence of your health and prosperity.

" Further,—may days of joy accord with your desire.
"   (Signed)   CANNING.

If, therefore, as acknowledged by Lord Dalhousie himself and again by Lord Canning, the first *direct* Representative of the British Crown in India, the Treaties concluded with the Nawab's ancestors are *existing* and *subsisting*, we may well inquire why has not the British Government insisted upon the Government of India fulfilling all the conditions therein named by restoring to His Highness and his family those rights and privileges of which they have been unjustly deprived by the officers of that Government? It was with the object of correcting the abuses practised by the officers of the East India Company that the Imperial Government took over the Administration of Indian Affairs, and it is matter of surprise that abuses still exist in India as evidenced in the case of the Nawab of Bengal and other Native Princes with whom solemn contracts were made by the East India Company. Her Most Gracious Majesty, after having assumed the Supreme Administration and Government of India, issued the following Proclamation to the Princes, the Chiefs, and the People of India, as an assurance that "*all Treaties and Engagements made with them by or under the Authority of the Honourable East India Company,*" were by Her accepted, and "*would be scrupulously maintained,*" hence the British Government is responsible for the faithful fulfilment of the same by the Government of India.

ALLAHABAD, *Monday, 1st November,* 1858.

THE RIGHT HONOURABLE THE GOVERNOR-GENERAL *has received the Commands of* HER MAJESTY *the* QUEEN, *to make known the following gracious* PROCLAMATION *of* HER MAJESTY *to the* PRINCES, *the* CHIEFS, *and the* PEOPLE OF INDIA.

PROCLAMATION OF THE QUEEN IN COUNCIL, TO THE PRINCES, CHIEFS, AND PEOPLE OF INDIA, VICTORIA, BY THE GRACE OF GOD, OF THE UNITED KINGDOM OF GREAT BRITAIN AND IRELAND, AND OF THE COLONIES AND DEPENDENCIES THEREOF IN EUROPE, ASIA, AFRICA, AMERICA, AND AUSTRALASIA.

QUEEN, DEFENDER OF THE FAITH.

Whereas, for divers weighty reasons, We have resolved, by and with the advice, and consent of the Lords Spiritual and Temporal and Commons, in Parliament assembled, to take upon Ourselves, the Government of the Territories in India heretofore administered in trust for Us by the HONOURABLE EAST INDIA COMPANY.

Now, therefore, We do by these presents notify and declare that, by the advice and consent aforesaid, We have taken upon Ourselves the said Government, and We hereby call upon all Our subjects within the said Territories to be faithful and to bear true allegiance to Us, Our heirs and successors, and to submit themselves to the authority of those whom, We may hereafter, from time to time, see fit to appoint to administer the Government of Our said Territories, in Our name and on Our behalf.

And We, reposing especial trust and confidence in the loyalty, ability and judgment of Our right trusty and well beloved Cousin and Councillor, CHARLES JOHN VISCOUNT CANNING, do hereby constitute and appoint him, the said VISCOUNT CANNING, to be Our first Viceroy and Governor-General in, and over Our said Territories, and to administer the Government thereof in Our name, and generally to act in Our name and on Our behalf, subject to such Orders and Regulations as he shall, from time to time, receive from Us through one of Our principal Secretaries of State.

And We do hereby confirm in their several Offices, Civil and Military, all persons now employed in the Service of the HONOURABLE EAST INDIA COMPANY subject to Our future pleasure, and to such Laws and Regulations as may hereafter be enacted.

We hereby announce to the Native Princes of India that all treaties and engagements made with them by or under the authority of the HONOURABLE EAST INDIA COMPANY *are by US accepted, and will be scrupulously maintained; and We look for the like observance on their part.*

We desire no extension of Our present territorial possessions; and while We will permit no agression upon Our Dominions, or Our Rights to be attempted with impunity, *we shall sanction no encroachment on those of others. We shall* **respect the** *Rights, Dignity and Honour of Native Princes as Our own;* **and We** desire that they, as well as Our own subjects, should enjoy that prosperity, and that social advancement which **can** be **secured** by internal peace and good government.

We hold Ourselves bound to **the Natives of Our Indian Territories** *by the same obligations of* **duty** *which bind Us to all Our other subjects; and those obligations,* **by the Blessing of ALMIGHTY GOD** *We shall faithfully and* **conscientiously fulfil.**

Firmly relying Ourselves on the truth of Christianity, and acknowledging with gratitude the solace of Religion, We disclaim alike the Right and the desire to **impose Our convictions on any of Our subjects.** We declare it to be **Our Royal will and** pleasure **that none be in any**wise favoured, none **molested or** disquieted, by **reason of** their religious faith **or** observances; **but that all** shall alike enjoy the equal and impartial protection **of the** Law: and We do strictly charge and enjoin all those who may be **in** authority under Us, that *they abstain from all interference with the religious belief or worship* of any of Our subjects, **on** pain of Our highest displeasure.

And **it** is Our further will that, so far as may be, **Our** subjects, of whatever **Race or** Creed, *be freely and impartially admitted* **to** Offices in **Our Service, the** duties **of** which they **may** be qualified, **by their education,** ability, **and** integrity, duly **to** discharge

We know, and respect, the feelings of attachment with which **the** Natives **of** India regard the **lands** inherited by them from their Ancestors; and we desire **to protect them in all** rights connected therewith, *subject to the equitable demands* of the State: and We will that generally, in framing and administering the **Law, due** regard **be** paid to the **ancient Rights, Usages, and Customs of INDIA.**

We deeply **lament the** evils and misery which have **been brought** upon INDIA **by the acts of ambitious men, who have deceived their countrymen by false reports, and led them into open rebellion. Our** power has been shown by the suppression **of that** rebellion in **the** field; We desire to show Our mercy, **by pardoning the** offences of those who have been thus misled, but **who desire to** return to the path of duty.

Already in one Province, with a view to stop the further effusion **of blood,** and to hasten the pacification of our Indian Dominions, **Our Viceroy** and Governor-General has held out the expectation of pardon, on certain terms, to the great majority of those who, in the late unhappy disturbances, have been guilty of offences against Our Government, **and** has declared the punishment which will be inflicted on those whose crimes place them beyond the reach of forgiveness. We approve and confirm the said act of Our Viceroy and **Governor-General,** and do **further announce and** proclaim as follow :—

Our **Clemency will be** extended **to** all offenders, save and except all those **who have been,** or shall be, convicted of having directly taken part in the **murder of** British Subjects. With regard to such the demands of Justice forbid the exercise of **mercy.**

To those who have willingly given asylum to murderers, knowing them to be such, or who may have acted as leaders or instigators in revolt, their lives alone can be guaranteed; but in apportioning the penalty due to such persons, full consideration will be given to the circumstances under which they have been induced to throw off their allegiance, and large indulgence will be shown to those whose crimes may appear to have originated in too credulous acceptance of the false reports circulated by designing men.

To all others in Arms against the Government, we hereby promise unconditional Pardon, Amnesty, and Oblivion of all offence against Ourselves, Our Crown and Dignity, on their return to their homes and peaceful pursuits.

It is Our Royal Pleasure that these terms of Grace and Amnesty should be extended to all those who comply with these conditions before the First Day of January next.

When, by the Blessing of Providence, internal Tranquillity shall be restored, it is Our earnest Desire to stimulate the peaceful industry of INDIA, to promote Works of Public Utility, and Improvement, and to administer its Government for the benefit of all Our Subjects resident therein. In their Prosperity will be Our Strength; in their Contentment, Our Security; and in their Gratitude Our best Reward. And may the GOD of all Power grant to Us, and to those in authority under Us, Strength to carry out these Our wishes for the good of Our People.

The British Government, under the Proclamation of 1858, took over the whole of the obligations contracted by the Honourable East India Company, whether by Treaty or otherwise, and undertook to scrupulously maintain the same. Hence the Nawab Nazim of Bengal is *justly* entitled to claim from Her Majesty and the Government compensation for all the losses, pecuniary or otherwise, sustained by himself and his family, having on his part always adhered to the obligations set forth in the several Treaties and Agreements.

But the present Nawab Nazim has greater claims upon the British Government than a mere acknowledgment of Treaty Rights or redress for the wrongs inflicted upon him and his Predecessors by the Government of India, for he has (as expressed at two of our public banquets in the City of London by Lord Cairns and also by Lord Lawrence, once Governor-General of India,) "*earned the gratitude and sympathy of the British nation by his loyal attachment and faithful adherence to the British Crown in seasons of danger and trial,*" and by the services he rendered to the State by his assistance and example "*during the great Santhal Rebellion of 1855, and of the more serious crisis which followed, the Mutiny of the Native Troops of the Bengal Army in 1857.*"

The following letters exhibit a few out of the many services rendered by His Highness when all his countrymen around him were rising up in arms and throwing off their allegiance to the British Government.

From The Secretary to the Government of Bengal to LIEUTENANT-COLONEL MACGREGOR, C.B., *Agent to the Governor-General at Moorshedabad.*

Fort William, 14th July, 1855.

Sir,

The Lieutenant-Governor has received your demi-official communication announcing that the Nawab Nazim has placed at the disposal of the Authorities, to aid in suppressing the disturbances that have arisen in the Northern part of the Moorshedabad District, the Sepoys and Troopers of His Highness' guard, together with a number of elephants, and I am instructed to request that you will convey to the Nawab Nazim the *cordial acknowledgments* of Government for his *prompt co-operation,* and assure him that the desire which he has thus manifested *to assist by the resources at his disposal the efforts of the Authorities to maintain the peace of the district,* **and to** *quell the unfortunate outbreak which has occurred, is warmly and highly appreciated.*

I have, &c,
(Signed) W. GREY,
Secretary to the Government of Bengal.
(True Copy)
(Signed) G. H. MACGREGOR,
Agent to the Governor-General.

From the Secretary to the Government of Bengal to the Agent to the Governor-General at Moorshedabad.

Fort William, 28th September, 1855.

Sir,

I am directed to acknowledge the receipt of your letter No. 83, dated the ——— instant, bringing to the notice of Government the amount of assistance rendered by the Nawab Nazim to the Authorities, from the commencement of the Santhal outbreak up to the present time.

2. In my letter No. 1612, dated the 14th July, I communicated to you the *high sense entertained by the Lieutenant-Governor of the prompt and useful co-operation of the Nawab Nazim in the measures then taken for the suppression of the Santhal insurrection*, and the Lieutenant-Governor now directs me to state in reply to your present letter, "*that he agrees with you that the course pursued by the Nawab*
" *Nazim on this occasion as detailed in your letter, clearly shows His*
" *Highness' anxiety to promote the service of Government by every*
" *means in his power.*"

I have, &c.,
(Signed) W. GREY,
Secretary to the Government of Bengal.
(True Copy)
(Signed) G. H. MACGREGOR,
Agent Governor-General.

From the Secretary to the Government of Bengal to the Agent Governor-General, Moorshedabad.

Fort William, the 4th August, 1857.

Sir,

With reference to your letter, No. 63, of the 25th June last, I am directed by the Lieutenant-Governor to forward herewith a copy of a letter, No. 81, of the 3rd instant, from the Secretary to the Government of India in the Military Department, and to request that you will lose no time in communicating to the Nawab Nazim of Moorshedabad, the acknowledgments of the Right Honourable the Governor-General in Council for the services rendered by His Highness on the occasion alluded to therein.

I have, &c.
(Signed) A. R. YOUNG,
Secretary to the Government of Bengal.

To the Secretary to the Government of Bengal.

Sir,

I am directed to acknowledge the receipt of your letter, No. 743, of the 30th ultimo, submitting for the information of the Government of India a copy of a letter from Lieutenant-Colonel Macgregor, C.B., bringing to notice the assistance rendered by the Nawab Nazim to the European Detachments, and in reply to request that you will move the Honourable the Lieutenant-Governor of Bengal to convey to His Highness the acknowledgments of the Right Honourable the Governor-General of India in Council for his great assistance on the occasion in question, as also for the readiness with which he was prepared to co-operate in preventing a disturbance which was anticipated (though without good reason) at Berhampore, on the 21st instant.

I have, &c.,
(Signed) R. J. H. BIRCH COLL,
Secretary to the Government of India in the Military Department.

(True Copy)
(Signed) G. H. MACGREGOR,
Agent Governor-General.

From the Secretary to the Government of Bengal to the Agent to the Governor-General at Moorshedabad.

Fort William, the 20th Oct., 1857.

Sir,

I am directed to acknowledge the receipt of your letter, No. 95, of the 9th instant, forwarding copy of a communication with translation addressed to you by His Highness the Nawab Nazim, in which he offers to place at the disposal of Government twenty-five of his elephants, and tenders his services in any other way in which they may be required.

2. The Lieutenant-Governor has perused with *much gratification the Nawab Nazim's address, and desires me to request that you will be so good as to convey to His Highness the expression of His Honour's* CORDIAL THANKS *for the* READINESS *with which His Highness has come forward to carry out the wishes of Government* ON THIS AS ON EVERY PREVIOUS OCCASION. The Lieutenant-Governor is *fully persuaded of the sincerity of His Highness' proffer of services, and of the* LOYAL SPIRIT *by which he is actuated.*

3. The Elephants should be forwarded to Raneegunge as soon as may be convenient to His Highness.

I have, &c.,
(Signed) A. R. YOUNG,
Secretary to the Government of Bengal.

(True Copy)
(Signed) G. H. MACGREGOR,
Agent Governor-General.

From the Secretary to the Government of Bengal, to the Agent Governor-General at Moorshedabad.

Fort William, 2nd November, 1857.

Sir,

I am directed to acknowledge the receipt of your letter, No. 104, dated the 22nd ultimo, reporting that at your request, His Highness the Nawab Nazim had furnished Captain Chapman while proceeding from Berhampore to Soory with a Guard of the Nizamut troops for the protection on the journey of certain horses selected by that officer at Moorshedabad for the use of the Bengal Yeomanry Cavalry, and soliciting sanction to the payment of Rs. 100, one hundred, as a present to the Guard for having well performed their duty.

2. In reply, I am desired to state that the Lieutenant-Governor authorizes the expenditure above proposed, and at the same time to request that you will convey His Honour's acknowledgments to the Nawab Nazim for the assistance rendered by him to Captain Chapman on the occasion.

I have, &c.,
(Signed)   A. R. YOUNG,
Secretary to the Government of Bengal.

From the Junior-Secretary to the Government of Bengal, to A. PIGOU, ESQ., in charge of the Office of Agent to the Governor-General at Moorshedabad.

Fort William, the 30th December, 1857.

Sir,

I am directed to acknowledge the receipt of your communication, No. 126, dated the 19th inst., *bringing to notice the good conduct* of a detachment of the Nawab Nazim's Troops while escorting Government horses to Raneegunge, and to convey to you the Lieutenant-Governor's sanction to the payment of a reward of 150 Rupees to the Native Officer and men of the detachment as recommended by you.

2. You mention also in the same letter, His Highness's co-operation in conveying a party of seamen to Berhampore.

3. *The Lieutenant-Governor has had frequent occasion to acknowledge the prompt and willing assistance rendered by the Nawab Nazim to the Officers of Government during the present disturbances, and desires once more to convey through you his acknowledgments for the service rendered on these two occasions.*

I have, &c.,
(Signed)   C. T. BUCKLAND,
Junior Secretary to the Government of Bengal.

Moorshedabad Agency, dated the 8th Jan., 1858.
True Copy,
(Signed)   A. PIGOU,
In charge of the Office of Agent to the
Governor-General.

Berhampore, July 27th, 1859.

Your Highness,

As I am about to leave Berhampore, permit me to thank you for the attention and kindness I have received from Your Highness.

You are aware of the circumstance that occasioned my coming, and the *promptitude* with which you sent elephants, oxen, &c., to meet the detachment under my command *was most gratifying*, and had it not been for the sudden rise of the river, *would have greatly aided our rapidly reaching Berhampore.*

On my arrival in Calcutta *I shall take special care to mention to Lord Canning, Your Highness' zeal on this occasion.*

* * * * * *

Believe me to remain your Highness' most obedient and faithful servant.

(Signed)   KENNETH D. MACKENZIE,
Lieut.-Colonel, 92nd Highlanders.

To His Highness, the NAWAB NAZIM *of Bengal, Behar, and Orissa.*

From E. H. LUSHINGTON ESQ., *Officiating Secretary to the Government of Bengal to the Officiating Agent to the Governor-General, Moorshedabad.*

Fort William, 8th November, 1859.

Sir,

I am directed to forward for your information and for communication to His Highness the Nawab Nazim the accompanying copy of a letter from the Secretary to the Government of India in the Foreign Department No. 6195, dated the 7th ultimo, announcing the honours which His Excellency the Governor-General in Council, has been pleased to confer on the Nawab Nazim and on *his Dewan* Roy Prosunno Narain Deb Bahadoor, and expressing the *high sense which the Government entertains of the faithful services rendered by His Highness during* the late disturbances

2. As directed in the 6th Paragraph of Mr. Beadon's letter, the Lieutenant-Governor desires me to observe that the Nawab Nazim in applying for the repeal of Act XXVII of 1854, appears to have misunderstood the operation of that Act, and that the annexed Extract paragraphs 36 to 53 from a minute recorded by the late Lieutenant Governor on the 18th September, 1858, will, it is hoped, satisfy His Highness that the repeal of the Act in question, would not produce all the effects which he supposes, and would besides have other consequences which are not desirable.

I am further directed to transmit herewith a Khurretah addressed by His Excellency to the Nawab Nazim, and to request that you will be so good as to deliver the same to His Highness. A copy of the Khurretah is forwarded for record in your office.

The Sunnud conferring the title of Rajah Bahadoor on the Dewan of His Highness will be forwarded as soon as received,

I have, &c,

(Signed)   E. H. LUSHINGTON,
Officiating Secretary to the Government of Bengal.

From C. BEADON ESQ., *Secretary to the Government of India, Foreign Department, to the Secretary to the Government of Bengal.*

7th October, 1859.

Sir,

I am directed by the Governor-General in Council, to acknowledge the receipt of your predecessor's letter, No. 3716, enclosing a minute by the late Lieutenant-Governor, relative to the conduct of the Nawab Nazim of Bengal during the rebellion, and to the reward which should be conferred on His Highness.

2. His Excellency in Council agrees generally in the views expressed in that minute, both as to the *faithful services of the Nawab Nazim* and the manner in which the *high sense which the Government entertains of those services,* can best be shown.

3. Already, when the Nawab Nazim was recently in Calcutta, the Governor-General in Council so far practically assented to the recommendations of the Government of Bengal, as to give His Highness a salute of nineteen guns on his departure from the Presidency, and His Excellency in Council has now much pleasure in formally declaring that His Highness is entitled to a salute of that number of guns, on all future occasions.

4. The Governor-General in Council is also pleased to cancel so much of the orders of the Government of India, dated the 6th December, 1854, as requires that when the Nawab Nazim may leave Moorshedabad, his camp shall be accompanied by a responsible officer of police on the part of the Government, and direct that the practice under which, previous to 1854, the expense of His Highness' hunting excursions was defrayed from the Nizamut Fund shall be revived.

5. These concessions, together with others which have lately been made to the Nawab *in consideration of his loyal conduct, will satisfy His Highness of the high estimation in which his services are held, and of the sincere effective desire of the Governor-General in Council to mark his appreciation of them.*

6. His Excellency in Council cannot consent to make any alteration in the Law as it stands; but he desires, that with the permission of the Lieutenant-Governor, it may carefully be explained to the Nawab as set forth in Mr. Halliday's minute, that the repeal of Act XXVII of 1854, would not produce all the effects His Highness supposes, and would have other undesirable consequences.

7. With reference to Mr. Secretary Edmonstone's letter, No. 2149, dated the 14th July, 1858, I am directed to state, that the Governor-General in Council has now been pleased to confer on Roy Prosunno Narain Deb, *the Nawab Nazim's Dewan*, the title of Rajah Bahadoor. The usual Sunnud will follow.

(True Copy)
(Signed) THOMAS JONES,
Register Bengal Secretariat.

(True Copy)
(Signed) C. MACKENZIE,
Officiating Agent Governor-General.

Services of H.H. the Nawab Nazim.

Extracts from a Minute by the Lieutenant-Governor of Bengal.

The Right Honourable the Governor-General has directed me to report " in full detail the services rendered by the Nawab Nazim, or under his direction, and the particular occasions on which His Highness assisted the local officers in their endeavours to enforce their authority and maintain tranquillity in Berhampore and its vicinity."

2. These services have been rendered on two occasions; *first*, on the occasion of the Santhall rebellion in 1855; and *secondly*, on the occasion of the mutiny of 1857.

3. The following are the detailed circumstances belonging to the *first* of these occasions:

4. On the 10th July, 1855, when disturbances broke out in the northern part of the Moorshedabad district, the Nawab Nazim lent to the magistrate of that district some of his light and fast boats to convey that officer and his establishment to the scene of the disturbance (expressing at the same time a desire to place all his resources at the disposal of the local authorities).

5. Twenty of his troopers were sent to accompany the magistrate, and thirty of his elephants to convey the camp equipage and ammunition of the right wing of the 7th Native Infantry, which had been ordered to proceed by forced marches to the disturbed district.

6. The Magistrate having reported to the Agent on the 11th July that the rebels were in great force, His Highness at once sent one hundred of his Sepoys to the former officer.

7. His Highness likewise supplied 124 stand of arms to the European soldiers of the recruit depôt at Berhampore.

8. The citizens of Moorshedabad having been alarmed by false rumours to the effect that the rebels were advancing in large numbers to plunder the city, His Highness sent his officers to give them confidence; sent fifty Sepoys to assist the police, and ordered the rest of his troops (350 men) to hold themselves in readiness to aid the authorities, if necessary.

9. On Mr. Bidwell assuming charge of his duties as Special Commissioner, he asked for more elephants, whereupon His Highness lent not only the remainder of his own animals, but also some of those of his relatives, in all fifty-seven in number.

10. The troopers above alluded to subsequently accompanied the right wing of the 7th N.I. in their several operations.

11. The hundred Sepoys first marched to Mohutpore, thence to Ponkour, Kudumsar and Paliehat, and had altogether served for a month and twenty-two days, when they were withdrawn by Mr. Bidwell.

12. Of the elephants some appear to have been retained for short periods, but twenty-seven remained with the troops at different places till about the end of January, 1856, and were returned after the Santhal field force was broken up.

13. The acknowledgments of the Government for the above services were conveyed to the Nawab Nazim through the Agent, Colonel

Macgregor, first on the 14th July, and then again on the 28th Sept., 1855, and in the meantime the Magistrate of Moorshedabad also thanked His Highness in a letter dated 9th August, 1855.

14. The details of the *second* occasion are as follows :—

15. When a detachment of Her Majesty's 64th Regiment, under the command of Captain Francis, was sent to Berhampore in June, 1857, His Highness assisted Government by lending forty-five elephants and all his camels, for the conveyance of the Detachment from Allatollee Ghaut to Berhampore.

16. A Detachment of Her Majesty's 35th Regiment, under the command of Capain Tisdall, was also sent up to Berhampore during the same month. His Highness sent down thirteen pairs of his carriage horses to enable this party to reach its destination.

17. On the 21st June, when His Highness was under the impression that the two native regiments at Berhampore had mutinied, and when there was a general excitement at Moorshedabad caused by the same impression, he at once made all his preparations for resisting the supposed mutineers in case they went to Moorshedabad, and also took measure to prevent any rising in the city, co-operating with the Magistrate with promptitude and zeal for that purpose.

18. While reporting the above services, the Agent, Lieutenant-Colonel Macgregor, C.B., stated: "It is with great pleasure that I have observed that His Highness has *always been most anxious to render every assistance* in his power to the British Government *on any emergency.*"

19. For the assistance rendered by His Highness in the above instances, the thanks of the Governor-General in Council were conveyed in letters from the Secretary to the Government of India.

20. On the occasion of the Magistrate of Moorshedabad undertaking the task of disarming that city in the early part of August, 1857, after the troops at Berhampore had been disarmed, the Agent to the Governor-General requested the Nawab Nazim to disarm his disciplined troops, who were men of the same kind as those of the regiments that had mutinied. His Highness most readily and cheerfully gave the order for disarming: and it was promptly and effectually carried out by the Nizamut Dewan, who sent the arms to Berhampore through the Agent. The Government of Bengal gave credit for this to both the Agent and the Nawab. The measure produced so excellent an effect, that the Magistrate accomplished his difficult task without resistance and without the aid of European troops.

21. In September, 1857, Colonel Macgregor had occasion, under orders from Major-General Sir James Outram, K.C.B., to despatch 20,000 rounds of service musket cartridges, with a due proportion of percussion caps, to Darjeeling *viâ* Kishengunge. The Colonel did not deem it advisable to entrust the ammunition to any guard from either of the regiments at Berhampore, and he accordingly asked the Nawab Nazim for a guard, when His Highness furnished a party of his own followers, consisting of sixteen confidential men, who safely escorted the stores and delivered them to the Deputy Magistrate at Kishengunge. The men were rewarded by the Government with presents to the amount of seventy rupees. Two Nizamut beaulcahs appear to have been used on this occasion.

22. In September, 1857, the civil authorities were directed to procure elephants from the zemindars and others in their several districts for use in the military operations which were then about to be undertaken. Colonel Macgregor having communicated with the Nawab Nazim on the subject, His Highness placed twenty-five of his elephants at the disposal of Government, intimating at the same time that *he could not consent to take compensation should any of the animals die in the public service* as offered by Government, and that besides elephants, he would be happy to offer any other aid that it was in his power to give, if required.

23. The Lieutenant-Governor's thanks were conveyed to His Highness on this occasion.

24. Two of the Nawab's relatives lent two elephants each.

25. In October, 1857, Captain Chapman of the Bengal Yeomanry Cavalry, who had selected seventy horses at Berhampore for his corps out of those belonging to the dismounted men of the 11th Irregular Cavalry, required a guard from the Nizamut troops to protect the cattle on their way to Soorie, the Nawab Nazim readily complied with Colonel Macgregor's request for the guard, by ordering a party of one havildar, one naik, and twenty-four men. The guard behaved well, and performed their duty in a satisfactory manner, but suffered some pecuniary loss by an accident in crossing the Bhagurutty; they were, therefore allowed a present of one hundred rupees. The acknowledgments of the Lieutenant-Governor were also conveyed to the Nawab Nazim for furnishing the guard

26. Again in December, 1857, another detachment of the Nawab's troops, consisting of the adjutant (Mr. Ryan), one subadar, and forty Sepoys, was allowed, to escort a large number of the Government horses of the 11th Irregulars, selected by Captain Pester of the 63rd N. I., to Raneegunge. These guards also satisfactorily performed their duty, and were rewarded with a sum of one hundred and fifty rupees.

27. During the same month His Highness also assisted the progress to Berhampore of the party of twenty sailors, under Captain Smart, sent to that station, by lending his elephants and servants to bring them up.

28. For the assistance rendered on the last two occasions, the Lieutenant-Governor's acknowledgments were again conveyed to the Nawab Nazim through Mr. A. Pigou.

29. The Nawab Nazim readily lent his house at Alipore for the accommodation of refugees from the North-western Provinces, and it was largely taken advantage of.

(Signed) J. F. HALLIDAY.

Extract from a Letter from the GOVERNOR-GENERAL OF INDIA *to* HIS HIGHNESS THE NAWAB NAZIM OF BENGAL.

My Friend,

In consequence of your numerous and valuable services rendered to the British Government during the Santhal rebellion in 1855, and at the more serious crisis which followed, the mutiny of the Bengal army army in 1857, services which are well known to all, and for which Your Highness has from time to time received the thanks of the Government, as well as recognitions of a more public and *permanent* kind, I consulted the honourable the Lieutenant-Governor of Bengal as to what special mark of the favour of the Government it would be expedient to confer on Your Highness, so that it might be manifest to all men that *Your Highness' loyal services and faithful attachment to the British Government* are duly appreciated, and that *the Government is not unmindful of the good offices* rendered by Your Highness in a *season of trouble.*

The Lieutenant-Governor of Bengal has laid before me in a minute a complete record of all that Your Highness and Your Highness's servants did on these two occasions; and this minute, recorded in the archives of the Government, will serve as a *perpetual remembrance* of Your Highness's active and zealous support, and of the *firm friendship which exists between Your Highness and the British Government.*

My friend, I have read *this record of Your Highness's friendly acts with the most lively satisfaction;* and, entirely agreeing in the views expressed by the Lieutenant-Governor, I have directed that Your Highness shall henceforth always receive a salute of nineteen guns, and that certain rules which are now in force as regards Your Highness's recreations shall be wholly removed.

By these and other tokens of favour which Your Highness has received in consideration of your *loyal services, Your Highness will be satisfied of the high estimation in which those services are held, and of my sincere desire to mark my appreciation of them.*

I have only to add, in conclusion, that, on the recommendation of the Agent and of the Lieutenant-Governor, I have had the pleasure of conferring upon Your Highness's Dewan, Raie Prosunno Narian Deb Bahadoor, in recognition of the ability and zeal with which, under Your Highness's direction, he co-operated with the British authorities to restore and maintain tranquillity on both the occasions above referred to.

I have, &c.,

(Signed)   CANNING.

From A. T. MACLEAN, ESQ., *Officiating Magistrate of Moorshedabad to the Agent to the Governor-General, Moorshedabad.*

Berhampore, 11th September, 1862.

Sir,

I have the honour to request the favour of procuring the information required in the annexed descriptive and valuation roll of elephants lent to Government by His Highness the Nawab Nazim during the Mutiny, if there be any which have not been returned to him or paid for.

I have, &c.

(Signed)   A. T. MACLEAN,

Officiating Magistrate.

Memo. No. 87.

Forwarded to His Highness the Nawab Nazim for the necessary information required by the Collector.

(Signed) W. A. A. THOMSON, Major.
Agent Governor-General.

Berhampore, 15th September, 1862.

From His Highness the NAWAB NAZIM *of Bengal, Behar and Orissa, to* MAJOR W. A. A. THOMSON, *Agent to the Governor-General at Moorshedabad.*

My Friend,

With reference to your Memo., No. 87, of the 15th September last, which is subjoined to the letter, No. 746 from the Officiating Magistrate of Moorshedabad to your address, as also to your letter, No. 99, of the 5th instant, in which you require me to fill up a Form showing the names, height and prices of the elephants, which I had placed at the disposal of Government during the Mutiny, and which, whilst employed in this service have died, I beg to state, I consider it the duty of every loyal subject to assist the Government to maintain good order and the public peace, and as in my case, in rendering aid to the State in the Santhal war, and again during the Mutiny, I was only fulfilling the conditions of the Treaties entered into by my ancestors, I must decline to receive any pecuniary return for such services I have rendered to the British Government towards the protection and preservation of the dominions of Her Majesty in India.

I remain, &c.

(Signed) SYUD MUNSOOR ULLEE.

The Palace, Moorshedabad, the 7th November, 1862.

For the services rendered by him His Highness has received no consideration but the *thanks* of the Government of India, while the descendants of rebels and of those who opposed the establishment of British Power in the East have been liberally dealt with, and even one of His Highness's servants (a creature of the Government of India) was honored by having the distinguished title of Rajah conferred upon him.

But apart from all political considerations under which the British Government has bound itself to India, there must in a commercial point of view be something

P

radically wrong in the system under which India has been governed, when sacred bonds and agreements have been unscrupulously set aside, and Native Princes, who have abided by their engagements, and magnanimously refused to accept pecuniary compensation for losses which they have unavoidably sustained in their duty to the Government, have been neglected, and all their petitions to the Government of India for redress have been either entirely disregarded or the claims set forth therein ignored without a fair and equitable inquiry. Surely all men should have justice done to them whether they are princes, or merchants, Asiatics, or Europeans; and as it is for justice only that His Highness the Nawab Nazim now appeals to the British nation, all distinctions of nationality or caste prejudice should be put aside, and after full inquiry all demands that are legitimately claimable from the Indian Government ought to be paid to the Nawab and his successors for ever. The British Government should, we think, be ever ready to listen to such appeals for justice, lest, by turning a deaf ear to entreaty and the just claims of Native Princes in India, a spirit of disaffection may again arise, and bring about a recurrence of those fearful events which in 1857 exposed the lives of so many of our countrymen, and nearly destroyed the British Empire in the East.

But since His Highness the Nawab Nazim of Bengal has proved by his acts his loyal adherence to the British Crown, he therefore deserves especial justice at the hands of the British Government, and it is to the consideration of his claims, as drawn up in 1858 by an officer of the Indian Government, the Agent Governor-General, and afterwards reported upon by him for the information of the Government, that we would now direct attention.

When Colonel Mackenzie took charge of the Agency at Moorshedabad, he found, among other papers, a Memorial which the Nawab Nazim had sent to Government regarding his claims and rights : and as it was supported by a mass of treaties, agreements, and letters from Government, it naturally excited interest. The Agent, therefore, entered fully into the spirit of the Memorial, and, having examined all the papers attached thereto, and found them correct, he felt it to be his duty, as Agent Governor-General, to represent the matter to the Government, in justice to the Nawab Nazim. He accordingly printed the whole subject; but before giving it publicity he sent a rough copy to Mr. Edmonstone (then Foreign Secretary to Government), requesting him to lay it before the Governor-General, in order to have the whole matter thoroughly sifted. This was done by Mr. Edmonstone, who afterwards wrote to the Agent, and stated,—

"The narrative is extremely useful, and should awaken the attention
" of Government to the position of the Nawab and the state of rela-
" tions with him. The whole subject has been more than once under
" the consideration of the Governor-General, and has also been dis-
" cussed with me as often ; but no final decision has been recorded,
" although I believe the Governor-General has made up his mind on
" the matter. I am not, of course, at liberty to inform you of the
" opinion the Governor-General appears to me to have formed, but I
" may say confidentially that it is not unfavourable. I wish you well
" in your endeavours to right His Highness, and have little doubt that
" you will succeed in some measure."

Narrative of NIZAMUT *Affairs, Compiled by* COLONEL COLIN MACKENZIE, *Acting Agent to the Governor-General at Moorshedabad in* 1858-9, *referred to by* MR. EDMONSTONE, *Foreign Secretary to the Government of India in the above quotation.*

1. When after the tragedy of the Black Hole in Calcutta, it was found impossible to place any reliance on the Nazim of Bengal, Serajud Dowlah, Clive entered into a treaty with Jaffier Ali Khan, the Bakshi of the Army, in consequence of which the latter drew off a considerable portion of Serajud Dowlah's troops during the battle of Plassy, and the Company's Government in return acknowledged him as Subah of Bengal, Behar, and Orissa. (The Great Mogul confirmed Meer Jaffier as the legitimate Nawab.)

2. It was always the practice of Native Princes to have a Dewan, or Minister who managed all their affairs. In 1765 the Emperor Shah Allum conferred the Dewani, *i e.*, the Civil Government of these Provinces on the East India Company on certain conditions, one of which was "that there shall be a sufficient allowance out of the said revenues for supporting the expense of the Nizamut;" and the Nawab

Nazim Dowlah (son of Jaffier Ali) agreed to accept the sum of seventeen and half lacs of Sicca Rupees for his own expense, and a further sum of thirty-six lacs for the maintenance of such Troops, Burkundauzes, &c., as may be thought necessary. The East India Company thus became His Highness's Agents or Managers.

3. The Nawab Syefu Dowlah, brother of Nazim-ul-Dowlah, on his accession in 1766, concluded a treaty with the Governor and Council, ratifying former engagements. The 2nd Article says, "I, having an entire confidence in them, *i.e.* (the English East India Company), " that nothing whatever be proposed or carried into execution by them " derogating from my *honour, dignity, interest*, and the good of my " country, agree that the protecting of Bengal, Behar, and Orissa, " be entirely left to their good management in consideration of their " paying to me the sum of seventeen lacs," &c. The remaining sum for the Nawab's Sawarie was diminished to twenty-four lacs.

4. In 1770 a minor son of Jaffier Ali, named Mobaruk-ul-Dowlah, succeeded his brethren, whose mother, Mani Begum, was considered the head of the house and managed all the affairs of her young stepson. She was styled the "Mother of the East India Company." A treaty was made with the young Nawab to the same effect before, but diminishing his personal stipend to fifteen and half lacs, and sixteen lacs for his Sawari.

5. The next year, however, the Court of Directors sarcastically reproached their Governor (Mr. Cartier) with not having taken advantage of the nonage of the new Subadar to reduce his stipend to sixteen lacs "*while a minor*," and this was done in defiance of the above treaty, and although on His Highness coming of age he repeatedly applied for the fulfilment of the treaty of 1770, he never obtained any addition to his reduced stipend, although the Court had expressly stated this reduction should take place *during his nonage*. The late Nazim Humayun Jah, in a letter to Lord William Bentinck, described this transaction in the following dignified manner:—" In 1770 the Government of India had entered into a treaty with the minor Nazim Mobaruck-ul-Dowlah, and about two years after, Mr. Cartier, their Governor, had the unpleasant task of informing the Nazim that the Court of Directors were of opinion that a sum something under sixteen lacs was quite sufficient for the Nawab Nazim during his nonage, his income was curtailed accordingly. I forbear offering any observation on this transaction. Your Lordship's own mind will suggest what must have been *felt*, and what might have been *said*. The Mani Begum remonstrated as strongly as she could, and Mr. Hastings (then Governor-General) promised that on the Nazim's coming of age, his situation should be taken into consideration;" but the promise made by him, and virtually contained in the order of the Court of Directors, which referred to the youth of the Nazim, as the sole ground of reduction, has been unredeemed. In 1786, 21st July, the Court desired that relief might be afforded to the Nawab either by better management of his stipend, or even by an immediate augmentation of it.

6. In consequence, Lord Cornwallis (3rd September, 1790) proposed various economical arrangements with a view of liquidating His Highness's debts, and proposed that the Nazim should lay by two lacs per

anuum for this purpose, and to provide for his increasing family. But at that time the Nawab's establishment cost about twelve lacs, nearly four lacs more being devoted to the pensions of Mani Begum and other relations and dependants, that His Highness was never able to lay by anything. The Governor-General declared the stipends of the *relations* of the Nawab hereditary after having "inquired of the Nawab Nazim the names of those he wishes to dismiss from the Establishment;" but the pensions of *dependants* were to be "at the option of the Prince to withdraw, and on their demise it shall rest with the Nawab to continue them *in toto*, or in part to their heirs, and of such pensions as by his own determination shall be resumed one-half to the payment of his debts." The Governor-General lays down the principle that the disposal of stipends should not "*in any wise be at the pleasure of Government* further than to prevent partiality." He adds,—" I propose that there shall be *no other check* over the Nawab in the disposal of the sums left to him (which included the stipends of his relations and dependants) than shall prevent the misconduct of his servants, and this I think sufficient by the interference of the Governor-General *in case of complaint.*" This was the first time the Government interfered with the disposal of His Highness's income of sixteen lacs.

7. In 1802 a Committee appointed by Lord Wellesley to act in concert with His Highness the Nawab and Mani Begum, to revise the whole system of the Nizamut, had recommended that on Her Highness Mani Begum's decease, her stipend of 1,44,000 sicca rupees per annum should be appropriated for the payment of the Nawab Nazim's debts, and for building expenses, marriage portions, and other purposes for which the Government had hitherto made advances.

In 1813 the Mani Begum died, and in 1816 Mr. Edmonstone drew up a Memorandum, showing the want of due superintendence over Nizamut affairs, the impossibility of the Judge affording this superintendence, and recommending the appointment of an officer of high rank and peculiar qualifications " for this purpose." "The salary of this officer should be high, not less than 36,000 rupees per annum, exclusive of a sum for house-rent and Establishment. It should be in point of salary above the office of Magistrate of a City or Zillah, especially at a station so expensive as Moorshedabad, where he would be obliged to maintain a certain appearance, and this, in order to avoid frequent changes in the agent, which would be a great public inconvenience. In a situation where illicit advantages would be so abundantly held forth, and might be so securely enjoyed, a liberal salary should on general principles be assigned." Mr. Edmonstone recommended this arrangement, on the ground that it would impose no financial burden on the Company, and would accomplish an effectual reform in the Nizamut. The amount of stipends which has lapsed was upwards of five lacs, chiefly arising from the arrears of Mani Begum's stipend since her death. To this it was proposed to add two lacs, said to be due by the Nazim to the Government, and to be paid out of Mani Begum's personal property. Mr Edmonstone remarks that "the question is not whether the Company is bound permanently to apply the sum of sixteen lacs to the support of the

Nizamut, on which point forcible arguments might be advanced on both sides" (although the treaty with Mobaruck-ul-Dowlah and his predecessors would appear to settle this point in favour of His Highness's successors for ever), "but the actual question was, whether lapsed stipends should be applied to an arrangement, *the exclusive object* of which is *the prosperity and the pecuniary benefit* of the Nizamut. The mode of such application has always been determined by Government." This minute was approved by the Governor-General in Council. Mr. Monckton was deputed to ask His Highness's consent, which was given, and the proposed sum of seven lacs was invested. It was stipulated that "the advantage arising from *the discount* on paper will belong to the Nizamut, and *is to be accounted for to His Highness the Nawab*" (Governor-General in Council).

The Nawab requested "an assurance from the Governor-General that these funds should be considered as appertaining to the Nizamut, and not liable under *any change of circumstances* to be diverted to purposes foreign to the interest of the house of Jaffier Ali Khan." The Governor-General assured His Highness that this fund is, and will be considered as *the inalienable property of His Highness's family* over and above the sixteen lacs of rupees assigned for its support. Regarding the right of the Nawab Nazim to 16,00,000 per annum, and also to the money thus invested, there can be therefore no question.

In 1823, the Governor-General pledged himself in a letter to the Nawab Nazim to a *scrupulous adherence to subsisting engagements*, and to the obligations of public faith and honour. This assurance was repeated *verbatim* by Lord Auckland.

8. In 1823, the arrears of Mani Begum's stipend from 1816 to 1823 amounted to seven and a half lacs in the Collector's Treasury. The Governor-General in Council desired that "six lacs may be invested to the best advantage, and the paper *held in deposit in the same manner* as that provided for the payment of the Agency." This sum formed Mani Begum's Deposit Fund. It was invested "for the benefit of the Nizamut, and is clearly on the same terms as the Agent's Deposit Fund, the inalienable property of His Highness's family." It was intended principally, "in the first instance, to build a palace for His Highness, to which the Government considered itself pledged."

9. At this time, those who had received the largest stipends, such as Mani Begum and Bubbee Begum, being deceased, the annual amount of lapsed stipends amounted to nearly three lakhs of rupees. Other allowances had been granted by the Nazim and sanctioned by the Supreme Government: but after deducting these there remained upwards of *two lakhs per annum*, and the Governor-General in Council proposed to the Nazim that "on condition of Government *withdrawing from all* interference in auditing his accounts, His Highness should consent to allow this sum of *two lakhs per annum* to accumulate in the Collector's Treasury instead of being spent in his own." "The Governor-General pledged himself that the British Government will, in that case, undertake the payment in future from that fund of *all charges for new buildings or other* expenses legiti-

mately claimable from it." Some " of these are previously specified ; a lakh was granted for renewing any part of His Highness's establishment, which may be defective," portioning the daughters of the family was named, and the object of the fund is stated to be " to place in the hands of Government a means for relieving any *exigencies* in which the family might be involved." The Deposit Fund formed from lapsed stipends was styled " *a Sacred Inheritance of the Nizamut.*"

The Government *proved* they did not wish to increase the Deposit Fund above two lakhs. by ordering that the one lakh remaining of the accumulated stipends, should be made over " to His Highness to meet " the stipends of the daughters of His late Highness," &c , with full liberty to appropriate any " **excess to purposes connected with the** " **splendour and credit of his exalted station.**"—" It is by no means " the desire of Government to increase indefinitely the appropriations " for the benefit of the Deposit Fund to two lakhs of rupees, *i.e.*, one-" eighth of the entire Nizamut stipends, and the Governor-General in " Council *would not wish to make it larger*, at the same time it would " not be advisable to reduce the Fund below one lakh and a half, or to " trench on the amount of Mani Begum's stipend, which has for so " long a time been set apart for the purpose." It is evident that Mani Begum's stipend was part of the annual two lakhs. " The " British Government will relinquish *all desire to increase the fund*, " *pledging itself on the lapse of any future stipend to consider the sug-* " *gestions of His Highness* as to its allotment, and, except under " special circumstances, *to assign the whole for the benefit of the family* " and its dependents."

His Highness's patronage and influence amongst the members of the Nizamut will be strengthened by the knowledge that his recommendations on behalf of individuals *will be sure of due attention.* The interest was to be re-invested. The Court of Directors sanctioned the arrangements made. They pronounce the Deposit Fund " *the property* " *of the Nizamut generally,*" and add, " the knowledge that you do " *not contemplate any further* increase of the Deposit Fund, and your " resolutions for applying it will probably obviate any recurrence of that distrust which appears to have existed in the minds of successive Nazims on the subject of your intentions with respect to that fund "

Thus from the arrears of Mani Begum's stipend three distinct funds have been formed—the first styled *Agency Deposit Fund*, set apart in 1816 for the payment of the Governor-General's Agent and his establishment ; the second called *Mani Begum's* or the *Nizamut Deposit* the *Lapsed Stipend or Nizamut Pension Fund*, which was to consist of the arrears of Mani Begum's stipend and others, which might lapse up *to the extent of two lakhs per annum* and *no more*, was intended for " the benefit of the Nizamut generally, including the Nizamut personally."

10. But the accumulation of lapsed stipends, which ought to have taken place in the Nawab's Treasury to complete the annual sum of two lakhs, was by no means regular. Mr. Sterling, in a note placed on record in 1833, recommends " that all demands on this account should be *relinquished*, and that the whole of the Nizamut stipends should be made over to the Nawab, with the exception of one pension of 60,000 rupees, and Mani Begum's stipend, thus limiting the accumulations of

the fund to Mani Begum's stipend of Sa. Rs. 1,44,000 a year. He adds—"I imagine the latter amount Sa. Rs. 1,44,000 is adequate to the "legitimate purposes of the fund, **viz.**, buildings and the occasional "relief and benefit of the different members of the family, including "His Highness himself, and *I do not see that we have any right* to keep "back from the Nazim a larger portion of the sixteen lakhs assigned "by Treaty than suffices for the above objects." That the sum proposed was, as Mr. Sterling considered it, ample, is proved by the difficulty that has since been felt in disposing of the Deposit Fund.

11. At this period the Nazim's income was insufficient. His establishment cost nearly fourteen lakhs annually. Even during the long minority of Humayun Jah, when the Governor-General, as represented by his Agent, was guardian and managed everything, "the sum considered applicable to the Nazim's own household was quite insufficient to maintain it on the scale fixed by the Committee (in 1802) and considered proper by the Government" (N. N. to G. G. 1st December 1834). The accounts were so confused that no one could understand them; and in spite of the pledge that "the Government would withdraw from all interference in auditing His Highness's accounts," and although the Governor-General considered that it might perhaps be sufficient to secure the due payment of stipends, that the agent should be *ready to receive complaints*," yet the interference had been so constant and so minute that it had deprived the Nazim of all power over his own affairs. His Highness had consented to the formation of the Deposit Fund, but so far from "the remainder of the sixteen lakhs being delivered to him to be disbursed *according to his pleasure*" in the time of Humayun Jah, the Nawab Nazim had no control over his own servants! He could not dismiss a man on three rupees a month, or even dispose of a few loose discoloured pearls and precious stones, without the sanction of Government. Captain Thoresby says, "according to the complicated undefinable forms now in force, the exertion of an efficient control on the part of the Nazim would be *next to impossible*."

During the minority of Nawab Nazim Humayun Jah, although the expenditure was under the Agent Governor-General's special management, a very large debt had been incurred. No accurate accounts had been kept, and no effectual supervision exercised. On the ground that this debt was incurred under the guardianship of the Agent to the Governor-General, it was paid out of the surplus of the Deposit Fund (Court of Directors, No. 40, 10th February, 1836) This proves that no amount of interference (for at this time accounts of every item were required from His Highness) was found effectual to introduce order.

12. Captain Thoresby, therefore, proposed that the Agent to the Governor-General should pay all the stipends, and that His Highness should receive the remainder of the sixteen lakhs for his personal expenditure, without the obligation of giving any account thereof. A new arrangement was, therefore, entered into between the Nawab Nazim and the Governor-General in Council to the following effect:—
1st. Customary perquisites under the name of Mamulats Zamostami, &c., given by His Highness should be commuted to cash payments, and on the decease of the recipients, "If there are no heirs entitled to succeed to it, the reversion shall be to the *Nizamut Treasury, i.e.*, to the Nawab Nazim."

5. Also that pensions which *have been*, or may hereafter be, assigned to servants and dependants shall *revert to the Nizamut Treasury* as casualties occur, and be at *the entire disposal of His Highness*: stipends were to be kept separate from the sum devoted to His Highness's personal expenses, and the Treasurer was to be answerable to the Agent as well *as to the Nawab Nazim* for the correctness of his issues and the existence of the balance." The Nawab Nazim was to have full liberty to modify his establishment at his pleasure, and "with regard to entertaining or discharging his servants he is at liberty to act as he pleases, *without any* interference whatever." His Highness formally consented (17th February, 1834), and it was settled and explained that "although His Highness was thus relieved from all responsibility connected with the stipends, every facility should be given for his making himself acquainted with the *minutest details*, and *his wishes regarding grants from the Deposit Fund would be signified to the Agent, and attended to as heretofore*." Sir Charles Metcalfe, in giving his formal consent to this agreement, informs the Nawab Nazim that " Agent Governor-General has been directed to consider it *as the rule* under which Nizamut affairs are *hereafter to be administered*."

13. His Highness, actuated by fear that his income might be indefinitely encroached upon, and in the deepest distress and anxiety " regarding the position and income which would be left to his son," addressed Lord William Bentinck, then Governor-General, in a private letter, requesting "that the income set apart for his own use should be secured to him and to the Nazims for ever, the younger sons of the family falling back into the rank of Akrobas, and being provided for as usual out of the Deposit Fund."

The Agent writes, " I think he apprehends that if he reduces his expenses a smaller income than he now receives will, after a year or two, be considered sufficient for him." To this Lord William Bentinck, replied by proposing to "confirm to the Nazim and his successors the sum now actually received, provided the remainder of the Nizamut Fund shall ever hereafter be at the absolute disposal of the British Government, subject only to the condition of providing for existing collateral branches of the Nizamut Family, and completing the Palace." The Nazim naturally objected to these hard and novel terms, and never answered the Governor-General's letter. The reason of this silence was inquired, but although His Highness expressed his wish that Captain Thoresby's plan for paying his relations, through the Agent's Office should be carried out, he *could not be persuaded to entertain the Governor-General's proposition*, and when pressed for an answer expressly declined it. In a private letter to the Agent, His Highness remarked " this is a strange arrangement and an odd way of fulfilling promises, 24th November, 1835.

The Mamulats, or perqusites given by His Highness to his relations, were worth about 1,20,000, and these being paid together with the stipends by the Agent, only about five and a half lakhs were left at His Highness's disposal. On discovering how small the Nazim's income would be, Sir Charles Metcalf reiterated Lord William Bentinck's proposal for fixing the Nazim's income, offering in case of his consenting, *to pay the mamulats* out of the Deposit Fund. But His Highness's mind was made up *not to enter into any agreement of the nature proposed.* His Highness not only rejected this proposition in words, but his payment of the mamulats himself undeniably proves that he did so, and yet this rejected proposal has several times been ignorantly spoken of as a valid agreement. Had he wished to do so, His Highness had no right to enter into such an agreement, for the Agency Deposit Fund had been declared " the inalienable property of His Highness's family," Mani Begum's Deposit Fund was held in deposit *in the same manner for the benefit* of the Nizamut, the lapsed stipend Fund was pronounced by the Governor-General in Council a " *sacred inheritance of the Nizamut,*" and the Court of Directors acknowledged the whole Deposit Fund as " the property of the Nizamut generally, and not public money." The Nawab Nazim had therefore no power to make over this fund to Government, as it was of the nature of an entailed estate, in which he himself had only a life interest. Captain Thoresby's agreement is, therefore, *the last entered into.*

14. The Agreement of 1834 was scarcely concluded when both it and that of 1823 were violated. Government directed that 62,640 rupees lapsed stipends, should be added to Mani Begum's stipend to make up the two lakhs a-year payable to the Deposit Fund by the agreement of 1823, but in opposition to the repeated pledges then given that " no more" than two lakhs should be the *foundation of another Deposit Fund, which will receive continual accessions* from the decease of the different stipendiaries. It has just been agreed that all pensions of dependents were to revert to His Highness and be at his sole disposal. The pensions of relations had been hereditary since 1796, and when lapsed were to be assigned for the benefit of the family and according to His Highness's suggestions, 1823.

The British Government in 1823 *relinquished all desire to increase the fund. This was an express and formal agreement with His Highness,* who honourably fulfilled his part of it, but Sir Charles Metcalfe in 1836, *without any agreement* with the Nazim, affirms that " the Deposit Fund *will increase every year by the* savings arising from all lapsed stipends accumulating in the Collector's Treasury."

15. His Highness in the new plan for paying stipends through the Agent being carried out, expressed a very strong wish that he should continue to give receipts for the whole amount of the stipend of sixteen lakhs. He seems to apprehend that the right of the family to the whole amount may be rendered less secure by his granting receipts for a part only. This was approved, and His Highness continues to grant receipts for the whole sum to the present day.

16. In 1837, the interest on the Deposit Fund being (upwards of three lakhs, one lakh of which was clearly due to His Highness) much larger than was required for ordinary purposes, the permanent charge being only 72,000 rupees, the Agent to Governor-General desired " that part should be employed in municipal improvements, roads, tanks, &c., which would tend to the comfort, convenience and credit of the Nizamut." There was also a surplus of above three lakhs in the collector's hands which was applied towards the palace, Immambarah, and minority. Lord Auckland sanctioned the union of the three Deposit Funds under the title of Nizamut Deposit Fund, but declined to make any rules for " appropriating the surplus income as it

may be lapsed; that, without any formal appropriation of the surplus, *His Highness the Nawab Nazim will be induced to accede to any reasonable propositions for its disposal:* such as building or repair of houses belonging to the Nizamut family, marriage portions, or municipal improvements;" thus clearly recognizing "the Nazim's right over the Deposit Fund." It is spoken of by the Agent as "not the property of Government," this being then an acknowledged fact. The Court of Directors, in 1840, required a more liberal application of the Deposit Fund to the relief of individuals than at present practised : for example in relieving the distress caused by inundation. "The Deposit Fund is not (as stated by the Deputy-Governor) *public money, but a part of the assignment by treaty of the family,* of which part is allowed to accumulate for its general benefit." Not only should grants in favour of the dependents be more *more freely made,* but a revision of the general allowances of the family should take place, with a view of increasing the provision of those whose stipends are *inadequate to their rank* or to the claims on them, or whose conduct entitles them to a mark of approbation from Government. Thus administered, the Fund might be made an instrument of moral discipline, for which no other obvious expedient presents itself. The Court thus distinctly reproves the Deputy-Governor.

For at least four years after the conclusion of the new arrangement in 1834, 1838, and 1839, the amount deducted from the Nawab Nazim (upwards of 8 lakhs) was fully spent on stipends, fresh ones having been granted, as was customary, to the family of Humayun Jah on that prince's decease. But *during the minority* of His present Highness stipends began to lapse, and were absorbed *for the first time* into the Deposit Fund, contrary to all previous agreements.

After his majority His Highness remonstrated vehemently against the infringement of his rights, especially on the death of grand aunt, Bahu Begum, when he claimed her stipend of Rs 2,000, and her mamulat of Rs. 1,900, as property reverting to himself, both as Nawab Nazim and as her sole heir.

His Highness entered fully into the question of his rights in 1837 ; and considering that His Highness, after the regular necessary disbursements of his establishment have been defrayed, has only Co.'s Rs. 1,400 a month at his disposal for all usual expenses, religious festivals, clothes, &c., it is not to be wondered at that, as the Agent to Governor-General naïvely complains, he should always revert to the subject of the lapsed stipends, "neither should it be forgotten that the government of the country was confided to the British, on the faith that the Nizamut of Bengal, Behar, and Orissa should be suitably maintained."

17. But under **Lord Dalhousie's** administration matters were entirely reversed. He was *the first* who affirmed that the Deposit Fund was at the *entire disposal of Government,* and that the Nawab Nazim had *no claim to or any control over it.* "In consequence lapsed stipends began to be spoken of as reverting *to Government."*

In **1854** the Agent of the Governor-General brought to His Lordship's notice that **the sum** of nearly **24 lakhs was** lying *undrawn* in the Collector's **Treasury,** and requested to know if this should not be invested so **as to give** His Highness's family the benefit of the interest.

In former days investments were ordered to be made *to the best advantage*. Even the unused interest on the Deposit Fund was to be re-invested; even "the discount on these transactions *belonged to the Nizamut* and *was to be accounted for to His Highness*." The Agent was directed to "*invest* all minority savings for the benefit of the minor." Lord Dalhousie considered the Deposit Fund unnecessarily large; and, instead of fulfilling the obvious obligation of restoring all but two lakhs per annum to the Nazim, he ordered that *no more of the capital should be invested*, but that it should henceforward be considered as a mere *book-debt bearing no interest*.

Since then grants from the Deposit Fund have been refused for the very objects for which it was instituted, *ex. gra.* for saving the burial-grounds of His Highness's family and other buildings belonging to the Nizamut from destruction by the annual encroachments of the river. This is one flagrant case. There are others.

One fertile source of these infractions of solemn agreements appears to have been the frequent change of Agents which took place just at the time of the last arrangements. There were no less than six changes in the Agent Governor-Generals from July 1833 to April 1836. A new Agent appears often to have misunderstood or been ignorant of the rights of the Nawab, and others unwittingly to have misled the Supreme Government into breaches of faith such as the above.

That this was involuntary, and arising from ignorance, is manifest by Mr. Melville at one time recommending the resumption of mamulats, and yet expressing himself as follows:—"One principal duty of the Agent under the instructions in force has always appeared to me to be *to protect this Prince* from the perpetual tendency of subordinate authorities to encroach upon such rights and privileges as it has been deemed just and expedient to reserve to this family."

But a breach of faith can never become a precedent or rule. These must be sought in deliberate stipulations and promises, and it is surely enough for a just Government that on the accession of His present Highness, he was proclaimed under authority of the Government of India to be Nazim and Soubadar of Bengal, Behar, and Orissa, and to have assumed and to exercise the authorities, dignities, and privileges thereof, 12th December, 1838, and that the late Governor-General solemnly promised, on his arrival, to promote the interests and *establish the authority* of all the Native Princes by *strict observance of* and enduring fulfilment of, *compact and treaty in terms of existing conditions, stipulations, and articles, arranged and concerted*.

On the 31st March, 1853, His Highness the Nawab Nazim Ferodun Jah, was out on a shooting excursion with a suite of about 2,000 persons. During his absence, one Hossaini missed a box belonging to his master (one of His Highness's eunuchs, named Miah Arjum), and Maddi, a lad, was seized on suspicion, and being beaten, pointed out a beggar, named Hingoo, as his accomplice. Both the prisoners repeatedly gave false information as to where the missing property was, and each time the discovery of their deceit was followed by unmerciful beating. They were beaten several times in or near the tents of the eunuchs (which was about 50 yards from that of His Highness with an outer konath or wall of canvas between), a native doctor was called on to attend them, who gave them poultices, &c,, but on the 5th and 6th April, they died, in the little tent of Etwari, the father of Maddi, which was three or four yards beyond the tent of the meahs or eunuchs.

On the 5th May, a petition was presented to the Sherishtah Dewani, or Dewan's Office of the Nizamut, purporting to be from the mother of Maddi, accusing Aman Ali Khan, His Highness's chief eunuch, then acting Dewan, and several others, of the murder of her son. The Nazim issued immediate orders for an enquiry. All the witnesses stated that the lad had died of cholera, in spite of the administration of laudanum and calcined gold, which the doctor Zummuik candidly confesses did not do him much good. The doctor stated that ten or twelve other persons had died of cholera in the camp, and many more in the villages. The brother and mother of Maddi deposed that she had presented no petition to the Agent or any one else, and her seal was not on the one produced. Etwari, the father of the lad, declared that he had seen him die of cholera. His Highness naturally believed this, especially as Aman Ali Khan had been with him from childhood, and His Highness reposed " entire confidence in him."

The accused persons were tried at Moorshedabad in September, 1853. On a careful perusal of the proceedings, the following conclusions can scarcely be avoided.

1st. That although Maddi and Hingoo were most cruelly beaten, and it is in the highest degree probable that they died from the beating, there is no *positive proof* that they did so.

2nd. There was apparently no *concealment* in the matter; they were beaten openly.

3rd. The only persons who accuse Aman Ali of having been concerned in beating these unfortunate men, are Hossaini, the approver, who had lost the box and (who had undoubtedly beaten them himself,) a leper, a temporary cook, and a discharged Burkundauz, who lived chiefly by begging, and an elephant-driver who had tied up the accused. These men all gave contradictory evidence. The Judges of the Sudder Nizamut felt constrained " to discard the evidence of the first four witnesses *in toto*." The leper affirmed that he saw Aman Ali Khan, the first of His Highness's officers in rank and authority, cutting a bamboo with his *own hands* and then beating the prisoners with it; a statement bearing the strongest marks of improbability on the very face of it; his evidence was pronounced by the Sessions Judge not entitled to much credit, as the discrepancies in it are irreconcileable. The discharged Burkundauz declared that Maddi and Hingoo were brought before His Highness who ordered their release, but that Aman Ali countermanded it, and threatened to blow them away from a gun! His evidence to use the words of the Court " teemed with improbabilities and gross contradictions." Three witnesses (in a much more respectable station in life) denied that Aman Ali Khan had beaten the two accused men; and testify that on hearing they had been beaten, he had at two different times sent orders that *they should be released.* George Shapcott (His Highness's coachman, whose evidence was universally acknowledged as trustworthy) testified that when Maddi at Naugeriah accused a third person named Janghi, the latter was seized, and would have been beaten by the camel-driver, who had most cruelly beaten Maddi, when Shapcott interfered and by the use of Aman Ali Khan's name effectually stayed the meditated injustice.

4th Aman Ali had no motive for taking up the matter with any violence. The box was not his, and was apparently of little value. At the same time he had, as the favourite of the Nazim, innumerable enemies asking his downfall.

The Mahoumedan Law Officer found Aman Ali Khan guilty of "instigating the beating on violent presumption," and of privity to the crime on full proof.

There was clearly no proof that Aman Ali Khan had ordered the men to be beaten, and the Sessions Judge gave his opinion as follows:—"After carefully weighing the whole of the evidence against him, I am not satisfied with that part which would implicate him as the instigator; which he would be, if it were satisfactorily proved that he gave orders for the two men to be beaten," and pronounced that he was only proved to have been an *accessory after the fact*.

The Sudder Nizamut considered that it was proved that the prisoner had forbidden the ill-treatment of the victims, and that there was *no proof of his being accessory* "after the fact and *acquitted him*. They also found the convicted prisoners guilty of culpable homicide," not of murder, for by their calling on a doctor to attend the victims and dress their wounds, it appears that in spite of their inhumanity that they had no intention of causing death. It was not to be wondered at that His Highness should be satisfied with the verdict of the Court and should have believed Aman Ali Khan innocent, and treated him accordingly. The Nazim had in the meantime appointed Rai Prosonno Narain Deb Bahadoor to the office of Dewan, which Aman Ali Khan had exercised without being formally invested with it. Lord Dalhousie, in defiance of the solemn verdict of the highest Court of Justice in India, decided that Aman Ali Khan *was guilty*, and that the act of His Highness in agreeing with the Sudder Nizamut by believing him innocent, was a proof of his own complicity in the murder. His Lordship might quite as reasonably have come to the same conclusion regarding the Judges themselves. He called for an explanation from the Nazim, and the expressions he used in so doing sufficiently show that he had made up his mind not only as to the guilt of the acquitted eunuchs, but as to that of the Nawab Nazim himself.

It was quite necessary in His Lordship's opinion "that the Nawab Nazim under whose *very eyes* this monstrous outrage of humanity has been perpetrated, should be required to give an explanation of his conduct in the matter, that measures should be taken to mark the sense entertained by Government of such proceedings, and that safeguards should be provided against repetition of them in future."

Again, the Nawab Nazim was required to state "why he failed to exert his authority to prevent the perpetration of so outrageous a crime, *almost in his very presence*," thus *taking for granted that* His Highness had been cognizant of it. These words demonstrate that His Lordship had come to a foregone conclusion, and that any explanation would be wholly ineffectual.

The Governor-General pronounced not only that Aman Ali Khan "had failed to use the influence he had to prevent the crime" (though the Sudder Adawlut had pronounced him *ignorant* of it) but that "from His Highness's tent being only 50 yards from where the men were tortured" and from his having the eunuchs daily to "*dine with him*," *he must* have been himself cognizant of the torture, of the death that ensued from the torture, and of the falseness of the rumour which ascribed the death of these men to cholera!

The first reason for this string of accusations was that the Nazim's tent had been pitched about 50 yards from the place where the unfortunate victims had been kept. His Highness's known gentleness and humanity of character, which are such that he cannot prevail upon himself to kill the camel at the Bakri Eed, but merely touches it with a lance and then withdraws while it is slaughtered, his European education and ideas, the facts that he was absent from his tent during the greater part of each day, and that much, if not most of the cruelty took place *at a distance from Camp*, availed him nothing. It was forgotten how unlikely a few cries were to attract attention amid the bustle of a large Camp. Even had they been heard, which, considering how completely the double walls of a large double-poled tent deaden sound, especially at such a distance, and that there was moreover an outer high wall of canvas between the two tents, and that His Highness was scarcely ever in his tent save at dinner, when he was serenaded all the time by his band, retiring to rest immediately afterwards, was not very probable. His Highness in talking the matter over freely with an old friend, related that he had on one occasion (he did not say whether in or out of his tent) heard some cries, and inquired the reason, to which Aman Ali Khan replied that it was a case of cholera, and, added the Prince, "of course I believed him."

The second reason was that the eunuchs had "*dined daily with His Highness*." Would any one, especially any Prince, like to be made responsible for all the acts of those who dined daily with him? Is it then probable that these men, had they committed or been aware of this atrocity, would have chosen their humane master as their confidant instead of carefully concealing the matter from him? It is to be remarked that the only evidence which proves that Aman Ali Khan knew of the accused persons being twice beaten, proves that on each occasion he gave orders forbidding their ill-treatment. It is nowhere proved that he knew the extent of the cruelty, or that it had resulted in death.

Mr. Trevor, the Prosecutor for Government, whose letter to the Secretary to Government against the decision of the Sudder Adawlut, appears to have been in some degree the basis of the Governor-General's opinion, considers that the acquitted Eunuchs were guilty of nothing more than privity (*i.e.* knowledge without consent of any crime), and that the ends of justice would have been fully answered *by a slight fine.*

The truth seems to have been that Aman Ali Khan knew of at least two beatings which he sent to put a stop to; that these beatings were continued and inflicted chiefly at a distance from Camp, as at Noughuria, beyond what Aman Ali Khan and the other eunuchs knew of. That the perpetrators themselves did not intend to kill their victims; that when they found they had gone too far, they called in the native doctor to endeavour to cure the unfortunate men, and that probably their death, and certainly the cause of it, was concealed from their superiors, and most especially that His Highness, as he affirms (and his character gives him every right to be implicitly believed) was *in total ignorance of the whole matter.*

The Governor-General's agent writes on this occasion,—" His Highness has invariably declared that he was never made cognizant of the fact that death ensued in consequence of the maltreatment which the unfortunate creatures, Maddi and Hingoo, received." Major Macgregor quoted testimony of General Raper, who perhaps knew the character of the young Nawab better than any one, and who observed that " as a boy he had *never shewn the smallest propensity to cruelty or mischief,*" and adds, " former agents, and every one who knows the Nazim, speak of him as kind, generous, and humane."

Major Macgregor's opinion was that the Nawab Nazim " *must* have heard a false account of the affair," but it seems unnecessary to suppose that he had heard any other than the account which was received by the Sudder Nizamut Court, and he could not be blamed for coming to the same conclusion. On receiving the Governor-General's letter, the Nazim immediately discharged five of the accused eunuchs, suspended Aman Ali Khan from his various employments, and desired him to give in his accounts as soon as possible.

In his answer to the Governor-General, His Highness expressed his grief at being held responsible for the conduct of his servants, and simply states the undeniable facts that during his shooting expedition, it was his habit to start early in the morning, take his breakfast on his elephant, return overcome by fatigue, and soon retire to rest, and that consequently he knew very little of what went on in Camp, to which Mr. Garrett, the Judge of Beerbhoom, the Honourable Mr. Eden, now at Baraset, and other gentlemen who had accompanied him, could bear witness. He solemnly declared that it never came to his knowledge that a murder had been committed, and mentioned that he had caused inquiries to be made immediately the matter was brought to his notice, when it appeared that Hingoo and Maddi had died of cholera. In reply to Lord Dalhousie's inquiry " why he continued to show favour and countenance to those who (*in His Lordship's opinion*) were concerned in the murder," the Nazim naturally replied that " when they were acquitted by the Sudder Court, after being so strictly tried, *I really thought them to be not guilty.*" His Highness seems at first to have understood that the Governor-General had ordered the dismissal of the eunuchs, though nothing is said of this in Lord Dalhousie's letter, but hearing nothing of the matter during an interval of four months, and having information that the affair had been referred to the Court of Directors, he thought they never would sanction such an injustice as punishing men for a crime of which they had been acquitted, nor such an interference with his own domestic arrangements, and therefore instead of depriving himself wholly of old and favourite attendants, he allowed them to continue among his retinue, although not exercising their functions, until the matter should be finally decided. This turned out a most unfortunate step. The Agent reported that they were still in His Highness's service, and that Aman Ali Khan had resumed his duties as chief eunuch.

At length in March, Lord Dalhousie pronounced the Nawab Nazim's explanation, which bears truth on the very face of it, to be most unsatisfactory (though one does not see what else an innocent man could have said) and the case aggravated by the favour His Highness continues to show Aman Ali Khan and the other eunuchs. The Nazim was peremptorily required "**to** dismiss them altogether from his service," and to "hold **no** further communication with any of **them.**" The Agent was required **to** "report within **one** week" whether this "requisition had **been complied with or not.**" His Highness was refused **permission to go to Dinagepore for** change of air, although Dr. Kean said he wanted exercise, and the excursion would do him a **vast deal of good,** "**and His Lordship** refused to sanction *under any* ***circumstances***" the usual disbursement from the Deposit Fund for His Highness's travelling expenses.

The question is not whether the **eunuchs were** innocent **or guilty,** but whether having been declared **innocent** by the highest **Court of** Justice in India, **any one had** a right **to** pronounce them guilty and to punish them as such, **and** even to go the length of punishing a defenceless Prince, because **he** coincided in opinion with British Judges! His Highness had an undoubted right to be of the same opinion as the Sudder Nizamut, but this Lord Dalhousie would by no means permit, and being in the only position in the world in which a British Sovereign or subject can punish those who have been legally acquitted, **he** decided that the eunuchs were guilty, and punished His Highness for believing them innocent, not only by depriving him of air and exercise, and of his right to have his travelling expenses paid from the Deposit Fund, but by recommending to the Court of Directors **to** diminish His Highness's stipend, to take away the salute of nineteen **guns due to** his **rank as** the acknowledged equal and brother of **the Governor-General, or at least to** diminish **it to** thirteen, "so that **the Nawab should no longer receive** in public **as** he now does, higher **honours than the Members of the** Supreme Government of India!" **He even declined to comply with an** Indent **for** Military Stores required for the **Nazim's use, and brought in a Bill** depriving His Highness, his **family and relations, including the** ladies, **of** all immunities and rights which had been **secured to them** by Treaties, by pledges from successive Governors-General, and by no less than four Acts of Council. The Treaties with the first four Nazims of Bengal have been already given, Lord Dalhousie repealed all those Regulations and even condescended to **use** the plea that these "privileges were **a serious** impediment to the **course** of justice."

How this could be the case as they extended only to Civil and **Revenue** cases, and did not extend to criminal cases, was not explained, **nor how the** Acts of 1805 **and** 1806, which regulated the form of address **to be used to the Nazim and** his family, could possibly affect the course **of justice!**

In vain **His** Highness and the chief ladies in his family remonstrated. His Highness remarked **it too** plainly appeared "that His Lordship's mind is still intent **on my** degradation; *the new Act completes the humiliation and distresses of this friend* by his depression and degradation with his family and friends, *irrespective of the obligations and provisions of ancient Treaties.*" Not only the injustice, but the

Q

excessive severity of this treatment, is remarkable, when we recollect that the Prosecutor for Government considered that the ends of justice would have been *fully answered by a slight fine*, inflicted on those whom he considered guilty *only of privity*, to the crime; but whom Lord Dalhousie appears to have considered as guilty of murder, thus going far beyond even the Prosecutor.

The persons accused were to be fined, the Prince in whose service they were was to be *degraded* in the eyes of all his countrymen, deprived of his most valued privileges.

The Court of Directors sanctioned all Lord Dalhousie's proposed measures except that instead of abolishing the salute—" it appeared sufficient that the number of guns be reduced from nineteen to thirteen," and that they declined interfering with His Highness's income *during his lifetime*, thus causing the most serious alarm as to what they might be pleased to do afterwards.

Summary.

The breaches of faith of which His Highness complains are, 1st depriving him of his just due of sixteen lacs per annum: By unduly increasing the Deposit Fund beyond the limit of two lacs yearly, contrary to solemn and reiterated stipulations and promises. This was done by resuming stipends, Mamulats, Mutynats, &c., which ought to have reverted to His Highness.

This was done by Sir C. Metcalfe in 1836.

2nd. Misappropriation of stipends.

3rd. Depriving him of all control over the Deposit Fund, and making it a book-debt without interest.

This was done in 1854.

4th. Depriving him and his family of their rights and privileges regarding suits in our Courts.

5th. Depriving him of the salute due to his rank as the acknowledged equal and brother of the Governor-General.

Summary.

The Nawab Nazim's right to sixteen lacs per annum is as clear as human pledges can make it.

It rests upon the treaties with Jaffier Ali Khan and his first three successors, upon the pledges of successive Governors-General, and the confirmation of the Court of Directors.

For instance, Lord Minto, on the accession of Nawab Nazim Zayenood-deen Ali Khan, assures him that "*the stipend* fixed on the accescession of your august father, by the Honourable East India Company will be continued to *Your Highness without any difference*," viz., at the annual *allowance of sixteen lakhs* in monthly issues as usual. The same pledge is reiterated by Marquis of Hastings in 1821, by Lord Amherst in 1825.

Lord Amherst says, " Your Highness may be assured that *the annual fixed allowance* and the other mutually settled points will remain and *continue* as approved and sanctioned by the Home authorities, namely, *sixteen lakhs of rupees per annum.*"

So late **as 1840, the** Court of Directors speaks of the sixteen lakhs as the assignment *by treaty*, of the family. His Highness' right to the income of sixteen lakhs rests upon the same basis as our right to Bengal, Behar, **and** Orissa, of which territories it is the stipulated price.

The Nawab Nazim *still gives receipts for the whole sum*. This income has been withdrawn from His Highness by unduly increasing **the** Deposit Fund, chiefly by *resuming lapsed stipends*, Mamulats, or perquisites granted by his predecessors **to** the Deposit Fund, instead **of** to His Highness' own treasury, **as** repeatedly stipulated, and by *resuming Mutayanats* or hereditary stipends left to dependants on condition of service, all of which are illegal **and contrary to treaties and agreement.**

I. Increasing the Deposit **Fund beyond the sti**pulated limit of two lacs per annum was an open violation **of the agreement** of 1823, which had been sanctioned by the Court of **Directors.** This was Sir Charles Metcalfe's doing.

Mr. Stirling **pronounced that** two lacs **were** more than **necessary,** and that we have *no right* to withhold from the Nazim any more than is positively required. The Honourable W. L. Melville, Agent to the Governor-General, saw *no reason* for augmenting the capital of this **Fund,** and there has always been considerable difficulty in disposing **of the** surplus, while at the same time His Highness has a very insufficient share of his own income for his personal and family expenses. The amount at first deducted from His Highness in 1836 was upwards **of** eight lacs yearly, out of which 56,000 of lapsed stipend, and *no more,* ought to have been set apart to make up with Mani Begum's stipend two **lacs** per annum. At first this sum was fully spent on stipends, but since **then** a very large surplus has annually **remained.** This has not been invested at all, and **consequently in April, 1858, there** remained **a balance of** about **23,80,000** *undrawn* from the Collector's Treasury. Of this, about **twelve lacs** is the result of the annual appropriation **to complete the sum of two lacs per annum.** The remainder, that is nearly **twelve lacs, clearly belongs to His Highness the Nazim.**

That so large an accumulation is quite unnecessary, **is** shown by the fact of its being *undrawn.* There is a further balance of upwards **of** fifteen and a half lacs from Mani Begum's stipends, which, as the **Nawab** Nazim justly observed, ought to revert to him, if not available **for** his relations. Stipends to the relations and dependants as well as the Mamulats, or perquisites, were originally fixed by the Nazim. On many occasions stipends were refused from the Deposit Fund and granted out of His Highness's privy purse. All stipends passed through the Nawab Nazim's hands up to 1833, 1834, and the new arrangement **that** they were to be paid by the Agent was only to ensure regularity, **and** not to place them at the disposal of Government. Subsequently all **these** stipends were taken into the hands of Government, and when they lapse are not returned to the Nizamut.

It is evident **that** no more ought to be set apart for relations, &c., than is actually required, as the **whole fourteen** lacs belong to the Nazim, and of course **when there remains no one to claim a** stipend, it naturally ought to revert to **the Prince by whom it has** been granted. This was the case in Lord Cornwallis's time, half of such pensions as by His Highness's own determination were resumed were to go to his privy purse, half to the payment of his debt. Lord Cornwallis declared the stipends of the Nawab Nazim's relations hereditary, and those of dependants at the option of the Prince, and the whole were declared not in any wise at the pleasure of Government further than to prevent partiality. Lord Amherst speaks of the distribution of pensions according to the judgment of both Sirkars. By the last agreement made with the Nawab Nazim which was declared to be the rule under which Nizamut affairs are henceforward to be administered, "all *Mamulats* and perquisites to relations" on the decease of the recipient without heirs, and all pensions to dependants are to *revert to the Nizamut Treasury* and be at the *entire disposal of His Highness;* yet when in 1849, the young Nawab Nazim addressed the Agent on the subject of the lapsed stipend of his grand-aunt, the Babbee Begum, to whose personal allowance of 2,000 a month and 1,900 on account of Mamulat, he considered himself entitled, as she had left no heir but himself, the Agent pointed out that the Mamulat was resumable to the credit of the Deposit Fund by orders of Government, 6th December, 1836, quite overlooking the fact that this order was issued without the consent of the Nazim and in open violation of the agreement made with him in 1834.

This agreement is the Rule now in force, but it has of late years been completely set at defiance. Even Mutayanats, or stipends left by Mani Begum, Babbee Begum, and others to old retainers, which are considered hereditary (the descendants continuing in the service of the Government, and against His Highness's wishes and remonstrances, and in spite of the express provision in the order of 18th July, 1838, for resuming stipends to the Deposit Fund *unless when they are dependants of the deceased,* the support of whom would be a duty incumbent on relations. Thus depriving the retainers in question of bread, and His Highness of their services. What is worse than that, many of these stipends have been resumed in *the lifetime* of the recipients. For instance on the decease of the Mariumnissa Begum, all the Mutayanats of the servants who were in attendance on her ceased. Even the Dhye, who had nursed her, lost her pension of ten rupees. The same was the case on the death of the Dulin Begum, and will occur on the recent occasion of the decease of His Highness's grandmother, unless the Right Honourable the Governor-General should be pleased to revert to the old mode of dealing. The second grievance of which His Highness complains is the misappropriation of stipends.

1. By resuming them arbitrarily without considering His Highness's wishes or suggestions, on the claims of heirs and dependents.

The Nawab Nazim's rights to the disposal of stipends was never doubted, and consequently exercised until 1852. Of this the proofs are innumerable. In 1795, pensions are to be assigned as His Highness the Nawab Nazim recommends. The following year the Governor-General in Council approves of the appropriation of the hereditary allowances therein recommended by the Nawab Nazim. In 1823 the Government *pledged* itself, on the lapse of any future stipends, to consider the suggestions of His Highness as to its allotment, and, except under special circumstances, to assign *the whole for the benefit of the family*, and accordingly requests the opinion of His Highness the Nawab Nazim on the propriety of continuing to the family of a pensioner "the allowance, or any part of it." Stipends were resumed on His Highness's recommendation, distributed as he proposed. Compensation to the Begum's was to be discussed with Nawab Nazim 15th May, 1834.

The Agent to Governor-General, in concurrence with Nawab Nazim, recommends 300 rupees per annum additional to Badurulnissa Begum. 31st December, 1836.

After the completion of the new arrangement for paying stipends from the Agent's office, Government instructed the Agent that "with regard to the distribution of allowances, it will be proper to consult the Nawab Nazim as to the individuals who are to receive it; and the wishes of His Highness, except where decidedly objectionable, should be attended to as heretofore (9th June, 1836). Stipends to relations were declared hereditary in 1795. Government *pledged itself* in 1823, on the lapse of any future stipend, to assign the *whole for the benefit of the family*." Even in 1838, the very order for resuming to the Deposit Fund the stipends of those who die without heirs acknowledged them as *hereditary*, when heirs exist, and an exception is made to their resumption *when there are dependents of the deceased*. But of late years all the stipends of any value have been diminished on the death of the holder. His Highness has been gradually obliged (in order to avoid the utter rejection of his recommendation) to name only a portion of the stipend to be assigned to the family and heirs. The Nazim has himself been obliged to support the dependents of his grand-aunt, the Bahu Begum, for years, only a very small portion of the expense being allowed him from the Deposit Fund.

3. *Depriving the Nawab Nazim of all control over the Deposit Fund, and making it a book-debt without interest.* This was the act of Lord Dalhousie.

The Deposit Fund was recognised as the inalienable property of His Highness's family over and above the sixteen lakhs assigned for its support as "the sacred inheritance of the Nizamut," "the property of Nizamut generally, *not the property of Government*, and solemnly declared by the Court of Directors to be *not public money*, but *a part of the assignment by treaty of the family*."

"The Governor-General in Council, with a view to uphold the due efficiency and dignity of the Nawab Nazim's station, deems it proper to declare *as a rule for future observance* that *all applications for aid from the Deposit Fund should be addressed to His Highness*, and by him forwarded, *if he thinks proper*, to the Agent, for the eventual orders of Government." The Governor-General in Council required that "every facility should be given for His Highness making himself acquainted *with the minutest details; and his wishes regarding grants from the Deposit Fund were to be signified to the Agent and attended to as heretofore;*" and speaks of the Agency Treasurer as accountable to the Agent of the Governor-General as well as to the Nawab Nazim for the disbursement of stipends. Not long ago His Highness's consent was requested, even before applying a portion of the Deposit Fund to supplying medical aid to the Nizamut School. This was given in a private note to Humayan Jah.

Lord Auckland **fully acknowledged** the Nawab Nazim's right over *the Deposit Fund*; yet, in defiance of these acknowledged rights, Lord Dalhousie asserted "*that the Deposit Fund is at the entire disposal of Government, and that the Nawab Nazim has no claim to nor any control whatever over it.*" The Lieutenant-Governor of Bengal adopted the same opinion: "I am directed to observe that, *under the condition of the Deposit Fund, it is a resource over which the Nawab Nazim has no sort of control;* and he should not therefore be allowed to recommend that disbursements may be made from it!!"

The contrast between the solemn stipulations entered into with the Nawab Nazim and the above assertions is too obvious to render any comment necessary. Refusing to invest the enormous sum belonging to the Nizamut, and making it merely a debt-book, has caused many to look upon it as Government property, and grants made from it as made from the public funds, and is in strong opposition to the principles laid down. So late as 1838 "the Government is, in respect to the Deposit Fund, *the Trustee responsible* for its application in the manner which will make it *most beneficial* to the family.

4. So late as 1834, the Vice-President in Council **speaks of** the Nawab Nazim **as a Prince** *whose* **independence has** been recognised by a Treaty with one of his predecessors, and adds, "Government considers it *unjust and unlawful* that a Prince who is not subject to the jurisdiction of the Supreme Court should be made to plead before it."

The inconvenience, insult, and injustice, which are the unavoidable results of the abrogation of a privilege inseparably connected with His Highness's rank have been fully pointed out elsewhere.

5. Even when morning guns were discontinued at the neighbouring station of Berhampore, "*it was never contemplated by* Government to withhold the usual salute to His Highness the Nawab Nazim," for which **express purpose two** 6-pounders were permanently attached **to the stations.**

The Marquis of Hastings, among other Governors-General, solemnly promised that "the *honours and distinctions* due *to the exalted rank* of His Highness's family *will always be paid* and faithfully observed."

Lord Amherst pledged himself "to maintain *the honours* of His Highness, and that "the respect due to the rank and the honours and distinctions appropriate to the high and eminent family of Your Highness, will be always kept in view and observed."

Sir H. Hardinge, on taking the reins of Government, writes,—"Be assured *the same honours and distinctions* paid to support **your** rank and authority will be observed *and continued.*"

His Highness feels the degradation the more keenly as the honour of **a salute of 19** guns, which he and his predecessors had so long enjoyed, **was** recently accorded to Maharajah Jung Bahadoor, who **is** only **a great** chief in Nepal, and not a hereditary Prince. So keenly does **His** Highness feel the disgrace to which Lord Dalhousie thus subjected him, that he has never left the precincts of his residence since, although his prolonged abstinence from exercise and change of air has had a very prejudicial effect on his health. He has, therefore, never submitted to receive the diminished salute.

On the above Narrative of Nizamut Affairs being placed before Lord Canning, Major Colin Mackenzie, Agent Governor-General, was called upon by the Lieutenant-Governor of Bengal to report officially on Nizamut Affairs, he was, however, prevented from noticing the Murder case. Subjoined is the Agent's official opinion on the subject of the Nawab Nazim's grievances and claims:—

From MAJOR COLIN MACKENZIE, *Acting Agent Governor-General at Moorshedabad, to* A. R. YOUNG, ESQ., *Secretary to the Government of Bengal.*

Dated Fort William, the 23rd May, 1859.

SIR,—I have the honour to acknowledge your letter, No. 119, dated the 2nd April, 1859, calling for my opinion on Nizamut affairs, together with the enclosures as per margin.

2. The force of the first two documents is considerably neutralised by their rejection in the third and last; but, as His Honour the Lieutenant-Governor has invited me "to make my remarks upon them, which they may seem to require," I have the honour to forward, for the consideration of Government, a narrative of the principal facts connected with Nizamut affairs, which I have for months past been engaged in compiling from a mass of ill-arranged records, in anticipation of a desire on the part of my superiors to have fuller information as to the facts of the case than has hitherto been afforded them.

3. I beg to premise that in offering this detail, I earnestly disclaim all intention of thrusting my opinion on the attention of Government, or of presumptuously dictating the course which ought to be pursued. If, in my endeavours to put the merits of the case clearly before the eyes of the deciding authorities, I have used little circumlocution, I trust that my plainness of speech may be viewed in a favourable light, and that it will be seen that my sole motives are concern for the *honour* and consequently for the *real interests* of my country, and of the Government which I have the honour to serve, and the necessity of putting aside all selfish considerations in the performance of *so sacred a duty*.

4. The papers before me, and referred to in the 1st paragraph of this letter, consist of a Note, signed by the Secretary to the Government of Bengal, and a Minute based upon it by Lord Dalhousie, dated 9th November, 1853. The Governor-General speaks of the note as "having given him, for the first time, a full view of the arrangements of the Nizamut." It was therefore the more to be regretted that the note itself was *incomplete*, and made no allusion to

several most important documents and facts which must have materially altered the conclusions arrived at. This incompleteness could scarcely have been avoided, unless the drawing up of the memorandum had been confided to the Agent Governor-General at Moorshedabad, or to some one who could command the leisure to peruse the mass of documents relating to Nizamut affairs, which are dispersed in the Offices of the Agent, of the Nizamut, and of the Bengal Government, and which, I may safely say, require the labour of months to become fully acquainted with.

5. After giving an outline of the three Treaties between the East India Company and the three sons and successors of the Nawab Jaffier Ali Khan, the writer of the Note came to the conclusions:—

1st.—That "no Treaties or agreements had been made with any of the five Nawabs, who have since ascended the Musnud."

2nd.—That "none of the above engagements were otherwise than personal," and that therefore "there never was any guarantee, expressed or implied, to continue the payment of Lacs 16,00,000 to the Nawab and his family for ever," which the late Governor-General states that "it is beyond question that the Nawab *has no right or title whatever to any allowance* by 'treaty or compact,'" or "by virtue of any agreement," but that he and his predecessors have received the stipend of 16 lacs, "of the free grace and favor of the British Government, in the same manner as the King of Delhi."

He supports his opinion by the remark that the amount of the allowance was changed for the worse from 56 to 43, and subsequently to 31 lacs; but although on a cursory glance these conclusions may appear well founded, they were apparently formed in the unconsciousness of the *grand fundamental treaty* of all, *i.e.*, the tenure on which the British hold the vast provinces of Bengal, Behar, and Orissa.

6. This is the *basis* of all our relations with the Nazim. It is the *Firmaun* of SHAH ALUM granting to the East India Company the Dewani or Civil Government of Bengal, Behar, and Orissa, "as a free gift and altumgau," with the *conditional Jagheer* "*of whatsoever may remain* out of the revenues thereof" after the payment of 26 lacs per annum (by the Nawab) to the royal revenue, "and *after providing for the expenses of the Nizamut*," securing them from dismissal, and granting the said office to the Company, "*from generation to generation, for ever and ever.*"

7. Upon this *Firman*, two supplementary agreements were based, carrying out its provisions—one between the Nawab Nudjim ul Dowlah and the company, and the other between SHAH ALUM and the Company. The former runs thus:—The King having been graciously pleased to grant to the English Company the Dewani of Bengal, Behar, and Orissa, with the revenues thereof, as a free gift for ever, on certain conditions, whereof *one is* that there *shall be a sufficient allowance out of the said* revenues for supporting the expenses of the Nizamut. Be it known that I do agree to accept of the annual sum of Sa. Rs. 53 lacs *odd as an adequate allowance.*" "This agreement by the blessing of God I hope will be inviolably observed as long as the English Company's factories continue in Bengal."

In the second agreement (between the SHAH and the Company)

the latter, in consideration of His Majesty having been graciously pleased to grant them the Dewani of Bengal, &c., do engage to be security for the regular payment of the sum of 26 lacs per annum, which the Nawab had agreed to pay to the King. This engagement having lapsed, owing to the downfall of the sovereignty of Delhi, does by no means affect the separate agreement between the Nazim and the Company, the former having fulfilled all his engagements, and the Company having enjoyed all the benefits contemplated therein.

8. From this it appears evident—

1st.—That Bengal, Behar, and Orissa, were granted to the Company as a *conditional Jagheer;* the full force of which term may be gathered from the fact that the Jagheer granted to Lord Clive is expressly styled an "unconditional Jagheer," and the grant to the Company of the Northern Circars in the same year is stated to be by way of *inam*, or free gift.

2nd.—That which was granted was not the whole revenue of these provinces, but "*whatsoever may remain after* remitting the annual tribute (which the Nazim or Viceroy was bound to pay to the Imperial Court) and providing for the expenses of the Nizamut." Thus the "expenses of the Nizamut" were the first charge upon the revenues of Bengal, and the Company were entitled *only to* "*what remained*." Had the treaty been purely personal and applicable only to the reigning Nazim, the expression used would have been the expenses of the Nawab Nazim Nudjim o Dowlah, but the phrase, "expenses of the Nizamut is a *generic* one, and has always been employed to include those who should inherit or appertain to the Nizamut;—the Nizamut exists, though Nudjim o Dowlah has been long dead.

3rd.—The grant being made "*for ever and ever*," the conditions of it are evidently *perpetual also.*

4th.—The stipulation was a sufficient or *adequate* allowance for the expenses of the Nizamut, and the amount was settled by mutual agreement. To annul, modify, or in anywise change a treaty so carefully worded, and on which such great interests depend, as the annexation of three provinces, which might be styled kingdoms, must obviously require the consent of both the contracting parties. The contracting parties were equal—*they are so in theory still.* The Nazim is now weak; but what made him so?—This very treaty! Shall we therefore break it? Who is to decide what is suitable or adequate? Evidently not only the paramount power, but both.

9. Accordingly this has been the invariable practice, with one marked exception. The Nawab Syfoo ul Dowlah ratified and confirmed the treaties entered into with his Father and Brother " as far as is consistent with the true spirit, intent, and meaning thereof," which is, if I mistake not, the custom whenever a supplementary article or modification is added to a treaty or agreement between contracting parties in Europe, and by no means implies that the treaty would not have been binding on the successors of the prince who made it without such confirmation. A further article was added, to the effect that "having entire confidence in them (*i.e.* the English), that nothing whatever be proposed or carried into execution by the Company derogating from his dignity, interest, and the good of his country," he made over the military defence of the country to the Company, and

in consequence, while receiving the same sum as his predecessors, viz., Rs. 17,78,000 for his household expenses, he agreed to diminish the portion for his Sowarr to 24 lacs instead of 36, as he no longer had to maintain the same number of horse and foot. This latter sum had never been considered fixed, the expression used in the agreement with Nudjim o Dowlah being, should "*such an expense hereafter be found necessary to be kept up.*" The change, therefore, cannot be said to be "for the worse," neither does it prove anything but that it was lawful to modify the former treaty by the consent of both parties.

10. The terms of both agreements denote their permanency, "so long as the English factories continue in Bengal." The treaty in 1770 with the minor Nawab Mubaruck o Dowlah was still more solemnly confirmed. Owing probably to the infancy of the Nazim, his stipend was reduced still further, but this agreement which the Governor-General in Council affirmed shall, by the blessing of God, be "*inviolably observed for ever*," was about two years after broken by the Court of Directors, and the allowance of the Nazim reduced to sixteen lacs. To use Lord Dalhousie's words, it was set aside by their sole authority, without any acquiescence, signified or asked, from the Nawab. But this transaction which His Lordship, apparently not being aware of the solemn *fundamental treaty* of SHAH ALUM, was thus led to adduce as a proof of right, was one of those instances of wrong which causes our early Indian history to be adduced as rather *a chart of shoals* than as an *armoury of precedents*. I think His Honour will agree with me that in order to act in accordance with the higher political morality of the present day, and especially with the pledge for the observance of treaties and engagements so recently given by Her Majesty, we must refer to the compacts made by our predecessors rather than to their mode of observing them.

11. The result of long and careful researches into voluminous ill-arranged records has been the establishment of the following facts; that although the engagements with the five subsequent Nazims were not in the shape of formal treaties, yet there have been *several solemn agreements and compacts*, especially 1790, 1823, and 1834, and each successive Governor-General on assuming the reins of Government, as also on the accession of a new Nazim, has confirmed *the existing treaties and engagements*, and reiterated the assurance of "a scrupulous adherence to *subsisting engagements*, and to the obligations of public faith and honour."

The late Governor-General solemnly promised on his arrival "to promote the interests and establish the authority of all Native Princes, by strict observance, enduring fulfilment of compact and treaty in terms of existing conditions, stipulations, and articles arranged and concerted."

In fact, with slight variations of expressions, every successive Governor-General has publicly assured each successive Nawab Nazim, that "the honour and dignities due to your hereditary rank, and the prescriptive privileges of your high station, guaranteed by the stipulations of *subsisting treaties and long-established relations*, observed and cherished by former Governors-General, will on the part also of this sincere friend, be fervently fostered and punctually fulfilled."

12. The 16 lacs to which the Nazim's stipend was reduced in 1772, have been *repeatedly recognized* as belonging to him *by treaty*.

The agreement promises " not to derogate from the honour, dignity, or interest of the Nawab Nazim," certainly include not diminishing his income, since both his dignity and interest would suffer by the curtailment of it.

Lord Cornwallis, after " inquiring of **the Nazim the names of those** whose pensions he wished to discontinue," **declared the stipends of** the relations of the Nazim hereditary. If **the stipends were to be** hereditary, the funds from which **they were paid must be hereditary** also.

Express pledges made.

Lord Minto, on the accession **of Nawab Nazim** Ali Jah, "**assures** him that the stipend fixed on the accession **of your** august father, by the Honourable East India Company, will **be** continued **to** Your Highness without any difference, viz., at the annual allowance of **16** lacs, in monthly issues as usual." The same pledge is reiterated **by** the Marquis of Hastings in 1821, and by Lord Amherst in 1825.

Lord Amherst says, " Your Highness may be assured that the regular fixed allowance and the other mutually settled points will **remain** and continue as approved and sanctioned by the home authorities, namely, 16 lacs of rupees per annum."

Lord Moira gave a formal assurance that the Agency Deposit Fund **would ever be** considered " as the inalienable property of His High**ness's family,** *over and above* the 16 lacs of rupees assigned for its **support."**

In 1836 the Government instructed the accountant of the **Revenue** Department " **that** the stipend of the Nawab Nazim and the **Nizamut** Pensioners **having** formed matter of *express engagement* **in** *a treaty, &c.*"

In 1840 **the Court of Directors corrected the Deputy-Governor who** had styled **the Deposit** Fund **"public money," and affirmed that " the** Deposit Fund **is not** public **money, but a part of the assignment** *by treaty* of the family." See narrative, passim.

Even had there been no treaties the 16 lacs are sufficiently **secured** by " long established relations ;" and Government has repeatedly pledged itself to " the strict observance and enduring fulfilment of existing conditions, stipulations, and articles arranged and concerted."

No change in the amount of the allowance has been made since 1772, and no change of any importance has ever been made even in the allotment of it, without a formal agreement with the **reigning** Nazim.

13. The principal agreements, omitting several **which proved abortive,** have been three in number.

By the *first*, seven lacs, chiefly arising from Mani Begum's Stipend, were invested for the payment of the Agent of the Governor-General and his establishment. His Highness gave his consent, on receiving from the Governor-General "an assurance that this Fund is and will be considered the inalienable property of His Highness's family, over and above **the 16 lacs** assigned for its support."

In 1823 the Governor-General proposed that two lacs of **rupees per** annum should be invested for the benefit of the Nizamut, **and be con-**

sidered as "a sacred inheritance of the family." His Highness consented, on the British Government "relinquishing all desire to increase the Fund" beyond *one-eighth* of the entire Nizamut Stipend.

The *third* and latest agreement which has been entered into between the "two Sirkars" is that of Captain Thoresby, in 1834, which stipulates that "all *perquisites*, mamulats," &c., *as well as present or future pensions*, should *revert to* and *be at the entire disposal of* "*His Highness.*"

That the stipends of relations and dependants should be distributed by the Agent, although the entire sixteen lacs are still paid to His Highness's receipt, the treasurer being answerable henceforward to the Agent, as well as to the Nawab Nazim; that His Highness should have full control over his own household and his own expenditure without the obligation of giving any account of either.

This was acknowledged by Government as "the rule under which Nizamut affairs are to be henceforth administered."

14. I.—To sum up the subject as a mere matter of account, it seems clear that an adequate allowance "for the Nizamut" is secured *by treaty* as the first charge on the revenues of Bengal, Behar, and Orissa.

II.—That the right of His Highness to at least sixteen lacs per annum rests, not only on ancient usage, "long-established relations," and prescriptive rights since 1772, but *on many formal stipulations and agreements*.

III.—That two lacs per annum, and no more, are by contract to be deducted from His Highness's stipend; the accumulations and balance of interest to be "invested in the securities of the British Government, who is the trustee responsible for the disposing of this money for the benefit of the family, especially for buildings, travelling expenses, and dowries. This is admitted in Lord Dalhousie's order, for he styles it "*a debt*," although he would not allow it to bear interest.

IV.—That the remaining 14 lacs, with all lapses and accumulations therefrom from 1836, only deducting such pensions as he and his ancestors have allotted to their relations and dependants, belong to the Nazim for the time being, whosoever that may be. and should be made over to him. It appears that if a portion of the money properly belonging to the Nazim has been withheld from His Highness, and made use of by Government, he has a claim not only to the principal, but also to the usual rate of interest.

15. The foregoing remarks and the subjoined narrative will, I venture to hope, enable Government to discern and weigh the merits of this important case, and to arrive at a conclusion befitting the magnitude of the interests debated, and the enduring influence of the principles involved. I will not dwell on the impression likely to be produced by this and similar decisions *upon the native mind*, *and it may be on that of the public at home*.

16. I cannot conclude without remarking that it is impossible to disconnect the interests of the Nawab Nazim from the proceedings adopted in connexion with the famous Murder case in the year 1853—4. But I am not authorised to enter upon this subject, although if called upon to do so I believe I could throw some additional light on it.

17. I beg permission to add, lastly, that my position is one of *peculiar difficulty and delicacy*. As Governor-General's Agent, my first duty is to Government, and *I heartily desire to avoid even the appearance of opposition to their acts or policy*. Of course I mean the Government which I have at present the honour to serve, as no man would be considered blameable for openly disapproving by-gone measures, such as the abolition of flogging in the native army, or the invasion of Afghanistan. At the same time I believe that His Excellency the Viceroy placed me in my present appointment with a view to my carrying out the very object for which the office was instituted, viz., *the protection of the interests of the Nawab Nazim as inseparably connected with the honour of the British name*. Indeed the Governor-General in Council in 1816, fully coincided with Mr. Edmonstone in declaring that the exclusive object "of the Governor-General's agency at Moorshedabad," *is the prosperity and pecuniary benefit of the Nizamut;* and it is on this ground alone that the Nazim consented to the formation of the Agency Deposit Fund out of his own revenues for the payment of the Government Agent and his establishment.

It is, therefore, with perfect confidence that I ask the indulgence of His Honour the Lieutenant-Governor, for having entered so fully into the subject, as also for any imperfection in the manner of doing so.

I have the honour to be,
Sir,
Your most obedient servant,
(Signed)   COLIN MACKENZIE,
Acting Agent to the Governor-General
at Moorshedabad.

Fort William,
23rd May, 1859.

The above statements having been drawn up by an *independent* officer of the Government, who had free access to all documents pertaining to the Nizamut and Collectorate, must necessarily bear the impress of truth and contain indisputable data for arriving at a correct conclusion as to the justice of His Highness's claims, which have been advanced by the Nawab himself in three Memorials; the first to the Court of Directors in March, 1857; the second to the Right Honourable Sir Charles Wood, Bart., Her Majesty's Secretary of State for India in Council, in April, 1860, supported by further appeals in December, 1862, and February, 1863; and the third and last to His Grace the Duke of Argyll, K.T., Her Majesty's Secretary of State for India in Council, in July, 1869, to which His Highness awaits a reply. A copy of the last Memorial will be found at the end of this narrative.

In the last Memorial now before Her Majesty's Secretary of State for India in Council, allusion is made to two social questions, to which with some correspondence relating thereto it will be necessary here to refer in order that all His Highness' grievances may be fully explained, and the arbitrary action taken by the Government of India against the Nawab in connection therewith fully exhibited.

The first matter was an affront supposed to have been offered (quite unwittingly !) by the Nawab to the Agent Governor-General (Page 327), and which the Nawab afterwards apologized for.

On the 14th of May, 1861, Colonel Mackenzie, Agent Governor-General, with some friends, drove at an early hour in the morning from Berhampore (where he resided) to the Nazim's Palace at Moorshedabad having expressed his intention of so doing to His Highness, verbally through the Dewan, Rajah Prosunno Narian Deb. His Highness sent a message back by his chief eunuch, Darab Ali Khan, to say that he would try and meet the Agent, if possible, after breakfast; but, as he was not very well, he could not say positively whether he would be able to go. His Highness, feeling worse as the day advanced, was obliged to forego the pleasure of meeting the Agent, and sent a message to this effect. This apparently offended the Agent, who construed it into an insult offered to the Representative of the Viceroy, and reported the matter to the Government. Two days afterwards the Agent called upon His Highness for an explanation, which was given, and accepted as an ample apology by him; but he required His Highness to pay him a return visit as a mark of respect, which His Highness did not think absolutely necessary in his official position, as the Agent had not paid him an official visit.

Extract from a Letter dated 8th June, 1861.

From LIEUTENANT-COLONEL C. MACKENZIE, *Officiating Agent Governor-General,* to HIS HIGHNESS THE NAWAB NAZIM, *&c.*

Para. 1. I have received Your Highness's letters of 22nd May and 4th June, and I understand their contents. *I cannot but accept the apology* contained in the first letter, and regret the severity of Your Highness's sufferings as you describe them. But the fact remains, that I never received a proper message by a proper messenger announcing the impossibility of Your Highness's meeting me in the Palace, and I therefore trust Your Highness will issue such orders to your Officers as will prevent a repetition of *the appearance of disrespect* to the Representative of His Excellency the Viceroy.

Extract from para. 6 *of letter No.* 18, *dated the* 14th *January,* 1861, *from the* GOVERNMENT OF INDIA *to the* LIEUTENANT-GOVERNOR OF BENGAL.

With regard to the affront offered by the Nawab Nazim to the Agent on his occasion of visiting the palace in May last, the Governor-General in Council agrees with the Lieutenant-Governor in thinking, that it has by no means been atoned for by the very unsatisfactory explanation which *has been accepted* by Lieutenant-Colonel Mackenzie *as an apology* to himself. For that affront, offered to the Government in the person of its Agent, His Excellency in Council will not be satisfied with imperfect excuses. Nothing short of a full admission of error, and an unreserved expression of regret, can be received by the Government as a sufficient apology, and the Nawab should be told that until such an apology has been forwarded by him, and accepted by the Lieutenant-Governor, neither will the request which His Highness has made for permission to visit the Governor-General be considered, nor will the letters, which he addressed to His Excellency on the 16th and 25th October be answered. The Agent also will be withdrawn for the present, and all Official communications between the Government and the Nawab will be made through the Collector of Moorshedabad until an Agent regularly appointed, can, with propriety, resume his functions.

From His Highness the Nawab Nazim of Bengal, &c., *to* The Honourable John Peter Grant, *Lieutenant-Governor of Bengal.*

His Highness the Nawab Nazim of Bengal is informed by the letter from the Officiating Secretary to the Government of India, to the Secretary to the Government of Bengal, dated Fort William the 14th January, 1862, No. 28, of which an extract was enclosed to the address of His Highness, and forwarded to the Palace of His Highness, on the evening of the 20th, that His Honour the Lieutenant-Governor of Bengal considers an affront to have been offered to Government, in the person of its Agent, on the 14th day of May last, by His Highness. His Highness also learns (from the same source) that His Excellency the Governor-General in Council agrees with His Honour the Lieutenant-Governor in that view, and His Excellency in Council has declared that His Excellency will not be satisfied with imperfect excuses; that nothing short of a full admission of error, and an unreserved expression of regret, can be received by the Government as a sufficient apology. His Excellency, therefore, directs that His Highness the Nawab Nazim do apologise in a way that shall be satisfactory to His Honour the Lieutenant-Governor for the affront offered (as His Excellency has decided) by His Highness to the Representative of the British Government.

His Highness the Nawab Nazim feels, that it will ill become His Highness to dispute, or to seem to cavil, with the decision of His Excellency in Council. *His Highness feels perfectly acquitted in his conscience of any thought of offence to the British Government, or to any Representative of the British Government.* His Highness hereby tenders his complete and unqualified apology for what has been held by the best authority to have been an affront on the part of His Highness. His Highness feels that a serious error must have been committed by him, and His Highness asks of His Honour the Lieutenant-Governor, that this His Highness's unqualified apology and unreserved expression of regret be accepted.

    (Signed) Syud Munsoor Ullee.
Palace, Moorshedabad,
 The 27th January, 1862.

This unfortunate affair led to an estrangement between the Nawab and the Agent Governor-General, who up to that time had supported the Nawab's claims; and further, it brought about the second social matter referred to by the Nawab in His Memorial (Page 329). His Highness' Dewan, who is a clever Hindoo, took advantage of the existing circumstances for exercising a degree of authority which he had not before done, and at last his acts became so intolerable that His Highness was forced to dismiss him from his service, which as his paid servant he certainly had a right to do. The Agent, however, thought otherwise and took the Dewan's part against his master. Some angry correspondence resulted, and at last the question was referred by the Agent to the Governor-General, who, while supporting his Agent, tacitly showed his disapproval of the action he had taken, by removing him from his office with its large emoluments, and placing him in a much inferior appointment. This naturally irritated the Agent, who, unfortunately for the Nawab, ever afterwards showed himself inimical to his interests.

I.

On the 8th June, 1861, the Agent Governor-General addressed the Lieutenant-Governor of Bengal on behalf of the Dewan Rajah Prosonno Narain Deb Bahadoor, against His Highness the Nawab Nazim, and alluded to "the Nazim's suicidal estrangement from him," &c. The Agent also wrote the following:—

II.

From LIEUTENANT-COLONEL C. MACKENZIE, *Officiating Agent Governor-General,* To HIS HIGHNESS THE NAWAB NAZIM, &c., *After Compliments.*

2. Your Highness has frequently assured me that you prefer plain speaking, and that when you do wrong you would be much obliged by my telling you so without circumlocution. I have done so in my last letter, and it appears from the tone of your reply that it has made you angry. I can make every allowance for a feeling of irritation, but I think Your Highness is bound to remember three things, *viz.*, 1st, that in warning you against any particular line of conduct, I have only your interest at heart, the nature of which I understand better than yourself; and 2nd, that during the last three years you have, through my explanations to Government, in a great measure, regained the position which you had lost, and acquired advantages of

no ordinary value and importance, on which you had set your heart, and 3rd, that so far as I can see, you should not now have been in a worse position than that in which I found you, but for the untiring industry, sagacity, and fidelity of Rajah Prosonno Narain Deb Bahadoor, your Dewan, bearing in mind as I do, the numberless times that you have acknowledged to me that the Rajah is almost the only man near you whose opinion you respect, and in whom you can place confidence, I could not believe that your present estrangement from him emanated from yourself, and I, therefore, in common with all around you, attributed it to the evil influence of Huqueem Abool Hosain. You say that you sent away this man with honour. Your Highness may have done this secretly, but at the time of his dismissal my worst impressions as to his character were derived from Your Highness's representations. Moreover, it is well known that he is a most unworthy person, and quite unfit to sit down in Your Highness's presence, far less to act as your Counsellor, seeing that his only object as a stranger and irresponsible adventurer must be to enrich himself at the expense both of Your Highness's purse and most vital interests. Nevertheless, it is, as I have often told Your Highness, your right to take the medicine of any physician you have selected for yourself, your Begums and children : only let the physician beware of interfering with public business, and thereby compromising Your Highness's interests and dignity.

3. While strongly objecting to the exercise of any pernicious influence over Your Highness on the part of Her Highness the Nuwab Begum, I have always been glad to encourage a filial feeling on your part towards her. Without dwelling on this rather delicate subject I am happy to be able to apprise Your Highness that the Nuwab Begum has informed me that she heartily concurs in all my views.

4. I know that Your Highness possesses good sense and good feeling, but I also know that *you have frequently deplored* to me, *that facility of disposition, which makes it easy for artful and intriguing persons,* especially your own attendants, *to impose on you for their own advantage.* My object is now what it always has been, *viz.,* to guard you from the machinations of such villains, and, to secure your interests and dignity as the *Rais* or chief of the Nizamut. But unless you listen to, and follow my advice, and the suggestions of your own better sense and feelings, disappointment must result to all parties concerned.

I am, my Friend,
Your Highness's Sincere Friend,
(Signed) C. MACKENZIE,
Officiating Agent Governor-General.

Berhampore,
The 8th June, 1861.

III.

On the 18th June His Highness the Nawab Nazim dismissed his Dewan, and appointed Rajendra Narain Deb to manage his private affairs, assisted by his own two eldest sons.

IV.

On the 11th June the Agent Governor-General wrote to the Lieutenant-Governor of Bengal: "*I feel it my duty to support the Dewan* against the fickleness and unreasonableness and groundless dissatisfaction of the Nazim; and I trust that I myself may look to similar support from the Lieutenant-Governor, or otherwise it is likely that the Nazim may be betrayed into blunders equally mischievous to himself and vexatious to Government." And he further suggested that "an admonition from Government might bring His Highness to his senses."

V.

On the 24th June the Lieutenant-Governor of Bengal wrote in reply, and expressed his regret at "the coolness between His Highness and his Dewan, and hoped that His Highness would soon restore the latter to the place in his confidence which his good conduct merits," but would not interfere in the matter.

VI.

On the 25th June the Agent Governor-General warned His Highness that "he had no power to dismiss the Dewan without the permission of the Supreme Government," and that, in appointing Rajendra Narain Deb, "he knew he was breaking through a stringent regulation of Government, which enacts that he can *neither correspond with nor receive any native of consideration nor any European whatever* without the cognizance and consent of the Agent Governor-General." This regulation could not be so applied, for it was made for the benefit of the Nawab Nazim, "to protect him from intrigues." The Agent further wrote a series of letters to the Government, expressing his opinion as to the nature of the office of Dewan, and also took up the Dewan's case as a personal matter.

VII.

From LIEUTENANT-COLONEL COLIN MACKENZIE, *Officiating Agent Governor-General, Moorshedabad,* to HIS HIGHNESS THE NAWAB NAZIM OF BENGAL, &c.

Berhampore, the 25th June, 1861.

MY FRIEND,—I have received the letter Your Highness has sent this morning by the hand of a Chobdar, and understand its contents.

Your Highness has yourself made it impossible for me to correspond with you officially in Persian, as the proper channel of business communications, viz., your Dewan is disowned for the present by you. Until, however, we receive the orders of Government, by which we must abide, I have no objection to receive letters from Your Highness and to reply to them in English. I have no doubt that Mr. Browning will be happy to render you the service of reading my letters, and of writing those of Your Highness.

I must conclude by once more advising Your Highness to remember that it is honourable to confess an error. I am sure that you feel in your heart that you have done wrong. Do not think, because you have, after waiting for more than a month, forced me to report all that has taken place to Government, that I am your enemy? I would still, if possible, extricate Your Highness from the difficulties into which wicked men have plunged you.

Let me ask one question. Did I forsake Your Highness when you were in distress? Why should I forsake the Dewan, who is the best friend you ever had, now that Your Highness, being deceived, is acting towards him with cruelty and injustice? I have too much regard for him, for Your Highness's true interests, and for my own character and conscience to do any thing so base.

I am, my Friend,
Your Highness's Sincere Friend,
(Signed) C. MACKENZIE, *Lieut.-Col.*,
Acting Agent Governor-General.

VIII.

From HIS HIGHNESS THE NAWAB NAZIM OF BENGAL, *&c., to* LIEUTENANT-COLONEL COLIN MACKENZIE, *Officiating Agent, Governor-General, Moorshedabad.*

Moorshedabad, 27th June, 1861.

MY FRIEND,—Your letter, dated the 25th of June, has reached me. I regret that you refuse to receive any Persian letters relative to Nizamut affairs, save through the hands of my late Dewan Rajah Prosunno Narain Deb Bahadoor, whom, as you are aware, I have dismissed from office. Your resolve will plunge the Nizamut into considerable difficulties, and perhaps I shall suffer, in addition, much loss. Your suggestion that I should correspond with you in English through Mr. Browning is quite impracticable. He is the tutor to my children, and has not sufficient time at his disposal to carry on so voluminous a correspondence as would necessarily devolve upon him. I have an efficient staff of Persian writers, and it is through them alone that I desire to correspond on Nizamut affairs.

You have informed me that the dismissal of my Dewan rests not with me, but the Government. I have repeatedly written to you for any documents that may be in your possession establishing your views. You have, however, sent me no such papers, and I, therefore, conclude that I am in the right, and that I can dismiss for his misconduct or for incompatibility of temper any of my servants without any formal application to Government.

You mention that you have reported the matter to Government. It is, perhaps, advisable, therefore, that I shall state my case to you, it is simply this:—

My late Dewan *gives me ample cause of offence.* I lose all my confidence in **him, suspect** him of malpractices, abolish his office, and call upon him **for an** account of the large sums of money, jewels and Government securities, that have, from time to time, passed through his **hands.** I also **demand** from him all papers and documents relating to **the Nizamut which are** in his custody. *He does not reply to my communications, and adds to all his offences, by disobeying my orders.*

In this posture of affairs I am sorry to state that *you, so far from giving me aid, side entirely with the late Dewan, and now refuse to transact any business save through him. I sincerely wish that these matters could have been arranged without an appeal to Government, not for my own sake, but for yours. For it has always been my aim to secure your good opinion, and, indeed, so far as possible, the goodwill and esteem of all with whom I am brought into contact.* Should I suffer any loss through your determination, and should any valuable papers now in the possession of Rajah Prosunno Narain Deb be not eventually forthcoming, to whom may I ask am I to look for reparation save to you, who are appointed by **Government to watch over my interests?** I would ask you, therefore, once more to take the whole matter into consideration, and to let me know on what authority you say that I can neither appoint nor dismiss my Dewan.

In conclusion, I request that you will be pleased to send **me a** copy **of your** representation to Government, that I may learn precisely its nature, at least so far as it affects myself. You will be pleased to submit this **letter, and** the rest of the correspondence in Persian and in English on **the** question, **since** May last, to His Honour the Lieutenant-Governor.

I am, &c.,
Syud Munsoor Ulee.

(Signed)

IX.

From His Highness **the** Nawab **Nazim of** Bengal, &c., *to* Lieutenant-Colonel Colin Mackenzie, *Officiating Agent to the Governor-General.*

My Friend, in continuation of my letter of the 27th ultimo, I beg to state, that, *I need only be convinced that I have done wrong, and I shall most gladly confess my error, for in doing so, it shows a greatness of mind;* if by your supposing me to have **done wrong, you** allude **to** my dismissal of my Dewan, I freely open my **heart to** you in stating, that, *I feel myself the party wronged against; I always regard my servants as my children, and in that feeling passed over many causes of provocation which* **my** *Dewan has* **given** *me, and smiled at his sauciness and even insolence; you* **cannot but** *be aware, how in many such instances* **I have** *pardoned him,* **and even** *dismissed some of my old and faithful servants* **who** *happened to come in his way.*

But *pampered by* **your** *indulgence and secure of your support, he entirely forgot* **his** *position, and attempted to be, and in fact became, the sole master of the Nizamut,* **he** *would treat me as a child and* *assume over me the* **power of** *a superior authority, a censor, a spy, and a jailor; to make me succumb to his will* **he** *would plume himself upon his influence* **with the Government** *and daunt me with threats,* and to give them the show of action, would, *with audacious impudence,* hold forth before **me** letters procured from you (private and demi-official), replete **with abuses and reproaches** *against me;* he also succeeded in coercing **my** servants to regard him as the **Nawab** and *absolutely to disobey me.*

I shall not disgust my feelings by dwelling on *the humiliating picture of a master placed at the mercy of a servant,* whose tenure of service depends upon his will, but **hasten** to add that *the late Dewan not only offended me by his overbearing insolence and all absorbing ambition, but has lost all my confidence.* I have **strong** grounds to believe that *he has grossly abused his trust,* and that *if* the accounts be properly examined, they would reveal startling facts. Promptitude is absolutely necessary in making such revelations, but I deeply grieve to find that *you have only in contravention to the solemn Agreement of* 1834 *contested my authority to* **dismiss my own** *servants, but interdicted the Dewan to render me an account* **which** *I have called for,* and which the longer he delays to give me the **greater** chance there is of my interest being injured.

I am sure *the just and humane British Government would regard with anything but pleasure your supporting my steward* in his refusal to render me an **account** under any circumstances, *especially when I suspected him of misappropriating my property.*

I cannot help remarking here that *you have pained and grieved me by* **refusing to** *attend* **my** *Durbar according to custom* on the day of the **Eed festival,** *although asked by myself,* and the Nawab Nazir Darab Ally Khan, *and you paid a visit on the afternoon of that very day to* **my late Dewan.**

I recoil from the idea of hurting an innocent **man much less** in recommending you to do so. Keeping apart **my** suspicion of the official malfeasance of Rajah Prosonno Narain **Deb,** *his insolence and insubordination are too potent to suffer* **me to see** *his face again.* Instead of being cruel and unjust **as you suppose,** *I have acted towards him* **as** *the most lenient and indulgent* **master.** God knows what efforts **I had to make,** to command my temper in *putting up with his* **insults** and **to** forget **his faults.**

In conclusion, I request you will be pleased to forward a copy of this letter, as well as the accompanying letter, to the Honourable the Lieutenant-Governor of Bengal.

I remain, my Friend,
Yours sincerely,
(Signed)   SYUD MUNSOOR ULLEE.

Palace, Moorshedabad,
The 2nd July, 1861.

X.

From LIEUTENANT-COLONEL COLIN MACKENZIE, *Officiating Agent Governor-General,* To HIS HIGHNESS THE NAWAB NAZIM OF BENGAL, *&c., Berhampore, the* 28*th June,* 1861.

MY FRIEND,—I beg to acknowledge the receipt of Your Highness's letter of the 27th instant, and in reply desire to remind Your Highness that it is not I who have put a stop to our official correspondence in Persian, but yourself, inasmuch as you blocked up the only channel through which such correspondence can, in accordance with the arrangement of Government, flow, namely, your present Dewan Rajah Prosonno Narain Deb Bahadoor. Your Highness requests me to observe that you have dismissed the Dewan, and you wish me now to furnish you with copies of former Government orders respecting the appointment of, and power of dismissing that officer. Your Highness seems to forget that in despite of my warning that you have no power to appoint or dismiss a Dewan without the consent and orders of Government, you have chosen to act independently in this matter from first to last. I can no more transact business with Your Highness in the Persian Department through any channel but that of your Dewan, than General Showers could receive Your Highness's Persian letters sent direct to him, and not through the Agent, for I am well aware of the secret correspondence which Your Highness has attempted to carry on with that gentleman and other persons, this being contrary, as you well know, to the express orders of the Governor-General in Council.

2. I again, as the Representative of the Viceroy, beg to inform Your Highness that there never was a real Dewan appointed or dismissed by any Nazim without the concurrence of the Agent. The only case in which a properly constituted Dewan was dismissed without the sanction of Government was that of Seeta Nauth. That transaction was concealed from Government by the Agent, and his death and that of the Rajah alone prevented a reversal of the irregularity.

3. Allow me to point out to Your Highness that you are mistaken in supposing that I wish to carry on the business of the Nizamut with you in English. By referring to my letter you will observe that as an exchange of English letters between you and me is still possible, I suggested that occasional communications of that kind might take place. I mentioned the name of Mr. Browning merely because I supposed that he would have no objection to help Your Highness, and because you might prefer his assistance, as that of an educated and talented gentleman, able and willing to perform a friendly office for you.

4. As Your Highness's fiat alone can no more dismiss Rajah Prosunno Narain Deb than mine could, he is still the Dewan Nizamut, and as such he cannot, with reference to the interests of Your Highness, and his duty to you, to the Government, and to himself, hand over charge of the departments entrusted to him to the irresponsible men pointed out by Your Highness, and certainly not to Your Highness's sons who are mere children. In this matter the Rajah has acted

by my directions given in presence of the Nawab Nazir Darab Ally Khan.

5. Throughout the whole of this disagreeable affair, the unpleasant consequences of which I have been most anxious to avert from you, Your Highness has totally overlooked the important fact, that for the time being, any Official declaration proceeding from the Agent carries with it the full authority of the Governor-General in Council, and that in defying the Agent you have literally defied the British Government. Your proper mode of action ought to have been *implicit acquiescence* in all my Official intimations (even supposing that you did not choose to follow my private friendly counsel), and then to have patiently awaited the decision of Government, who would certainly have attended to any reasonable appeal on the part of Your Highness.

I am, my Friend,
Your Highness's sincere Friend,
(Signed) C. MACKENZIE, *Lieut.-Col.*,
Acting Agent Governor-General.

XI.

From HIS HIGHNESS THE NAWAB NAZIM OF BENGAL, &c., *to* LIEUTENANT-COLONEL COLIN MACKENZIE, *Officiating Agent to the Governor-General.*

MY FRIEND,—I have to acknowledge the receipt of your letter, dated the 28th ultimo, and, in reply, beg to state that I do not see how I have put a stop to our official correspondence in Persian. I am not aware of any orders of Government, which provide that the channel of Persian correspondence of the Nizamut, is the Dewan. If you allow occasional correspondence in English, I do not understand why the same cannot be carried on in Persian, and that as often as the Nizamut affairs require. Mr. Browning, as tutor to my children, can ill afford time to become also my correspondence writer. Communications in English have always passed between me and my old friend and tutor General Showers (in your time as well as before it), with the assistance of my late Dewan, Rajah Prosonno Narain Deb, but as I cannot avail myself of the Rajah's assistance now, I correspond with the General in Persian. With regard to the Nizamut accounts which my late Dewan keeps back under your directions, I have to request you will kindly recall this order, which is sure to prove detrimental to my interests; and ask the Dewan to render the accounts, which is what I have repeatedly called for.

I remain, my Friend,
Yours sincerely,
(Signed) SYUD MUNSOOR ULLEE.

Palace, Moorshedabad,
The 5th July, 1861.

XII.

From HIS HIGHNESS THE NAWAB NAZIM OF BENGAL, &c., *to* LIEUTENANT-COLONEL COLIN MACKENZIE, *Officiating Agent to the Governor-General.*

MY FRIEND,—I have to acknowledge the receipt of your letter, No. 120, dated the 27th ultimo, with its enclosure, and to request you will be pleased to send me particulars of the charges brought by Aslan Khan against the late Dewan, as also a copy of your letter, No. 69, dated the 11th ultimo, alluded to in the letter of the Junior Secretary to the Government of Bengal for my inspection.

I remain, my Friend,
Yours very sincerely,
(Signed) SYUD MUNSOOR ULLEE.

Palace, Moorshedabad,
The 3rd July, 1861.

XIII.

No. 6.

From HIS HIGHNESS THE NAWAB NAZIM OF BENGAL, &c., *to* LIEUTENANT-COLONEL COLIN MACKENZIE, *Acting Agent Governor-General, Moorshedabad.*

Moorshedabad Palace, the 3rd July, 1861.

MY FRIEND,—I have to request you will be good enough to intimate to the Collector of Moorshedabad, that my stipend for the future is to be paid on the receipt and seal of Coomar Rajendar Narain Deb, whom I have appointed to the post of Madar-ul-aham instead of Rajah Prosonno Narain Deb. An impression of the Madar-ul-Maham's seal is herewith enclosed.

I remain, my Friend,
Yours sincerely,
(Signed) SYUD MUNSOOR ULLEE.

XIV.

Extract from a Letter No. 132, *dated 4th July,* 1861.

From LIEUTENANT-COLONEL COLIN MACKENZIE, *to* HIS HIGHNESS THE NAWAB NAZIM OF BENGAL.

Para. 3. In Your Highness's letter you desire that intimation should be given to the Collector that your income should, for the future, be paid to the receipt and seal of Coomar Rajender Narain Deb. Hitherto Your Highness's income has been paid to the receipt and seal of *your present Dewan* **Rajah Prosonno** Narain Deb Bahadoor, and until I receive the **orders** of Government on the subject, it is impossible for me, with every wish to accommodate Your Highness, to change the usual official channel.

(Signed)   Colin Mackenzie,
Acting Agent Governor-General, Moorshedabad.

XV.

Extract of a Letter No. 6, dated July, 1861, *from* His Highness the Nawab Nazim of Bengal, &c., *to* Lieut.-Colonel Colin Mackenzie, *Officiating Agent Governor-General, Moorshedabad.*

Para. 2. With reference to my stipend, which you refuse to accommodate me with pending the orders of Government, allow me to state for your information that my stipend, before this, was on different occasions paid to the receipt and seal of my Treasurer, Baboo Ramsoonder Sein; and I do not see how you can object to the withdrawal of my stipend by any person whom I choose to appoint. *I regret to observe that you have of late assumed towards me an unfriendly tone which is hurtful to my feelings and injurious to the interests of the Nizamut, which it is your duty to protect.* By delaying the issue of my income you put me to the greatest inconvenience imaginable, particularly as this is Mohorum time and all the inhabitants are *Tajiadars,* or celebrators of the festival. *By compelling me to raise money on high interest to carry on the expense* of the Nizamut and the Mohorum festivities, *you subject the Nizamut to a considerable loss, for which I must look to you for reparation.*

(Signed)   Syud Munsoor Ullee.

XVI.

From His Highness the Nawab Nazim of Bengal, &c., *to* Lieutenant-Colonel Colin Mackenzie, *Agent to the Governor-General, Moorshedabad.*

Palace, Moorshedabad, the 15th July, 1861.

My Friend,—I have written to you twice for my stipend, and your non-compliance with my requisition has put me and the people connected with the Nizamut to great inconvenience, and *driven me to the necessity of raising funds on high interest* to meet the expenses of the **Nizamut** and the Festival.

I remain, my Friend,
Yours very sincerely,
(Signed)   Syud Munsoor Ullee.

XVII.

Extract from a Letter dated **16th July, 1861.**

No. 141 of 1861.

From **LIEUTENANT-COLONEL MACKENZIE,** *Acting Agent to the Governor-General, Moorshedabad,* **to** **HIS HIGHNESS THE NAWAB NAZIM OF BENGAL.**

MY FRIEND,—Par. 1. I beg to acknowledge Your Highness's letter of yesterday's date, in which you complain that you suffer inconvenience because it is not in my power to authorise the payment of Your Highness's income and other monies, except to the authorised receipt of your Dewan Rajah Prosunno Narain Deb Bahadur.

2. I am sorry for this, but it cannot be helped until Your Highness chooses to retrace the false steps you have, under ill advice, taken, or until I receive the orders of Government authorising me to comply with Your Highness's request.

XVIII.

From **LIEUTENANT-COLONEL COLIN MACKENZIE,** *Officiating Agent to the Governor-General, Moorshedabad, to* **HIS HIGHNESS THE NAWAB NAZIM OF BENGAL.**

Dated Berhampore, 4th July, 1861.

MY FRIEND,—I have the pleasure to acknowledge receipt of two letters from Your Highness of yesterday's date without any numbers.

2nd. In one, Your Highness requests copies of certain papers sent by Government for the information of Rajah Prosonno Narain Deb Bahadur. I regret that I am not justified in complying with Your Highness's requisitions. Perhaps, Your Highness is not aware, that the object of Government in handing over the documents in question to the Rajah is, that he may bring an action against Auslan Khan for libel, which, of course, the Rajah will do ere long, even though his long-established character for honesty and integrity cannot be affected, either in the eyes of Government, or of the numerous gentlemen in high office, with whom he has been connected, by the baseless slanders of disappointed and envious knaves and intriguers.

4th. I beg once more to remind Your Highness that you are persisting in a course which involves great disrespect to, and defiance of, the British Government, seeing that you have refused to listen to my official warning that you cannot dismiss your Dewan and appoint another (changed only in name but not in office) without the sanction of the Governor-General in Council. Your Highness's present advisers are quite incompetent to the task they have undertaken, and are only striving to, as I have told you again and again, to aggrandise and enrich themselves, even though **it involve the ruin of** Your Highness and the Nizamut of which you are *Rais*.

I remain, my Friend,
(Signed)   C. MACKENZIE,
Officiating Agent Governor-General.

XIX.

From HIS HIGHNESS THE NAWAB NAZIM OF BENGAL, &c., *to* LIEUTENANT-COLONEL COLIN MACKENZIE, *Officiating Agent Governor-General, Moorshedabad.*

Dated 6th July, 1861.

MY FRIEND,—I have to acknowledge the receipt of your letter, dated the 4th instant, and in reply beg to state with regard to the matter of Auslam Khan, whom Rajah Prosonno Narain intends to prosecute ere long for libel, you ought to have, out of courtesy at least, furnished me with details of the charges brought by one servant of the Nizamut against another, especially as those charges concern the Nizamut property, and my knowing the merits of the case would not have altered the position of the Rajah.

2nd. In conclusion, I have to request that, should you still differ with me with respect to the points above mooted, you will be good enough to submit this letter and the rest of our correspondence since May last to His Honour the Lieutenant-Governor of Bengal.

I remain, my Friend,
Yours sincerely,
(Signed)   SYUD MUNSOOR ULLEE.

P. S.—I beg to remind you that, you have not as yet complied with my requisition to supply me with a copy of your Representation to Government to enable me to vindicate my character against any imputation that might have been cast **upon it.**

XX.

On the 6th July His Highness invited the Agent to the Palace, and regretted not having been able to visit him at Berhampore in consequence of indisposition. The following reply was sent:—

XXI.

Extract from a letter dated 6th July, 1861 :—

No. 141 of 1861.

From LIEUTENANT-COLONEL COLIN MACKENZIE, *Acting Agent to Governor-General, to* HIS HIGHNESS THE NAWAB NAZIM OF BENGAL.

Par. 3rd. If Your Highness supposes that I am, or have been, in any way actuated by personal **feelings** during the late unpleasant discussions, **you** are greatly **mistaken**. Of course the disreputable and intriguing persons, who, under the guise of loyalty and attachment to Your Highness, are *doing their best to effect your ruin*, and that of the Nizamut, will endeavour to persuade Your Highness to adopt the contrary opinion: but I greatly fear that unless Your Highness speedily shakes yourself free from **such pernicious influences, you will regret** it when perhaps it is **too late.** Once more I solemnly warn **Your** Highness, and **this in the spirit of a true friend, that it is in vain for you to expect me to set at nought the orders of the Government which** I serve (and **to which you are as amenable as men of** inferior rank) even were it **not evident, that from first to last Your** Highness has been miserably **misled.**

5th. I am now compelled, **with infinite regret, to** apprise Your Highness distinctly that *it would be impossible for me, under any circumstances, to receive you, privately or publicly, even were you disposed to come,* until the final orders of **His Excellency** the **Viceroy, and His Honour the Lieutenant-Governor of Bengal, arrive.**

XXII.

On the 16th July the Agent wrote to the Lieutenant-Governor as follows:—

"1. **In continuation of my** Despatch No. 71, dated the 25th June last, I have the honour to state, for the information of His Honour the Lieutenant-Governor, that H. H. the Nawab Nazim of Bengal, up to the present **time,** persists in repudiating the authority of Government with **regard to** all **the steps which he** has lately taken, and in turning **a deaf ear to my solemn warning and** advice."

"3. He persists **in thinking that, although he is at liberty to put aside my** authority **as Agent, yet that I can act independently of the orders and wishes of Government.** One cause of great dissatisfaction to His Highness is that **I have refused to allow money to be paid into** his treasury except to the customary **and authorised receipt and seal of** the Dewan, Rajah Prosonno-Narain **Deb."**

XXIII.

From **His Highness the Nawab Nazim** of **Bengal,** &c., to **the Honourable J. P. Grant,** *Lieutenant-Governor of Bengal.*

My Friend,—In my former letter, dated 2nd instant, **I** have already mentioned, for Your Honour's information, the reasons which induced **me to** abolish the office of Dewan, and make **other arrangements for the** management of the Nizamut's business. It is necessary that I **should now** state the causes which led **me to withdraw my** confidence from the **late** Dewan.

2. In 1853, Rajah Prosonno **Narain Deb** Bahadoor applied for the place of Dewan Nizamut, and **obtained it,** upon the recommendation

of Colonel G. H. Macgregor, the then Government Agent. I reposed implicit confidence in him, vested him with such powers from time to time as his position required, and made him valuable presents on divers occasions; in short, *never was a servant treated with greater kindness* than Rajah Prosonno Narain; *but the return which I got for all those favours is what no servant ever made to his master.*

3. For some time after his appointment Rajah Prosonno Narain discharged his duties to my satisfaction; but *his zeal was short-lived; it was succeeded by an insatiable passion to aggrandize himself at my expense.*

4. Vain of his absolute authority over the Nizamut, *secure of the Agent's support*, and believing everything to be within his reach, he soon forgot his position and became unsteady, overbearing, and insolent. I attempted to correct him by good counsel, but without success.

5. I will first allude to those circumstances, trifling as they are, which *led to a misunderstanding, in creating which my Dewan*, Rajah Prosonno Narain, had *not an insignificant share.*

6. On the 14th of May last a message was brought to me that the Agent, with some of his friends, intended to call at the Palace. I was then living at Hoomayoon Munzil with my family, and on the previous day had taken physic, in consequence of which I felt very weak: and when the notice arrived I was labouring under a severe attack of headache. I had every wish to see the Agent, notwithstanding my indisposition; but as the day advanced, and I felt more and more unwell, and the distance between my Palace and the Munzil exceeded two miles, I was compelled to forego the pleasure of meeting the Agent, to whom a message of my inability to come was accordingly sent. This slight accident, over which I had no control, was magnified into a serious offence and personal slight; and the Agent, instead of following the dicates of his own sense, evidently listened to the counsels of designing men when he wrote the Persian letter, of which the accompanying is a copy (marked A). *In this letter the Agent makes use of such insulting terms to me as ill become the representative of the British Government.* I regretted much that the simple circumstance should have caused such difference of feeling, and *offered an ample apology* (although I was then smarting under the gratuitous reflections of the Agent) for the disappointment of which I was the innocent cause (*vide* my Persian letter, dated the 21st May, marked B). The Agent was not satisfied with my explanation, as the following extract from his letter, dated the 8th June, will show: "I cannot but accept the apology contained in your letter, and regret the severity of Your Highness's sufferings as you describe them. But the fact remains, that I never received a proper message by a proper messenger announcing the impossibility of Your Highness's meeting with me in the Palace; and I therefore trust Your Highness will issue such orders to your officers as will prevent a repetition of *the appearance of disrespect* to the representative of His Excellency the Viceroy."

7. Now from this it is clear that the Agent is not pacified. I really do not comprehend how and in what way he expects the message. It was sent by me through Nawab Nazir Darab Ally Khan, who is a very respectable officer of my Court, and he communicated it to the Agent.

That this trifling occurrence still rankles in the mind of the Agent is evident from the tone of his letters, both Persian and English, which he has written to me since, as also from the circumstance of his having refused to attend my Durbar on the occasion of the Eed festival, although personally asked by the Nawab Nazir Darab Ally Khan, and written to by myself. I cannot help mentioning here, that out of respect to the Agent, I stopped the holding of the Durbar on that day; but the Agent, I regret to say, returned the compliment by passing that very evening in the house of my late Dewan.

8. But there are other more direct and substantial proofs of the Agent's bias against me, a bias which I owe not to any dereliction or omission on my part, but to the machinations of my Dewan.

9. I shall now describe a proceeding, *the result of a conspiracy*, which I am sure cannot but disgust your Honour. Rajah Prosonno Narain Deb procured a private letter from the magistrate, Mr. Cockerell, to the address of the agent, copy of which is appended (marked C), for which the latter thanks his favourite in his private letter (marked D). The magistrate exhausts all his armoury of threats; *he would punish me* with the imposition of income tax, the jurisdiction of the police in my killa, with no immunity from the Arms Act, and the various undefined marks of the displeasure of Government. The huqueem (native physician in my service) is assumed to be a *budmash*, a term with which it is now the fashion to brand a person whom one wishes to crush in the absence of any definite charge to lay against him; other persons are mixed up with him whom the Dewan would see ruined.

10. Some letters are then addressed by the Agent to Rajah Prosonno Narain, apparently private and in confidence; but, as the sequence will show, *with the view of insulting me*, through the Dewan, magnifying his importance in my eyes and overwhelming me with stormy threats. The Dewan sends me these letters, the copies of which are herewith annexed (marked D, E, F, G, H); in one of them the Agent speaks of his being sick of my "folly and evasions;" in another he calls me "the foolish and ungrateful Nazim;" in the postscript of a third he asks of Prosonno Narain for the marriage contracts, and adds, contrary to good breeding, "I trust no forgery may be attempted, as that is transportation;" so much for abuses and insults; then there are threats imminent, and future, defined and vague, in the execution of which Rajah Prosonno Narain is to take more or less an active part; thus, in one letter the Agent says he "he thinks of going down to Calcutta to hold a talk with the authorities there touching the Nazim;" in another, "To-morrow I shall take the business up. I agree with Mr. Cockerell's letter to me, and thank you for it. *I shall be glad to see you in the afternoon, and to talk to you about the step you contemplate.* The Nazim is fast justifying Lord Dalhousie's treatment of him, and inviting fresh punishment from Government;" and, to crown all, it is made out that I have "insulted Government and trifled with him" (the Agent), and then he throws his ægis over his protégé by telling him, "Do you be pleased not to trouble yourself."

11. Whoever dreamt that a descendant of the Nuwab Meer Mahomed Jaffer Khan, than whom a more staunch ally to the English is

not to be found in India, would be subjected, for the sake of one of his own servants, to such degradation, after all the rights, privileges, and immunities, which the said Nuwab, Meer Jaffer, and his descendants, had enjoyed.

12. I owe all **this to Rajah** Prosonno Narain and to the blind partiality **of** the Agent **for him.** I winked at Rajah Prosonno Narain's faults, **but he** took **an unfair** advantage of my indulgence. **He** dismissed **most of my old and** faithful servants, and reinstated those whom I have **turned out; he disposed** of places without my knowledge, and committed **a series of irregularities,** for which the several departments **of the Nizamut have suffered considerable** injury

13. Reports **of** *enormous spoliations of my jewels and other property have, from time to time, been brought against the Dewan,* but which, **for** want of sufficient evidence, **I** could not entertain. Prosonno **Narain** *drew from my treasuary large sums of money on different occasions,* **for** the purpose of purchasing Government Securities, an account of which, however, he has **not yet** submitted to me, although frequently called upon to do so.

14. **The Nawab Nazir Darab** Ally **Khan** Bahadoor did, on several occasions, *demand* from **Prosonno** Narain, **both** verbally and in writing, *a receipt for the jewels, gold, and* silver *articles* (the property of the Nizamut) which he had, from time to time, taken from him, but *without success.*

15. **The repetitions of** *such accusations* proceeding from different quarters *did not fail to excite a latent* suspicion in my mind, and so *long as he does not render* any account of his stewardship, I have every reason to complain of his conduct. Prosonno Narain was several times questioned by me *as to* the disposal of the monies, above alluded to, but *he always evaded me* by giving vague replies. When constrained by **all these** circumstances, I dispensed with his services, and called upon him, by a written parwannah, dated the 19th of June last, which was repeated on the 24th ultimo (copies of both purwannahs **are** annexed, marked **I, J**), **to** render me an account of all the pecuniary transactions that had passed through his hands. *Due* notice *of his discharge from my* service, *and* the **call for the** submission **of an** *account, were given to the Agent,* but the result is the following reply from him under which the Dewan seems to have taken shelter :

16. "**As Your Highness's fiat alone can no more** dismiss Rajah Prosonno **Narain Deb than mine could, he is still the** Dewan Nizamut, **and as such** *he cannot,* **with reference to** the interest of Your Highness, **and his duty to** you, **to the Government and to himself,** *hand over charge of the* departments entrusted to him **to the irresponsible men pointed** out by Your Highness, **and certainly not to your Highness's sons,** who are mere children. *In this matter the Rajah has acted by my* direction given in presence of the Nawab Nazir Darab **Ally Khan."**

17. The Agent has not only *encouraged the Dewan not to render an account of my property,* but has gone to the length of putting a stop to my Persian correspondence with him. He says in his letter, dated 25th June, 1861 :—

18. "Your Highness has made it impossible for me to correspond with you officially in Persian, as the proper channel of business com-

munications, viz., your Dewan is disowned for the present by you. Until, however, we both receive the orders of Government, by which we must abide, I have no objection to receive letters from Your Highness, and to reply to them in English."

19. Your Honour is aware that *the Persian is my language and the language of the Nizamut. I have thus been deprived of the privilege of representing my views in my own tongue; that under an enlightened Government is not denied even to a felon.* How far this prohibition has proved disadvantageous to me, it is impossible to give you an adequate idea.

20. To the Agent's kind interference I owe another unpalatable boon. Not content with disputing my authority to dismiss my own servant, the Agent has of late refused to pass my stipend on the ground that the same can be alone paid to Rajah Prosonno Narain Deb, and not to any other person whom I choose to appoint for the purpose (*vide* letter marked K). I would like to ask the Agent whether, on previous occasions, the stipend was not paid by my cashkeeper? If so, what could be the motive, except that of putting me to trouble and expense for the sake of his favourite, that induced the Agent to keep back my stipend?

21. The Agent, in his zeal to serve Rajah Prosonno Narain, is betraying himself into acts which I am sure your Honour will construe rightly.

22. Because by virtue of the explicit authority of the solemn agreement (which, as far as I know, does not contain any prohibitive clause) *I have dismissed my own servant and desired him to render me an account, under suspicion of his having abused his trust,* because I have entertained in my service Huqeem Abool Hossain under the sacred right of a prince to select his own physician, whose treatment has been very successful in my family, and who, like every man, has a right to be considered honest unless otherwise proved, am I to be treated as I have been? *Surely, my unswerving allegiance to Her Most Excellent Britannic Majesty, my loyalty so often acknowledged and rewarded, never merits such maltreatment at the hands of the representative of His Excellency the Viceroy.*

23. I appeal to your Honour, **whom I look** *upon as my judge, my advocate, and my friend. For the Agent sides with my dismissed servant*—a servant whose face, *come what may,* I have sworn not to see again. *To whom can I look for advice and help but to that Government which regards me* **as** *the representative of its old and* **faithful ally?** *Upon your fiat depends the protection of my interests and the sustenance of my honour, which I hold dearer than life.*

I remain, my friend,

Yours most sincerely,

(Signed) SYUD MUNSOOR ULLEE.

Palace, Moorshedabad, 17th July, 1861.

P.S.—In addition to the letters above adverted to, I take the liberty to append the rest of my correspondence (18 in number) with the Agent, relative to the question now before your Honour, to come to a right understanding of my case.

XXIV.

From HIS HIGHNESS THE NAWAB NAZIM OF BENGAL, &c., *to* THE HONOURABLE J. P. GRANT, *Lieutenant-Governor of Bengal.*

Palace, Moorshedabad, the 18th July, **1861**.

MY FRIEND,—The Agent to the Governor-General having withheld from me a copy of his representation to Government, touching the dismissal of the Dewan Nizamut, I have to request Your Honour will order a copy of the said representation to be given to me from your office to enable me to ascertain my position and justify myself, if necessary.

I remain, my Friend,
Yours very sincerely,
(Signed) SYUD MUNSOOR ULLEE.

XXV.

From HIS HIGHNESS THE NAWAB NAZIM OF BENGAL, &c., *to* LIEUTENANT-COLONEL COLIN MACKENZIE, *Agent to the Governor-General, Moorshedabad.*

Para. 2nd. You have more than once taxed me for listening to the counsel of "disreputable persons and intriguers." May I ask you their names? I am not aware of having any but honest and honourable men about me, and if you know of any person who deserves the epithets above quoted, I shall be obliged by your enlightening me without delay.

3rd. I have to assure you that I follow nobody's counsel but my own, and if ever I was misled, it was by my late Dewan.

4th. I really do not understand how you have made out that I expected you "to set at naught the orders of the Government which you serve.

5th. If the explanation which I gave you, for not meeting you on the occasion of your last visit to my Palace does not satisfy you, I can only say that I am extremely sorry for it, and your attempt to make it a Government cause will, I doubt not, prove futile, for I would be insulting that august body who rule the destinies of India were I to suppose them capable of viewing the matter in the same light as you do.

6th. You have been once a sincere friend to me, and our present difference of feeling will, I am sure, cease to exist when the cause of our dispute, namely, the Dewan, is finally removed by orders of Government.

7th. In conclusion, I have to request you will be pleased to forward copies of this letter, and the one under notice, to the Honourable the Lieutenant-Governor of Bengal.

I remain, yours sincerely,
(Signed) SYUD MUNSOOR ULLEE.

Palace, Moorshedabad,
The 18th July, 1861.

XXVI.

From HIS HIGHNESS THE NAWAB NAZIM OF BENGAL, &c., *to* LIEUTENANT-COLONEL COLIN MACKENZIE, *Officiating Agent to the Governor-General, Moorshedabad.*

Palace, Moorshedabad, 23rd July, 1861.

MY FRIEND,—I have to bring to your notice that the office table, used by the late Dewan Nizamut, has been assailed in different places by white ants, and unless the drawers are opened and the contents examined (and this can alone be done by the Dewan who has the keys), I have every reason to fear the valuable documents which the table is said to contain will suffer material injury.

2nd. I have to add that the Dewan has in his custody keys of certain Almirahs, Chests, &c., appertaining to the office, and containing important papers, which also ought to be examined.

3rd It is expected that you will make the necessary arrangements to ensure the safety of the papers in question.

4th. I beg to state further that agreeably to instructions conveyed in the letter of the Secretary to the Government of India, dated the 11th September, 1852, the then Government intimates to me in the Persian letter, dated the 16th September, 1852, that it is not the intention of the Governor-General to interfere in the appointment or dismissal of the Nizamut servants, but it is necessary that the Agent should report to Government the appointment or dismissal of such superior Officers as the Dewan Nizamut.

5th. In conclusion I request you will be good enough to send an early reply to this letter, and forward a transcript of the paragraph 4th, for the information of His Honour the Lieutenant-Governor of Bengal.

I remain, my Friend,
Yours sincerely,
(Signed) SYUD MUNSOOR ULLEE.

XXVII.

On the 30th July, 1861, the Agent wrote to the Lieutenant-Governor on behalf of the Dewan, and forwarded the Dewan's Petition to Government.

XXVIII.

On the 2nd September, the Agent wrote to His Highness about the Nizamut accounts, and received the following reply.

XXIX.

From HIS HIGHNESS THE NAWAB NAZIM OF BENGAL, &c., *to* LIEUTENANT-COLONEL COLIN MACKENZIE, *Acting Agent Governor-General, Moorshedabad.*

MY FRIEND,—You are aware that, under your own instructions, my late Dewan, Rajah Prosonno Narain Deb Bahadoor, has in his keeping all the chests and boxes containing the Nizamut accounts and other papers, and that I have on several occasions solicited you to order him to render them up to me, as my affairs have been brought to a stand-still for want of those papers, but that you have not been kind enough to favour me with any reply to my address on the subject, nor has the Rajah Prosonno Narain surrendered to me the papers. You will, therefore, no doubt see that, under these circumstances, that is, so long as Rajah Prosonno Narain retains the custody of my papers, and in consequence I am debarred from access to them, it is impossible for me to carry into effect the orders of the Bengal Government as communicated to me in your letter No. 166 A., dated the 2nd instant, as I will be unable to compare the statement now forwarded to me with my own accounts.

I beg to solicit you will be kind enough to submit a copy of this letter to His Honour the Lieutenant-Governor of Bengal with the view of apprising His Honour of the reasons which preclude me from obeying his orders with that despatch with which he requires it should be done.

I remain, my Friend,
Yours sincerely,
(Signed)   SYUD MUNSOOR ULLEE.

Palace, Moorshedabad,
The 4th September, 1861.

XXX.

On the 4th September, His Highness wrote to the Agent inquiring about the Berah Festival, and not receiving a reply, wrote again.

XXXI.

From HIS HIGHNESS THE NAWAB NAZIM OF BENGAL, &c. *to* LIEUTENANT-COLONEL C. MACKENZIE, *Agent Governor-General, Moorshedabad.*

Palace, Moorshedabad, the 11th September, 1861.

MY FRIEND,—On the 4th instant, I did myself the honour of addressing you a letter, and then sent Darab Ally Khan Bahadoor to wait upon you with a verbal message communicating that the Berah festival would take place on the 12th. The Khan Bahadoor informed me on his return that you would favour me with a written answer on the subject. Up to this moment, however, I have not received it. I beg, therefore, to inform you that I have postponed the celebration of the festival till Thursday week, the 20th September, and hope to hear from you on the matter within that time.

I remain, my Friend,
Yours sincerely,
(Signed)   SYUD MUNSOOR ULLEE.

XXXII.

After a lengthy correspondence on various questions relating to His Highness' Dewan, and other matters, the Agent received the following communication on the 17th January, 1862 :—"*It is not the intention of the Governor-General, in Council, that Lieutenant-Colonel Mackenzie should resume charge. He is directed to abstain from all further interference in Nizamut affairs. The grave doubts of His Excellency in Council as to Colonel Mackenzie's unfitness for the position he now holds have been already recorded, and the present correspondence clearly shows that any hope of his ever obtaining a salutary influence over the Nazim is out of the question.*"

XXXIII.

(No. 406.)

From the SECRETARY to the GOVERNMENT OF INDIA, with the GOVERNOR-GENERAL, to the SECRETARY to the GOVERNMENT OF BENGAL.

Dated, Simla, 6th July, 1863.

SIR,—I am directed to reply to your letter, No. 1158, dated March 11, reporting on the Petition of Rajah Prosonno Narain Deb, Bahadoor, Dewan, Nizamut of Moorshedabad.

2. The points on which a report was called for by his Excellency the Viceroy and Governor-General were four :—

    1st. Attempts on the part of the Nawab Nazim to deprive the Dewan of his official residence.

    2nd. Non-recognition of the Dewan's official title by the Nawab Nazim.

    3rd. The Dewan, being deprived of the management of certain pensions and certain tomb payments, which are a charge on the Nizamut funds.

    4th. The Dewan being accused of delay in rendering the Nizamut accounts.

3. On the first point, the following appear to be the facts of the case. When the house was erected, the understanding was that *the Dewan was to have it as long as he continued to exercise the functions of Dewan.* The land on which the house was built belonged to the Nizamut, and not to the Nawab Nazim, but there were some ruined buildings on it which the Nawab Nazim bought with his own money. The house itself was built from a grant of Rs. 7,000. from the Nizamut Fund, and from old materials, to which the Nawab Nazim added some money from his own pocket, on the understanding that when the Dewan ceased to use it, the house was to become available for one of his sons. After the quarrel with the Dewan, the Nawab Nazim tried to oust him, but the Bengal Government decided that, as the house was required for the use of the Dewan Nizamut, it could not be vacated. After this decision the Nawab Nazim appealed twice to the Agent Governor-General, offering to repay all the money spent from

the Nizamut Fund in the building and repair of the house. But as the Nawab Nazim laid claim to the house on the the ground that it was built for one of his sons, an assertion which the Agent could not for a moment admit, the matter was allowed to drop.

4. The Lieutenant-Governor has not favoured His Excellency the Viceroy with any opinion on the subject. The Dewan, however, occupies the house under the orders of the Bengal Government, and has a right to expect protection from being either ousted or molested in its occupation. This question is distinct from any proposition on the part of the Nawab Nazim to secure an indisputable title to the premises, by paying what the house cost the Nizamut Fund. The offer of the Nawab Nazim to repay the amount expended from the Nizamut Fund was in itself an admission of the weakness of his claim. But it is not clear to His Excellency the Viceroy and Governor-General on what conditions the Nawab Nazim contributed towards the expense of the construction of the house. The matter is one which, under present circumstances, should not be allowed to drop, but should be cleared up, and *the Nawab Nazim's claim, to whatever extent it may exist, be clearly proved, and should be fully satisfied.*

5. As regards the non-recognition of the official title of Dewan Nizamut, held by Rajah Prosunno Narain Deb, Major Thomson reports that the Nawab Nazim had in several letters spoken of the Dewan Nizamut as the Agent's Dewan, but the Agent was unwilling to notice what he thought was not intended as an affront. But at last, on receiving a letter in which the Nawab Nazim spoke with disrespect and *distrust* of the Dewan, he, on 1st December, 1862, wrote to the Nawab Nazim, insisting that, in official correspondence, he would write of the Rajah as the Dewan Nizamut. He reports that ever since then the Nazim has given the Dewan his proper title, and the Dewan never complained to the Agent *officially* on the subject.

But I am to point out that when the memorial of the Dewan Nizamut was submitted to Government on 20th November, no steps had been taken by the Agent Governor-General to secure the recognition of the Rajah's title. Moreover, in the month of August, the Nawab Nazim had written to the Agent a much stronger letter than that which called forth the Agent's remonstrance of 1st December, and in that letter wrote of the Dewan with the most studied insolence as the "ex-Dewan," and "your Dewan," and charged him with forgery. It was the Agent's duty to have remonstrated against that letter, and to have protected from gross insult an officer who possessed the confidence of Government and with respect to whom the orders of Government were, "the Governor-General in Council will not allow His Highness another opportunity of treating with injustice and contumely a high native officer appointed with the sanction of Government and still possessing its confidence." It is further to be remarked that the Nawab Nazim's reply to Major Thomson's letter of 1st December expressed no intention of recognising the Dewan's title, but merely repeated his strong objection to receive messages through Rajah Prosunno Narain Deb Bahadoor in private matters, and his intention to attend to the Agent's wishes in these matters, and to conduct his private affairs himself, if the Agent would correspond with him direct. Morover in the fourth Paragraph of his fresh memorial to the Secretary of State, dated 1st December, which **notwithstanding** the remonstrances **of the** Agent Governor-General, **the Nawab Nazim** has refused to modify, the Nawab Nazim again talks of the Dewan Nizamut as the ex-Dewan.

You will, therefore, instruct the Agent to the Governor-General to inform the Nawab Nazim that, in future, all letters from His Highness will **be** returned unanswered in which, when writing of the Dewan Nizamut, the Nawab Nazim does **not** give **that** officer **his** proper **title** of Dewan Nizamut, **or** gives him any other **title.**

6. The third **point** on which a Report was called **for** was the transfer of the management of certain pensions and tombs from the Dewan Nizamut to the Nawab Nazim. It is nowhere distinctly stated what these pensions, &c., **are.** But so far as His Excellency can gather from the papers before him, the pensions **appear to** be what are called **the** Akrobah, and the Tombs appear to **be the** Tombs kept up in memory of the family of Aliverdi Khan, and the charge on both accounts appears to be on the Nizamut Fund, and not on the Nawab Nazim's personal stipend. Up to 1848 **the** Nawab Nazim seems to **have** had some voice **in their** management, but owing to frauds then practised, and the non-report of many lapsed pensions, their distribution appears then **to** have been limited entirely to the Dewan. His Honour, the Lieutenant-Governor, appears at first to have considered their distribution a part of the Dewan's duties, under the orders of 14th January, 1862, for in March of that year, when certain petitioners asked that their pensions might be distributed through the Nawab Nazim instead of through the Dewan, and suggested that **they** should be paid through the Agent's office. On this His Honour, **the** Lieutenant-Governor, ruled that their distribution should be left **to the** Nawab **Nazim.**

The facts **have been gathered** from remarks scattered **over the** correspondence. In **the Report now** before His Excellency, **the Viceroy** and Governor-General, **no grounds** whatever **are** given for **the decision** *that the distribution of the pensions,* &c., *should be left to the* **Nawab** *Nazim.* His Excellency, however, **is** of **opinion** that the best course which Government can follow in its dealings **with** the Nawab Nazim, is to adhere strictly to the principles laid down in the orders of 14th January, 1862, unless they shall be modified by Her Majesty's Government. The private affairs of the Nawab Nazim, and the Nizamut affairs, should be kept entirely distinct, and the responsibility for the administration of the latter should in the first instance rest on the **Dewan Nizamut.** If, therefore, as His Excellency supposes, the expense **of the pensions** and Tombs referred to are charged to the Nizamut **Fund, and not to the** Nawab Nazim's personal stipend, His Excellency **requests that the** administration of them, and of all expenditure **similarly charged, may** be restored to the Dewan Nizamut, who cannot **be relieved of any portion of** responsibility attaching **to** him under the orders of 14th January, 1862.

7. On the fourth and last point, the alleged delay in rendering the accounts, **the Dewan had** explained:—1st. That, as he could not go in person to **the palace, he,** with the concurrence of the late Agent, the Magistrate **of** Berhampore, and the Nawab Nazim himself, sent Mr. Vivian, the superintendent of buildings, with **an** English writer, to deliver over the accounts to Messrs. Knott **and** Montriou on behalf

of the Nazim; but after some of the papers had been examined Messrs. Knott and Montrieu raised objections, and Mr. Vivian was so discourteously treated that he refused to go back again. 2nd. That thereafter the Nazim went to Calcutta, and of course the accounts could not then be made over. 3rd. That the Dewan next employed an attorney, Mr. Judge, to make over the accounts; but as the chest was sealed with the Nazim's own seal, affixed after the Dewan had been precluded from access to the papers, Mr. Knott would allow no one but the Dewan, or some one on his part, to break the seal, and Mr. Judge was of opinion that this could not be done. 4th. That when at last the Bengal Government ordered the boxes to be made over in presence of the Agent, Mr Knott commenced by laying before the Agent a box, and alleging that the Dewan had abstracted the Agreement of 1834, yet that agreement was found in its proper place in this very box; that Mr. Knott charged the Dewan with the responsibility for several missing accounts, yet these were afterwards found in the palace, but when so found Mr. Knott asserted that *the signature of approval on them was not genuine.*

With respect to these complaints, His Excellency desired a report to be submitted "in the accusations made with respect to delay of accounts and non-production of papers which it would seem were found to be in their proper place." The Agent Governor-General, however, touches upon no single point which it was important should be fully entered into. Not a single statement of the Dewan is impugned, but *the Agent contents himself with pronouncing* that, as stated in his letter to the Bengal Government, No. 80, of 26th July last, no copy of which is furnished, *both parties are to blame.*

I am to refer to the correspondence noted in the margin, and to inform you that so far as appears from the records of this office, the explanations of the Dewan Nizamut in regard to the delay in rendering the accounts are quite correct, and that, as at present informed, His Excellency acquits the Dewan Nizamut of blame in this matter.

8. With reference to the 2nd and 3rd paragraphs of your letter, I am to observe that the Dewan Nizamut has been placed in a position of considerable difficulty by the irritating manner in which the Nawab Nazim has acted towards him, and *although he has in some instances erred in point of discretion, His Excellency the Viceroy and Governor-General does not think that he has been seriously to blame,* or that he has forfeited his claim to the support of Government.

10. I am to request that a copy of the first eight paragraphs of this letter may be given to the Dewan Nizamut in reply to his Memorial.

I have, &c.,
(Signed) H. M. DURAND.
Secretary to the Government of India.
(True copy.)
THOMAS JONES,
Registrar, Bengal Secretariat.
(True copy.)
W. G. BUCKLE,
Agent Governor-General.

One false step led to another, and the Agent Governor-General not only supported the Dewan against the Nawab, but also withheld His Highness' stipend for a long time without a just cause (Page 249). His Highness was therefore obliged to borrow money at a high rate of interest (Page 250) to meet the current expenses of his large family, and on applying afterwards to the Government for compensation, he was referred to the ex-Agent. The ex-Agent refused to pay, so the Nawab instructed his solicitors to try the issue in a Court of Justice, but the proceedings were at once stopped by the Government (Page 268), and the Nawab was compelled to sustain the whole loss without a prospect of redress from any quarter! Thus was the Nawab a second time debarred from appealing to a Court of Justice for the recovery of that which every right-thinking man must consider he was justly entitled to! The following letters throw some light on the subject :—

Correspondence relating to the interest paid by His Highness for the use of money during the stoppage of his Stipend.

I.

No. 58 A.

From HIS HIGHNESS THE NAWAB NAZIM OF BENGAL, &c., *to* MAJOR W. A. A. THOMSON, *Agent to the Governor-General, Moorshedabad.*

MY FRIEND,—I beg to subjoin a statement, showing the sums of money I was obliged to borrow from Bankers and others, and the interest which was paid for these accommodations, to enable me to meet the pressing necessities of the Nizamut for the period, namely, June to December, 1861, during which Lieutenant-Colonel Colin Mackenzie, the late Agent to the Governor-General unwarrantably stopped the payment of my monthly stipend.

It would be needless for me to repeat all that had transpired in relation to this matter, and of the indignities and inconveniences I experienced at the time. I, therefore, refer you to the correspondence noted on the margin, from which you will perceive, that I had protested against this act of the Agent, and warned him that I should "look to him for reparation." This warning will be found in my letter, No. 6, dated 5th July, 1861, to his address.

The least reparation I can now seek from Government is the reimbursement to me of Rupees 7,167-5-3, the amount of interest which I had paid for the monies advanced to me by the parties during my embarrassment.

I remain, &c.,
(Signed) SYUD MUNSOOR ULLEE.

Palace, Moorshedabad,
The 30th October, 1862.

II.

No. 97.

From MAJOR W. A. A. THOMSON, *Agent to the Governor-General, Moorshedabad, To* HIS HIGHNESS THE NAWAB NAZIM OF BENGAL.

Dated Berhampore, 1st November, 1862.

MY FRIEND,—In reply to your letter, No. 58 A, of the 30th ultimo, I beg to remind Your Highness that *Government never gave the slightest sanction to the suspension of your Monthly Stipend*, and would, therefore, decline to pay the amount of interest mentioned by Your Highness were I to forward your letter.

I remain, &c.,
(Signed) W. A. A. THOMSON, *Major*,
Agent Governor-General.

III.

No. 63A.

From HIS HIGHNESS THE NAWAB NAZIM OF BENGAL, &c., *to* MAJOR W. A. A. THOMSON, *Agent to the Governor-General, Moorshedabad.*

MY FRIEND,—I am in receipt of your letter, No. 97, of this date, in which you inform me, that Government not having sanctioned the late Agent's act, by which *my stipend was suspended for seven months*, it would decline to pay to me the interest I had incurred for money borrowed to meet the urgent wants of my family and establishment.

Lieutenant-Colonel Mackenzie, having, in the capacity of Agent to the Governor-General, done me a wrong, and, **he, in his** letter, dated 28th June, 1861, having instructed me, that, "**for** the time being, any official declaration proceeding from the Agent, carries with it the full authority of **the** Governor-General in Council," it became my duty, if not, an act of courtesy towards Government, **on my** part, first, to make known my claims to Government, **and, on** Government directing me to **hold** Lieutenant-Colonel Mackenzie responsible **for** *the consequence of his unauthorized act,* I could then take **the** necessary measures for recovering from him such damages as I have suffered.

Under such circumstances I beg you will lay my previous letter before the Government, and communicate its decision thereon.

I remain, &c.,

(Signed) **SYUD MUNSOOR ULLEE.**

Palace, Moorshedabad,
The 1st November, 1862.

IV.

No. 2634.

From THE HONORABLE A. EDEN, *Officiating* Secretary *to the* Government *of* Bengal, *to* THE AGENT **TO THE** GOVERNOR-GENERAL, *Moorshedabad.*

Fort William, the 27th November, 1862.

SIR,—I am directed to acknowledge the receipt of your letter, No. 116, dated **13th inst.**, with enclosures, being an application from the Nawab Nazim **to be allowed a** compensation of Rupees 7,167-5-3, being the amount of interest he **has had to** pay for money advanced to him by money-lenders, during **the** period **of** the payment of **his** monthly stipend was stopped, and in reply to state **that the Lieutenant-Go**vernor is unable to comply with His Highness's **request.**

I have, &c.,

(Signed) A. EDEN.
Offg. Secretary to **the Govt. of Bengal.**

No. 121.

Copy forwarded for **the information of** His Highness the Nawab Nazim, with reference to his letters of the 30th October and 1st ultimo, Nos. 58 and 63 A.

(Signed) W. A. THOMSON, *Major,*
Agent Governor-General.

Berhampore,
8th December, 1862.

V.

No. 8.

From THE AGENT TO THE GOVERNOR-GENERAL, *Moorshedabad,* to HIS HIGHNESS THE NAWAB NAZIM OF BENGAL, *Berhampore, 30th January,* 1863.

MY FRIEND,—I have been directed by His Excellency the Governor-General in Council to ask Your Highness whether Messrs. Remfry and Rogers are acting with your knowledge and by your authority in the prosecution now being made against Colonel C. Mackenzie, late Agent to the Governor-General at Moorshedabad, and if so, what are your reasons for departing in matters purely Official from the usual and prescribed course.

2. I am further directed to inform Your Highness, that, if Messrs. Remfrey and Rogers are acting by your authority, *the Governor-General in Council must view with displeasure any proceedings which, on the face of them, give trouble and annoyance to an Officer of Government, who did nothing more than his duty;* moreover, that it is the intention of Government to support Colonel Mackenzie in this matter, and that it will be well for Your Highness to re-consider the step you have taken and withdraw from the vexatious proceedings to which you have given rise.

I remain, &c.,
(Signed) W. A. A. THOMSON,
Agent Governor-General.

VI.

No. 12.

From HIS HIGHNESS THE NAWAB NAZIM OF BENGAL, &c., to MAJOR W. A. A. THOMSON, *Agent to the Governor-General, Moorshedabad.*

MY FRIEND,—I have to acknowledge the receipt of your letter No. 8, of yesterday's date, in which you inform me that *His Excellency the Governor-General in Council would view with displeasure the prosecution of my intended action against Colonel Colin Mackenzie, for the recovery of the interest I had paid on sums of money I was compelled to borrow, when my stipend was suspended for a time.*

In reply, I beg to intimate to you, for the information of His Excellency the Governor-General, that *I have adopted the only course open to me, namely, of directing my solicitors to drop the action* they were about to institute on my behalf.

I remain, &c.,
(Signed) SYUD MUNSOOR ULLEE.

Palace, Moorshedabad,
31st Jan., 1863.

There is little doubt that the above circumstances must have militated very much against the interests of the Nawab, if (as they probably were) they were looked upon in a *personal* light by the Governor-General. We maintain that personal feelings should not have actuated any man (particularly one high in office like a Governor-General of India) in the performance of his *official* duty, and whatever may have been the nature of the supposed affront offered to the Government in the person of the Agent, the Nawab having fully apologized, privately and officially, had more than made every atonement for his error, and no further notice should have been taken of the subject. But the Governor-General was evidently not appeased, for he entirely changed his views of the Nawab's claims, and refused to accord that justice which His Highness had been led to expect at his hands.

The first Memorial of 1857 presented by His Highness was never replied to, and the second of 1860, after lying on the table of the Foreign Secretary's Office in Calcutta for twenty-one months, was partially answered by Lord Canning in the following manner—pending the decision of the Secretary of State thereon :—

Extract from a letter from the Officiating Secretary to the Government of India to the Secretary to the Government of Bengal, dated, Fort William, the 14th January, 1862. No. 28.

1. I am directed by the Governor-General in Council to acknowledge the receipt of your letters relative to the recent dismissal of the Dewan by the Nawab Nazim of Bengal, and to the conduct of His Highness towards the Governor-General's Agent, Lieutenant-Colonel Mackenzie.

2. On the first point, I am directed to express the general concurrence of His Excellence in Council in the view taken by the Lieutenant-Governor, both *as to the constitution of the office of Dewan*, and, as to

the course which *the Nawab Nazim's proceedings towards the present Dewan*, impose upon the Government.

3. Heretofore, *no Dewan has ever been appointed, or removed, by the Nawab Nazim, without the concurrence and approval of the Government*, or, its Agent, and, although *the Government has always assumed the power of appointing and removing the Dewan, in opposition to the wishes of the Nawab*, yet, the power has in no case been exercised, except, after previous communication with the Nawab, and, a full consideration of his objections.

4. Therefore, in summarily dismissing the Dewan without enquiry and without any just cause, in opposition to the remonstrances of the Agent, and in violation of his own promise, on abolishing the office of Dewan, and in appointing his two sons to "conduct the affairs of the Nizamut" aided by another functionary under the title of Madar-ul-Maham, *the present Nawab Nazim has not only departed from a long established usage, but has usurped an authority which does not belong to him, and, was never even claimed by any of his predecessors*. The proceeding is one, which, to say the least of it, is not respectful to the Government.

5. The Governor-General in Council is not, in the least, disposed *to interfere with the Nawab's management of his own private affairs*, nor does His Excellency desire, any longer, to have a voice in the appointment of the persons by whom the expenditure of the Nawab's personal stipend is to be controlled. His Highness is at liberty to spend his income as he pleases, so long as he keeps out of **debt**, and he is equally free to choose his own servants, to dismiss them, and to designate them by any names that he deems appropriate. But the Governor-General in Council will not allow His Highness another opportunity of treating with injustice, or contumely, a high native officer, appointed with the sanction of Government, and, still possessing its confidence, *nor, will the Nawab, in future, be consulted as to the appointment of the officer by whom the general business of the Nizamut is managed under the superintendence of the Agent*.

6. The Nawab Nazim, therefore, should be informed, that, the Government will take no cognizance of the arrangement he has made for the management of the affairs of his own household, and that the expense of it must be defrayed from the funds at the disposal of His Highness. *The Nawab should also be told, that the Dewan will not be allowed in future to interfere in the private affairs of His Highness, but, that he is the only officer whom the Government will recognize as the Dewan of the Nizamut, and through whom the business of the Nizamut, generally, will be transacted. The Dewan will continue to receive the salary he has hitherto drawn, but, it will be paid to him from the Nizamut Fund. The office will be maintained on this footing so long as it is held by Rajah Prosono Narain Deb*, but, when a vacancy occurs, **it will** have to be considered whether the duties are not such as may be performed by a less expensive agency.

The Nawab Nazim's stipend, *together with all arrears that may be due to him, should be paid at once to his own receipt*, if this has not been already done, consequent upon a communication which lately passed between the Governor-General **and the** Lieutenant-Governor. With regard to the affront offered by the Nawab Nazim to the Agent on the occasion of his visiting the Palace in May last, the Governor-General in Council agrees with the Lieutenant-Governor in thinking that it has by no means been atoned for by the very unsatisfactory explanation which has been accepted by Lieutenant-Colonel Mackenzie as an apology to himself. *For that affront* offered to the Government in the person of its Agent, *His Excellency in Council will not be satisfied with these imperfect excuses. Nothing short* **of** *a full admission of error, and an unreserved expression of regret* **can be received** *by the Government as a sufficient apology*, and the **Nawab should be** told that, until such an apology has been forwarded to **him, and accepted** by the Lieutenant-Governor, neither will the **request which His Highness** has made for permission **to** visit the **Governor-General** be considered, nor will the letters which he addressed **to His Excellency** on the 16th and 25th October **be** answered. *The Agent*, **also**, *will be withdrawn for the present*, and all official communications **between the** Government and the Nawab will be made through the **Collector of** Moorshedabad, until an Agent, regularly appointed, can, **with** *propropriety, resume his functions.*

7. I am directed to take the opportunity of referring **to the** Nawab Nazım's Memorial to the Secretary of State, and to **the** correspondence ending with your letter No. 421, dated the 6th July last, relative to the Accounts of the Minority, and to the allegations made by **His** Highness in respect to the late Mr. Torrens.

8. The Nawab should be informed that *his Memorial*, **though** *expressed in language far from respectful, will be forwarded* **to** the Secretary of State for the consideration of Her Majesty's Government, *together with such remarks as the unfounded pretensions it sets forth, and the erroneous statements and inferences it contains*, **have** *rendered necessary.*

9. At the **same time it** should be **clearly** explained to **His Highness** that *the Governor-General in Council entirely rejects his* **claims so** *far as they are founded on the assertion of any Treaty-rights,* **or of** *any sovereign or hereditary titles*, and 'that his recognised position **in** regard to the sum of sixteen lacs of **Sicca** rupees, now annually **set** apart for Nizamut purposes, and to the accumulations thereof, is as follows :—

1st. Since 1771, *sixteen lacs* of rupees have been granted for Nizamut purposes. *The continued payment of this sum is guaranteed by no Treaty, and, it has hitherto been paid of the free will, grace and favour of the British Government. It may cease, or may be diminished, whenever the Government shall determine, but there is no intention of making any change in the present arrangement during the lifetime of the present Nawab.*

2ndly. Though *there is no guarantee for the continuance of the above payment in whole, or in part, yet, certain pensions*, now charged upon it, *were declared by* Lord Cornwallis, in 1790, *to be*, and *are, therefore, hereditary.*

3rdly. Out of the above-mentioned sum of sixteen lacs, somewhat *less than seven lacs of Sirca Rupees, a year, are now paid to the Nawab* for his own purposes. This money is at the Nawab's disposal without control unless he falls into debt, in which case the Government may step in and take the management of it; *any pension granted out of* his annual sum, reverts to the Nawab, on its discontinuance. This arrangement, however, is only for the lifetime of the present Nawab, and will be re-considered at his death.

4thly. *The rest of the sixteen lacs,* after deducting the amount paid to the Nawab, *is carried to the credit of the* Deposit Fund.

5thly. *Everything once paid in the* Deposit Fund, *is held at the disposal of the Government* as a means of providing for the collateral branches of the Nizamut family (exclusive of the Rajmehal branch), and for other purposes connected with the Nizamut.

10. The only other point in the Nawab Nazim's Memorial which it is necessary to notice now is, that which relates to the charges brought by His Highness against the late Mr. H. Torrens. It is alleged by the Nawab that Mr. Torrens, in his capacity of Agent of the Governor-General, prevailed on His Highness, on his coming of age, to agree to the sale of certain Government Securities, amounting to *upwards of nineteen lacs of Rupees,* the invested savings of his personal stipend, during his minority; that he caused the Securities to be sold and held for some time in his own name by the Calcutta firm of Mackenzie, Lyall and Co; and that *he was, at least, a consenting party to the reckless plunder and dissipation of nearly the whole amount.* **The statements** of the Nawab and of Lieutenant-Colonel Mackenzie on this subject, as contained in the enclosures of your letter No. 421, **dated** the 6th July last, *reflect, most painfully, on the character and conduct of Mr. Torrens,* and, if that gentleman were now alive, it would have been obviously imperative on the Government to make a strict and searching inquiry into the whole facts and bearings of the case. There certainly are, as the Lieutenant-Governor observes, grounds for presuming that he acted on good faith for the Nawab's benefit, though altogether without authority, and with the most culpable imprudence and disregard of all official propriety; that he was imposed on by others, and that notwithstanding *the suspicion that necessarily attaches to some of his acts,* he himself derived no personal advantage from the transactions in question. But, at the least, *the appearance of the* **case** as regards him, judged by his own letters to Mackenzie, Lyall and Co., *is most discreditable.* Still, under the circumstances, *it does not appear to the Governor-General in Council that any good object can be gained by further inquiry.* Mr. Torrens has been dead for more than eight years, and, so far as the Nawab is concerned, it is clear, from his own admission, that, after he became of age, he gave Mr. Torrens full authority to deal with the accumulated savings; that he made no objection or complaint in Mr. Torrens' lifetime as to the way in which the money was being disposed of, though His Highness might, in such a case, as he has recently done, have **addressed** the Governor-General direct; that he allowed several years to elapse, after Mr. Torrens' death, before he accused that officer of having aided to pillage him, or otherwise brought his proceedings to the knowledge of the Government; and that the statements, in regard to Mr. Torrens, made by His Highness in his Memorial to the Secretary of State, were not brought forward in the way of complaint, but were merely incidental to the subject-matter of the Memorial, and intended to illustrate the manner in which his interests were injuriously affected by the action of the law of 1854. *The matter may, therefore, be allowed to drop.*

11. With reference to your letter No. 490, dated the 17th of September last, *I am directed to request that the Nawab Nazim may be urged to give a discharge* for the Minority Accounts, the correctness of which in no way depends upon circumstances which occurred after His Highness came of age,

12. In a preceding paragraph *it has been directed that the Agent should be withdrawn*, the Governor-General will not entertain the question of any Agent residing at Moorshedabad, until the Nawab Nazim shall have apologized in a way that shall be satisfactory to the Lieutenant-Governor, for the affront offered by His Highness to the representative of the British Government. Lieutenant-Colonel Mackenzie should, therefore, be directed to leave Moorshedabad directly, and repair to Calcutta; he should make over charge of his office to the collector of Moorshedabad, who, with the assistance of the Dewan, will make the usual payments to stipendiaries, and others, and discharge the current duties of the Agent's office, but will hold no communication with the Nawab except such as may be required by law.

(A True Extract.)
(Signed) C. MACKENZIE, Lieut.-Colonel,
Offg. Agent to the Governor-General at Moorshedabad.

As correct inferences can only be drawn upon written statements by a fair and free discussion of them, it will be necessary here to enter into details which may throw light upon the opinion expressed by Lord Canning in the above letter.

In Paras. 1, 2, 3, 4, 5, and 6, His Lordship's endeavours to support the action taken by the Agent Governor-General against the Nawab in favour of the Dewan; but as the Dewan was the paid servant of the Nawab (Page 245), no doubt can possibly exist as to the Nawab's right to dismiss him at pleasure without even informing the Agent of his intention so to do. The assertion that no Dewan had ever been appointed or removed by the Nawab without the approval of the Government is not quite borne out by Lord Cornwallis's letter (Page 42), wherein it is stated that "*the Government left His Highness the free choice of his own Dewan;*" besides, we may gather from the Treaties that the

Dewan in whose appointment the Government claimed any interference (Pages 24 and 27) was vested only with the disbursement of such sums as were set apart for the Nawab's state and rank, and had no control over His Highness's personal stipend—the Government, therefore, when during the minority of Nawab Mobaruck-ul-Dowlah it withheld the Nawab's state allowances, forfeited all claim to interference in the appointment or dismissal of the Dewan, whom the Nawab might wish to select for the disbursement of his own personal stipend—hence the argument of His Lordship is unsupported by facts, and the action taken by the Government of India against His Highness can only be looked upon as an *arbitrary measure*, especially when it is remarked that "*the office will be maintained on this footing so long as it is held by Rajah Prosonno Narain Deb,*" &c.; a man who owed his rank and elevation to the Nawab, and for whom provision was thereafter to be made *without the Nawab's sanction* out of the Fund established for the benefit of the Nawab's Family. It is, moreover, a strange fact, that this man receives £150 a year more than his superior officer, the Agent, who is at the head of the Nizamut Affairs!

This Dewan appears to have been a great friend of the Agent Governor-General (Page 243), who was no doubt led away by *personal* feelings to support his authority, for it is the only instance on record where the Agent advocated the cause of the Dewan in opposition to the Nawab's wishes, but having once committed himself, it may be seen that the Governor-General for whom he acted was in a measure bound to support him, although he expressed his displeasure afterwards by quietly removing him from his lucrative appointment, and giving him a subordinate one elsewhere (Page 261). The order to pay the Nawab all arrears due to him has not yet been carried out by the Government of India. As to the affront alluded to, it can only be looked upon by disinterested people as *a personal question* between the Agent and the Nawab, which, though *unintentionally* offered, was *fully* apologized for to the Agent, who accepted the apology (Page 239); hence we cannot see that His Lordship the Governor-General was justified, on so slender a pretext, in subjecting the Nawab to the indignities which the Government thereafter heaped upon him.

There is little doubt, we think, from a perusal of the records (Pages 52 to 72), that the object of the Government in establishing the appointment of Agent Governor-General, in 1816, was to regain that control over the Nizamut Affairs which they had abandoned during the Soubahship of Nawab Mobaruck-ul-Dowlah—the Agent, therefore, can only be looked upon as acting in the room of the Dewans who before the time of Nawab Mobaruck-ul-Dowlah had been appointed by the Government. Virtually, then, the Agent is the Government Dewan, though he may be recognized under a different official title, and in the appointment or dismissal of this officer, the Nawab has never claimed any voice, although in fairness he ought to be consulted since the Agent is paid out of the Nawab's money.

With regard to the Memorial submitted by His Highness in 1857 being (as stated in Para. 8) " expressed in language far from respectful," it might certainly be called disrespectful if *an exposure* of the naked truths and facts which it exhibits (in plain English) against the injustice practised by the Indian Government upon the Nawabs Nazim, from generation to generation, can be considered so; moreover, the style in which His Lordship speaks of the Nawab's claims must convince every careful reader of the existence of some powerful bias in His Lordship's mind having more of a *personal* than an official character.

The arbitrary nature of the remarks in Para. 9, "*the Governor-General in Council entirely rejects the Nawab's claims so far as they are founded on the assertion of any Treaty rights, or of any sovereign or hereditary titles,*" &c., may readily be observed by a comparison with His Lordship's letter of the 11th March, 1856, (Page 194) "*just regard to the honours and dignities due to your hereditary rank, and the prescriptive privileges of your high station, guaranteed by the stipulations of subsisting Treaties and long-established Relations,*" &c., and, therefore, requires no comment!

As to the sum of sixteen lacs which, since 1771, have been granted for Nizamut purposes, His Lordship's statement is *literally correct*, that the payment of *that* sum is guaranteed by no Treaty, although the Court of Directors and the officers of the Indian Government frequently alluded to *that* sum as "*the Assignment by Treaty of the Family*" (Pages 97, 108), but it is noticeable that His Lordship does not allude to, or deny, the validity of the Treaty of 1770 which guaranteed the payment for ever, *not of sixteen lacs,* but of Rupees

31,81,991-9, and which Treaty was upheld by the Indian Government so late as 1834 (Page 93) in order to prevent the Nawab being personally subjected to the ordinary processes of the Supreme Court in Calcutta, which at that time was the only direct emblem of Her Majesty's Power in the East.

Again, His Lordship stated *"that certain Pensions declared by Lord Cornwallis in 1790 as hereditary are hereditary;"* yet some of these have been absorbed into the Nizamut Deposit Fund in accordance with Mr. Trevelyan's Minute of 1836 (Page 101) without just cause. And further, it is remarked that *"any Pensions granted out of his annual sum reverts to the Nawab on its discontinuance;"* this was not, however, the practice before the present Nawab's time; as the reader will no doubt have observed; nor was this arrangement intended to be carried out after the death of the present Nawab, though no reason is adduced in justification of the intention.

With respect to the *"balance of the sixteen lacs, after "deducting the amount paid to the Nawab, being carried to "the credit of the Deposit Fund, and that Fund being held "at the disposal of the Government as a means of providing "for the collateral branches of the Nizamut Family,"* &c.; no remark can be offered except the *arbitrary* manner in which the Nawab's income was reduced from *sixteen* lacs to *seven* lacs without a corresponding advantage to the Nizamut Family, for which the Nawab agreed to set aside two lacs of rupees annually and no more. (Pages 79, 85, 323).

We now turn to Para. 10, in which the Governor-

General endeavours to subvert the claim advanced by the Nawab against the Government in respect of certain monies misappropriated by the Agent Governor-General in his *official* capacity, and His Lordship assumes that on the death of the Agent, the Government was released from responsibilities incurred by him during his lifetime, remarking, at the same time, "*it does not appear to the "Governor-General in Council that any good can be obtained "by further inquiry." "The matter may therefore be allowed "to drop.*" If this be a standard for meting out justice to an injured individual, we can only observe that it is directly opposed to the principles of truth and honour upon which the Courts of Justice in this country are upheld; and it is to be hoped that Her Majesty's Government will take a fairer view of this claim of the Nawab's than was taken by His Lordship, when issuing the instructions conveyed in the above letter. The whole letter *savours of irritation produced from some personal cause*, and does not bear the impress of a *just* verdict in answer to the claims advanced by the Nawab in his Memorial.

Having thus laid before our readers an impartial view of the statements contained in the foregoing letter, we will proceed to notice the opinions expressed upon the same subjects by Her Majesty's Secretary of State for India in reply to the communications forwarded to England by the Government of India.

On receipt of the Despatch from Her Majesty's Secretary of State for India by the Governor-General, the following Extract was forwarded for His Highness's information:—

Extract of a Despatch from the Right Honourable the Secretary of State for India to His Excellency, the Right Honourable the Governor-General of India in Council, No. 30, dated India Office, London, the 17th June, 1864.

1. The letters of the late Governor-General and Viceroy, dated 24th September No. 66 A. and 66 B., 1863, terminate a long series of official papers received from your Government during the last two years, relating to the affairs of the Nawab Nazim of Bengal

2. *All the correspondence necessary to the formation of a correct opinion with respect to the special questions which they illustrate, having now been received,* I proceed to communicate to you the views of Her Majesty's Government.

3. The Nawab Nazim having addressed to me more than one Memorial in which he claims the recognition of the British Government of certain rights, power, and privileges which he alleges to belong to him and to his family under Treaty or engagements, it is necessary that I should review all the circumstances of His Highness's position.

4. The present Nawab Munsoor Ullee Khan, styled the Nawab Nazim of Bengal, *is admitted to be a descendant of Meer Jaffir Ali,* who, when the East India Company were first *invested with* the Dewanee of Bengal, Behar and Orissa, was at the head of the Nizamut of those Provinces which he had attained through the influence and assistance of the British Government. A Firman of the Emperor of Delhi *made it one of the conditions of the grant of the Dewannee that provision should be made "for the expenses of the Nizamut,"* that is, that a part of the revenues of those provinces should be appropriated to the payment of the department of the administration distinguished by that official name. But *subsequently by special arrangement the Company undertook to perform the duties of the Nizamut,* and made provision for its expenses by paying their own servants to do the work which had before been done by the servants of the Nazim. The office of the Nizamut being thus practically abolished, and its duties merged into general administration of the country, *the stipulation of the Imperial Firman ceased with the objects for which it was intended to provide.* I am of opinion, therefore, that the family of the Nawab Nazim of Bengal, have, under the Firman of Shah Allum, no claim upon the British Government.

5. But *the administrative duties of the Nizamut having been transferred to the Company, a personal provision was made for the family of the Nazim.* It was *right* that consideration should be shown to the sons of Meer Jaffir Ali though they were not called upon, after the death of the eldest Nujum-ood-Dowlah, to discharge the high official duties of the Soobadar or Viceroy of Bengal, Behar, and Orissa. Accordingly, *treaties were entered into with the younger princes,* Syefood-Dowlah and Moobaruck-ood-Dowlah successively, *by which the Company undertook to secure to them the Soobadaree of the Provinces of Bengal, &c., and to pay them a certain "annual stipend."*

In each of these Treaties, the Nawab expressly indicated himself as the person to whom these advantages are to accrue, and *I cannot perceive that in either case the Nawab, who was party to the Treaty,* had any regard to other interests than his own. It is true that at the end of the Treaty of 1766, the Nawab Syef-ood-Dowlah says, "this agreement, (by the blessing of God), I hope will be inviolably observed as long as the English factories continue in Bengal," and that the Nawab Moobaruck-ood-Dowlah says, "That this agreement, (by the blessing of God), shall be inviolably observed." But as the agreement in both cases, was of a specifically personal character, *it appears to me that the intention was to secure the strict observance of the Treaties during the lives of the persons interested, that is to say that they should last as long as the objects for which they were intended to provide.* The Treaty obligations therefore of the British Government ceased in both instances with the life of the other party; and that this was practically acknowledged at the time is evident from the fact that the amount of stipend payable to the Nawab was revised upon the death of Syef-ood-Dowlah with the full *consent* of his successor, a proof that the previous Treaty was not considered to confer any hereditary rights. And if the Treaty of 1766 was not an hereditary Treaty that character cannot be claimed for the Treaty of 1770 which was couched in the same general terms. I concur therefore, in the opinion with Your Excellency's Government that under these Treaties, the Nawab Nazim of Bengal has no *acquired* rights.

6. In 1772, *by an order of the Court of Directors* of the East India Company, passed on a review of the proceedings of the Bengal Government upon the occasion of Moobaruck-ood-Dowlah, and of the treaty concluded with him by the Indian Government, *the stipend of the Nawab Nazim was fixed at the annual amount of sixteen lacs of rupees*. No treaties of a later date than 1770 were entered into with the descendants of Meer Jaffir, but on the occasion of each succession, the member of the house *entitled to succeed* by Mahomedan law has been recognized by the British Government as Nawab Nazim, and the stipend of sixteen lacs of rupees has continued to be appropriated to the benefit of the Nawab Nazim and other members of the family. By whatsoever terms strictly defined the Nawab Nazim may hold the titles and privileges which he now enjoys, it is obvious to me that they could not be interfered with or altered, during good conduct, without a violation of the spirit, at least, of the assurances which have been given to him by our Government, and departure from the whole tenor of our transactions with him during a long course of years. I perceive with satisfaction, therefore, that your Government have no intention of disturbing subsisting arrangements for the pecuniary provision of the Nawab Nazim and his family, and the maintenance of the titular dignity of His Highness.

7. It appears that *the personal allowance of the Nawab Nazim himself is about seven lacs of rupees*, that from the remaining nine lacs, provision is made for the members of the family, and that *the balance goes to the formation of an accumulating fund* known as the "Nizamut Deposit Fund."

8. It is *unnecessary* to trace further the history of the Fund. Its *accumulations*, representing as they do the unappropriated portions from year to year, of the sixteen lacs stipend, *unquestionably belong to the Nawab Nazim and his family, and can properly be expended only for their benefit*. But this does not confer upon the Nazim himself

any right to dispose or to superintend the disposal of these balances. This right belongs to the Government, *under the conditions upon which the Fund* **was** *constituted.* It was assumed in the first instance mainly for the benefit and protection of the Nazim and his family; and I am of opinion that it is to the advantage of His Highness and his family that this system should be maintained. At the same **time** *it would seem to be desirable*, and I believe, that to **some extent, it has been the** practice in past time, for your Government, **through the Agent at** Moorshedabad *occasionally, to consult the* **Nazim with respect to any** *extraordinary expenditure from* **the Nizamut Fund.**

9. In connexion with this question **of administration of the Nizamut** Funds, I may here consider the **object** of the **claim advanced by the** Nawab Nazim to appoint and dismiss his **Dewan at pleasure.** If the Dewan, over whom this absolute **authority has been claimed, were** charged with the administration only **of His Highness' own share of** the stipend, or if the Nawab Nazim had **established his** right to exercise control over the Deposit Fund, his claim with respect to the appointment and dismissal of the Dewan might **be** tenable. But the Dewan has hitherto administered both His Highness' personal stipend and the general financial affairs of the Nizamut, including both the distribution of the separate stipends of other members of the family, **and** the management of *the Deposit Fund*, which *has been ruled to be under Government control.* It was necessary, therefore, that *the Government* **which** *was responsible for the Administration of the Funds*, and was **bound to maintain the** rights and interests of those in whose favour it **had deemed it necessary** to interfere, should have authority over the appointment **of the** minister charged with the executive details. Practically, *it appears to have been the* **custom** *for the Government and the Nawab Nazim, in* **communication** *with each other, to appoint or dismiss a Dewan, and as the official salary was paid from His Highness' stipend, it was doubtless right that he should be* **consulted.** But *inconvenience has resulted* from **this arrangement.** The **Nawab Nazim,** presuming upon the fact **that the Dewan has been** officially **styled the "Dewan of** the Nawab Nazim," took upon himself summarily **to dismiss the Dewan** Rajah Prosunno Narain Deb, and to place the financial administration in the hands of his own sons. In consequence of this act, **you have appointed the Rajah, Dewan of the Nizamut,** and *charged the Deposit Fund with the payment of his salary*, and you have communicated to **the Nazim that the Government have no** desire to interfere between **him** and his servants, or with his manner of expending his own personal share of the Nizamut allowances, and that he may appoint a Dewan for the **management** of his own personal affairs. This very obvious arrangement **is well calculated to meet the** existing difficulty, and to prevent the recurrence of **similar conflicts;** but *it is worthy of the consideration of your Excellency's Government whether for the more effectual prevention of future misunderstanding, it might not be desirable to confer upon the officer acting upon* **the part of** *Government a wholly different official designation.*

10. But, although the Nawab Nazim, apparently influenced by evil advisers, both European and native, has, in summarily dismissing his Dewan, acted in a disrespectful manner towards your Government, I am not without hope that **by** the exertions of your present **Agent at**

Moorshedabad, he **may yet be brought to a** better state of mind and express regret for his past conduct. *It is not to be forgotten that during the period of the Mutiny of the Bengal Army, the conduct of His Highness was* **marked by loyalty** *and fidelity to* **the** *British Government, and that as far as lay in his power he rendered assistance to the* **authorities of the District.** I would not, therefore, on account of what I hope may be regarded as an exceptional departure from his ordinary behaviour towards your Government, deprive him of any of the dignities or privileges of his position, among the most highly prized of which is the appointment of a British officer of rank to be the channel of his communications with your Government.

11. But whilst Her Majesty's Government are desirous that, unless the future conduct of the Nawab Nazim should call for such a measure upon your part, His Highness should not be deprived of any of the honours and privileges of which he is now in the enjoyment; they are at the same time of opinion that *it would be inexpedient to restore to him, those of which he was deprived* in 1854 by a special legislative enactment, *in consequence of an outrage, which was considered at the time* by the Government, both in India and in England, *to have been attended with a large amount of culpability on the part of the Nazim.* Her Majesty's Government cannot consent to the restoration of exclusive privileges of this description, the existence of which has been found from experience to be *inconvenient* and liable to abuse. His Highness' salute, which was at the same time reduced, has now been again replaced on its original footing, in consequence of his loyalty and good conduct during the mutiny; but he must be informed that Act XXVII. of 1854 can on no account be repealed.

* * * *

13. In conclusion, I have only to observe that I concur in opinion with Your Excellency's Government, that *the extent of this correspondence is out of all proportion to the magnitude of the interests involved. Much of it relates to matters of a vexatious, and in some respects of a frivolous character,* and I cannot but regret that so much of the time of the Government, both of India and Bengal, has been expended in such unprofitable discussions. *I trust, however, that your Excellency by endeavouring to remove as far as can be done, consistently with the public interests, all causes of irritation,* especially in connexion with small matters, from the mind of the Nawab Nazim, *will soon be able to place your relations with His Highness on a more satisfactory footing.*

14. I cannot close this despatch without referring to the terms in which the Nawab Nazim has adverted to the circumstances under which the arrears, accumulated during his minority, were dissipated upon his becoming of age. *The statement of these circumstances in the despatch* of the Government of India, dated 5th May, 1854, *has not satisfied me that His Highness had not good ground of complaint against the Agent, by whose proceedings so large a sum was placed in jeopardy and ultimately lost.* Had those circumstances been more early known to your Government, they would, as observed in the despatch referred to, have called for a strict and searching inquiry, but the decease of Mr. Torrens, the Agent in question, having precluded such an enquiry at the time, *I am reluctantly driven to the conclusion*

at which you have arrived, that no benefit will arise from reopening the consideration of that subject.

         I have, &c.,
       (Signed) C. Wood,
      (Signed)   C. U. Aitchison,
      Under-Secretary to the Government of India.

(True Copy) (Signed) Maurice Power,
      Assistant in charge office on Tour.

(True Copy) (Signed) W. B. Buckle,
      Agent Governor-General.

Paragraph 12 of the above despatch **not furnished with copy**, forwarded to the Nawab Nazim contains **the following important information** :—" I am of opinion that the future **position of Nawab Nazim's,** " sons should be fixed and defined with **as little delay** as possible. Her " Majesty's Government desire to have **the views of** Your Excellency " on this subject. Your Excellency *is aware that this Government* " *are fully sensible of the* INCONVENIENCE OF PERPETUA- " TING IN THIS OR ANY OTHER FAMILY **A** LINE OF " TITLED STIPENDIARIES *without power and responsibility,* " *and without salutary employment, &c., &c.,* it would seem to be the " wish of the Nawab Nazim that his sons should be trained to some " **useful** occupations, I should be glad if arrangements could be made " **for** enabling them to become useful members of Society. *The accu-* " *mulations of the Nizamut Deposit Fund* MIGHT *afford permanent* " *endowment to a certain extent.*"

It must appear to all observing men that the above despatch was written to support the opinions expressed by the Governor-General in 1862, and not to do justice to the Nawab. It was with a view of having his claims *reconsidered* that His Highness came to England and addressed Her Majesty's Secretary of State for India by a Memorial, dated 18th July, 1869.

Her Majesty's Secretary of State for India in Para. 2 of the above despatch distinctly stated "*All the correspondence necessary to the formation of a correct opinion with respect to the social questions which they illustrate had then been received,*" yet it will hardly be credited that after His Highness has been put to the trouble and expense of visiting England to personally appeal to the Government, his Memorial has been sent to India for a Report from the Local Government. Many months have since elapsed, but up to the present moment no reply has been given by the Imperial Government to His Highness either for or against his claims, which appears very extraordinary. The claims must be either righteous or groundless; if the former, it would be creditable to acknowledge them; if the latter, they should be repudiated at once, and the honour of the British Nation vindicated, for no possible advantage can arise from delay or by offering a passive resistance to the Nawab on the subject of his claims.

In Para. 3 the receipt of the several Memorials is acknowledged, and the purport of them set forth; but no reason is even given for not having furnished His Highness with replies thereto.

The legitimacy of the descent of the present Nawab from Meer Jaffir Ali Khan is boldly admitted in Para. 4, and also the stipulations of the grant of the Dewanny which was conferred upon the English East India Company as *" a conditional Jaghire "* (*gift*) *whereby they agreed to pay on behalf of the Nawabs Nazim a certain fixed " tribute to the Court at Delhi, and provide for the expenses of " the Nizamut, reserving whatever might remain out of the " revenues of the three Provinces after paying the above for " their own use."* The writer of the Despatch is, however, a little in error as to the time when the Dewanny was conferred; it was not given nor even applied for until after the death of Meer Jaffier, and during the reign of his son Nudjm-ul-dowlah who *accepted of a certain fixed amount in full of all demands for himself and successors as an adequate allowance for the expenses of the Nizamut, to be regularly paid as long as the English Company's Factories continue in Bengal.* The gift of the Dewanny was only *the appointment to the office of collecting the* **Revenues**, and, consequently, did not in itself entitle the servants of the Company to usurp any authority without the sanction of the Nawab for whom they merely acted as managers. It would be as reasonable to suppose that the Chancellor of the Exchequer in England should govern the whole of the country, because he is at the head of the Revenue Department as that the East India Company were entitled to deprive the Nawabs of their rights. That the Company took advantage of the *trust* reposed in them by the Nawab is obvious; but that is no reason why the British Government should follow their example, for the feelings of Englishmen must naturally revolt at the idea of taking mean advantage of those who are now powerless, and to whose ancestors we owe our dominion in the East. The object for which the Imperial Firmaun was intended to provide, viz.: the Nizamut has not died out, and until this is the case, or the Nizamut rebels, the Imperial Firmaun must be binding on the British Government in respect of the Provinces of Bengal, Behar and Orissa. The Company may have undertaken to perform the *executive* duties of the Nizamut, but for this *they were fully recompensed* by the Nawabs who permitted their stipends to be cut down to meet the extra expenses entailed on the Company until the year 1770, when *a permanent settlement was mutually agreed upon*, and evidently considered by the Government of India as a fixed deduction from its revenues. It might be urged that since the British

Government took over the Supreme Administration of India, the Imperial Firmaun of 1765 became invalid. This argument, however, cannot hold good, but would rather act in favour of the Nawab who so nobly sided with our Government during the Rebellion of 1857, when he might have been in a measure justified in opposing it and supporting the King of Delhi with whom it was at variance. For *this act of loyalty alone* to the British Crown, which no doubt saved for it the Provinces of Bengal, Behar and Orissa, we think the British Government ought to do justice to the Nawab, and support him in his claims upon the Indian Government.

The general inconsistency of the arguments in Para. 5 of the Despatch must to commercial men appear obvious, for if two parties enter into an agreement, the duration of that agreement, *if expressed*, can in no way be affected by the interests involved—hence the Agreements with Nawab Nudjm-ul-dowlah or Syef-ul-dowlah would hold good so long as "the English Company's Factories continue in Bengal" (Pages 22, 24). But the duration of the Agreement of 1770 was even more clearly expressed, for it concluded in the unmistakeable words: "*This Agreement, by the blessing of God, shall be inviolably observed for ever*," (Page 27) therefore the other contracting party to the Agreement, the East India Company, were in their peculiar position of trust legally bound to pay Nawab Mobaruck-ul-dowlah and his successors "for ever" whatever consideration or Civil List was named in that Agreement. The all-important words "for ever" in the last Agreement, may have been ingeniously left out by the writer of the Despatch, in order to give an apparent consistency to his argument, but this omission cannot in any way affect the legality of the document alluded to, for in a Court of Justice it would rather tend to support the Agreement itself, and throw a doubt on the Despatch on the principle adduced in common law respecting documents " falsus in uno falsus in omnis."

Again by comparing Para. 6 of the above Despatch with the Order contained in the Despatch from the Court of Directors, dated 20th April, 1771 (Page 31)—which is evidently referred to for the purpose of showing that the Agreement made in 1770 with Nawab Mobaruck-ul-dowlah by the Bengal Government was invalid—it will be seen that the Court of Directors did not attempt to withdraw from the responsibility their legally constituted agents in India had imposed upon the Company, but merely censured the Governor-General for not having made better terms, and also ordered him, as the guardian of the young Nawab, to keep back (while he was a minor) that portion of his stipend appointed for his state and rank, and only pay him sixteen lacs until he reached his majority; hence the conclusions drawn in that Paragraph must be incorrect, and the Agreement of 1770 should, in justice, hold in its entirety unless indeed as hinted in the latter part of the Paragraph, the Government of India can use *might* against *right*, and refuse to act up to their obligations.

From Para. 7, it would be supposed that the *Nawab Nazim himself has a personal allowance of seven lacs of rupees* (£70,000), and that all the other members of his family are provided for from the balance of the sixteen lacs; such, however, is not the case, for His Highness, out of the seven lacs, provides for his own family and connexions (145 souls), besides meeting all the expenses of his palace, guards, servants, and retinue; therefore, instead of having any surplus *for himself*, has to provide for a large deficit from the private revenues of some of his relatives, while the Government of India absorbs nearly six lacs of rupees (£60,000) annually into the Nizamut Deposit Fund, instead of two lacs (£20,000), as agreed upon (Page 79). Can we, therefore, wonder at His Highness having so frequently pressed his claims upon the attention of the British Government?

For an explanation of Para. 8 of the Despatch, we must refer our readers to Pages 52 and 86, where the formation of the several Funds is fully entered upon. These unquestionably belong to the Nawab, and ought surely to be under his supervision, as they have been formed from the accumulations of *his own* money; but even this privilege has been denied him, and of late years, excepting a grant to His Highness for his journey to England, little benefit has been derived from the Funds either by himself or the members of the Nizamut Family.

The remaining Paras. 9, 10, 11, 13, and 14, in which some strange assertions are made, will be fully understood by a reference to His Highness's last Memorial of July, 1869, Page 329 and Page 303, or to the large copy of His Highness's Memorial, with appendices, printed for private circulation, which was forwarded to the India Office in July 1869, for the purpose of enabling Her Majesty's Secretary of State for India in

Council to reconsider the subject of His Highness's claims which had been set aside by the Despatch of June 1864, and from which this work has been compiled. As to the extent of the *correspondence being " out of all proportion to the magnitude of the interests involved,"* this can only be looked upon as a private opinion, for in the cause of justice every pains should be taken to arrive at the truth, and every evidence (documentary or otherwise) brought to bear upon the subject, in order to arrive at a correct conclusion regarding the interests involved, be they large or small! Besides, as the National Faith has been pledged, and the credit of the Nation is of paramount importance, the interests involved are immense! British Honour and Faith are at stake (Page 93), and cannot be neglected to suit the capricious opinion of any Government official.

The foot note to the Despatch which was found amongst some papers connected with a lawsuit in which His Highness is now engaged, exhibits the policy proposed for doing further injustice to Indian Princes by withdrawing from them that support which has been guaranteed to them by the terms of Solemn Treaties and Engagements, as fully set forth in the following Memorial.

From HIS HIGHNESS THE NAWAB NAZIM OF BENGAL, BEHAR AND ORISSA, *To* HIS GRACE THE DUKE OF ARGYLL, &c., &c., SECRETARY OF STATE FOR INDIA IN COUNCIL.

MY LORD DUKE,

With a firm reliance on the honor and justice of the British Government, which from generation to generation gained the unbounded confidence of my ancestors and other Princes of India, I have been led to visit England in order to personally memoralize Her Majesty's Government in respect to certain grievances and acts of injustice to my family, for which I have vainly endeavoured to obtain redress in India. I now, therefore, beg respectfully to address Your Grace as the Secretary and Representative of Her Majesty's Government for India, and to lay before Your Grace a narrative of facts with my views thereon, in the earnest hope that Your Grace will give the subject your wise consideration, and accord to me and my family such justice as, in the opinion of Her Majesty's Government, the merits of our case are deserving of.

In reply to the several Memorials submitted by me through the Indian Government for the consideration of Her Majesty's Government, the Extracts (Pages 269 and 279), were forwarded to me by the Secretary to the Government of Bengal for my information and guidance; and although from Extract (Page 279) it is clear that the late Secretary of State for India acknowledges my descent from Nawab Meer Jaffir Ali Khan, yet there are certain points of vital importance to myself and my family which have been wrongly represented, and these, I trust, may now be fairly inquired into and equitably adjusted by Her Majesty's Government, so that I and my successors may realize the truth of the assurance given me in 1856 by the Viceroy, His Excellency (the late) Lord Canning, in the following words :—

" *Your Highness may be assured that the consideration, respect and* " *friendly interest in the prosperous administration of your affairs,* " *and just regard to the honors and dignities due to your hereditary* " *rank, and the prescriptive privileges of your high station, gua-* " *ranteed by the stipulations of subsisting Treaties and long-estab-* " *lished Relations, observed and cherished by former Governors-* " *General, will, on the part also of this sincere friend, be fervently* "*fostered and punctually fulfilled.*" (Page 194)

A reference to the Extracts alluded to will give an insight into the grievances which this Memorial purports to set forth; but that Your Grace may be able to inquire into each specifically, I beg to advance them under separate heads, as follows :—

I. THE HEREDITARY NATURE OF CERTAIN TREATIES, AND THE CHANGE IN THE VIEWS OF THE GOVERNMENT WITH REGARD TO THEM.

II. THE UNJUSTIFIABLE ATTITUDE ASSUMED BY HIS LORDSHIP THE MARQUIS OF DALHOUSIE TOWARDS MYSELF ON ALL QUESTIONS RELATING TO THE NIZAMUT, ON A MISCONCEPTION OF MY BEING IN SOME WAY CONNECTED WITH A BASE OUTRAGE COMMITTED BY SOME MENIAL SERVANTS, OF WHICH I WAS NOT EVEN COGNIZANT AT THE TIME.

III. THE ABROGATION OF THE REGULATIONS OF 1805, 1806, AND 1823, BY ACT XXVII OF 1854.

IV. THE NIZAMUT DEPOSIT FUND, ARBITRARILY CONVERTED INTO A "BOOK-DEBT BEARING NO INTEREST;" AND GENERAL MISAPPLICATION OF THE FUND TO PURPOSES ALTOGETHER FOREIGN TO ITS TRUE INTENT AND OBJECT.

V. THE UNJUST AND HARSH TREATMENT I EXPERIENCED FROM THE INDIAN GOVERNMENT DURING THE LATTER PERIOD OF THE ADMINISTRATION OF LORD CANNING, AND THE SPECIFIC LOSSES AND DEPRIVATIONS I HAVE SUFFERED IN CONSEQUENCE.

VI. EXTRAORDINARY TRANSACTIONS OF MR. TORRENS, AGENT GOVERNOR-GENERAL.

These, Your Grace, being the principal subjects I desire to bring to the notice of Her Majesty's Government, I will proceed to explain each one fully.

I.—THE HEREDITARY NATURE OF CERTAIN TREATIES, AND THE CHANGE IN THE VIEWS OF THE GOVERNMENT WITH REGARD TO THEM.

Before entering upon the details of the Treaties in question, I would respectfully ask Your Grace to consider the exact meaning of the word Treaty.

A Treaty is a formal league, or contract, between two ruling powers or sovereigns, for the adjustment of differences, or for forming an agreement for their mutual benefit, and cannot in honor be broken through by either power so long as their respective successors exist. It differs from an ordinary agreement in so far that whereas in an ordinary agreement heirs and successors are particularized—in a Treaty no allusion is ever made to such—since with ruling powers it is never contemplated, that the succession will die out, nor would it be politic when a Treaty is being framed to even hint at the death or extinction of either ruling power.

When the representatives of two Governments conclude a Treaty, they are bound to observe good faith towards each other, not personally as individuals, but as the respective heads of the Powers they represent in continuous succession, and no Treaty can in honor be modified without the consent of both the ruling powers therein represented.

The Treaties (Pages 6, 9, 12, 15, 22, 23, 26) referred to in my former Memorials, were entered into by the Honorable East India Company with my ancestors, Nawabs Meer Mahomed Jaffir Ali Khan, Nudjm-ul-dowlah, Syef-ul-dowlah, and Mobaruck-ul-dowlah, and are dated respectively 4th June, 1757, 10th July, 1763, 25th February, 1765, 30th September, 1765, 19th May, 1766, and 21st March, 1770.

Treaties (Pages 6, 9 and 12) were drawn up between the English East India Company, a *constituted* ruling power of the one part, and Nawab Meer Mahomed Jaffir Ali Khan a *constituted* ruling power of the other part, and having been entered upon by them in good faith, as the representatives of two Governments for mutual benefit, (as set forth in the Treaties) were in honor binding on them and their successors. On the death of Nawab Meer Jaffir Ali Khan, his eldest surviving son Nawab Nudjm-ul-dowlah, ascended the musnud as the legitimate successor; but, as the country was in an unsettled condition, in consequence of the war then carrying on against Nawab Shujah-ul-dowlah —the ruling powers evidently deemed it expedient for their mutual security, to add some special clauses to the Treaty with Nawab Meer Jaffir, which they accordingly did by the supplementary Treaty and Agreement of 1765, after going through the preliminary form of ratifying and confirming the original one, which really was the basis of their operations, and was intended to last for ever, or at least so long as their successors acted in concert with one another and observed mutual friendly relations.

Soon after the accession of Nawab Nudjm-ul-dowlah, the grant of the Dewanny was conferred upon the East India Company by the King of Delhi, under certain stipulations to which they, as well as the Nawab, acceded, viz.: "*They would remit the sum of twenty-six lacs of rupees annually to the Royal Government, and provide for the expenses of the Nizamut, reserving whatever balance might remain out of the revenues of the three provinces of Bengal, Behar, and Orissa, after paying the above, for their own use*" (Page 21). This necessitated a new clause in the Treaty with the Nawab, which was added in Sept., 1765. The object of this clause is obvious from its wording. The East India Company being men of business and unwilling to run the risk of clashing with their firm allies, the house of Meer Jaffir, by an undefined settlement of accounts, at once proposed a fixed amount in full of all demands, as the Nizamut's share of the revenues of the provinces, which was, after due consideration, accepted by the Nawab, who reposed implicit confidence in the honour of the British nation, and its representatives, and agreed to the sum named "as an adequate allowance for the support of the Nizamut," to be regularly paid, not only during his lifetime, but "*as long as the English Company's factories continue in Bengal.*" (Page 22)

On the accession of Nawab Syef-ul-dowlah some further additions were found necessary for the mutual benefit of the ruling Powers, and accordingly another supplementary Treaty and Agreement was drawn out, and connected with the original Treaty of Nawab Meer Jaffir, and also the additional ones with Nawab Nudjm-ul-dowlah by an article ratifying and confirming them all. The object of the additional clauses is clear. The East India Company, seeing the disadvantages of a Government with divided responsibilities, *undertook the whole of the military*, as well as the civil duties of the Provinces, in consideration of the Nawab allowing them to take twelve lacs of rupees annually from his stipend for the support of the troops, and this Agreement was also intended to be observed "*as long as the English factories continue in Bengal.*" (Page 24)

When Nawab Mobaruck-ul-dowlah ascended the musnud, the last

Supplementary Treaty was drawn out, and also connected with the original Treaty with Nawab Meer Jaffir, and the other supplementary ones, by the leading article ratifying and confirming them all. The object of this Treaty was evidently *to secure a permanent pecuniary arrangement* with the house of Meer Jaffir, on more favourable terms to the Company; for by this time the Hon. East India Company, having had the entire collection of the revenues of the Provinces for five years, were enabled to form a pretty correct idea of the returns available, after paying the Royal Government, and meeting the expenses of their Civil and Military Establishments, &c.; and as it is probable that they at the time had heavy demands upon their Treasury, owing to the unsettled state of the country, they no doubt proposed the reduction in the Nawab's share of the revenues to such a sum as they could always meet without being placed in difficulty themselves, they being the responsible financiers of the State. Thus far, all the modifications in the Treaties having been executed with the mutual consent of the contracting parties, were apparently plain and straightforward, and consistent with the principles of justice and honour, and since the sum last assigned for Nizamut purposes (Rs. 31,81,991-9) was so small a proportion of the revenues of the provinces that it need never have been reduced, the Treaty with Mobaruck-ul-dowlah, concludes by invoking a blessing from the Almighty as a guarantee that it would be "*inviolably observed for ever.*" (Page 27)

It is argued in the despatch (Page 279) that "the Company "*undertook to perform the duties of the Nizamut*, and *made pro-* "*vision for its expenses* by paying their own servants to do the "work which had before been done by the servants of the Nazim. "The office of the *Nizamut* being thus *practically abolished*, and its "duties merged into general administration of the country, *the stipu-* "*lation of the Imperial Firman ceased with the objects for which it* "*was intended to provide.* I am of opinion, therefore, that the family "of the Nawab Nazim of Bengal have under the Firman of Shah "Allum no claim upon the British Government. But *the administra-* "*tive duties of the Nizamut having been transferred to the Company*, "a personal provision was made for the family of the Nazim. It was "right that consideration should be shown to the sons of Meer Jaffir "Ali," &c. I would respectfully urge, Your Grace, that when examined without prejudice, the above argument will be found to be based on a misconception of the meaning of the word *Nizamut*. The word *Nizamut* is synonymous with the English term Royal Family, and can only be applied to the Nawabs Nazim, not as the Government, but merely as the titled heads of it, since they had no more to do with *the practical administrative duties* of the Government than the Sovereigns of Europe now have.

In proof of this, Your Grace, it is observable that in the second Supplementary Treaty with Nawab Nudjm-ul-dowlah, although the principal portion of the duties of the State, that is the Dewanny, or Civil Administration, of the three provinces of Bengal, Behar and Orissa, together with the revenues thereof, had been conferred on the English Company by the Emperor of Delhi, the grant was subject to certain conditions set forth in the Firman by which it was conferred, one of which was, "*there shall be a sufficient allowance out of the said revenues for supporting the expenses of the Nizamut,*" or Nazim's family; and again the Nawab agreed to a certain fixed sum "*as an adequate allowance for the expenses of the Nizamut,*" which expenses are distinctly specified under two heads, viz.: Rs. 17,78,854—1 for household or family expenses, and Rs. 36,07,277—8 for guards and personal palace attendants befitting his rank and station. Again, from the corresponding clause of the Treaty with Nawab-Syef-ul-dowlah, where the Nizamut stipend was fixed at the reduced figure of Rs. 41,86,131—9, in consideration of the Company having undertaken the *whole* of the military administration of the provinces, which the Nawab agreed should "*be entirely left to their discretion and good management,*" as he would thus be relieved from all pecuniary responsibility in the affairs of Government without lowering his political status as a titular prince, it is evident that the word *Nizamut* meant *the family of Nazims*, and not the Administrative Government.

The same fact may be proved from the last Treaty with Nawab Mobaruck-ul-dowlah; and since it was an agreement that was "*to be inviolably observed for ever,*" it is reasonable to suppose that the Nizamut stipend, as then fixed at Rs. 31,81,991—9, should *in honour and justice* have been regularly paid by the Government of India to each Nawab who has since succeeded.

It is further stated in the Despatch (Page 279), in allusion to the Treaties of 1766 and 1770:—" In each of these Treaties the Nawab " expressly indicated himself as the person to whom these advantages " are to accrue, and I cannot perceive that in either case the Nawab " who was party to the Treaty had any regard to other interests " than his own."

Surely, Your Grace, it is not reasonable to suppose that the Honourable Company and the Nawabs, when executing these Treaties, had no regard to their successors—for not only does the Despatch from the Honourable Court of Directors of 20th April 1771, contradict this view of the question, but the Treaties themselves being based on the Imperial Firman which expressly stipulated for the "*providing for the expenses of the Nizamut*" did not require the insertion of any special clause to secure this object—particularly as it had, in the first instance, been expressed in the Treaty with Nawab Nudjm-ul-dowlah at the time of the grant of the Dewanny.

Again the supposition that "the Nawab who was party to the Treaty, 'had no regard to other interests than his own,' " is not borne out by the wording of the articles of the Treaties, inasmuch as, the Honourable Company's interests, as set forth in all the previous Treaties, were fully secured, while at the same time the Nawab relinquished much that he was fairly entitled to by those Treaties. Hence, on these grounds it cannot fairly be argued that the Treaties were of a purely personal character. But even supposing the Nawab Mobaruck-ul-dowlah executed the Treaty from "purely personal motives, regardless of the advantages derived by the Honourable Company"— yet the Honourable Company on their part having guaranteed that it would be "*inviolably observed for ever,*" were *in honour and justice* bound to fulfil the conditions therein named.

It may possibly be urged that the words "*for ever*" bear no signification and are redundant; but with respect to this, permit me to state, Your Grace, that Treaties are generally framed by rational beings, and when their effect is intended to be limited, such limitation is expressly notified, as in the Treaty, with the Nawab Nudjm-un dowlah, which contemplated an existence only "*so long as the Factories of the English continue in Bengal.*" Even this could never have been intended to cease with the life of Nudjm-ul-dowlah; but was concluded in those words rather as an inducement for his successors to continue to support the authority of, and remain the firm allies of the English, who, on their part, guaranteed to support the succession, and adhere to the terms of the Treaties so long as they continued in Bengal.

Again, it is irrational to suppose that in the last Treaty with Mobaruck-ul-dowlah, the solemn invocation to the Almighty asking His blessing on *the inviolable observance "for ever"* of the Treaty was accidental, and that the Treaty was really intended only to last during the life-time of the Prince who executed it. It would be as rational to suppose that the dissolution of the Government of the East India Company absolved the British Government from all obligations contracted by that august body while ruling in the East, since virtually the death of the representatives contracting the obligations had taken place: yet Her Majesty in the Proclamation of 1858, with the advice of both Houses of Parliament, accepted the obligation to "*scrupulously maintain*" all Treaties entered into by the Honourable East India Company.

It is not for a Prince in my position, crushed and trampled down as I have been, to presume to criticise the acts of a powerful Government, who have declared that it is by their "free grace and favour" alone that I hold my position: and who on my attempting, in 1860, to bring facts to their notice, were pleased to remark, that I was guilty of discourtesy and want of respect to the British Government. I, however, feel thankful that in this free country, where I now sojourn, I can lay my grievances at once before Her Majesty's Government in a true and faithful light, without fear of giving offence, and with a full assurance that justice will be done me without prejudice. I will, therefore, with Your Grace's permission, bring to the notice of Her Majesty's Government, an act of injustice which laid the foundation of all the pecuniary difficulties in which the successors of Nawab Meer Jaffier Ali Khan have since been involved, and led to the introduction of all the measures which have since tended to lower the political and social status of my family.

The Treaty with Mobaruck-ul-dowlah (even if considered, for the sake of argument, as a personal one between a powerful Government and a powerless Prince), was a solemn engagement binding the Government to pay him the full allowance of Rs. 31,81,991-9, during his lifetime. Yet the Government, during the minority of the Prince, withheld Rs. 15,81,991-9, on the ground that sixteen lacs were enough for any Nawab *during his minority*; and further when His Highness came of age, no portion of the sums withheld was restored to him, nor was his stipend raised to the amount stipulated for in the Treaty although the Munnee Begum repeatedly appealed to the Government on the subject, under an assurance from the Governor-General, Mr.

Warren Hastings, that the full amount would be paid when the Nawab reached his majority. The following quotation, from a Despatch to the Government of India will fully elucidate my remarks, and leave Your Grace in full possession of all the facts connected with this subject.

The Court of Directors wrote as follows:—"In noticing the "encomiums you pass upon your own abilities, we cannot but ob- "serve with astonishment, that an event of so much importance as "the death of Nawab Syef-ul-dowlah, and the establishment of a "successor in so great a degree of non-age, should not have been "attended *with those advantages to the Company* which such a "circumstance affords to your view. We mean not to disapprove "*the preserving the succession of the family of Meer Jaffir;* on the "contrary, *both justice and policy recommended the measure*, but "when we consider the state of minority of the new Soubadhar, we "know not on what ground it could have been thought necessary to "continue to him the stipend allowed to his adult predecessor; con- "vinced as we are, that an allowance of sixteen lacs per annum will "be sufficient for the Nawab's state and rank, *while a minor*, we "must consider every addition thereto as so much to be wasted. You "are, therefore, *during the non-age of the Nawab*, to reduce his annual "stipend to sixteen lacs of rupees." (Page 31)

From the above, it is evident that the Honourable Court of Directors considered themselves bound *in justice* to abide by the Treaties which *guaranteed the succession* to the descendants of Meer Jaffir, as also the payment of the full amount stipulated for, to the respective heirs when they arrived at their majority (although they ordered their representatives in India to withhold a portion *during the minority of Nawab Mobaruck-ul-dowlah*); I would, therefore, leave it for Your Grace to consider why this just conclusion was not afterwards acted up to: and I may here be allowed to draw a parallel between the history of the house of Meer Jaffir, in their relations with the Honourable Company, and that of any of the European Allied Princes or Noblemen in their relations with their Sovereigns. In Europe it was customary, during the early periods of Government, for Supreme Rulers to enter into treaties with their Allies (Princes and Nobles), and to give them grants of land, and privileges under Royal Warrant, or Charter, for the purpose of securing their allegiance, and that of their successors, or, as marks of Royal favour in return for services rendered to the Sovereign. The recipients of these ad- vantages were generally the heads of military bodies, and assisted in protecting the countries over which their Sovereign held sway. In process of time military organization underwent many changes, until at length, in the present day, all trace of the feudal system has been lost. Yet the Allied Princes and Nobles are allowed to retain all the advantages conferred upon their ancestors, from generation to generation, except in those countries where revolutions have destroyed the landmarks of ancient grandeur, and over-thrown the Ruling Power. But no revolution has overthrown the British Government of India: then why should the family and successors of Meer Jaffir, the faithful allies of the British Government, be trampled down? Your Grace, my ancestors were faithfully attached to the

British cause, and I myself have done all in my power to support the British rule in India, by placing my available resources at the command of the Government, *when circumstances required it* (vide Letters Pages 199 to 209.) Yet I have never solicited any reward or recognition of my services beyond what I consider I am entitled to by Treaty, and although other Princes have had titles conferred upon them, and even one of my servants was honoured with a distinguished mark of esteem, I myself have never received any consideration, nor has even justice been accorded to my claims, though I have earnestly entreated for it. Even the descendants of rebels, and those who opposed the British, and resisted their establishment in India, have been liberally dealt with, while I, following the good example of my ancestors, and *fully confiding in the good faith and honour of the British nation as expressed in Treaties, and in the written declarations of Governors-General*, have heard it said that all those statements were mere idle expressions, and bore no signification whatever. It is a hard matter, Your Grace, for an Eastern Prince, brought up to believe implicitly in the good faith and honour of the British nation, to hear any one say that Public Treaties, Proclamations, and Official Letters are used as means for practising Political deception. No, Your Grace, I cannot credit this, and rather than that such should be proved to me, I pray the Almighty may remove me from this world, so that I may die, as I have lived, in the firm conviction that *British honour and public faith are unimpeachable*, and that *the word and bond of the British can never be changed*. I will never believe that the Treaties drawn up with my ancestors are otherwise than binding on the British nation, since it is impossible that the representatives of a Christian Government calling themselves Christians, and fearing God, would invoke His Holy name for purposes of deception and spoliation.

I now desire to draw Your Grace's attention to the consideration of the question, whether the Treaties alluded to were regarded by the contracting parties as merely personal, or whether they were held to possess an *hereditary nature*. It is now said, that they were of a personal character, but I would ask: " Did the Honourable East India Company take this view of the Treaties? Did they allege, on the death of Mobaruck-ul-dowlah that all Treaty obligations between them and the Nizamut Family had ceased? On the contrary, so late as 1840, after I had succeeded to the Musnud of the Nizamut, the Honourable the Court of Directors refer to the annual stipend of *sixteen lacs* as " the Assignment by Treaty of the Family." (Page 108)

Again, reviewing the Treaties, it will be seen that there was no need for a fresh Treaty on the death of Mobaruck-ul-dowlah, since the policy which dictated the acquisition of the entire Administrative Government of Bengal, Behar, and Orissa, by means of Treaties, had by that time been crowned with a success as unprecedented as it was complete.

The last Treaty confirmed the transfer of the military defence of the Provinces from *the Nizamut* to the Honourable East India Company in perpetuity and *guaranteed a permanent compensation* for this; there was, therefore, nothing more to treat for; and it is not to the point to enquire now, why the Honourable Company did not, in 1770, take possession of the Provinces *by right of the strongest*, and at once ignore the necessity of making Treaties! On the contrary, it is this fact that demands attention, that by Treaty the Honourable East India Company gradually obtained possession of these Provinces, and when the last of these Treaties was framed they in return specially engaged in making it binding "*for ever.*" It may well then be enquired, whence the necessity for new Treaties when so clear a guarantee had been given of the duration of the last one executed? For it is sufficiently proved that the contracting parties recognised *the existing ralidity* of the last Treaty, as shown in the Honourable Court's Despatch, dated the 24th April, 1840, and also from the uninterrupted harmony of succession up to my period!

Again, from the following extract of a letter (quoted at length under the third head of this Memorial) written on 20th February, 1834, by Mr. (now Sir Charles) Trevelyan, Your Grace will observe that the Governor-General in Council admitted the existence and application of the Treaty of 1770, and in alluding to the prescriptive rights and privileges of the Nawab Nazim as secured by that Treaty said, " It will " be observed from the Treaty (1770) of which a copy is annexed, that " His Highness the Nawab has been recognised by the British Govern- " ment as an Independent Prince, and that the National Faith is " pledged, '*for nothing being proposed or carried into execution dero-* " *gating from his honour.*'" And when commenting on the unadvisedness of allowing the Supreme Court to have jurisdiction over the Nawab Nazim, His Lordship remarks: "As the Government has no " power to regulate the proceedings of this Court towards persons ac- " knowledged to come within its jurisdiction, if the liability of the Na- " zim were to be admitted, there is no degree of indignity which might " not be inflicted upon him by its ordinary processes, *in contravention of* " *the pledged National Faith, and of the respect which is obviously due* " *the representative of our oldest ally on this side of India.*" His Lordship further states in the last para. of this letter, " the Nawab " Nazim is a Prince whose independence has been recognised by a "Treaty with one of his predecessors." It is very evident from the above (exclusive of other documentary evidence) that the Government of India acknowledged without reservation that the Treaty of 1770 was binding in perpetuity, and instructed their officers to view it in the same light, and to plead the same under their authority in Her Majesty's Supreme Court at Calcutta. Surely, Your Grace, there can be no doubt about the truth of the above assertions, for the Government would never have used them for the purpose of misleading the Supreme Court (at that time the only emblem of Her Majesty's authority in the East.) Had they been expressed to an Indian Prince, they might have been considered as licenses of rhetoric; but such could not possibly be the case when addressed to a Court, presided over by British judges of the highest legal qualifications, at the head of whom was the venerated Chief Justice Sir Edward Ryan. (Page 93).

Further, Your Grace, Her Majesty, in Her gracious Proclamation of the 1st November, 1858, to the Princes, Chiefs, and People of India, accepted the obligations of the Honourable East India Company with respect to Treaties with the Princes of the land; and it is therefore very difficult to surmise whence arose the doubt that led the

Government of India in 1862 to assert, that the Nizamut existed alone "by the free grace and favour of the British Government." The fact is, Your Grace, that recently, most unfortunately for myself, circumstances have placed me in a most invidious position with respect to the Government of India, and it is a just and impartial review of these circumstances, which alone will place me in the position I ought to occupy with respect to that Government.

These circumstances will, in the course of this Memorial, form separate heads needing separate investigation; so, before bringing them to Your Grace's notice, I will proceed to lay before Your Grace some documents which clearly exhibit the Political position of the Nawab Nazim, as recognized by the Indian Government of the Honourable East India Company, up to the last Governor-General appointed by that august body. Leaving aside all others which are to the same purport, I beg to adduce the following letters addressed to me by their (late) Lordships the Marquis of Dalhousie and Earl Canning, on their respectively assuming the Administration of India; letters which are, in fact, the ratifications of the Treaties with my ancestors. The first of these is dated the 12th January, 1848, and is as follows:—

"Nawab Sahib, of high worth and exalted station, my good brother, "may peace be with you.

"After expressing wishes, words cannot describe, for a joyful meet"ing; what I have now the pleasure officially to announce, you will "have heard through the ordinary channel—my appointment of "Governor-General of India; I arrived at Calcutta, and assumed the "duties of my office on the 12th January, 1848.

"Your Highness may be assured this friend is desirous, and bent "heart and soul to do all he can to knit the ties of attachment and "friendship, and to connect the bonds of harmony and concord be"tween the Honourable East India Company and your Highness, and "that personal sentiments of the highest regard and esteem, should "confirm the relations between us, while zealously striving to promote "the interest, establish the authority, and maintain the best under"standing between all the States and Sirdars of Hind, and the Deccan, "and this High and Paramount Power, by strict observance of word "and bond, and enduring fulfilment of compact and treaty, in terms "of existing conditions, stipulations and articles arranged and con"certed."

(Signed) "DALHOUSIE."

The second is dated the 11th March, 1856, and is as follows:—

"Nawab Sahib, of high worth and exalted station, my good brother, "I wish you peace."

"After expressing devoted desire beyond description for a happy "interview, I would announce what you will have gleaned from the "newspapers of the 29th February last, that this friend has been ap"pointed to succeed the most noble, the Marquis of Dalhousie, K.T., "as Governor-General of India."

"Permit me to add, this friend entered Calcutta, the seat of Government and assumed the duties of this high office on the 26th February, 1856, corresponding to the 22nd Jumadee-ul-Sanee, 1272, H."

"Your Highness may be assured the consideration, respect, and friendly interest in the prosperous administration of your affairs, and just regard to the honors and dignities due to your hereditary rank, and the prescriptive privileges of your high station, guaranteed by the stipulations of subsisting Treaties and long-established relations observed and cherished by former Governors-General will, on the part also of this sincere friend, be fervently fostered and punctually fulfilled,"

(Signed), "CANNING."

It is for Your Grace to decide whether these letters do not bear strong internal evidence of the *hereditary* nature of the Treaties? and whether, in the words "*the prescriptive privileges of your high station, guaranteed by the stipulations of subsisting Treaties, and long-established relations,*" there is not overwhelming evidence to set aside the supposition that those Treaties were of a personal character?

There is one more quotation with which I will trouble Your Grace, and it is in such plain and unmistakeable language as appears to me to admit of no misinterpretation. It is as follows:—

PROCLAMATION.

"Fort William, Political Department,"
"19th December, 1838."

"By order of the Government of India, the Deputy-Governor of Bengal notifies to the Public, and to the Allies of the British Government, and to all friendly powers, that Nawab Shooja-ool-Moolk, Ihtisham-ood-dowlah, Humayoon Jah, Syud Moobaruck Ali Khan Bahadoor Feroze Jung, having departed this life at Moorshedabad, on the 3rd October, 1838, his son, the Nawab Syud Munsoor Ali Khan, has succeeded to the hereditary honors and dignities of the Nizamut and Subadary of Bengal, Behar, and Orissa; and His Highness is hereby declared, under the authority of the Government of India, to be the Nazim and Soobadar of Bengal, Behar, and Orissa, and to have assumed, and to exercise the authority, dignities and privileges thereof, and under the style and title of Moontazm-ool-Moolk, Mohsen-ood-Dowlah, Fureedoon Jah, Syud Munsoor Ali Khan Bahadoor Nusrut Jung.

"Published and proclaimed by
"His Honor the Deputy-Governor of Bengal,"
(Signed), "H. T. PRINSEP,"
"Secretary to the Government of Bengal."

"*General* **Order by** *the Honorable the Deputy-Governor* **of**
"*Bengal, under date the* 19*th December,* **1838."**

"The Honorable the Deputy-Governor of Bengal has been pleased
"to direct that **a salute of 19 guns** be fired from the ramparts of Fort
"William at 12 o'clock this day, in honor of the accession of His High-
"ness Syud Munsoor **Ali Khan to** the Musnud of the Provinces of
"Bengal, Behar, **and Orissa,** and that the above **Proclamation** be read
"at the head of **the troops in garrison at sunset this evening under a**
"**salute of three volleys of musketry.**"
 (Signed)   "H. T. Prinsep,"
   "Secretary to the Government of Bengal."

The above Proclamation and General Order appeared in **the** *Calcutta Gazette* of Wednesday, 19th December, **1838,** and **it is for Your Grace** to consider what interpretation should **be** put upon the words "succeeded" and "hereditary" which occur in the body of this Proclamation. Were these words used in the full belief of *the Rights of the Nizamut being based on certain Treaties,* or is **no** importance to be attached to their signification?

Only three years previous **to** the date of this Proclamation, the Government of India **in the person** of Lord William Bentinck, addressed his Highness, my father Nawab Humayoon Jah, in the **following** words :—

"Your Highness will experience the **same disposition to cultivate and**
"improve **the** existing harmony and good understanding between the
"two Governments, **and** *an inviolable adherence* **to** *the engagements by*
"*which your Highness* **and** *the Honorable Company are* **indissolubly**
"*connected.*"

And again a year later, Lord Auckland wrote as follows :—

"Your Highness may be assured that I am cordially disposed to
"maintain the relations of harmony and friendship subsisting between
"the two States, to establish the utmost degree **of** individual friend-
"ship with your Highness, and to seek the confidence of all the States
"and chiefs of Hindostan and the Deccan, *by a scrupulous adherence*
"*to subsisting engagements, and to the obligations of public faith and*
"*honor.*"

It is the relations between the Honorable East India Company and the Nizamut that I would solicit an investigation of. What were the views the Government of India entertained of the obligations and engagements between it and the Nizamut? **Lord** Bentinck **is** most clear on this point, when in the letter quoted **above,** he pledges himself to "**an** inviolable adherence **to the** engagements by which your High-
"ness **and the** Honorable Company are indissolubly connected."

The **next point to** which I deem it right to draw Your **Grace's attention while** on this subject, is that portion of the **Despatch (Page** 280), where **it has** been argued that the Treaty **with His Highness** Moobaruck-ul-Dowlah fell through, for **as** the Nawabs Nazim since then have **received** the reduced allowance of sixteen lacs **the Treaty** ceased to **have effect.**

I would gladly forbear discussing this question; but since it has been so prominently put forth to my prejudice, I consider it proper to bring it to Your Grace's notice as a breach of faith, and to inquire whether this breach of one of the Articles of the Treaty was at the instance of the Nizamut?

The young Nazim was a minor, a mere child, without power to redress his wrongs, and the only person about him who exercised control in his affairs was the Munnee Begum, "the Mother of the Company," as she was styled by that August Body, on account of her deep attachment and sincere devotion to their solid interests. She, poor infatuated lady, was led to believe by Mr. Warren Hastings, that the arrangement which thus reduced the Treaty allowances to about one-half, was simply *a temporary one to last during the minority of the young Nazim*, and so she lived on in this vain hope, confiding to the last in the good faith of the Honourable Company, that all would come right in the end. The Court of Directors did not ignore the Treaty, they merely rebuked their Governor for not taking advantage of the "non-age of the Nawab to reduce the annual stipend during "his minority," and ordered: "You are, therefore, *during the non-"age of the Nawab*, to reduce the annual stipend to sixteen lacs." In even this, though there was not a breach of Treaty, there was an apparent breach of faith unsought, unmerited, and unatoned for. The Treaty obligations, it is very evident, were never meant to be set aside, because "both justice and policy recommended the measure of "preserving the succession of the family of Meer Jaffir." Yet successive Governors-General, from that period up to the last Governor-General of the Honourable Company, have admitted the annual allowance *of sixteen lacs only* as "the Assignment by Treaty of the "family," though each, and all of them have recognised "the en-"gagements by which the Nizamut and the East India Company were "indissolubly connected."

But the question may suggest itself to Your Grace: What could have led the Government of India to alter its views on this subject?

If Lord Dalhousie, in 1848, acknowledged "the strict observance of "word, and bond, and enduring fulfilment of compact and Treaty, in "terms of existing conditions, stipulations, and articles," how came His Lordship, in 1853, to urge that the Nizamut existed "on the "free grace and favour of the British Government?" The answer to this question will be found in the second head of my grievances, to which I now beg to draw Your Grace's attention, viz.:—

II.—THE UNJUSTIFIABLE ATTITUDE ASSUMED BY HIS LORDSHIP, THE MARQUIS OF DALHOUSIE, TOWARDS MYSELF ON ALL QUESTIONS RELATING TO THE NIZAMUT ON A MISCONCEPTION OF MY BEING IN SOME WAY CONNECTED WITH A BASE OUTRAGE COMMITTED BY SOME MENIAL SERVANTS, OF WHICH I WAS NOT EVEN COGNIZANT AT THE TIME.

In Para. II. of the Extract of the Despatch No. 30, dated the 17th

June, 1864, the late **Secretary of** State of Her Majesty's Government, in noticing the abrogation of certain enactments that protected *the rank and dignity of the Nizamut* expressed himself in the following words: "that Act XXVII of 1854," which repealed those enactments, "can on no account be repealed in consequence of an outrage which "was considered at the time by the Government both in India and "in England to have been attended with a large amount of culpability "on the part of the Nawab Nazim."

Your Grace will, I trust, take an impartial view of this matter as I cannot allow such an aspersion on my character to pass unnoticed. I therefore solicit your attentive perusal of the following statement of facts connected with that deplorable case, in proof of the absence of any knowledge on my part of the occurrence adverted to.

On the 31st March, 1853, I was out on a shooting excursion with a suite of about 2,000 persons, and during my absence, one Hossainee missed a box belonging to his master, Meah Urjoomund, one of my eunuchs. It appears that a lad named Muddee was suspected of having stolen the missing property, and he was seized and beaten. I most solemnly declare that I knew not a word of all this at the time, for the chastisers, well-knowing my disposition, and the certainty of incurring my utmost displeasure if the matter came to my knowledge, most carefully concealed it from me. However, as it afterwards appeared, on being beaten, the lad Muddee pointed out a vagrant, named Hingoo, as his accomplice in the theft, and this man was similarly seized and beaten. Up to a full month after their death, I knew not a word about the matter, nay I pledge myself that I was not even made acquainted with the circumstances of any person's property being missing. On the 5th May following, a petition was presented to the Dewance Sherista, or Dewan's office of the Nizamut purporting to be from the mother of the lad Muddee, accusing Aman Ali Khan, my chief eunuch (who at the time was acting Dewan), and several others of the murder of her son. It was thus, and then, that I came to hear of the matter, and at once ordered a strict inquiry to be made, which, had I wished to screen the accused I would not have done. All the witnesses deposed that the lad had died of cholera. The Hakeem **Jumook** deposed that he had treated the lad for cholera, by administering laudanum and calcined gold. And he (the doctor) further stated, that ten or twelve other persons had died of cholera in the camp, and many more in the villages in the neighbourhood. The brother and mother of Muddee deposed that she had presented no petition to any one, and that her seal was not on the one produced. Etwari, the father of the lad, declared he had seen him die of cholera. All these statements led me to believe that the lad had actually died of cholera, more especially as Aman Ali Khan, the person particularly accused, had been with me from my childhood, and I having been accustomed to repose entire confidence in him, naturally concluded that the writer of the petition was one of his enemies, who had thus sought to prejudice me against him.

That Aman Ali Khan had a great many enemies, owing to his elevation, I was well aware of, and I will candidly own that I was biased considerably in his favour by this fact, and therefore regarded the petition, after hearing the declarations of the witnesses, as a got-up slander. Besides, the declaration of Etwari, the lad's father, left no room for my young and inexperienced judgment (for I was only twenty-five years of age then) to arrive at any other conclusion than that some designing persons had adopted this nefarious method of doing an injury to an old officer of my establishment, and the one of all others whom I had been taught from my earliest childhood to regard with entire confidence. At this stage stopped all further active interference on my part with the case.

The accused persons were tried at Moorshedabad in September, 1853. On a careful perusal of the proceedings, the following conclusions can scarcely be avoided, viz.:—

1st. That although Muddee and Hingoo were said to have been most cruelly treated, and there was a probability that they died from the effects of the ill-treatment they received, there was no positive proof that they did so.

2ndly. There was apparently no concealment in the matter, as they were beaten openly. This might be urged against me, for not having been able to determine a fact, admitted in Court, to have been done openly; but the admission was a subsequent one, doubtless by the direction of counsel, when the accused stood on their defence on a most serious charge; whereas, in the investigation made before me, the accused probably did not contemplate that matters would take so serious a turn, and hoped, by concealment from me of every fact connected with their atrocious conduct to escape my displeasure, and their own certain dismissal and punishment.

3rdly. The only persons who accused Aman Ali of having been concerned in beating the poor unfortunate men, were Hossainee, the approver, who had lost the box (and who had undoubtedly beaten them himself) a leper, a temporary cook, a discharged Burkundaz (who lived chiefly by begging), and an elephant-driver (who had tied up the deceased). These men all gave contradictory evidence, and the Judges of the Sudder Nizamut felt constrained to discard the evidence of the first four witnesses *in toto*. Your Grace will observe the improbabilities in the evidence given, thus: The leper affirmed that "he saw "Aman Ali Khan, the chief of our officers in rank and authority, first "cutting a bamboo with his own hands, and then beating the deceased "with it!" A statement bearing the strongest marks of improbability on the face of it, so much so that the Sessions Judge pronounced this man's evidence "not entitled to much credit, as the discrepancies "in it are irreconcilable." The discharged Burkundaz declared "that "Muddee and Hingoo were brought before me, and I ordered their "release, but that Aman Ali Khan countermanded the order, and "threatened to blow them away from a gun." This person's evidence, to use the words of the Court, "teemed with improbabilities and gross "contradictions;" and such was the evidence for the prosecution.

On the other hand, three witnesses, in a more respectable station in life, declared on oath than Aman Ali Khan had not beaten the deceased; and they further testified that he, on hearing that the men had been beaten, at once ordered their release. George Shapcott, my coachman (whose evidence was universally acknowledged as trustworthy), testified under oath, "that when Muddee, at the village of

"Nowguriah accused a third person, named Hingoo, the latter was "seized, and would have been beaten by the camel-driver, who had "most cruelly beaten Muddee, when Shapcott interfered, and by the "use of Aman Ali's name, effectually stayed the meditated injustice."

This witness was a European and a Christian, and his evidence, which was given "in a plain straightforward manner," as recognized by the Court, was "infinitely more trustworthy than either that of the "approver Hossainee (the real delinquent) or of the camel-driver, and "others for the prosecution." These wretched men were no doubt the real offenders, and both circumstantial and material evidence point to them as the guilty parties; but a chain of circumstances furnished them the opportunity of becoming witnesses for the prosecution, in the hope of extricating themselves from the difficulty their deeds had placed them in, when the case assumed a more serious aspect. The camel-driver was one of those sentenced to a long period of imprisonment, notwithstanding his most vigorously perjured efforts to lay the blame on one whose high station, he thought, would doubtless palliate the compliance to so overt an act. And it is a most singular fact, that the most interested parties, the father and mother of Muddee, do not appear as principals in the prosecution. It may be argued that they were bought over to silence, but this is an unnatural assumption, and is not tenable when it is taken into consideration that it was on the mother's supposed representation that the concealed facts came to form the subject of judicial enquiry. That Muddee and Hingoo came to a premature end, from the effects of the beating, may readily be supposed, but that Aman Ali was in any way mixed up in the affair cannot be credited for many reasons.

4th. There is an entire absence of motive to permit the assumption of Aman Ali's complicity in the death of these unfortunate men. The box which was stolen was not his, nor was it of material value. It belonged to a very subordinate officer in my service, and there is an air of improbability which militates against the supposition that a person in Aman Ali's position would have so interested himself about the recovery of a paltry article, the property of an insignificant officer, as to order the use of torture for the purpose of extorting a confession. At the same time, it is to be remembered that Aman Ali, as my confidential servant, had a host of enemies constantly seeking his downfall; hence, the Mahomedan Law Officer found Aman Ali "guilty of in-"stigating the beating on violent presumption, and of privity to the "crime on full proof." But there clearly was no proof that Aman Ali had ordered the men to be beaten, and the Sessions Judge gave his opinion as follows:—"After carefully weighing the whole of the "evidence against him, I am not satisfied with that part which would "implicate him as the instigator, which he would be if it were satis-"factorily proved that he gave orders for the two men to be beaten," and pronounced "that he was only proved to have been an accessory "after the fact."

The Sudder Nizamut, the highest Court of Justice in the country, considered that it was proved that the prisoner had forbidden the ill-treatment of the victims, and that there was "no proof of his being "accessory after the fact," and accordingly acquitted him. And since, with all the means of arriving at a just conclusion, the judges of the

Sudder Nizamut had pronounced Aman Ali innocent, surely there was nothing to be wondered at in the circumstance of my believing him to be innocent. I merely recognized the verdict of the Court; and Aman Ali, on being acquitted, was treated by me as innocent of any crime; for I should have considered it very harsh to have treated the man as guilty, when a body of duly qualified and highly competent judges had pronounced that "there was no proof of his being even "accessory after the fact." In the meantime, I had appointed another person to fill the office of Dewan, in place of Aman Ali, who had acted in that capacity without being formally invested with the duties of it, and I must now earnestly crave Your Grace's attention to the action taken by the Governor-General on this deplorable and much to be regretted case, since I must for ever abide by the decision of Her Majesty's Government as to whether it was just or unjust; whether all the circumstances of the case, when viewed together, admitted of my name being coupled with the atrocious villains who were convicted, and whether the Government acted arbitrarily or not, in depriving me of certain of my prescriptive rights on the groundless supposition of my being, in some way or other, culpable in the case, of which I have endeavoured to give Your Grace a true and faithful review.

Lord Dalhousie, in utter defiance of the solemn verdict of the highest Court of Justice in India, decided that Aman Ali was guilty, and that my act in agreeing with the Sudder Nizamut, and believing him innocent, was a proof of my own complicity in the murder. His Lordship might quite as reasonably have come to the same conclusion regarding the judges themselves, and summarily have suspended them, or discharged them, from their offices. His Lordship called for an explanation from me, (Page 129) and the expressions he used in so doing sufficiently show that he had previously made up his mind, not only as to the guilt of this acquitted eunuch, but also to my complicity in the affair. It was quite necessary, in His Lordship's opinion, "that the Nawab Nazim, under whose eyes this "monstrous outrage on humanity has "been perpetrated, should be required to give an explanation of his "conduct in the matter, that measures should be taken to mark the "sense entertained by Government of such proceedings, and that safe- "guards should be provided against a repetition of them in future." I was also required to state why I "failed to exercise my authority to "prevent the perpetration of so outrageous a crime, almost in my "very presence," thus taking for granted that I had been cognizant of it. These words clearly demonstrate that His Lordship had come to a premature conclusion, and that no explanation would alter his decision. The Governor-General pronounced that not only "had Aman "Ali failed to use the influence he had to prevent the crime" (though the Sudder Court had declared him ignorant of it), but that "from "his Highness's tent being only fifty yards from where the men were "tortured, and from his having the eunuchs daily to dine with him, "he must have been himself cognizant of the torture, of the death that "ensued from the torture, and of the falseness of the rumour which "ascribed the death of these men to cholera."

The first reasons assigned for this series of accusations, was that my tent had been pitched about fifty yards from the place where the unfortunate victims had been kept. Your Grace, my known gentleness and humanity of character, which are such that I cannot prevail on myself even to perform in *propriâ personâ* the sacrifices enjoined by our religion; my European education and ideas, the fact that I was absent from my tent during the greater part of each day, and that much, if not most, of the said cruelty took place at a distance from the camp, availed me nothing in His Lordship's opinion; though the evidence which proved that the men were beaten, established also that they were beaten:—

1st. In camp and before His Highness returned from shooting.
2nd. At a shop in the village.
3rd At the River Nowguriah.
4th. After His Highness returned and in a garden at some distance from the camp.
5th. Next day, and after His Highness had gone out shooting.
6th. Again at the river at Nowguriah.

On no occasion did it appear that the men were beaten while I was in camp; and even supposing such had been the case, it should not be forgotten how unlikely a few cries were to attract attention amid the noise and bustle of a large camp. What with the trumpeting of elephants, of which upwards of sixty were in the camp, the shouting of servants and camp-followers, of whom there were about 2,000, and last, though not least, the vigorous efforts to please of a full brass band, which played almost incessantly while I was within hearing, I maintain, Your **Grace**, that in the midst of a concatenation of such discordant noises, the possibility of hearing any particular cries was certainly rather remote.

Then, again, my tent was a double-walled one, surrounded again with a high Kanat, or thick cloth enclosure, and these facts should not be lost sight of in determining whether I could possibly have heard the cries of the men at the distance specified where the torture was said to have been inflicted. I can assure Your Grace, that such was the thickness of my tent, that it would have been impossible to distinguish cries outside it, even if no other noises prevailed around; but apart from my own assertions, it was clearly elicited from the entire evidence in Court, that the unfortunate men were never beaten in my presence nor in my hearing; and even supposing that they were clandestinely confined in a tent fifty yards from mine, yet it would by no means be inconsistent with all the collateral circumstances to believe that I was entirely ignorant of the matter. How frequently do occurrences of the greatest moment transpire almost under our very eyes, without our being at all cognizant of them; nay, more, the annals of how many trials record the evidence of individuals to certain facts, while the same persons swear to an ignorance of others, which it might be inferred they were assuredly acquainted with. Persons living in the upper story of a house have sworn positively to their not hearing cries of distress from the inmates of a lower story, and their testimony has been recognised as genuine in the Highest Courts and Tribunals of England, where every one receives due justice.

In this case the circumstances were of a nature that more than allowed the supposition of my utter ignorance of the atrocious crime committed, as it was not likely that the wretches, who were culpable, would communicate their guilt to their master, whose known humanity would have at once become the instrument for bringing them to the hands of justice, where they would meet with such punishment as their crime deserve. It was hardly probable that they would have had the temerity to come to their master and say, we have beaten two men to death, do you put your ægis over us to protect us from the consequences; nor is it likely that even those of my servants who were acquainted with any of the circumstances would make a confidant of me; on the contrary, as was really the case, their utmost vigilance was directed to a careful concealment of every fact, so that I might not obtain even an inkling of it.

The second reason his Lordship adduced, in accusing me of complicity, was, that the accused and acquitted eunuchs had "dined " daily with His Highness!" Would any one, especially the Prince, like to be made responsible for all the acts of those who dined daily with him? Would such persons be likely to choose, as the topic of their conversation on such occasions, their own implications in so atrocious an outrage as the one under notice supposes? It is to be remarked, that the only evidence which, in any way, might prove that Aman Ali knew of the accused persons being twice beaten, proved also that on each occasion he gave positive orders forbidding their ill-treatment. It was nowhere shown that he knew of the extent of the cruelty inflicted, or that it had resulted in death.

The truth seems to have been (from the Report of the case), that Aman Ali had heard of two beatings, which he, on both occasions sent to put a stop to; but that these beatings were continued, by the cameldriver and Hossainee, in whose charge the missing box had been, at a distance from the camp (as at Nowguriah), Aman Ali and the other eunuchs were at the time quite unaware of it. That the perpetrators themselves did not intend to kill their victims is also evident from the fact that, when they had gone too far, they called in the Hakeem to endeavour to cure the unfortunate men; and that the death of the poor men, and certainly the cause of it, was carefully concealed from my officers, and most especially from me. I thus remained in total ignorance of it, until the petition was presented to the Dewance Sherista.

Major MacGregor, the Governor-General's Agent, in writing on the subject to Government, remarked that, "His Highness had invariably " declared that he was never made cognizant of the fact that death en- " sued in consequence of the mal-treatment which the unfortunate " creatures, Hingoo and Muddee, received." On the same occasion, Major-General Raper, who perhaps knew my character, and understood my disposition better than any one, and who observed that, "as " a boy he had never shown the smallest propensity to cruelty or mis- " chief," and further added that, " former Agents and every one who " knows the Nazim speak of him as kind, generous, and humane."

Major MacGregor's opinion on my decision of the matter was " that the Nawab Nazim must have heard a false account of the " affair;" but I had heard no other than the account which was received by the Sudder Court, and I maintain I could not be blamed for coming to the same conclusion as that arrived at by the Honorable the Judges of that Court. However, that the Government might have no just ground of complaint against me, I immediately dismissed all the accused eunuchs, and on receipt of the Governor-General's letter, suspended **Aman Ali Khan** from his various employments, ordering him to give in his accounts as soon as possible. More than this I could **not** have done ; I could not have sent Aman Ali away at once, as he had to render his accounts of the Dewanship, so I suspended him, and nominated another officer to his post.

In my reply to the Governor-General, I expressed my grief at being held responsible for the conduct of my servants, and simply stated the undeniable facts, that during my shooting excursion it was my habit to start early in the morning, take my breakfast on my elephant, and, returning in the evening overcome by fatigue, soon retire to rest, and that, consequently, I knew very little of what went on in the camp. To these assertions, Mr. Garrett, the Judge of Beerbhoom, the Honorable Mr. Eden, late Secretary to the Government of Bengal, and other gentlemen who accompanied me, and who knew no more about the affair than I did, could have borne witness. I, at the same time, solemnly declared that it never came to my knowledge that a murder had been committed, and I further mentioned that when the subject was brought to my notice, I immediately instituted an enquiry, and it appeared from several statements that Muddee and Hingoo had died of cholera. In answer to the Governor-General's inquiry, why I "continued to show favor and countenance to those" (Aman Ali) "who" (in His Lordship's opinion) "were concerned in the murder," I very naturally said that when they were acquitted by the Sudder Court after being so strictly tried, I really thought them to be not guilty.

At first, under the impression that the Governor-General required the dismissal of the eunuchs, (though nothing is said of this in His Lordship's letter,) I discharged them all : but hearing nothing of the matter during an interval of four months, and then having information that the affair had been referred to the Honorable Court of Directors, and thinking that that just and humane body of gentlemen would never sanction such an injustice as punishing men for a crime of which they had been acquitted, nor sanction any interference with my own domestic arrangements, I, instead of depriving myself wholly of the services of the old and faithful attendants, permitted them to continue among my retinue, under a proviso that they should not exercise the functions of their several offices until the matter should be finally decided.

Importunity, and a natural feeling of attachment to old servants who had nursed me from my infancy, and whom I really thought to be perfectly innocent, led me to take this probably imprudent step : but the consequences of it, both to myself individually, and to my whole family, as the sequel will show, were most disastrous ; neither my rank nor dignity were spared, nor the right of the female members of my household recognized ; but everything was done to degrade me in the estimation of the whole country, for the Agent reported the matter to Government ; and stated, that "the eunuchs were still in my service, and that **Aman** Ali had resumed his duties as chief eunuch."

At length, on the 23rd March, 1854, the Governor-General pronounced my explanation "most unsatisfactory," and although I knew not of what fault I had been guilty, nor could I have urged anything beyond what I did in proof of the innocence of my servants, yet I was peremptorily ordered "to dismiss them altogether" from my service, and "to hold no further communication with any of them;" and the Agent was required "to report within one week whether this requisition had been complied with or not." Further, I was denied the privilege of going for change of air to Dinagepore though my health required it, as testified by Dr. Kean the Civil Surgeon of Moorshedabad, and his Lordship refused to sanction "under any circumstances," the usual disbursements from the Deposit Fund for my travelling expenses.

Such were the immediate steps taken by the Government with respect to me; but those which quickly followed, and were sanctioned by the Honorable Court of Directors at the instigation of the Administration in India, led to the lowering and disgrace of myself and my family. It may not be to the point, at so late a period as the present, to enter upon a discussion as to whether the eunuchs were innocent or guilty, but I hold, Your Grace, that they were innocent when declared to be so by a body of British Judges, and when such a decision was given in open Court, it became the duty of all persons to recognize and respect it in its entirety. Your Grace will, I hope, agree in my opinion, that it ill became the Head of the Government to furnish such an example to the community at large, as to call in question the patient investigations and findings of its own August Courts of Judicature, and to brand with incapacity its highest Officers of Justice, yet such was virtually the case, and a climax was attained when that Government went so far as to punish a defenceless Prince for doing his duty loyally in recognizing the Judgment of its Highest Tribunal.

Probably His Lordship supposed the eunuchs to be morally guilty; but it is to be borne in mind that the law, in its endeavours to suppress crime by punishing the guilty, affords a great latitude with respect to evidence, and even circumstantial and collateral facts are not disregarded by the Officers of Justice, particularly in a Court where legal acumen and evidence of various kinds are the predominant elements in deciding a case. Such was the Sudder Nizamut Court. It was presided over by British Judges of known worth, and was unencumbered with the risk of a packed jury. Its decisions were by the law and evidence, and in the case of the eunuchs, neither the law nor the evidence established their culpability; they were acquitted because they were innocent, and the really guilty parties were condemned to suffer as the law directed.

We frequently hear of persons being taken up on suspicion of having committed crimes, yet after trial, if they are declared innocent, they are as free as any other subjects of the realm, and are privileged to again move in society, and no society would condemn and brand as felons, men whom a twofold trial had declared innocent. Yet I was required, nay ordered, to summarily dismiss those eunuchs, and thus brand them with ignominy as guilty parties. It mattered little to the community at large whence this measure proceeded, and to the masses, its true cause was unknown. No one supposed that the summary ejectment of some of my oldest servants from my household was the act of the Governor-General, but each and all were impressed that I had acted harshly in believing them to be guilty contrary to the issue of a severe criminal trial. I had dismissed them, and my act in the estimation of the people of Bengal had unjustly branded them with a crime. Thus was the Nawab Nazim made to occupy a false position by the Act of the Government in 1854.

That I had been deeply wronged by the Government I felt convinced of; but at the same time I never contemplated the addition of an insult to that injury, as conveyed in the words of the late Secretary of State for India, which I have quoted at the opening of this subject.

As I desire to bring to Your Grace's notice the various encroachments made on my just rights by the Government, in consequence of the unjust supposition of my culpability in the atrocious outrage I have reviewed, I will, in the first place, notice them categorically, so that Your Grace may be enabled to view them in juxta position with the erroneous hypothesis on which they were based:—

1. I was summarily deprived, together with my family, (including the ladies), of all immunities and rights, which had been secured to us by Treaties, by solemn pledges from successive Governors-General, and by no less than four Acts of Council.

2. These four Acts were at once annulled.

3. It was urged that my rights and claims were not secured by the stipulations of Treaties.

4. The Deposit Fund, created by my ancestors, the former Nawabs Nazim, and punctually contributed to by me alone in the sum of sixty lacs of Rupees, was declared to be public money.

5. The Nizamut Deposit Fund was to be arbitrarily converted into a Book Debt bearing no interest, in direct opposition to the terms of the Trust.

6. A system of encroachment was initiated, which the Government have since constantly striven to mature, to the extinction of every privilege that was at one time mine by virtue of my rank and dignity.

These, Your Grace, are the consequences of the action taken by the Governor-General against me in 1854, and with your permission I will notice them *seriatim* in the course of this Memorial, my last appeal to the British Government for redress and justice; and in the meantime I pray Your Grace to move that Government, by a just setting forth of the facts of my case as laid before you, to cancel the harsh imputation conveyed in the words of the late Secretary of Her Majesty's Government for India, which I have quoted at the opening of this address.

III.—THE ABROGATION OF REGULATIONS OF 1805, 1806, AND 1823, BY ACT XXVII., OF 1854.

Your Grace, I beg to state that the abrogation of the Regulations above stated has directly had the effect of depriving me of the civil privileges and insignia of rank, "guaranteed by subsisting Treaties and long-established customs," and that the substitution of Act XXVII. under the Administration of Lord Dalhousie, if *justly and equitably* viewed, can be regarded only as a breach of that promise, which every Governor-General had repeated *to uphold the interests, dignity, credit, and prescriptive privileges* of the Nazims, and all the members of their family.

The three Regulations of 1805, 1806, and 1823, repealed by Lord

Dalhousie, defined the proper form in which the Nazims should be addressed, and the manner in which they were to sue and to be sued in Civil Cases. In conformity with that of 1823 all actions were carried on by the Governor General's Agent, upon whom also all processes were served. It was in addition provided that "*no security* "*should be required of the Nawab on any attachment issued against* "*the Nawab, or against the Agent.*" Without entering upon a discussion of the merits of the question, I will merely state for Your Grace's information that all native gentlemen in India consider themselves lowered in the estimation of the public by being compelled to appear before a Court of Justice in their own proper persons, whether as Plaintiffs or Defendants; and indeed such is the feeling in this matter, that inevitable loss will be contemplated, and met with perfect resignation, in preference to the degradation so much dreaded, of being forced into Court at some stage of the proceedings in a suit. I mention this only to show the general feeling of *the respectable classes of the natives of India* on the subject, and while I admit myself not prepared to argue the merits or demerits of a conventionality which tolerates such a feeling, I would merely pause to suggest, that if such a state of feeling be shared in by the *ordinary respectable classes of natives*, then how great a derogation from my rank as Nawab Nazim, must it be in the opinion of my fellow-countrymen when I am deprived of the privilege which properly raised me above the level of my menials. I need not assure Your Grace, that men of much inferior rank to myself, will make any sacrifice, by laying out large sums of money, and, in short, be prepared to do anything to escape the dreaded downfall of their reputation by having to appear in Court, and such being truly the case, how acutely must I, as the Nawab Nazim of Bengal feel in this matter, while the feeling of bitterness is enhanced by the reflection that the arbitrary measure of one Governor-General, framed in entire violation of the promises acted up to by all previous Governors-General, and also in opposition to measures, "*guaranteed by subsisting Treaties and long-established* "*Relations*" at once, and without just cause, deprived me of the privileges secured to me by the three Regulations, which were the only Legislative Enactments protective of the dignity attaching to my position. Thus in my case, the shame of deprivation of the privileges enjoyed by my ancestors, was added to the original prejudice, which I will frankly admit, has its influence with me, as with every other respectable native of India, otherwise I would be despised by all my countrymen.

According to the provisions of the Enactments of 1805, 1806, and 1823, it was ruled that all actions should be carried on by the Governor-General's Agent, and that all processes should be served upon him. I take the liberty to draw Your Grace's attention here to the fact that in 1823, in the time of my father, it was deemed expedient to provide by legislation for the rank and dignity of the Nawab Nazim, but in 1854 the aid of legislation was sought to deprive me of those very privileges which over and over again were recognized by the Government through a century, and were only after 1854 disregarded by the Honourable Court of Directors. The only boon conferred, as I have before stated, by the above named enactments, was the substitution of the Agent's name for mine in Civil Suits; it, of course, being held in view that all liabilities should be mine; then surely by taking into consideration the peculiar constitution of the office of Agent, and the resources whence he is paid, together with the incontestable fact that it is his duty "*to watch over and protect the interests and dignity of the "Nawab Nazim* and *to advance the welfare of the family*," it is not difficult to conclude that the boon secured me by the act, with respect to the services of the Agent, involved no extraordinary latitude of indulgence. I would here ask Your Grace to take into consideration the constitution of the office of Agent to the Governor-General, and to notice the result of the repeal of the three Regulations. I am now subjected to the indignity of being summarily summoned to the Courts of the pettiest Judicial officers, men who in the scale of Indian society would venture no further of themselves than to stand in my presence, and yet in their official position can legitimately issue orders and injunctions to me, and compel my attendance in their Courts, if I would avoid judgment going by default. Thus, in innumerable instances, I have been compelled by the arbitrary force of circumstances entailed by the repeal of these protective Enactments to make sacrifices and forego the process of law (which is necessary for the defence of unfounded claims and pretentions), and to think myself fortunate if compromises could be effected. All this might have been easily provided against by the insertion of a protective clause in the Legislative Enactments, and such a measure would have been in perfect harmony with "*existing Treaty rights*," which have over and over again been acknowledged as "*hereditary;*" for (and I do not seek to draw a wrong inference) if these previous Enactments flowed spontaneously from *a regard for the position of the Nawab Nazim, and with a view to maintain intact his dignity which various Treaties and solemn engagements distinctly provided for*, then the protection provided by the Government cannot but be held as binding now as it was in the time of my father. I therefore appeal with confidence to Your Grace's sense of justice against the policy initiated by Lord Dalhousie, and since then cherished and pursued by succeeding Governors-General with respect to these rights. It may be urged by the Indian Government against my argument, that I can claim exemption under the new code from attendance in the Civil Courts; but this exemption is a favour granted to innumerable native gentlemen, and ought I as Nawab Nazim to descend to the level of men of ordinary position, who will try to meet me on terms of equality? There is surely something more due to the Nawab Nazim of Bengal, the faithful Ally of the British Government, than to the ordinary Zemindar, who presents himself before the Nazim with a "Nuzzer" in his outstretched hands! Even social etiquette requires some mark of respect consequent on social position, as perpetuated through successive generations, and holding this fact in view, I might well pause to reflect on the policy of an Executive Administration that would simply ignore my social existence, and degrade me in the eyes of my countrymen, by forcing me to claim an exemption *which is mine by right;* for however practicable such a step might be in a European community, I need not assure Your Grace that in

India it is at once incompatible with my rank, which has been "*guaranteed*" by successive Administrations, dating from the history of the British rule in that country.

But if the repeal of these Regulations, and the substitution of another, has proved injurious to myself (in not lowering my status, but in forcing me to suffer pecuniary losses in the manner already described), then (holding in view the customs of my country), how infinitely more oppressive has this arbitrary measure proved to the ladies of my household. However, that Your Grace may realize the extent of this grievance, I will endeavour to show Your Grace that it is one which, if not provided against, must inevitably lead to the utter destruction in public estimation of that rank which I have inherited. Your Grace must be aware that according to the usages of Oriental society, the affording of security from impertinent curiosity to the female members of his family, is an obligation positively incumbent on an Eastern gentleman, but on none more so than a person of high rank, and an inevitable consequence of a dereliction of this duty is simply to expect isolation from social intercourse, or, at least, degradation in the estimation of the community from the status previously occpied. Such being the rule of Oriental society, it was wisely provided by the three legislative enactments already alluded to, that whenever it was necessary to take the evidence of any lady of the Nizamut family, *three creditable female members of the family conducted the inquiry and reported its issue*, but now, as the case stands, Her Highness my mother, or any other lady of rank, such as my wife or sister, may, on the most frivolous pretext, be subjected to examination by Commissions, which "may be issued to any officer of the Court or other person." One of the immediate results of such a state of things is the encouragement which is thus given to crafty adventurers to apply for commissions to examine the ladies of the Nizamut ; and as they know that I would be prepared for almost any sacrifice rather than permit a proceeding that would expose a lady of my house to the indignity of an examination by a petty officer of the Court, they take advantage of circumstances, and, by working upon my feelings, force me to accept their terms, and effect compromises at any cost.

Thus, Your Grace, feeling that I have been harshly treated without any provocation, I cannot but regard the sanction given by the Indian Government to *the repeal of the Regulations that protected my honor and dignity* as *a departure from the Treaty obligations*, and a confirmation of the unjust and cruel policy initiated by Lord Dalhousie ; I therefore, earnestly appeal to Her Majesty's Government in the fervent hope that I may be reinstated in the position I occupied before those Regulations were repealed, when *the Agent was formally interposed between the Nawab Nazim and the actual operation of the Civil Courts*, on the grounds set forth in the following letter :—

To H. PAULIN, ESQ., *Attorney to the Honorable Company.*

Sir,

 "I am directed to acknowledge the receipt of your letter of "the 17th inst., forwarding copy of the Advocate-General's

"opinion regarding the question of the liability of the Nawab
"Nazim to the jurisdiction of the Supreme Court."

"2. In reply, I am desired to transmit for the information of
"the Advocate-General, copy of a communication which has
"been received on the same subject from the Governor-General's
"Agent at Moorshedabad, and to state as follows :"

"3. His Honour in Council is decidedly of opinion that the
"*Supreme Court has no right to exercise jurisdiction over the
"Nawab Nazim of Bengal*, and should the attempt to move the
"Court to adopt this course of proceeding be persisted in,
"*it is requested that the Advocate-General will adopt every neces-
"sary legal means for resisting it.*"

"4. It will be observed *from the Treaty*, 1770, of which a copy
"is annexed, that *His Highness the Nawab has been recognized
"by the British Government as an Independent Prince, and that
"the National Faith is pledged, for nothing being proposed or
"carried into execution derogating from his Honour.*"

"In order to prevent his being *liable to any indignity* from
"subjecting his person, or property, to the process of the Zillah
"Courts, Regulation 19 of 1825 was passed, *prescribing certain
"rules under which alone he could sue, or be sued, in those Courts.*
"With regard to the Supreme Court, the case is very different.
"As the Government has no power to regulate the proceedings
"of this Court towards persons acknowledged to come within
"its jurisdiction, *if the liability of the Nazim were to be admitted,
"there is no degree of indignity which might not be inflicted upon
"him* by its ordinary processes, *in contravention of the pledged
"National Faith, and of the respect which is obviously due to the
"Representative of our oldest Ally on this side of India.*"

"5. Without intending to limit the discretion of the Advo-
"cate-General, as to the grounds of objection which should be taken
"up, His Honour in Council would wish every possible exertion
"to be made to establish *the Right of the Nawab Nazim to be
"exempted from the jurisdiction of the Supreme Court.* Any
"further information which can be procured from the Govern-
"ment Records, here or at Moorshedabad, shall be furnished to
"you on your requisition and the Vakeel of His Highness the
"Nazim, stationed at the Presidency, will likewise be directed
"to place himself in communication with you.

"6. The case of Raja Hurreenauth Rae, referred to by the
"Advocate-General, does not appear to His Honour in Council
"to bear any analogy to the present. *Raja Hurreenauth Rae
"was a subject of this Government, from whose gift he derived his
"title, while the Nawab Nazim is a Prince, whose Independence
"has been recognized by a Treaty with one of his Predecessors,*

"I have, &c.,
(Signed) "C. E. TREVELYAN,
"Deputy-Secretary to the Government.
"Council Chambers, 20th February, 1834."

Before concluding this head of my Memorial, I would respectfully ask your Grace to consider the opinion of the Government of India, as set forth in the above letter on the following points:—

1. The inability of any Court of Justice to exercise jurisdiction over the Nawab of Bengal.
2. The obligation of Government to resist any measure that might be adopted to enforce the liability of the Nawab Nazim.
3. The recognition of the British Government that the Nawab Nazim is an Independent Prince.
4. That National Faith has been "pledged to observe inviolably for ever" the Treaty of 1770, by which nothing can be proposed or carried into execution derogating from the honor of the Nawab Nazim.
5. That Regulation 19, of 1825, was passed by the Government to prevent His Highness being liable to any indignity, and certain rules were prescribed under which alone he could sue and be sued.
6. If the liability of the Nazim were to be admitted, there is no degree of indignity which might not be inflicted upon him in contravention of the pledged National Faith, and of the respect due to him, as the oldest Ally of the British Government in Eastern India.
7. The right of the Nawab Nazim to be exempted from the jurisdiction of the Courts is based on the fact that he did not acquire his title as a subject of the British Government, but as a Prince whose independence was secured by Treaty.

And now, Your Grace, without further remark on this question, permit me to lay before Your Grace the next head of my memorial, to which I would especially draw attention, as the subject of it appears to have been little understood by any of the Government officers who have commented upon it.

IV.—THE NIZAMUT DEPOSIT FUND ARBITRARILY CONVERTED INTO A BOOK-DEBT BEARING NO INTEREST; AND GENERAL MIS-APPLICATION OF THE FUND TO PURPOSES ALTOGETHER FOREIGN TO ITS TRUE INTENT, OBJECT, AND CONDITIONS.

Your Grace will observe that in November, 1853, His Lordship the Marquis of Dalhousie addressed a series of proposals to the Court of Directors, which were to the effect that there was "*no existing Treaty,* "*compact or agreement, relative to my rights, and consequently that I* "*had no claim to any stipend whatever,*" and proposed "*that no more* "*of the capital of the Deposit Fund should be invested, but that* "*thenceforward it should be considered a mere book-debt bearing no* "*interest.*"

From the above it is very clear that the Nizamut **Fund is a** "*debt,*" and from another document (Page 70) it is also very **clear** that the **Fund**, forming this debt "*is the unalienable property of His Highness's family.*" It is still further evident that the several funds which are said to have been amalgamated and **formed this** "**debt**" bore interest according to the terms of each respective trust, **and** from documentary evidence (Page 61) it can be proved that the Agency Fund was formed from "*assets pertaining to the Nizamut, and the advantages arising* "*from the discount on the paper (Government Securities) belonging to* "*the Nizamut were to be accounted for to His Highness.*" Further, these Government Securities were "*purchased on account of the Niza-* "*mut, and the Accountant-General was directed to have these Securities* "*invested as the property of the Nizamut*" (Pages 80, 82). From other **documents** it may be seen that the six lacs of Munnee Begum's Fund were to be "*invested in Public Securities for the benefit of the Nizamut*" (Page 83), **to be held** "**in deposit in the same** manner **as** the **Agency** "**Fund ;**" and, again, relative to the Nizamut Deposit **Fund it was ruled** that "*future accumulations from* **the** *Nizamut Deposit* **Fund** *were to be invested in* "*Securities of the* **British** *Government as the* "*funds may accrue.*" (Page 79).

The Honourable Court of **Directors**, although placed in the anomalous position of persons owing a "**debt**," and yet **declared not liable to** pay either interest or principal, as the term "*book-debt*" implies, refused to accede to so iniquitous a proceeding **as** that proposed by Lord Dalhousie. But His Lordship seemed determined to carry his point against all opposition, and disregarding the terms of the various trusts, setting aside the overwhelming documentary evidence which supported the fact of these trusts being the actual and **real** property of the Nizamut, invested to bear interest for the benefit **of** myself and family, and declining to act up to the instructions of his employers, who were a Court of Equity exercising a power beyond **that to** which **His** Lordship could lay claim, His Lordship ruled that **the Nizamut Fund** was "*a mere book-debt bearing no interest.*"

Thus, Your Grace, has the arbitrary **act** of one person laid **the foun**dation of a system which, if persisted **in**, would ultimately lead to the ruin of **every hope**, cherished **by the Nawabs** Nazim of **successive** generations. **My ancestors inaugurated and fostered this fund with** the most laudable motives, and *for special purposes*, **and I** myself have contributed to **it in** the **sum of two** lacs of rupees annually for the last thirty years, *irrespective* **of** *the* **numerous** *stipends that have been absorbed into it* arbitrarily, **and without** regard **to** my most pressing wants, to which these lapses **ought to** have been applied ; but now, after all, to labour under the uncertainty as to whether this fund, which by right belongs to me and my family, may be accepted by Her Majesty's Government as being a "*mere book-debt and public money*," is a climax I may well shudder at.

In corroboration of the fact that **the Nizamut Fund is neither a** "*book-debt bearing no interest*," **nor is it "***public money***,**" but that it is as declared to be by the late **Secretary of State of Her Majesty's** Government for India, in **the despatch of 17th June, 1864, Para 8,** "*the property* **of** *the Nizamut.*" I will, for Your Grace's information, quote the same.

8. "**It** is unnecessary to trace further the history of the Fund. Its " accumulations, representing as they do the unappropriated portions " from year **to year** of the sixteen lacs stipend, *unquestionably belong* " *to the Nazim and his family, and can properly be expended only for* " *their benefit.* But this does not confer upon the Nazim himself **any** " right to dispose, **or to** superintend the disposal **of these balances.** "This right belongs to the Government under the **conditions upon**

"which the Fund was constituted. It was assumed, in the first
"instance, mainly *for the benefit and protection of the Nazim and
"his family*, and I am of opinion that it is to the advantage of His
"Highness and his family that this system should be maintained.
"At the same time it would seem to be desirable, and I believe that
"to some extent it has been the practice in past time, for your Govern-
"ment, through your Agent at Moorshedabad, occasionally *to consult
"the Nazim* with respect to any extraordinary expenditure from the
"Nizamut Fund."

Your Grace will notice that in the above quotation, not only does the Right Honourable gentleman acknowledge *the just right of myself and my family to the proceeds of the Fund*, but he also tacitly admits that I *should be consulted as to the disbursement of the same;* and although it is argued that the fact of the Fund being my property does not confer upon me "the right to dispose, or to superin-"tend the disposal, of these balances," yet I think Your Grace will bear with me, when I observe that this argument is at variance with the several arrangements made with my ancestors in connexion with this Fund, and to a great extent even with the last one of 1834, embodied in the suggestions of Captain Thoresby, Agent to the Governor-General, forwarded to Mr. (now Sir Charles) Trevelyan, and adopted as the final arrangement for regulating the financial affairs of the Nizamut, particularly in the matter of lapsed stipends, pensions, and other savings. Attached to Captain Thoresby's letter is the following:—

"The form in which the Nizamut accounts are rendered through
"the Agent to the Government being unsatisfactory and productive
"of no good, and the present Nizamut system causing considerable
"inconvenience, a new arrangement, agreeably to the term of the fol-
"lowing paragraphs, has been devised *with the full concurrence of the
"Nawab Nazim*, Humayoon Jah, by the advice of the Agent of the
"Governor-General, and is approved and sanctioned by His Excel-
"lency the Right Honourable the Governor-General in Council to
"have effect from the commencement of the Bengal year, 1241, after
"the settlement of all former accounts, when a brief abstract of the
"Nizamut expenditure, according to a form *approved by the Nazim
"and Agent*, will be furnished generally for the information of Go-
"vernment in lieu of detailed accounts.

I. "All customary perquisites, comprehended under the names
"Mamoolat, Zumistani, &c., granted to the Ukrooba, besides their re-
"spective pensions, shall be commuted to cash payments from the
"beginning of the above year; and after the decease of the receivers
"of the compensation allowances, if there are no heirs entitled to suc-
"ceed to it, *the reversion shall be to the Nizamut Treasury.*"

II. "The stipendiary accounts shall be kept distinct from all others,
"and the monies on account of pensions shall be deposited in a sepa-
"rate chest appropriated to that purpose. The Khazanchee, or Daro-
"gah, appointed to the charge of it, and to make the disbursements
"and keep the accounts, shall be answerable *to the Agent as well as to
"the Nawab Nazim* for the correctness of his issues and the existence
"of the balance.

III. "It is earnestly *recommended to His Highness to introduce* a

" more simple and effective mode of keeping the Nizamut accounts,
" **and to** make such arrangements as may ensure the final settlement
" of the current expenses of the proceeding month in the course of
" the following month, including the salaries and wages of *every de-*
" *scription of servants,* so that there may be no debts incurred, and
" no dissatisfaction occasioned in consequence; such regularity will
" tend **to** the security of His Highness's interests as well as ease and
" comfort.

IV. " **Such** reductions and modifications of the different esta-
" blishments in the Nizamut *as shall be thought desirable and*
" *proper by the Nawab Nazim, either at the present time or here-*
" *after, shall be executed by him, and with regard to the salaries*
" *of his servants and the entertaining or discharging of them, he is*
" *at liberty to act as he pleases without any interference.*

V. " *Pensions* which have been, or may hereafter be assigned to ser-
" vants or dependents, *shall revert to the Nizamut Treasury as*
" casualties occur, *and shall, with other savings effected by retrench-*
" *ments, be at the entire disposal of His Highness, providing that no*
" *just dues or debts remain unsatisfied.*

VI. " The intent of the foregoing arrangement is, that by the intro-
" duction of method and order into the affairs of the Nizamut, which
" shall provide for the full efficiency of all departments, and prevent
" the recurrence of **pecuniary** embarrassments and debts, *His High-*
" *ness the Nawab* **Nazim** *may enjoy an increase of ease and happi-*
" *ness.*"

The next point for Your Grace to consider is whether Her Majesty's
Government will recognize the obligation to pay me *the interest* **on** *the*
"*debt.*" In the first place I would beg to bring **to** Your Grace's notice
the fact that there is ample **documentary evidence to** prove **that one of
the conditions of the** trusts was, *each one should bear interest* **in Public**
Securities; also **that** *these trusts did for a long course of time* (up to
1854) *bear interest;* and, lastly, that the Government undertook, as
Trustees of the Funds to put out **the money in the best possible way** *for the
benefit of those concerned.* I leave **Your Grace** to decide how far these
conditions have been fulfilled, **and whether** justice has been done to
myself or my family; for surely **we** are entitled to some explanation
in respect of the mutual relations and obligations that existed between
the Government of the Honorable Company and the Nizamut with re-
gard to these Funds, and the benefits accruing to us therefrom!

I have already drawn Your Grace's attention, in the first and **second
heads of** this Memorial, to one instance of *unjust curtailment of our hereditary* stipend, *by the reduction of the Treaty allowance of His Highness*
Nawab *Nazim Moobaruck-ul-Dowlah during his minority,* under a pro-
mise (from Mr. Warren Hastings), that the allowance would be restored
to the **full amount on** his coming of age; but this **never** having been
done, **naturally led to** disappointment, **and** was the origin of those
serious embarrassments that led Lord Wellesley, in 1802, to appoint
a Special Commission **to** *inquire into the financial difficulties of the
Nizamut.*

This Committee, acting **in** concert with His Highness Nawab
Nazim Bubber Jung, and Her Highness Munnee Begum, suggested
that on the death of Her Highness Munnee Begum, her **annual**

stipend of Sicca Rupees 1,44,000, should be appropriated annually towards "*the payment of the Nizamut Debts, building expenses, marriage portions, and other such purposes for which the Government had hitherto made advances.*" (Page 48) Had this arrangement not been entered into, *the reversion of Her Highness Munnee Begum's allowance would have been to His Highness the Nawab Nazim,* so that in point of fact, it was from the personal allowance of His Highness that this Fund was created.

Her Highness Nawab Munnee Begum died in January, 1813, and *a sum of two lacs of rupees, of Her Highness's private property, was at once set apart towards this Fund* (Page 62). It is needless for me to add that His Highness the Nawab Nazim being *the heir-at-law to the personal property of Her Highness, these two lacs were de facto His Highness's property.*

In 1816, the *accumulations* of Munnee Begum's allowance had amounted to *five lacs*, and to this sum was added the *two lacs* of Munnee Begum's *private property* referred to above, and thus was formed *the first Nizamut Fund.* This, according to the suggestion of Mr. Edmonstone, a Member of the Council in India, who had been appointed to examine into the financial difficulties of the Nizamut, and at the instance of Mr. Monckton, Persian Secretary to the Governor-General, was set apart to defray the expenses (in Mr. Edmonstone's own words) of "*a special officer of high rank and peculiar qualifications, who should be able to give his whole time and attention to the Nizamut Affairs.*" This officer was designated Agent to the Governor-General, and hence the Fund set apart for his support was styled *the Agency Fund* (Page 53).

Your Grace may readily believe, that on this Fund, which was originally established *as a resource to meet the contingent expenses of the Nizamut*, being subsequently proposed *to be diverted to a different purpose*—one altogether foreign to everything contemplated by the Committee of 1802—His Highness' mind was filled with justifiable apprehension, and as before observed, it was not till Mr. Monckton was sent by the Governor-General, that his Highness, through a misconception of the subject, *was prevailed upon to acquiesce in the arrangements.*

The Agency Fund was thus established for the purpose of paying the Agent Governor-General, the Agency Office, &c., and my grandfather's consent to its establishment, though given with much reluctance, was at length secured. The Extracts from Public letters bearing on the history and nature of this fund (Page 52 to 72), will throw more light on this subject than any remarks I might wish to make:

The Court of Directors having ordered the reduction of the allowance paid to the Agent, on the representation of Lord Dalhousie, this order was carried into effect on the appointment of the late Colonel Thomson to the Office of Agent Governor-General in 1862, without my knowledge, and was, perhaps, intended to be viewed as an economical measure—but unfortunately about the same time a subordinate appointment of Dewan Nizamut was created, much to my humiliation, as will hereafter be shown, and this officer, whose duties (as defined by the Government of India) were to act under the orders of the Agent Governor-General, yet draws a larger income with less responsibility than his superior officer! I would ask Your Grace if this is just either to me or to the Agent Governor-General? If the Nizamut Deposit Fund could not bear the payment of Rs 3,000 per mensem to the Agent, how does it meet the extra demand of Rs. 2,133.5-4 per mensem for the subordinate who thus draws now Rs. 133-5-4 per mensem more than his superior officer?

Ere I close my remarks on *this portion of the Nizamut Fund*, I would beg leave to draw Your Grace's attention to the following quotations which materially bear on the subject. Mr. Monckton, who was made to play a prominent part in the above transaction, thus expressed himself when writing to His Highness on the subject, in a semi-official manner: "*this fund will not be liable, under any change of circumstances,* "*to be diverted to purposes foreign to the interests of the House of* "*Jaffir Ali Khan*," and the Governor-General assured His Highness that "*this Fund is, and will be considered and recognized as the in-*"*alienable property of His Highness' family over and above the Six-*"*teen Lacs assigned for its support*" (Page 70). Now, as a concluding remark on this *Agency Fund*, I may observe to Your Grace, that Company's Papers (Government Securities) were purchased with the money realised, and of course these securities bore interest from which the expenses of the Agency were defrayed; and, that the Nawab Nazim should be made acquainted with the accounts under this head is clearly shown from the following quotation which lays this point down as one of the *absolute conditions of the trust*. In this the Governor-General himself proposed with regard to the formation of the Agency Fund that the "*Fund should be invested in Government Paper, and* "*that the advantage arising from the discount on the Paper will belong* "*to the Nizamut, and is to be accounted for to His Highness.*" (Page 61).

I would now beg to draw Your Grace's attention to the second of the Funds which on being amalgamated came to be called the *Nizamut* "*Deposit Fund.*"

This Fund consisted of the accumulation in the Collector's Treasury of Munnee Begum's allowances, and in 1823 these accumulations amounting to Six Lacs formed *a separate and distinct Fund*, the establishment of which I will endeavour to explain for Your Grace's information.

In 1817, as before stated, the accumulation or Munnee Begum's allowance of Sicca Rupees 1,44,000 had amounted to *five lacs* to which were added *two lacs of her private property*, and thus was formed the "*Agency Fund.*" From July, 1817, to May, 1823, or thereabouts, further sums accumulated amounting to *six lacs*, and *this sum was then set apart for the original purposes of the former accumulations of seven lacs, which had been diverted for* the support of the office of Agent Governor-General, and thus was instituted the *second* of the Trusts under consideration. The object and conditions of this Fund are so intimately allied with the third of these separate Trusts, and in fact as the "*Munnee Begum's Fund of six lacs*" very shortly after merged into another, owing to the annual accumulations of the 1,44,000 rupees, I find it necessary, after having explained how it came to be instituted, to ask Your Grace to consider it along with the last of the Trusts styled the "*Nizamut Deposit Fund.*"

The accumulations of the Munnee Begum's allowance (out of the

Y

Nizamut stipend of sixteen lacs) having amounted (between 1817 and 1823) to *six lacs*, as before observed, this sum was formed into a Fund, called *the Munnee Begum's Fund*, which was intended to meet *the debts of His Highness' building expenses, marriage portions, &c.*; but then arose the question, what should be done with the future accumulations of Munnee Begum's allowance? The Government of India, being fully sensible (from experience) that the reduction of the Nizamut stipend from Rs. 31,81,991-9 to Rs. 16,00,000-0 was in itself a permanent source of pecuniary embarrassment to the Nawabs Nazim and holding in view that the large family of the then reigning Nawab would eventually have to be supported by additional grants from the public revenues, (since in 1786 *the Honorable Court of Directors, feeling themselves bound to provide for the expenses of the Nizamut had ordered "an immediate augmentation of His Highness Moobaruck-ul-Dowlah's "stipend," which however was not attended to by the Governor-General*), at once proposed that all future accumulations of the Munnee Begum's allowance should annually be absorbed into *another Fund to meet the various liabilities of His Highness.* To this Fund His Highness was required to contribute the sum of 56,000 rupees annually to be also deducted from his stipend by the Collector of the Government Treasury, and in this manner was formed the "*Nizamut Deposit Fund*" *of two lacs annually which was the last of the Funds*, all of which in a general way for **convenience** are spoken of as "*The Nizamut "Deposit Fund.*"

I would now beg to draw Your Grace's attention to the following quotations which will enable Your Grace to perceive the accuracy of my observations with respect to the two last mentioned Funds. On the 2nd May, 1823, the Governor-General in Council made the following minute: " *It is by no means the desire of the Government to in-* " *crease indefinitely the appropriations for the benefit of* **the Deposit** " **Fund.** *Their net amount seems at present to exceed two lacs of* " *rupees, after allowing for all the augmentations and appropriations* " *sanctioned. This is one-eighth of the entire Nizamut stipend, and* " *the Governor-General in Council would not wish to make it larger;* " at the same time he conceives it would be **unadvisable** ever to reduce " the Fund below one lac and a half, or at any rate to trench on the " amount of Munnee Begum's stipend which has for so long a time " been set apart for this purpose. *In consideration of the British* " *Government withdrawing from the interference now exercised in* " *auditing the accounts of His Highness,* the Governor-General in " Council thinks it will be **necessary and** not too much to expect, that " **His Highness should consent to allow** *the above sum of two lacs of* " *rupees to accumulate in the Collector's Treasury.* The British " **Government** will in that case *undertake the payment in future from* " *that Fund of all charges for new buildings or other expenses legiti-* " *mately claimable from it; and further will relinquish all desire to* " *increase the Fund pledging itself on the* **lapse** *of any future stipend* **to** " **consider** *the suggestion of His Highness as to its allotment,* and " except under certain circumstances (**which may** demand a different " appropriation) *to assign the whole* **for the benefit** *of the family and* " *its dependents.*" (Page 85)

His Highness acquiesced in the above arrangement and the Honorable Court of Directors ratified it in the following unmistakeable words : " *The Deposit Fund shall consist of two lacs of rupees annually,* " whereof the Munnee Begum's stipend of 144,000 rupees, is intended " to form a part and the remainder, 56,000 rupees, is to be made up by " the Nazim's depositing that sum annually in the Collector's Treasury "

Your Grace will readily perceive that the Nizamut Deposit Fund was on no account to exceed *two lacs a year*, that this annual contribution was to consist *of Munnee Begum's stipend plus 56,000 rupees, to be deposited by His Highness*, and that the British Government undertook to pay from the Fund so instituted "*all charges* for buildings or other expenses *legitimately claimable from it ;*" yet when the new palace was erected, the cost of the furniture for it, amounting to about seven lacs of rupees, was charged against my stipend during my minority, although Mr. Dale, Agent Governor-General, in Para. 13, of a letter to Mr. Sterling, Persian Secretary to Government, dated 25th January, 1830, stated as a reason for not reducing the Nizamut Deposit Fund, the necessity of providing funds for this object.

I will now ask Your Grace to decide from the following extract whether the fund so created bears interest or not? The extract is from a letter addressed by His Lordship to His Highness in connexion with the above minute, and reads thus:—

" With regard to *the future accumulations on account of the De-* " *posit Fund,* I propose that they should be kept wholly in the Col- " lector's Treaty, and *invested in securities of the British Government* " *as the funds may accrue.* The present amount, which approaches to " *near three lacs of rupees per annum*, which, however, had only nomi- " nally lapsed, and nominally accumulated seems *unnecessarily large ;*" " on which account, *should you agree to allow the accumulations to* " *proceed* in the Collector's Treasury, I propose *to limit the amount to* " *two lacs, leaving you the remainder, with full liberty to appropriate* " *any excess, to purposes connected with the splendour and credit of your* " *exalted station.*" (Page 79)

It is very evident from the words of His Lordship, that this Deposit Fund would be "*invested in securities of the British Government*" as *the funds accrued*, thus constituting the British Government Trustees of the same, and guaranteeing that if the accumulation were allowed to proceed in the Collector's Treasury, *the Nawab Nazim had full liberty to appropriate any excess* (i.e., interest) *over the two lacs for any purpose* "*connected with the splendour and credit of his exalted station ;*" yet his Lordship the Marquis of Dalhousie, in another letter asserts that the Nawab Nazim had "*no claim*" on the Deposit Fund, and suggests the possibility of its being regarded as "*a mere book debt bearing no interest.*" It is for Your Grace to declare whichever course Her Majesty's Government considers honorable and right, and to accord me such justice as the merits of my case deserve.

Before leaving the subject of these two Funds, I deem it right to observe that they enjoyed *a nominally distinct character only*, and that, too, for a very short time : thus, the amount required for the support of the office of Agent Governor-General was considerably in excess of the interest derived from the capital invested for that purpose, so that the Munnee Begum's fund had to be drawn upon to supply the deficit, and in this and similar ways the Funds very soon lost their individuality, and became blended into a common Fund.

After the lapse of so many years, it would be a difficult task to enquire into the state of these Funds *in their distinct characters*. I would, therefore, solicit Your Grace's consideration of them *collectively, as forming one general Nizamut Fund*, and I leave it to the just and wise judgment of Her Majesty's Government to decide whether I have any claim or not to *the accumulations or interest arising from those Funds*, since the *conditions and practice* that were acknowledged prior to the ruling of 1854 point out a solution of the question, and Your Grace will, I trust, accept the same as being in perfect harmony with the Exalted Character and Acts of the British Government towards their Allies and Tributary Princes in India.

I have now to ask Your Grace to enter with me upon the history of another Fund, which was forced into existence in 1836 by a lamentable misconception of the nature and terms of the Nizamut Fund, and was styled officially the "*Lapsed Stipend Fund;*" and I will endeavour to show Your Grace how unjust to myself has been the creation of this Fund; how *it has been swelled to enormous proportions, while I have been reduced at times to the utmost necessity*; how every fraction absorbed under the pretext of lapses ought to revert to me, and how difficult (nay, impossible) I find it to provide, as becomes their rank, for the wants of the large family God has blessed me with, so long as this Fund is allowed to swallow up every stipend of my Akroba that lapses.

I must, in the first place, ask Your Grace to accompany me so far back in the history of my affairs as 1836. In that year was framed a minute on Nizamut affairs by Mr. Secretary (now Sir Charles) Trevelyan, and the subsequent proceedings of the Government, based on that minute, are those which have well nigh drained me of every resource I could fall back upon. The minute itself was based upon entirely erroneous premises, and, consequently, the Government, by simply taking this minute for their guide, have inadvertently been led into dealing harshly with me. To illustrate the errors in this minute, I would observe that at the outset it asserts that "*the Deposit Fund,* "*generally called the Nizamut Deposit Fund, consists of savings by* "*lapses in a Fund of about seven lacs, appropriated to the Nawab* "*Nazim's relatives,*" whereas it merely consisted, as concisely expressed by the Honourable Court of Directors, "*of two lacs of rupees* "*annually, whereof the Munnee Begum's stipend of* 1,44,000 *rupees* "*was 'to form a part, and the remainder,* 56,000 *rupees,' was 'to be* "*made up by the Nazim, depositing that sum annually in the* "*Collector's Treasury.*'"

Thus, as the minute alluded to is altogether at variance with the proceedings of the Government in 1823, and is unsupported by any authority up to the date of its origin in 1836, the only rational inference that can be drawn is that the writer based his views on a misconception of the whole question.

Another point in the minute to which I would draw Your Grace's attention is that "*the lapses from pensions which already amount to* "62,640 *rupees, will form the foundation of another Deposit Fund,* "*which will receive continual accession from the decease of different* "*stipendiaries, &c.*," and this, when contrasted with the minute of the Governor-General in Council, dated 2nd May, 1823, shows plainly that the writer must have been unacquainted with the subject in hand, and thus unwittingly misled the Government, who have ever since acted upon the minute, to my disadvantage and serious loss.

And now permit me to lead Your Grace into a general inquiry on the subject of this unnecessary "*Lapsed Stipend Fund.*" The Nawab Nazim had, as we have seen, made ample provision for all contingent expenditure by setting aside two lacs of rupees annually from his income above what had been invested for the support of the Agency, and the six lacs called the Munnee Begum's Fund. His Highness therefore relied on *the pledge of the British Government* that his income would no longer be interfered with, and that he would now be allowed to remain in undisturbed enjoyment of all those *pecuniary rights* that were his by virtue of his being the *head of the family*. It is also just to suppose that the Government in creating the "Nizamut Deposit Fund" had sufficiently relieved itself of the burden of meeting the increasing wants and demands of the Nizamut family; *whence then*, it may reasonably be inquired, *arose the necessity for trenching on the Nawab's income further, by resuming lapses of stipends to the formation of another fund?*

The Agreement of 1834 precluded any such arrangement, and yet *without just regard to what was the personal and private property of His Highness a new Fund was formed to absorb all lapses.*

The Governor-General's Agent having become the bursar under the Agreement of 1834 of the stipends given by His Highness to his relatives, *the opportunity was furnished for establishing a new system, and lapses instead of at once being made over to His Highness, were allowed to accumulate in the Collector's Treasury*, and when they had attained a high figure, were carried to the credit of *a new Fund, to the creation of which His Highness never gave his consent* as he had done when former arrangements of this nature were entered into, under assurances that they would tend to relieve His Highness of his debts, and ensure him "*an increase of ease and happiness.*"

Another fact to which I would beg to draw Your Grace's attention is, that these matters were set on foot in 1836, and, if I am not in error, did not begin to operate till the following year, a little while before my father's death, when I was but a child eight years of age, and wholly unable to protect my rights. Then followed a period of minority that permitted the resumptive process of curtailing the income of my office to proceed without let or hindrance, and by the time I arrived at man's estate, a proceeding that was clearly based on erroneous conceptions was acting vigorously. During my minority, the Agent withdrew the whole of the stipends, and those which lapsed remained undrawn in the Collector's Treasury instead of being paid over to the Nizamut Treasury. This might not have been the case had I been of age, as I could have drawn the lapsed stipends myself in accordance with Captain Thoresby's agreement.

On the death of my grand-aunt, Buboo Begum, I was deprived of her stipend, and Mamoolats, which ought to have reverted to me, not only as Nazim, but as her sole heir-at-law. Moreover, the Honourable

Court of Directors **had ordered** that *during my minority all savings from my income should be invested for my benefit*, yet though the lapsed stipends came under that head, they were suffered to lie idle; and not only so, but were, I believe, written off as a credit to the Deposit Fund. Thus, Your Grace, *a misappropriation which arose from an oversight of the Agent Governor-General during my minority, was turned by Lord Dalhousie into a rule* which has ever since deprived me of those pecuniary advantages, which I trust Her Majesty's Government will find to be my just claim.

I will now ask Your Grace to enter with me upon the consideration of the next head of my Memorial.

V.—THE UNJUST AND HARSH TREATMENT I EXPERIENCED FROM THE INDIAN GOVERNMENT DURING THE LATTER PERIOD OF THE ADMINISTRATION OF LORD CANNING AND THE SPECIFIC LOSSES AND DEPRIVATIONS I HAVE SUFFERED IN CONSEQUENCE.

His Lordship assumed the duties of Governor-General on the 26th February, 1856, and on the 11th March of the same year addressed me a letter, which I have already quoted under the first head of this Memorial. Soliciting a reperusal of that letter, I will proceed to state, Your Grace, that it bears on the face of it most clear and distinct testimony of His Lordship's views regarding the hereditary nature of my rank, and of the guarantee given to my prescriptive privileges by the stipulations of subsisting treaties; and Mr. Edmonstone, while Foreign Secretary to the Government of India, in writing to Colonel Mackenzie, Agent Governor-General, on the 8th of January, 1859, remarked as follows in respect to my rights, that he had "long "ago laid the narrative before the Governor-General" (Lord Canning), and "urged him to have the details tested by thorough examination," and "that Lord Canning seemed to acquiesce in the proposal." Mr. Edmonstone proceeds to say, "the whole subject (of my rights and "conduct) has been more than once under the consideration of the "Governor-General, and has also been discussed with me as often; "but no final decision has been recorded, although I believe the "Governor-General has made up his mind on the matter. I am not, "of course, at liberty to inform you of the opinion the Governor-"General appears to me to have formed; but I may say, confiden-"tially, that it is not unfavourable. I wish you well in your endea-"vours to right His Highness, and have little doubt that you will "succeed in some measure." It is very evident that His Lordship based his opinions and views, as expressed in his letter to me, on the actual terms of the treaties with my ancestors, and on a strict sense of my just rights without permitting himself to be biased by the views of his predecessor. This is further evident from the circumstance of His Lordship having shown a disposition to restore to me the exercise of those prescriptive rights which his predecessor had deprived me of. I allude to the restoration of my salute to its full complement of nineteen guns, which His Lordship's predecessor had reduced to thirteen; and I may here mention, your Grace, that my salute is one of the few privileges left me, and, in fact, under present circumstances, constitutes the principal insignia of my rank. Yet His Lordship did not hesitate in 1862 to endorse the arbitrary views of his predecessor expressed in the Despatch of November, 1854. Holding in view the two documents, His Lordship's political letter of the 11th of March, 1856, to my address, and His Lordship's minute of the 14th January, 1862, there certainly appears so great a contradiction as to give room for inquiry, and the inference is that there must have been some aggravating cause which led His Lordship to alter his views. This brings me, Your Grace, to a point of my Memorial that I would much rather have avoided; but as it is a subject which forms one of the links in the narrative of my recent relations with the Indian Government, and which has proved up to the present time the great stumbling-block to the assured prosperous administration of my affairs, I have no alternative but to stifle my feelings and recur to it, however unpleasant it may be to me to do so. On the 14th of May, 1861, a verbal message from my Dewan was brought to me by one of the eunuchs, to the effect that the Agent Governor-General with some of his friends intended visiting the palace. I was living at the time with my family at Hoomayoon Munzil, one of my garden houses, which is nearly three miles from the palace, and as I had been unwell on the day previous I was obliged to take medicine, and when the messenger arrived I was suffering with such a severe head-ache that I felt too poorly to venture out, more especially in the sun, which in the month of May is so trying in India, that few people will expose themselves to it between the hours of 8 a.m. and 5 p.m.

Nothing would have given me greater pleasure than to have met the Agent and his friends, who spent the day in the Palace, and partook of the usual hospitality which was provided by my orders for them; but as I was quite unable to be present myself, I sent a message to this effect by one of my principal servants, Nawab Nazir Darab Ali Khan, and I do not think, Your Grace, that there was any impropriety in my having so done, considering I myself had only received a verbal message, and that not direct from the Agent. Yet this trifling incident was magnified by the Agent into an appearance of disrespect to the Representative of His Excellency the Viceroy; and although on hearing that he had taken umbrage, I at once wrote to him on the subject, and made an apology for my unavoidable absence, which he afterwards accepted, he reported the matter to Government, and under the impression that I had been guilty of discourtesy towards the Representative of His Excellency the Viceroy, this opportunity was taken for lowering my Political status.

At the time, I could not understand the Agent's object in reporting the matter to the Government—as he had always shown the greatest consideration for me and my family by supporting our dignity and rank (as shown by the correspondence (Page 211 to 237), and, as a friend, even going beyond his official duty as set forth in a letter to the Nawab Nazim from the Marquis of Hastings, dated 5th July, 1817; but now that a considerable period has elapsed since the unfortunate misunderstanding occurred, and I have had an opportunity of reviewing all the collateral circumstances and correspondence. I am led to believe that the Agent acted as he did for the purpose of forcing me to reinstate (his friend) my Dewan (Raja Prosono Narain Deb) whom I had summarily dismissed on account of his bad behaviour towards me. I considered, Your Grace, that I had a right to dismiss this person under the provisions of the Fourth Article of the Agreement of 1834, which gave the Nazim exclusive power over his servants, and as the Dewan was a servant of mine *whose salary was paid by me out of my own personal stipend over which the Government did not claim any control*, I cannot see that my conduct was *officially* reprehensible, or that the Agent was justified in interfering in the matter; for surely a master has a right to dismiss a servant who has provoked his displeasure, without referring to a third party. Yet the Government of India, guided by the remarks of the Agent, (although it tacitly admitted its sense of displeasure at his interference by withdrawing him from his appointment, and putting him in another on a much lower salary), opposed my wishes and reinstated the Dewan by recognizing him as its own servant, and paying his salary out of the Deposit Fund, which was created for vastly different purposes, and is still being supported by me. Thus it may be said that I have virtually paid this officer, since his reappointment by Government eight years ago, upwards of two lacs of rupees, irrespective of the interest that would have accrued upon that sum if it had been invested in Government securities according to the terms under which the Deposit Fund was formed, and yet, Your Grace, objections have been raised on almost every occasion on which I have solicited grants from the Deposit Fund for my own use or for the benefit of my family!

I must now respectfully ask Your Grace to consider the justice of the action taken by the Government of India in the above matters, and also the uncalled for assertion that I had intentionally offered an insult to the Agent Governor-General, and had thereby incurred the displeasure of the Government.

Your Grace, surely there was nothing in my behaviour on the occasion of the Agent's visit to the Palace, that could be construed into an insult to him even as a private gentleman, much less as the Representative of His Excellency the Viceroy! I received a verbal message, and sent back a verbal reply. I was not asked to meet the Agent in his official capacity, even had I been well enough to do so, and as he did not visit the Palace on business but merely to show his friends through the building, I cannot see that *my presence was necessary*, either in my private or public position. Why, then, I may well ask was the matter taken up on Political grounds, as an insult to the Governor-General? (Page 240)

Yet, Your Grace, such was the apparently slight foundation on which His Excellency (the late) Lord Canning based the minute of 14th January, 1862 (Page 269), which was to a certain extent concurred in by the late Secretary of State for India in Despatch No. 30, of 17th June, 1864 (Page 279), and which, when contrasted with His Lordship's letter of 11th March, 1856, (Page 194) clearly indicates the bias under which His Lordship changed his views with regard to my rights as secured by subsisting Treaties.

I would here beg to observe, Your Grace, that the subsequent harsh measures of His Excellency's Government against the just and proper recognition of my Political status and prescriptive privileges, evidently emanated from His Excellency's determination to support the authority of the Agent Governor-General, who had pledged himself and the Government to recognize no other individual as Dewan Nizamut but my dismissed servant. However, the Government, by removing the Agent, expressed its displeasure at the action he had taken in espousing the cause of one of my servants in opposition to my wishes, which it probably looked upon as a Political error on his part; for during the lifetime of **Nawab** Mobaruck-ul-Dowlah, the Dewan was summarily dismissed without the Government questioning the Nawab's right to act without its consent (Page 42), and, even in my own time, a former Dewan was dismissed by me under almost similar circumstances, and with the entire approbation of the Agent, without a reference to Government. My dismissing my Dewan, therefore, in 1861, was not without precedent, nor did I think it imperative to consult the Agent, since in the Fourth Article of the **Agreement of 1834**, which I beg to quote for Your Grace's information it is clearly stated:

"Such reductions and modifications of the different establishments in the Nizamut as shall be thought desirable and proper by the Nawab Nazim, either at the present time, or hereafter, shall be executed by him, and with regard to the salaries of his servants, and the entertaining and discharging them, he is at liberty to act as he pleases without any interference."

I will now proceed to lay before Your Grace the specific losses and deprivations I have suffered by the proceedings of the Government in 1862, consequent on the above-mentioned occurrences. The management and disbursement of certain allowances had up to that period formed one of my *prescriptive privileges*, and this was summarily withdrawn from me and made over to the Dewan Nizamut—then no longer my servant—as one of his functions. This I cannot but regard as one of my most crying grievances, and you will perceive, Your Grace, in the course of the following notice of these allowances, that with their withdrawal from my control I at once ceased to have any influence among the members of my family. Nor is this all, I feel my dignity assailed when I see these trifling privileges, without any just cause, taken from me and delegated to one who before had been my servant. Surely some consideration might have been shown in the matter, and out of respect to my feelings some duly qualified Government official might have been appointed, subject to my approval, and at a much lower stipend, to perform the duties required, instead of subjecting me to the insult of having my affairs ruled over by a person who gained his position (as the following letters will shew) during his connexion with me as my servant.

A. "I have the honor to acquaint you, for the information of the Most Noble the Governor of Bengal, that His Highness the Nawab Nazim has expressed his desire of appointing Baboo Prosonno Narain Deb, Rai Bahadoor *to be his Dewan*." — Major Macgregor, 23rd Sept., 1853.

B. "The Agent at Moorshedabad reports the wishes of the Nawab Nazim to appoint the Rai Bahadoor of the Toshakhanah *as his Dewan*." — Hon. C. Beadon, 29th Sept., 1853.

C. "I am directed by the Governor-General in Council to request that during the remainder of the leave you are understood *to have* — Hon. C. Beadon, 1st Oct., 1859.

"*obtained from* His **Highness the Nawab Nazim**, you will accompany His Excellency to Lucknow and Cawnpore, in the capacity of Honorary Assistant Secretary in charge of the Toshakhanah, to which *temporary office* His Excellency has been pleased to appoint you."

<small>Calcutta Gazette, 8th Oct., 1859.</small>

D. "His Excellency in Council has been pleased to confer upon **Rai Prosouno Narain Deb** Bahadoor, *Dewan of the Nawab Nazim*, the title of Rajah Bahadoor in consideration of his services during the same period."

<small>Sec. to Govt. of India, 6th Dec., 1859.</small>

E. "I am directed to forward a copy of a letter addressed this day to Rajah Prosonno Narain Deb Bahadoor, *the Nawab Nazim's Dewan*, who has recently *with His Highness's permission*, been employed as Honorary Assistant Secretary to the Government of India. In communicating this letter to the Nawab Nazim I am desired to request that you will convey to His Highness, the Governor-General's acknowledgment *for his courtesy in allowing the Goverament to avail itself of the Dewan's services.*"

<small>Rajah Prosonno Narain Deb Bahadoor, 23rd June, 1862.</small>

F. "You will, I doubt not, perceive that it would be imprudent for me to sign documents which might in any way serve to increase the amount of my responsibility, besides, *when I was Dewar to His Highness*, the box without any list of its contents was delivered to the care of the Mahafez Khannah through me."

Besides, this arbitrary act of the Government was unsupported by any precedent and opposed to the terms of the Agreement of 1834, which has been the rule by which Nizamut affairs have been administered, with the exception only of such modifications as the foregoing, and others equally prejudicial to my prescriptive privileges. Para IV. of the Agreement of 1834, states "such reductions and modifications of the different establishments in the Nizamut *as shall be thought desirable and proper by the Nawab Nazim* at the present time or hereafter, *shall be executed by him*, and with regard to the salaries of his servants and the entertaining and *discharging* of them *he is at liberty to act as he pleases without any interference.*"

Surely, then, Your Grace, there was nothing in my conduct in this matter to warrant the removal from my control of such allowances and appointments as I have before had the entire management of, and I trust Your Grace will, in fairness and justice, restore to me the authority of which I have been unjustly deprived.

Among the allowances of which I have been deprived, are the four following, which will readily enable Your Grace to perceive the bearing of the whole question, viz. :—

(a) Mamoolats.
(b) Zemistance.
(c) Mutaynats or Dooriats.
(d) Mookhbarahs.

For an explanation of these terms, I beg to refer Your Grace to the glossary annexed to this Memorial ; and, in the first place, will ask Your Grace to consider the two first collectively.

During the minority of my father, Nawab Nazim Hoomayoon Jah, although the expenditure was under the special management of the Agent Governor-General, a very large debt had been incurred, which was subsequently paid out of the surplus of the Deposit Fund, on the ground that it was contracted under the guardianship of the Agent. I mention this to show that no amount of interference was found effectual to introduce order into Nizamut Affairs from the time that Nawab Moobaruck-ul-Dowlah's stipend was reduced. Capt. Thoresby, who was then Agent Governor-General, therefore proposed that all stipends to the members of the Nizamut family should be paid from his office, and that His Highness should receive *the remainder of the sixteen lacs for his personal expenditure, without the obligation of giving any account thereof.* A new arrangement was in consequence entered into between the Nawab Nazim and the Governor-General to the following effect:—

1st. Customary perquisites under the name of Mamoolat and Zemistanee, given by His Highness, should be commuted to cash payments, and on the decease of the recipients, "*if there are no heirs entitled to succeed to it, the reversion shall be to the Nizamut Treasury,*" i.e., to the Nawab Nazim. His Highness gave his formal consent to this *Agreement* on the 17th February, 1834, and it was settled and explained that "although His Highness was *thus relieved from all responsibility* connected with the stipends, every facility should be given for his making himself acquainted with the *minutest details*, and *his wishes regarding grants from the Deposit Fund* would be signified to the Agent, and *attended to as heretofore.*" Sir C. Metcalfe, in giving his official consent to this Agreement, informed His Highness that "the Agent Governor-General has been directed to consider it" (this Agreement) "*as the rule* under which Nizamut Affairs are hereafter to be administered."

The frequent changes of Agents Governor-General has been one of the most fertile sources of infraction of solemn Agreements, and on reference to the records it will be found that from July, 1833, to April, 1836, no less than six changes of this nature transpired. The consequence was that *Nizamut affairs and the Nazim's rights were little understood*, and as the Supreme Government relied on the representations of these officers, it was very frequently led into doing many acts of injustice, which, if it had been rightly informed, would never have been sanctioned. For instance, the Honourable Mr. Melville, who was Agent Governor-General in 1836, recommended the resumption of Mamoolats, a positive infraction of the Agreement of 1834, and yet expressed himself on the duties of Agent Governor-General in the following words:—"*One principal duty of the Agent under instructions in force has always appeared to me to be to protect this Prince from the perpetual tendency of subordinate authorities to encroach upon such rights and privileges as it has been deemed just and expedient to reserve to this family.*" If such was the duty of the Agent, how came it that, on his representation, the Government was led to resume those allowances, and thus to encroach upon rights which it was the Agent's duty to protect? I would ask Your Grace to consider whether it was *fair and just* that the Government should have disposed of that which was virtually my property? Since the Mamoolats and Zemistanee allowances are derived from the portion of my sixteen lacs stipend set apart annually for the payment of the members of the Nizamut family, to whom and to whose heirs these two allowances, among others, are perfectly legitimate.

To understand how the Agent became the bursar of these allowances, I must inform Your Grace that the Nawab Nazim and the other members of the Nizamut were not always on the best of terms; it therefore sometimes occurred that the Mamoolats and Zemistanee allowances were withheld from obnoxious members, and when given were not of the customary value; therefore, this money was entrusted to the Government for due disbursement through one of its officers, *merely as a guarantee of its regular payment*, so long as heirs were to be found, in absence of whom the *reversion* lawfully *would be to the Nawab Nazim*, as it was before the Government undertook the disbursement of the allowances. Under these circumstances, it certainly appears to me unjust that I should be deprived of these *reversions;* hence I bring the matter forward for Your Grace's consideration, as an infringement of the Agreement of 1834, which expressly states that " if there are no heirs to succeed, *the reversion shall be to the Nizamut Treasury*," or, in other words, to the Nawab Nazim. Then, again, so late as May, 1868, my son-in-law, Nawab Feroze Jung, was refused the allowances in question, though his father enjoyed them during his lifetime; and when he addressed the Agent and memorialized the Government, he received the inexorable answer, that " Such allowances " were resumable, and the memorialist could not be permitted to draw " them." If such a course, Your Grace, is to be followed, it is very evident that the ruin of my family is inevitable, as *the annual stipend is being gradually reduced by lapses* being absorbed, and although I myself only draw Rs. 7,32,000-0-0, *I am obliged to grant receipts in full for the whole sixteen lacs stipend*, which does not appear to me to be a *legitimate demand, though I am forced to execute it as a Government order.*

It is my province, Your Grace, as a memorialist to represent my grievances; it is yours to investigate and redress them; and with every hope of justice being done me, I will bring to Your Grace's notice the third allowance styled Mutaynats or Deoriats. Reverting again to the Agreement of 1834, it is therein stated that " all pensions " which had been or might be assigned hereafter to servants and de- " pendents *shall revert to the Nizamut Treasury* as casualties occur " and be at the *entire disposal of the Nawab*."

Surely Your Grace, it was never intended that *resumptions* should take place on the occurrence of any or all casualties among the servants and dependents paid from this allowance, nor was it contemplated that the Nawab and other members of his family in the enjoyment of this privilege, the Mutaynat allowance, should not be permitted to entertain or dismiss these dependents and servants—yet such is the case at the present moment. The allowance is derived from a source that can admit of no misconception viz: *my admitted stipend of sixteen lacs* in its different portionings to members of my family; hence I cannot see the justice of absorbing it for the credit of the Deposit Fund instead of making it revert to me according to the Agreement of 1834 Again, several members of my family have recently been harshly dealt with by the Government in consequence of the above error as to this allowance; take for instance a member of my family drawing 400 *rupees* and a Mutaynat of 36 *rupees;* in the event of any casualty occurring among the dependents who are the recipients of the Mutaynat, any remissness on the part of that member to report the matter, results in his becoming liable to forfeit the allowance together with a part or the whole of his hereditary stipend. Such a state of things is daily becoming the practice, so I consider it my duty, as the head of the Nizamut Family, to appeal against such unjust measures, and to solicit our right to entertain or dismiss any servant or dependent in our establishments *without interference.*

I have another grievance of an equally grave nature to lay before Your Grace in connection with the disbursement of this allowance, which I have always looked upon as *one of my prescriptive privileges*, and with advertence to such privileges it was ordered by Her Majesty's Government through the late Secretary of State for India, that "*His* "*Highness should not be deprived of any of* **the honors and privileges** "*of which he is now in the enjoyment.*" and in conformance with this order the disbursement of this allowance was restored to me; but in a few months, and in a most unaccountable manner, without a reason being assigned, it was transferred by order of the Agent from my rightful custody to that of the Dewan, whom I had dismissed from my service. Nothing could be more hurtful to my feelings than to be thus summarily deprived of one of my privileges, and to see it conferred on a man who had been my servant and had given me just cause for his dismissal. Silently I have suffered this bitter slight and humiliation, in the firm hope of eventually obtaining redress when I laid the matter before Her Majesty's Government, and it is now for Your Grace to consider the justice of my claim and to restore me to the position I ought to occupy according to subsisting agreements as guaranteed by Her Majesty's Proclamation of 1858

I may now trace the consequences of the removal of these allowances from my control:

The dependents who are supported by these allowances, being now paid by an officer *who has been removed from my control*, are made quite independent of my authority, and refuse to render me that service which, under the constitution of these allowances, they would be compelled to do; and, further, they are taught to believe that they are paid from a separate Government Fund instead of *a portion of my admitted stipend of sixteen lacs, over which I ought, in justice, to have some control.* Thus my prescriptive privileges, which have been so often guaranteed, have of late years been ignored to my prejudice. Further, Mutaynats or stipends left by the Munnee Begum, Bubboo Begum, and others to old retainers, and *which* were *hereditary* (the descendants of these retainers continuing in the service of the family) have recently, after being enjoyed by several generations, been resumed by orders of Government, in contradiction to an express provision dated 18th July, 1838, for resuming stipends to the Deposit Fund, "*unless when there are dependents of the deceased, the support of* "*whom would be a duty incumbent on the relations.*" Thus the immediate respect of the resumption is to deprive the retainers of their bread, and myself of their services; I therefore pray that these Mutaynat allowances, known also as Deoriat Pensions, be dealt with more liberally by the Government, that they be *restored to my control under the supervision of the Agent Governor-General,* as was the practice before the recent innovation.

I now come to the **4th head of allowances**, styled Mookhbarahs, which are set apart for **certain religious ceremonies** enjoined by our sacred writings at the **mausoleums of** deceased relatives, as also for the keeping of these **mausoleums in proper repair, and** *which, from their peculiar nature, ought to be under my special care as the head of the family by Muhomedan law.* Yet, Your Grace will barely credit that the disbursement of these *sacred* allowances was also made over to the **same officer** whom I discharged, and who is a *Hindoo*, a *persuasion* **which we are taught to regard with peculiar dread in** religious matters, as is well known by any reader of history—so that the fact of entrusting him (a Hindoo) with the management of Mahomedan rites, and the regulating and disbursement of allowances for prayers and offerings for the departed of my Faith, does in itself show to what **extent** arbitrary proceedings may be carried to support an officer *whose connection with my affairs cannot fail to be unpleasant to me*, **and** whose previous conduct led me to dispense with his services. Your Grace will now see with what little consideration I have been treated, and how much at variance the practices of late years have been with the promises held out to me in 1839, that "*the dignity and honor of the illustrious house which you* " *now represent will ever be an object of care* and solicitude to this " *Government.*"

And while on this point, Your Grace, I may add that *the courtesy which my rank entitles me to* in respect of my opinion being sought even in the most trifling matters relating to the affairs of the members of my family, *has been altogether abandoned*, and happen what may, whether it be the death of any member and the portioning of his stipend, or whether assistance be sought by some member from the Deposit Fund for any purpose, *the officer above alluded to, and who now holds the title of Dewan Nizamut is the only person required to report on the case, and my* **authority is** *entirely set aside*. The recommendations made by that officer are, **as** a rule, sanctioned, and *he thus enjoys an* **influence over the** *members of my family* (by exercising privileges that are mine prescriptively) *while I, the Nawab Nazim, and the head* **of** *the Family, am converted into a* **nonentity,** and the **Akrobah, as the mem**bers of my family are **termed,** finding that I have no voice in their affairs, have, with few exceptions, **forsaken me to go where they** are induced to hope for substantial recognition of their attentions, and *while my former servant has every respect shown him in consequence of his exercising my prerogative, my durbars are almost deserted,* and present at once the ludicrous, but to me painful, **spectacle** of empty seats, as hardly any of my **Akrobah will** attend them, actuated, no doubt, by fear of giving offence to the Dewan Nizamut, to whose clique they **profess to belong, in the hope** of receiving favours at his hands; for Your Grace is no doubt aware that *any officer supported under Government* **authority can** *exercise despotic sway over the minds of those natives* **who draw their** stipends *through him*, and it is for **Your** Grace to consider **whether** *this* **officer is** *still to exercise arbitrary control over my family*, **or** *whether in justice I may be permitted to resume that natural* **control over** *my affairs which the head of every family should exercise,* irrespective of other claims insured by Treaty or Agreement.

It may be urged, Your Grace, against my objections, that the management and disbursement of these allowances came within the duties assigned to the Dewan Nizamut, even while they were in my custody; true, but the Dewan, being then my paid servant, merely acted up to my instructions as a steward, and could not exercise the arbitrary disposal of them as he now does; and what I now pray for, Your Grace, is that the Dewan should be entirely under my control as before, and that I only may be held responsible to the Agent Governor-General for the *correct disbursement* of these allowances. This was the course *before I took the present Dewan Nizamut into my service*, and, as there was never any constraint imposed upon me before I selected this officer, *I little thought that he would ever have been made an instrument for my humiliation*. It is for Your Grace to decide whether I have been *justly* dealt with, and *whether the placing of this officer over my private affairs* as a permanent arrangement has been conducive to "*the honor and dignity of my exalted station*," as guaranteed by the Government. I am both ready and willing at once to resume the management and disbursement of these several allowances as prescribed, before their removal from my custody, and to submit all documents and papers connected with their management for the information and sanction of the Agent Governor-General, as was the practice before, and I trust that Your Grace will give me your considerate support for the restoration of this and my other prescriptive privileges, of which the only one that I am now honored with is my salute of nineteen guns, which was restored to me under circumstances stated in the following letter from His Excellency, (the late) Lord Canning.

"My Friend,

"In consequence of your numerous and valuable services rendered to the British Government during the Santhal rebellion in 1855, and at the more serious crisis which followed, the mutiny of the native troops of the Bengal Army in 1857, services which are well known to all, and for which Your Highness has from time to time received the thanks of the Government, as well as recognitions of a more public and permanent kind, I consulted the Honourable the Lieutenant-Governor of Bengal as to what *special* mark of the favour of the Government it would be expedient to confer on Your Highness, so that it might be manifest to all men that Your Highness' *loyal* services and *faithful* attachment to the British Government are *duly appreciated*, and that *the Government is not unmindful of the good offices rendered by Your Highness in a season of trouble.*

"The Lieutenant-Governor of Bengal has laid before me in a minute a complete record of all that Your Highness and Your Highness' servants did on these two occasions; and this minute, recorded in the Archives of Government, will serve as a *perpetual* remembrance of Your Highness' *active and zealous support*, and of the *firm friendship* which exists between Your Highness and the British Government.

"My Friend, I have read this record of Your Highness' friendly acts with the most lively satisfaction, and entirely agreeing in the views expressed by the Lieutenant-Governor, I have directed that Your Highness shall henceforth always receive a salute of nineteen guns, and that certain rules which are now in force, as regards Your Highness' recreations, shall be wholly removed.

"By these and other tokens of favour which Your Highness has received in consideration of your loyal services, Your Highness will be satisfied of the high estimation in which those services are held, and of my sincere desire to mark my appreciation of them.

"I have only to add, in conclusion, that on the recommendation of the Agent and of the Lieutenant-Governor, I have had the pleasure of conferring upon *Your Highness' Dewan* Rai Prosuno Narain Deb Bahadoor the title of Rajah Bahadoor, in recognition of the ability and zeal with which, under Your Highness' directions, he co-operated with the British authorities to restore and maintain tranquillity on both the occasions above referred to.

"I have, &c.,
"(Signed)   CANNING."

Before concluding this head of my Memorial, I may be permitted to offer a few remarks on that portion of the letter (Page 269), from His Excellency (the late) Lord Canning, which refers to the dismissal of my Dewan; and I would respectfully urge, Your Grace, that the line of argument adduced by His Lordship is based upon an erroneous supposition, that the Government had always exercised a control over the appointment of the Dewans Nizamut. A careful examination of the Treaties with Nawabs Nudjm-ul-Dowlah, Syef-ul-Dowlah, and Mobaruck-ul-Dowlah will show that *the Dewans who were appointed under the sanction of the Government were invested only with the control of that portion of the Nawab's allowances assigned for State purposes, or the support of his rank and dignity*, while the personal stipend of the Nawab (over which the Government did not claim any control) was left entirely at his disposal.

When the Government of India (after the receipt of the despatch from the Court of Directors, dated 20th April, 1771, ordering them to withhold that portion of the allowances of Nawab Mobaruck-ul-Dowlah, set apart for the support of the rank and dignity of the Nawab Nazims, and which they considered were unnecessary for him during his minority), deprived the Nawab of the State allowance which had been guaranteed by the Treaty in perpetuity, the Government control over the appointment of the Dewans (who had had the disbursement of that sum alone) ceased, and, moreover, it does not appear from any record that the Government ever afterwards claimed a voice in the appointment of the Dewans whom the Nawabs selected for the purpose of keeping their family accounts; but in 1816, when the Government thought proper to interfere, for the avowed purpose of extricating the Nizamut from pecuniary difficulties, Mr Monckton suggested that an officer should be appointed by the Government to control the affairs of the Nizamut, "*invested with dignity of a representative character, and enabled to devote his time and attention exclusively to the duties of his situation.*" A separate fund was formed from the Nawab's money for the support of this functionary, who was duly installed under the auspices of Government, and with the sanction of the Nawab, and styled the Agent to the Governor-General. Hence, Your Grace, it is very evident that the Agent, who was expected to control all the accounts of the Nizamut, was virtually the *Government Dewan*, and was the only officer connected with the Nizamut, in whose appointment or dismissal the Government could *justly claim* any interference.

Your Grace will, I trust, excuse me for having again introduced this subject, but as it is one that has materially affected my *social position*, I feel that it should be prominently set forward to attract the notice of Her Majesty's Government, and in the earnest hope that it will receive a just and impartial consideration, I will leave it to Your Grace's disposal, and introduce the sixth and last subject of my Memorial.

VI. EXTRAORDINARY TRANSACTIONS OF MR. TORRENS, AGENT GOVERNOR-GENERAL!

I regret having occasion to allude to Para. 14 of Despatch No. 30 of the 17th June, 1864, from Her Majesty's Secretary of State, to the Governor-General of India, on reference to which Your Grace will observe, that while the Secretary of State admits that I had good grounds for complaint against the conduct of Mr. Torrens, yet regrets that owing to the death of that officer, he, (the Right Honorable Gentleman) is "reluctantly driven to the conclusion, that no benefit will arise from "reopening the consideration of that subject." Your Grace, my complaint was not against Mr. Torrens in his private capacity, but as Agent Governor-General, and an officer acting for the British Government whose actions bore prima facie the authority of Government. Your Grace, the Most Hon. the late Marquis of Dalhousie, in the case of some of my servants who were declared innocent of any crime by the highest Court of British Indian Judicature, declared that I as their master was to be held responsible and punishable for what they had never done, and were proved never to have been privy to, yet in this instance where (Page 112) a high Government officer plunges into "intrigues," and instructs the doctoring and cooking up of accounts under the ægis of his official position, which effectually protected him from being personally indicted in the Supreme Court of Calcutta for fraud, both the Indian and Home Governments declare that there would be no benefit arising from an enquiry into the subject as the Agent is now dead; but Your Grace, Mr. Torrens in all he did acted in his *official capacity*, as evidenced by his own declaration to that effect, and although specific losses to the extent of upwards of £250,000 were sustained by me in consequence, I am desired to believe and admit that the consideration of the matter would not lead to any benefit. If by such expression be meant, that it would lead to the publication of a scandal, and exhibit the dereliction of the Government of India, in not interfering for my protection before the death of Mr. Torrens, or asserting that a mistake had been made in the selection of such an officer for the Post of Agent, I am prepared to admit that the Government of India would by no possible means derive benefit or credit from an enquiry into the matter; but, Your Grace, does this consideration prove that my losses are fictitious and not worthy of consideration?

A public trial in the Supreme Court compelled the production of the letter quoted on Page 118, and the accounts of the Agents, Messrs. Mackenzie Lyall and Co., fully substantiated my assertion that the accumulation of my minority money was squandered and misappropriated, under the sanction, knowledge and connivance of the very officer whose duty it was to watch over my interests and protect me from being imposed upon by others. Your Grace, surely the death of a Government Officer cannot diminish or remove the responsibility of the Government for whom he acted, and whom he personally represented; and although the existence of Mr. Torrens might have led to his being indicted in a Criminal Court and punished for his conduct, yet this done, the responsibility of the Government to make good the specific losses which his misdeeds had occasioned, would have been legitimately claimable in a Civil Court. My complaint against Mr. Torrens and the other parties implicated in these nefarious transactions was well known to the Government (vide Letter of 12th April, 1853, Page 122), and although I instituted a suit against some of the parties concerned for the recovery of my dues, the proceedings were stopped at the instance of the Government, and I was thus hopelessly debarred from claiming my rights. I trust, however, Your Grace will order a full enquiry to be made into the circumstances of the case by which her Majesty's Government may be enabled to decide what I am justly entitled to.

Having now laid before Your Grace the general details of my grievances, and a few documents (out of many that might be produced) in support of the justice of my claims—I will, for the purpose of facilitating inquiry, endeavour, with Your Grace's permission, to deduce certain points therefrom which I would beg respectfully to submit for the consideration of Her Majesty's Government.

1. With what object were the Treaties herein alluded to, executed between the Representatives of the two Governments? What *principles* were involved?

2. Were the Powers **bound *in honor*** to abide by the acts of their Representatives?

3. Who were the Representatives that executed the Treaties alluded to? What were their respective positions? What were the conditions and obligations implied in the Treaties?

4. What led to the modification of the Treaties during several generations? How were the relative positions of the Contracting Powers altered thereby?

5. What was the object of the additional Treaty with Nawab Nudjmul-Dowlah? Whence did it originate?

6. Was the Firmaun of the King of Delhi binding on the Honorable East India Company. On what terms was the Grant of the Dewanny conferred?

7. What led to the modification of the Treaties on the accession of Nawab Syef-ul-Dowlah: and again on the accession of Nawab Mobaruck-ul-Dowlah?

8. Was the last Treaty executed with Nawab Mobaruck-ul-Dowlah of so personal a character that the conditions named therein were only

binding on the then existing Government and Nawab? Why was it concluded with the words " for ever?" Was it acted up to during the lifetime of Nawab Mobaruck-ul-Dowlah?

9. What opinion did the Court of Directors offer in regard to the Treaty of 1770, being the basis of all their future operations with the Nawabs Nazim? Were their instructions carried out?

10. What led to the pecuniary embarrassment of Nawab **Mobaruck-ul-Dowlah**? **What** originated **all the measures that have since been** introduced by which the Political and social status of the Nawabs Nazim has been lowered?

11. What were the objects for which the several Funds were formed? Have these objects been carried out and the conditions fulfilled?

12. Is the **Nawab Nazim** entitled to receive the surplus of the Deposit Fund that may have accumulated by interest or otherwise over and above the Two Lacs per annum he has been and is still obliged to set apart for the objects of the Fund?

13. Does the condition of the Fund require that contributions should still be made to it by the Nawabs Nazim for the furtherance of its object? Under what circumstances is the Nawab Nazim entitled to receive pecuniary assistance from the Fund?

14. Is the Nawab Nazim justly entitled to the reversion of the lapsed Stipends?

15. Why was the **office of** Agent Governor-General established? What, strictly speaking, are the duties of that officer?

16. What were the duties of the Dewan after the appointment of the Agent Governor-General? Had the Nawab a right to dismiss him as his own servant, without reference to the Agent? Was the subsequent action taken against the Nawab Nazim just?

17. Were the **harsh measures** adopted by His Excellency (the late) Marquis of Dalhousie **against** the Nawab **Nazim based** on just and reasonable conclusions?

18. Were the circumstances that led to the estrangement between the Agent Governor-General and the **Nawab Nazim of so grievous a** nature as to justify the action taken by **His Excellency** (the late) Lord Canning, against the Nawab Nazim?

19. What are the meanings of the words hereditary and Nizamut so frequently used in the Treaties and in the letters from various Governors-General to the Nawabs Nazim?

20. On what grounds has it been asserted that the sum **of Sixteen Lacs** is the " Assignment by Treaty **of** the Family?" Is it **just to** demand a receipt from the Nawab Nazim for the whole sum of Sixteen Lacs, without **rendering him some** account as to its disbursement?

21. Were not the **Nawabs Nazim** declared **under the** authority of the Government to be Independent Princes and treated as such? What offence have they been guilty of on account of which their Political status has been lowered? Why have they been deprived of " the prescriptive rights, honours, and privileges of their exalted " station, guaranteed ' by subsisting Treaties and long-established re- " lations,' to be inviolably observed for ever."

I would here solicit the favour of Your Grace again considering the wording of the Treaties, from which it would appear that the Nawabs Nazim gradually ceded their power to the Honourable East India Company, for the better governing and protecting of their Provinces and People, and in return they received guarantees that the Honourable East India Company would secure their position as Princes, and that their "rights, honours, and dignity would be scrupulously "maintained." Thus, Your Grace, from voluntarily having placed themselves in the position of feudatories to the Nawabs Nazim, the Honourable East India Company eventually acquired the Supreme Administrative Government of the three Provinces of Bengal, Behar, and Orissa; but as they bound themselves to perform certain obligations, it is for the fulfilment of these promises by Her Majesty's Government, that I now pray; and although as a faithful Ally of the British, it is not for me to question the acts of their Exalted Government, yet as a powerless Prince, relying on the hopes and promises held out to my Ancestors by the Representatives of that Government, through which means the possession of the three Provinces of Bengal, Behar, and Orissa was secured to them by Treaty, without bloodshed, and thus (under the blessing of the Almighty) a way was opened for the introduction of good government, wise legislation, and profitable institutions, into a country which, for many ages, had been the scene of political intrigues, massacre, and bloodshed, I may be allowed to inquire whether Her Majesty's Exalted Government and the British Nation will now give their Sanction to the further carrying out of the system of oppression and injustice which has prevailed against myself and other Princes of India for some time past, under which it has even been proposed, in opposition to the principles of justice and honor, that the Government should withdraw entirely from the support of those titled stipendiaries, whose rank and dignity it has bound itself to protect! Nay, rather, Your Grace, would it not be more consistent with the Exalted Position and Magnanimous Principles of the British Government, to endeavour to elevate and educate the Princes and People of India in such a manner as might enable the former to hold offices under the Government, in which they would command respect and esteem, and be made useful members of society, and the latter be made acquainted with everything that is good and profitable, by which they might improve their social condition; for by such means the Government would remove all causes of disaffection, and the sense of injustice that is felt in many instances, and would eventually secure the affection and attachment of all classes of natives in India in perpetuity.

In conclusion, I would earnestly ask Your Grace to take an impartial view of my claims, so far as they are based on the principles of truth, honor, and justice, and if consistent with these principles, I pray that I and my family may be placed in the position we ought to occupy, so that I may feel and find that my wrongs have been redressed, and that the Exalted Government of the United Kingdom of Great Britain and Ireland has carried out the Assurances given by Her Most Gracious Majesty in 1858, that "all Treaties made by the East India Company "are by Us accepted, and will be scrupulously maintained," and We

" will respect the rights, dignity, and honor of Native Princes as Our
" own."

I have the honor to be,
Your Grace's sincere friend,
(Signed) SYUD MUNSOOR ULLEE.

Alexandra Hotel, London,
July, 1869.

This Memorial, instead of being dealt with on its own merits, has, as before stated, been referred to the Government of India for a Report thereon; but what further light the local Government of India can throw upon the subject of His Highness's claims, it is difficult to divine, since in Para. 2 of the Despatch of June, 1864, Her Majesty's Secretary of State for India declared that *"All the correspondence necessary to the formation of a correct opinion with respect to the social questions which they illustrate had then been received!"* Perhaps it was thought that the prospect of an English winter might induce an Eastern Prince brought up in luxury to leave England and return to his own native country, where once again under the jurisdiction of the local Government he might never again be allowed the privilege of visiting our *free country* to advocate his claims in person. But the Indian Prince, with hope to sustain him, has withstood the inclemency of our climate, and not having received a reply to his Memorial, or any consideration from the Indian Government, is now compelled to lay his grievances before the public, with a view of obtaining that sympathy and support to which he is justly entitled at the hands of the British Government and Nation, *not only as a right, but as an* act of gratitude for the services he rendered to our countrymen in the far East, in their season of trial and danger in 1857, when men of his own creed and country raised the standard of rebellion throughout the land, and endeavoured to throw off the British yoke in India.

Apart from all pecuniary compensation to which His Highness considers himself entitled at the hands of the Imperial Government there are other matters of a political and social character set forth in the Memorial, which being of a *less expensive* nature, ought, we think, to be entirely conceded to His Highness as an act of courtesy; but leaving these matters to be justly dealt with by Her Majesty's Government, we will give our readers an idea of the enormous losses sustained by the Nawabs and the gain effected for the East India Company, from 1757 to 1858, and since 1858 by the Indian Government through the infringement of those Sacred Treaties and Agreements made by the East India Company with the Representatives of the House of Meer Jaffier Ali Khan.

STATEMENT

Showing the Approximate Amount deducted from the Nizamut Stipend by the Government of India under various pretexts since the infringement of the terms of the Treaty and Agreement of 1770 in 1772.

		Rs.	As.	Pc.	£	s.	d.
1.	Accumulations of the difference between the Annual Stipend of Rs. 31,81,991-9 agreed on by Treaty *"for ever"* (Page 26) and the Annual Allowance of Rupees 16,00,000 paid as "Assignment by Treaty *of the Family*" (Page 280) from 1772 till 1870 . . .	15,50,35,173	2	0	15,503,517	6	3
2.	Accumulations of the monthly amount of Rs. 18,000 deducted from the "Annual Allowance" of the Nizamut from September 1790 to December 1816, by order of Lord Cornwallis (Page 29) for meeting the liabilities (Rupees 22,86,666-12-3) incurred by Nawab Mobaruck-ul-dowlah in consequence of his income having been unjustly curtailed in 1772	56,70,000	0	0	567,000	0	0
3.	Accumulations of Munnee Begum's Stipend and Private Property appropriated for the Agency Fund and *"invested in Government Securities"* by order of the Governor-General, as communicated in Mr. Monckton's letter of 19th December, 1816, (Page 62) . .	7,00,000	0	0	70,000	0	0
4.	Accumulations of Munnee Begum's Stipend "invested in Public Securities for the benefit of the Nizamut" by order of the Governor-General as communicated in Mr. Prinsep's letter, dated 28th Jan., 1823 (Page 83) deducting the						

		Rs.	As.	Pe.	£	s.	d.
	amount of Rupees 1,46,503 invested for building the new palace	6,00,000	0	0	60,000	0	0
5.	Accumulations in the Nizamut Deposit Fund "of sums of Rupees 2,00,000 deducted annually from the Nizamut Allowance of sixteen lacs from 1823 to 1870, which were also to be invested in Government Securities" by order of the Governor-General, communicated in Mr. Prinsep's letter dated 28th January, 1823 (Page 80 and 85) and which, as expressed in Para. 8 of the Despatch from Her Majesty's Secretary of State for India, dated 17th June, 1864, "unquestionably belong to the Nawab Nazim and his family, and can properly be expended only for their benefit"	94,00,000	0	0	940,000	0	0
6.	Accumulations of the several pensions which lapsed by the decease of members of the Nizamut, which were absorbed into the Deposit Fund at the suggestion of Mr. Trevelyan in letter dated 26th February, 1836 (Page 101).	1,50,00,000	0	0	1,500,000	0	0
	Total	Rs. 18,64,05,173	2	0	£18,640,517	6	3

Note.—As several of the above sums were invested in Government Securities bearing Interest, and the Interest was re-invested (Pages 72 and 80), the accumulations must have now reached enormous proportions.

The enormity of the injustice perpetrated by the Government of India against the Nawabs Nazim must strike every honourably disposed Englishman with surprise, and should, we think, for the sake of our National Credit, lead Her Majesty's Government at once to redress the wrongs which have been inflicted, and so patiently borne with for upwards of one hundred years by those Princes.

But it may be asked, why have not these wrongs before been brought to the notice of the British Public? This may be answered by referring the reader to a consideration of the political relations that existed between the Nawabs Nazim of Bengal and the Honourable East India Company in former years, whereby the latter held the former under absolute control, and prevented their appealing to the British Government, except through their own officers. The little notice taken of the present Nawab's Memorials by the local Government of India will sufficiently exhibit the manner in which Native Princes, faithfully attached to the British cause, are treated by that Government, and should awaken public attention to the fact that such a state of things must tend to act unfavourably on the minds of those Princes and may again produce that spirit of defection in India which probably was one great source to which the Rebellion of 1857 might be traced.

As the Nawab in His Memorial does not specify exactly what he requires, but appeals in general terms to the Government for justice and an acknowledgment of his claims so far as they are based on sound principles, we may venture to submit for our readers a statement of such demands as in our opinion might appear legitimately claimable from the Imperial Government by the Nawab.

1. *A recognition of the hereditary rank, dignity and privileges of himself and his successors as long as they continue to remain faithful to the British Government.*
2. *A guarantee that the titular dignity, social prestige and private rights of his family shall not in future be invaded by the officers of the Indian Government.*
3. *An admission that the Nawab Nazim, whoever he may be, is hereafter to have the entire control of the affairs of the Nizamut.*
4. *A settlement of his pecuniary claims upon the Government of India on a fair and reasonable appraisement, and the future payment to himself, his heirs and successors, of a stipend commensurate with their dignity, to be fixed by mutual agreement.*

Before concluding our subject, we will again briefly explain the general grounds upon which His Highness the Nawab Nazim of Bengal, Behar, and Orissa presses his claims upon the attention of the British Government.

The East India Company, having obtained the Executive Administration of some of the Provinces of India by deed of gift or right of purchase from the Native

Princes who ruled over them, were legally bound to pay those Princes and their heirs-at-law the several sums they had stipulated for as the price of the transfer, for such periods as were set forth in the Agreements executed between them and the Company, *by virtue of which alone the Company were legally* entitled to hold possession of the privileges that had been transferred to them; and the British Government having by Royal Proclamation in 1858 taken up all the obligations contracted by the East India Company has since that time been legally bound to fulfil all the engagements made by that august body while administering the affairs of India.

Such being the nature of the bonds now existing between the British Government and Indian Princes, we will leave the question of the Nawab's claims to be equitably adjusted by the Houses of Parliament, and in conclusion express a hope that as "our National Faith has been pledged," His Highness will receive that justice which, in our opinion, the merits of his case deserve, and on his return to India, will carry with him the conviction of his loyal Ancestors, that "British Honour and Public Faith are unimpeachable, and the Word and Bond of the British Nation can never be broken."

THE END.

www.ingramcontent.com/pod-product-compliance
Lightning Source LLC
Chambersburg PA
CBHW030345230426
43664CB00007BB/542